The Carnegie Foundation for the Advancement of Teaching

Founded by Andrew Carnegie in 1905 and chartered in 1906 by an Act of Congress, The Carnegie Foundation for the Advancement of Teaching is an independent policy and research center whose charge is "to do and perform all things necessary to encourage, uphold, and dignify the profession of the teacher and the cause of higher education."

The Foundation is a major national and international center for research and policy studies about teaching. Its mission is to address the hardest problems faced in teaching in public schools, colleges, and universities—that is, how to succeed in the classroom, how best to achieve lasting student learning, and how to assess the impact of teaching on students.

EDUCATING CITIZENS

*Preparing America's Undergraduates
for Lives of Moral and Civic Responsibility*

Anne Colby, Thomas Ehrlich,
Elizabeth Beaumont, Jason Stephens

o

Foreword by
Lee S. Shulman

First in a series published
in partnership with

The Carnegie Foundation for
the Advancement of Teaching

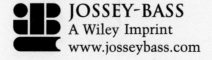

JOSSEY-BASS
A Wiley Imprint
www.josseybass.com

Published by Jossey-Bass
A Wiley Imprint
989 Market Street, San Francisco, CA 94103-1741   www.josseybass.com

Jossey-Bass books and products are available through most bookstores. To contact Jossey-Bass directly call our Customer Care Department within the U.S. at 800-956-7739, outside the U.S. at 317-572-3986 or fax 317-572-4002.

Jossey-Bass also publishes its books in a variety of electronic formats. Some content that appears in print may not be available in electronic books.

Library of Congress Cataloging-in-Publication Data

Educating citizens : preparing America's undergraduates for lives of
moral and civic responsibility / Anne Colby . . . [et al.] ; foreword by
Lee S. Shulman.
      p.   cm.
Includes bibliographical references and index.
      ISBN 0-7879-6515-4 (alk. paper)
   1. Moral education—United States.   2. Civics—Study and teaching
(Higher)—United States.   I. Colby, Anne, 1946-
      LC268 .E355 2003
      378'.014—dc21

2002152152

Printed in the United States of America
FIRST EDITION
HB Printing   10 9 8 7 6 5 4 3

CONTENTS

FOREWORD

EDUCATING CITIZENS is a new book inspired by an old and honorable tradition of American educational and political thought. It exemplifies The Carnegie Foundation for the Advancement of Teaching's commitment to a vision of education that integrates intellectual with moral virtues and connects the values of civic responsibility to the classic academic mission of higher education.

In his masterful biography of John Adams, the historian David McCullough gives special attention to one of Adams' most impressive accomplishments, his single-handed authorship of the Constitution of the Commonwealth of Massachusetts. McCullough (2001) characterizes this work as "one of the great, enduring documents of the American Revolution" and "the oldest functioning written constitution in the world" (p. 225). Perhaps the most remarkable passage in this work is Section Two of Chapter Six, which puts forward a conception of the state's obligations to educate its citizens.

> Wisdom and knowledge, as well as virtue, diffused generally among the body of people being necessary for the preservation of their rights and liberties; and as these depend on spreading the opportunities and advantages of education in various parts of the country, and among the different orders of the people, it shall be the duty of legislators and magistrates in all future periods of this commonwealth to cherish the interests of literature and the sciences, and all seminaries of them, especially the university at Cambridge, public schools, and grammar schools in the towns; to encourage private societies and public institutions, rewards and immunities, for the promotion of agriculture, arts, sciences, commerce, trades, manufactures, and a natural history of the country; to countenance and inculcate the principles of humanity and general benevolence, public and private charity, industry and frugality, honesty and punctuality in their dealings, sincerity, good humor, and all social affections, and generous sentiments among the people [McCullough, p. 223].

How refreshing and surprising to see one of our founding fathers call for an educational mission that not only seeks to inculcate the practical and theoretical arts, literature and the sciences, commerce and our national history; he also sees education as a process that must nurture "the principles of humanity and general benevolence," including such virtues as honesty, charity, sincerity, and even good humor! The wise John Adams understood that if a democratic society were to function as intended, as "a social compact, by which the whole people covenants with each citizen, and each citizen with the whole people," such covenants can only be entered into by an educated citizenry blessed with virtue as well as wisdom and knowledge. Absent such intentionally sought accomplishments, a functioning democracy might well become a shattered dream (McCullough, p. 221).

Colby, Ehrlich, Beaumont, and Stephens assert that achieving this combination of moral and civic virtue accompanied by the development of understanding occurs best when fostered by our institutions of higher education. It does not occur by accident, or strictly through early experience. Indeed, I would argue that there may well be a critical period for the development of these virtues, and that period could be the college years. During this developmental period, defined as much by educational opportunity as by age, students of all ages develop the tools and resources needed for their continuing journeys through adult life.

In an analogy that I find particularly provocative, the authors liken the college years to the planning and supply phase of a long and complex expedition. Those who embark on an expedition, like Lewis and Clark, must spend a considerable amount of time and energy to ensure that they have gathered the most useful material goods for the journey. Even more important, they must prepare themselves with the knowledge and skills needed to cope with a wide range of contingencies. In some ways, the preparations directly shape the trajectory of the subsequent journey. Maps direct the travelers toward one set of paths rather than another. Available tools dispose the explorers to seek out particular kinds of terrain. Their choice of comrades also opens up some options while foreclosing others. And the knowledge and values they acquire equip them to respond effectively to the unpredictable challenges and opportunities that will inevitably confront them in their travels.

Our authors present us with a striking array of institutional cases—colleges and universities that creatively provide settings for the moral and civic development of their students. At first glance, the institutions differ greatly from one another. Some are public, others private. Some are faith-based, others secular. Some are research and doctoral institutions, others liberal arts or community colleges. Yet, from the Air Force Academy to Portland State University, from Messiah College to Turtle Mountain Community College, from Duke University to Tusculum College, they share a commitment to integrating the highest of academic and civic commitments.

Educating Citizens stands as a carefully crafted set of "existence proofs" that this sort of integration is both possible and desirable. It highlights both the general principles that characterize moral and civic education in all these institutions and the local contexts and missions that give each program its unique and special quality. Taken together, this book offers its readers a vision of the possible, an inspiring and instructive vision of how such work can be undertaken.

What are the essential elements of moral and civic character for Americans? How can higher education contribute to developing these qualities in sustained and effective ways? What problems do institutions face when they seriously and intentionally undertake moral and civic education? What strategies do they employ to overcome them? As the authors state, "These are the questions we have wrestled with in writing this book. They are the issues at the heart of democracy's future in America."

When the research team began their studies in 1998, they could not have foreseen the intellectual, moral, and civic challenges that lay ahead for this nation after the events of September 11, 2001. How well have we as a nation been prepared for the challenges of this expedition? How well are we preparing the next generation for the opportunities they will encounter? The essence of moral and civic education is imparting the understanding that it is important to be generous and responsible to our family, friends, and neighbors, but that is not sufficient. It is critical that we are responsible, responsive, patriotic, and loyal to our nation and society, but that, too, is insufficient. Educated citizens must understand and accept their obligations to all humanity, to making this a nation worth defending in a world safe and promising for all its inhabitants. By combining attention to both moral and civic virtue, our authors remind us of how inextricably our duties to family, nation, community, and world are bound together.

Writing of the Massachusetts constitution, McCullough observes, "It was, in all, a declaration of Adams' faith in education as the bulwark of the good society. . . . The survival of the rights and liberties of the people depended on the spread of wisdom, knowledge and virtue among all the people, the common people, of whom he, as a farmer's son, was one" (p. 223). This book carries forward those dreams, those visions of the role of education in fostering a learned civic society.

As the first book in a new Carnegie Foundation series, *Educating Citizens* also continues the Foundation's historic journey to explore, inform, and even redefine important issues in education. It follows the same path begun by publications such as the *Flexner Report on Medical Education,* the Carnegie Commission reports under the leadership of Clark Kerr, and the many superb works of Ernest Boyer.

I am delighted to present this work as a striking exemplar of the Carnegie Foundation's century-long commitment to the support and improvement of education in America and the world.

Menlo Park, California   LEE S. SHULMAN
September 2002

PREFACE

LONG BEFORE they began the project on which *Educating Citizens* is based, the two senior authors on our team, Tom Ehrlich and Anne Colby, had been asking questions about the ways education can contribute to preparing people for lives of moral and civic responsibility—Tom from the perspective of higher education, Anne from the perspective of life-span developmental psychology, especially the psychology of moral development. In the course Altruism, Philanthropy, and Public Service, which Tom taught while president of Indiana University, he used a book about exceptional moral commitment that Anne had coauthored with William Damon, and wrote her a note of appreciation. Fortuitously, some years later both Tom and Anne moved to California and had the opportunity to work at The Carnegie Foundation for the Advancement of Teaching, which had also just moved to California, from Princeton, New Jersey. They were delighted to join forces to think about the contributions undergraduate education might make to educating responsible citizens. Tom and Anne were joined in 1998 by Elizabeth Beaumont and Jason Stephens, who brought to the team the perspectives of political science and educational psychology.

The four of us share the conviction that moral and civic learning should be a central goal for both liberal and professional education. We also believe that moral and civic messages are unavoidable in higher education and that it is better to pay explicit attention to the content of these messages and how they are conveyed than to leave students' moral and civic socialization to chance. At the time we began the Project on Higher Education and the Development of Moral and Civic Responsibility, dismay over excessive individualism in U.S. culture and growing civic disengagement was very much a part of public discourse, and many individuals were writing persuasively about the need for moral and civic renewal if the citizens of this country were to move toward a more cohesive and humane society. A number of national reports had been issued proposing steps to promote these goals and diagnosing the barriers to achieving them. We were struck, however, by the fact that many of these reports (see, for example, National Commission on Civic Renewal, 1998; Council on Civil Society, 1998) paid minimal attention to the role of higher education in shaping the moral and civic lives of students and U.S. culture more generally. In contrast, we believe that higher education has a critical role to play in shaping character and a sense of social responsibility in the U.S. citizenry because such a large share of the population attends college for at least some period of time.

Responses to early publications and conference presentations on our project, along with others' writing, particularly in the publications of Campus Compact and the Association of American Colleges and Universities, on the need for and importance of education for citizenship at the college level, have made it clear that many others share our conviction and are eager for opportunities to learn more about high-quality efforts to integrate moral and civic learning into undergraduate education. There has been significant attention for the past decade or two to moral and civic education at the elementary and secondary levels, where such education usually has two quite separate parts, with moral education framed in terms of character and civic education framed in terms of democratic maxims and political institutions. There are also a number of very useful books about service learning at the college level and many research papers exploring and documenting its impact (for example, Eyler & Giles, 1999). Recently Marcia Mentkowski and her associates (2000) have written about moral and civic development in college in the context of Alverno College's abilities-based approach to undergraduate education. But no studies had set out to describe in detail the broader efforts that some colleges and universities are making to support the moral and civic development of their students, nor were there any studies that spell out how educators can best understand the nature of that development, to outline the impediments institutions face when they do this work, and to offer guiding principles that can effectively shape such endeavors. Those, then, are the aims of this book.

At the heart of this book are a number of assumptions. First, we assume that although college is only one phase in any individual's lifelong process of moral and civic development, it can be pivotal, leading to new ways of understanding the world and one's place in the world, providing new frameworks through which later experiences are interpreted, and equipping the individual with a wide array of capacities for moral and civic engagement. Even for the many students who come back to college after years in the workforce, it is not too late to develop new modes of moral and civic understanding; new values, interests, and self-definitions; and new intellectual, social, and practical skills. We also argue that if it is to be most effective, moral and civic learning should be integrated into both curricular and extracurricular programs and that it does not require a trade-off with more narrowly academic goals. In fact we are convinced that the two strands of undergraduate education—disciplinary, or academic, on one hand and moral and civic on the other—can be mutually enhancing. Our fieldwork has also made it clear to us that moral and civic education can be implemented successfully in all kinds of institutions and can be shaped to fit a wide array of educational missions. Also central to our approach is the assumption that the moral and civic strands of education for citizenship cannot be separated. We discuss this key assumption in the first chapter. Our central conclusions and recommendations are summarized in the final chapter.

Audiences for This Book

In writing this book we have in mind three main audiences, who may read it for different purposes and from somewhat different, though interrelated, vantage points. One audience consists of those people who are interested in contemporary higher education broadly, including policymakers, scholars, and representatives of organizations concerned with the purposes and practices of U.S. higher education.

Both of the other two intended audiences involve those responsible for the education provided by a college or university. In any institution some people are in a strong position to take action at the level of the institution and are responsible for thinking about student learning from an institution-wide perspective. We hope this book will be helpful to these individuals, our second audience, who include not only the administrative leadership, such as presidents, vice presidents, and deans but also faculty who participate in curriculum reform, act as advisers and partners to the administrative leaders, and establish systems for cross-campus integration. This second group also includes staff members who work in campus centers of various kinds or in the office of institutional research and who play important roles in coordinating programs across the institution. Moreover, when any faculty members or program directors think carefully about the impact of their courses or programs on students, it is very helpful for them to pay attention to the broader context in which students are experiencing the course or program. And when faculty and student affairs personnel habitually take the institutional view, that can build a more unified sense of purpose and community on campus.

The primary responsibilities of some people in a university or college are grounded more in particular courses, programs, and departments than in the planning and implementation carried out by the institution as a whole, and most of their efforts will be concentrated at that level. In order to make the book useful for these readers, our third audience, we have included many examples drawn from our observations and fairly detailed information about courses in various fields, pedagogical approaches, and programs and practices in the domain of student life, with the idea that some readers may be most interested in learning how they might develop and implement programs and courses that promote moral and civic learning.

Organization of This Book

In Chapter One we discuss why explicit efforts to include moral and civic learning in undergraduate education are necessary, and we lay out the goals and rationale of that endeavor, with particular attention to the question of how higher education institutions in a pluralistic society can find some common values in which to ground these efforts. This chapter also describes the project that gave rise to this book, including our visits to twelve colleges and universities that take their students' moral and civic development very seriously.

Chapter Two addresses the broader higher education context in which contemporary efforts to support students' moral and civic development are taking place. A brief look at the history of these efforts makes it clear that moral and civic education for undergraduates is not new but has been pushed to the margins in most institutions. Moreover, some aspects of contemporary higher education are impeding efforts to bring it back from the margins. Allies of this work, including especially those who are calling for more searching attention to student learning and those who draw on the traditions of liberal education, are working to change some of these inhospitable conditions. Given the strong countervailing forces, the institutional impediments to this work will not be dramatically altered in the short run. Fortunately, our fieldwork convinces us that moral and civic education need not wait until all impediments have been removed.

Chapter Three describes twelve colleges and universities that take holistic and intentional approaches to undergraduate moral and civic education. Each has developed a distinctive definition of moral and civic maturity, one that grows out of the institution's own mission and history, along with multiple intersecting means for fostering that maturity. Three themes for moral and civic education emerge from an exploration of those twelve distinctive definitions: connections with communities of various sorts; moral and civic virtue, variously defined; and concerns for systemic social responsibility, or social justice. All of the twelve campuses place at least one or two of these themes at the center of their approach, and most incorporate all three in their moral and civic education to some extent. This chapter then turns to some key features in the ways these institutions accomplish their holistic, intentional approach. Leadership from administrators, faculty, and campus centers is central to their success, as is establishing a campus culture that supports positive moral and civic values.

In Chapter Four we review research and theory about moral and civic development and use that work to articulate a framework for thinking about the many dimensions that make up moral and civic maturity, the significance of those dimensions, and their potential for development during college. The multiple dimensions are heuristically clustered into three categories, even though the categories intersect and the dimensions interact. The clusters are moral and civic understanding, motivation, and skills.

We claim that moral and civic learning in the curriculum can touch not only the most obviously cognitive aspects of moral and civic understanding but also such motivational dimensions as identity and efficacy and such skills as negotiation and collaboration. In Chapter Five, we describe some pedagogical approaches that are especially well suited to supporting moral and civic growth and discuss why we consider them essential to a full palette of teaching methods and why we believe they will strengthen the broad range of academic learning as well as moral and civic learning. We explore the teaching of ethics as one example of how challenging the teaching of moral and civic understanding, motivation, and skills can be and the kinds of dilemmas faculty confront when they do this kind of teaching. In order to illustrate what teaching for moral and civic learning looks like in the context of an actual course, we describe four quite different courses in some detail.

Chapter Six begins with the assumption that institutions concerned with moral and civic education wish to reach the widest number of students and to reach them in sufficient depth to have a lasting impact. We argue that they are best able to accomplish this when moral and civic education is incorporated into the curriculum, both in general education and in academic majors. We describe a number of ways to structure general education programs to suit different institutional needs and constraints yet also provide a powerful developmental experience. We also review briefly some examples of approaches to moral and civic education in the arts and sciences, undergraduate professional education, and the fine arts. Finally, this chapter describes some efforts to help students integrate moral and civic learning across different courses and across disciplines.

This kind of teaching is difficult and demanding, and faculty are extremely busy even without taking on this additional set of goals. In Chapter Seven we ask what motivates those faculty who make this commitment, what they find rewarding in the work, and what kind of support they need to sustain this commitment.

As important as moral and civic learning in the curriculum is, it is at least as important for experiences outside the classroom to contribute to educating citizens. Chapter Eight addresses the question of how to provide guidance for and take advantage of extracurricular opportunities. Much of student life is outside the direct control of the administration; nevertheless these activities can be extremely powerful, and there is much colleges and universities can do to take best advantage of them—setting the stage before incoming students arrive on campus; establishing a climate through honor codes, residence hall experiences, and informal teachable moments; and drawing on the wide array of existing clubs and activities, especially service, religious, and political clubs and leadership development programs. Chapter Eight also discusses the ways some colleges help students maintain their moral and civic commitment at graduation time and beyond through graduation pledges, job placement services, and alumni programs.

After commenting on the assessment of student learning in courses that incorporate moral and civic goals, Chapter Nine addresses the question of how faculty and program leaders can assess the quality of curricular and extracurricular programs of moral and civic education in ways that will contribute to program improvement. Assessment of moral and civic education has a long way to go before it is fully developed, so we offer general directions, caveats, and descriptions of some ongoing assessment efforts rather than prescriptions.

Chapter Ten lays out in summary form some basic principles for undergraduate moral and civic education that have emerged from our observations and analyses. These principles address the questions of how institutions can be sure to support the full range of developmental dimensions—moral and civic understanding, motivation, and skills; how they can take advantage of the most useful sites for moral and civic education—the curriculum, extracurricular programs, and other aspects of student life outside the classroom; and how they can be sure to touch on the three basic themes of moral and civic virtue, systemic social responsibility, and community connections.

Acknowledgments

Many people helped in the preparation of this book and the study on which it is based. We are grateful to them all, and especially to the following:

Our colleagues at The Carnegie Foundation for the Advancement of Teaching provided a wonderfully collegial environment and wise counsel for our work. The leadership of the foundation has been supportive from the outset. Lee Shulman, John Barcroft, and Ann Fitzgerald have all provided invaluable assistance. Our particular thanks for reading all or portions of the manuscript, and for giving us their thoughtful comments, go to Gay Clyburn, Mary Huber, Pat Hutchings, Lee Shulman, Bill Sullivan, and Johanna Wilson. Mary, Lee, and Johanna also joined in some of our site visits and helped write descriptions of those institutions. Ruby Kerawalla, Lindsay Turner, and Sarah Durant all provided superb assistance to the project.

Our research assistants Hahrie Han, Daniel Gitterman, and Jennifer Rosner each did an outstanding job of reviewing the literature and many other tasks.

Eamonn Callan, Carol Schneider, and Jim Youniss reviewed our entire manuscript in draft and provided many insightful comments and suggestions. Bill Damon offered wonderfully helpful advice throughout our project and on many drafts of the book.

The faculty, students, and administrators at the twelve campuses we visited in depth gave freely of their time and attention, and we are much in the debt of many individuals at Alverno College; California State University, Monterey Bay; the College of St. Catherine; Duke University; Kapiʻolani Community College; Messiah College; Portland State University; Spelman College; Turtle Mountain Community College; Tusculum College; the United States Air Force Academy; and the University of Notre Dame. Other campuses that we visited and that helped in our study were Emory University, Lewis and Clark College, Miami University, San Francisco State University, Tufts University, the University of Minnesota, and the University of Pennsylvania. We also appreciate the thoughtful counsel of Harry Boyte, Ira Harkavy, Liz Hollander, and Judith Ramaley during the course of our study.

Jon Dalton and his colleagues at the Florida State University and other educators from throughout the country who joined us there at a conference connected with our project taught us a great deal about moral and civic learning. The campuses involved in that conference were the twelve case study institutions and also Mills College, Pitzer College, St. Mary's College, Stanford University, and the University of the Pacific.

Finally, we are enormously grateful to the foundations that provided funding for our work over the past three years: Surdna Foundation, Inc., Walter and Elise Haas Fund, Flora Family Foundation, The James Irvine Foundation, John Templeton Foundation, and of course The Carnegie

Foundation for the Advancement of Teaching. Our work would not have been possible without their support.

Menlo Park, California   ANNE COLBY
August 2002   THOMAS EHRLICH
                                           ELIZABETH BEAUMONT
                                           JASON STEPHENS

THE AUTHORS

ANNE COLBY joined The Carnegie Foundation for the Advancement of Teaching as a senior scholar in 1997. Prior to that, she was director of the Henry Murray Research Center at Harvard University, a longitudinal studies data archive and social science research center. She is the principal author of *A Longitudinal Study of Moral Judgment* (1983) and *The Measurement of Moral Judgment* (1987), coauthor of *Some Do Care: Contemporary Lives of Moral Commitment* (with W. Damon, 1992), and coeditor of *Ethnography and Human Development: Context and Meaning in Human Inquiry* (with R. Jessor and R. A. Shweder, 1995), *Competence and Character Through Life* (with J. James & D. Hart, 1998), and *Looking at Lives: American Longitudinal Studies of the Twentieth Century* (with E. Phelps and F. Furstenberg Jr., 2002). She holds a B.A. degree from McGill University and a Ph.D. degree in psychology from Columbia University.

THOMAS EHRLICH is a senior scholar at The Carnegie Foundation for the Advancement of Teaching. From 1987 to 1994, he was president of Indiana University. After retiring from Indiana University, he joined San Francisco State University as distinguished university scholar and held that position until 2000. In addition, he was provost at the University of Pennsylvania from 1981 to 1987 and dean of the Stanford University Law School in the 1970s. He also served from 1979 to 1981 as the first director of the International Development Cooperation Agency and from 1975 to 1979 as the first president of the Legal Services Corporation. He is the author or editor of eight books, including *The Courage to Inquire* (1996) and *Civic Responsibility and Higher Education* (2000). He is a graduate of Harvard College and Harvard Law School, was a law clerk for Judge Learned Hand, and has received four honorary degrees.

ELIZABETH BEAUMONT is a research associate at The Carnegie Foundation for the Advancement of Teaching and has worked on the Project on Higher Education and the Development of Moral and Civic Responsibility since 1998. She is currently helping to lead The Carnegie Foundation's Political Engagement Project, which investigates educational approaches to increasing college students' political knowledge, interest, skills, and involvement. She holds a B.A. degree in English Literature from Pomona College, and she completed her Ph.D. degree in political science, with a concentration in political theory and constitutional law, at Stanford University in 2000. Her research interests include democratic theory and its implications for civic and political education.

JASON STEPHENS is a doctoral candidate in educational psychology at Stanford University. He has been a research assistant on the Project on Higher Education and the Development of Moral and Civic Responsibility at The Carnegie Foundation for the Advancement of Teaching since 1998. In addition to the role and impact of higher education on undergraduates' moral and civic development, his research interests include moral reasoning, achievement motivation, and academic misconduct among high school students. He is a graduate of the University of Vermont (1991) and holds an M.Ed. degree (1994) from Vanderbilt University.

EDUCATING CITIZENS
IN A PLURALISTIC SOCIETY

WE BEGIN WITH the story of Virginia Foster Durr, who was a friend of the two senior authors of this book. Mrs. Durr, who died in 1999 at the age of ninety-six, was a remarkable woman not only in her contributions to racial justice and civil liberties but in the surprising direction her life took, given the culture in which she grew up. Virginia Durr was a white woman from a genteel (and racist) Alabama family, yet she became a major figure in the black civil rights movement. She helped integrate Washington, D.C., and Birmingham, Alabama, and fought for years to end the poll tax, which was used to prevent blacks, women, and poor people from voting in the South until 1964, when the Voting Rights Act was passed. We begin with this story not because Virginia was dramatically transformed in college but because experiences she had in college played a pivotal role in a longer process that began before her college years and continued much beyond them. Four things stand out in Virginia's account of her undergraduate years at Wellesley College in the early 1920s. They reflect the importance of the courses and faculty; the college's mission, cultural climate, and rules; and the connections students can make through clubs and interest groups.

First, as she studied history, political theory, and economics, Virginia became aware of dimensions of life that she had not known existed, developing an intellectual framework that persisted beyond her college years and affected the way she interpreted her later experiences. Some of her teachers deliberately connected their course material with social issues of the day and with the lives and concerns of their students. As she later recalled:

We had some excellent teachers at Wellesley. I had a marvelous teacher in economics, Professor Muzzy. . . . There were all kinds of tables and statistics that I had difficulty following. But I did get the impression that the great majority of people in the world had a pretty hard time. Once Muzzy gave me a paper to write. He knew that I came from Birmingham, so he said, "Mrs. Smith is the wife of a steelworker and her husband makes three dollars a day. Now tell me how Mrs. Smith with three children is going to arrange her budget so that they can live." Well, I tried to do it. I had to look up the price of food and rent and doctors. It was an active lesson in economics. I soon realized that Mrs. Smith couldn't possibly live on that amount of money. She just couldn't do it. When I handed in my paper, I had written at the end, "I've come to the conclusion that Mrs. Smith's husband doesn't get enough money, because they can't possibly live on what he is paid as a steelworker in Birmingham, Alabama." . . . These incidents at Wellesley had a delayed effect, but the main thing I learned was to use my mind and to get pleasure out of it. So my Wellesley education was quite liberating [Durr & Barnard, 1985, pp. 62–63].

When Virginia returned to Alabama and began the kind of charity work that was expected of young married women, the intellectual framework she had developed through this and other college courses led her to see the plight of the poor as a reflection of deep injustices in the U.S. economic and political systems rather than as a character defect of the poor themselves. This perspective later propelled her interest in the development of unions and her work in forging connections between the campaigns for civil rights and for workers' rights.

Second, a dramatic incident early in Virginia's sophomore year reveals the impact colleges can have when they set clear moral expectations for their students and rigorously enforce those expectations. One evening Virginia went down to the dining room for dinner and was shocked to see a black girl seated at the table to which she had been assigned. She immediately told the head of the house that she "could not possibly eat at the table with a Negro girl" (Colby & Damon, 1992, p. 99). The head of the house calmly explained that the rules of the college required her to eat at that table for a month, and if she did not comply she would have to withdraw from college. When Virginia explained that her father would "have a fit" if she ate at that table, the head of the house responded, "He's not our problem. He's your problem. You either abide by the rules or you go home" (Durr & Barnard, 1985, p. 57). Mrs. Durr later reflected that that was the first time her values regarding race had ever been challenged, and it made a big impression on her. As she said: "The incident may not have been crucial at the time, but it was the origin of a doubt. It hurt my faith, my solid conviction of what I had been raised to believe" (p. 59). This experience did not immediately lead to a new perspective on race relations and civil rights, but it did move Virginia a perceptible step in that direction. The college had forced her to interact with an educated, middle-class black girl for the first time, and she realized that the girl was intelligent and cultured. She became aware that her views on segregation were not shared by the community she had joined, a community she prized very highly. Although she remained racist until many years later, the incident lodged in Virginia's memory, creating a fracture in her convictions about race that contributed to their later destruction.

Virginia's mind was more thoroughly opened to issues of gender equality during college—the third important experience college offered her. Through a combination of coursework, admiration for strong women faculty, and the ethos and mission of Wellesley, she came to see gender roles in an entirely new way, questioning the norms and assumptions that so severely constrained women in the early twentieth century, especially in the Deep South. She learned to care passionately about women's rights, including their rights as citizens: "I realized for the first time that women could be something. This was the real liberation that I got at Wellesley" (Durr & Barnard, 1985, p. 59).

After Virginia returned to Alabama, she eagerly went to the polls and was shocked to learn that she had to pay a tax in order to vote. Virginia was outraged by the tax and the way the entrenched political establishment used the tax to maintain its control. When she moved to Washington, D.C., with her husband a few years later, she joined the Women's Division of the Democratic National Committee in a bitter, extended, and ultimately successful campaign to abolish the poll tax. She initially joined that struggle solely for the sake of women's rights; her action was a direct result of her college experiences. Although she much admired Eleanor Roosevelt and the other women on the committee, she was still a self-described racist and initially disagreed with them about race. Because of the coalitions that formed around the voting rights issues, however, Virginia soon found herself working closely with black organizations and distinguished black women such as Mary McLeod Bethune and Mary Church Terrell. Over time these working relationships led her to change dramatically her perspective on race and to look back on her earlier views with a sense of shame.

A fourth critical college influence resulted from Virginia's participation in an extracurricular activity, the Southern Club, through which she formed relationships with other southern students who had come north to college. This might have insulated her from the benefits of encountering a new culture, but almost by chance, it led to further growth. In the Southern Club, Virginia came to know and admire a Harvard student, Clark Foreman, who later became an activist for racial equality, after having studied abroad and then having witnessed a lynching upon his return to the United States. He and Virginia renewed their friendship some years later while they were both living in Washington, D.C. Just at the time that Virginia began her work with the Democratic National Committee, Foreman also confronted and seriously challenged her segregationist views on race, opening her mind still further and helping to draw her into the struggle for racial justice.

Some of the important developmental experiences Virginia had while a student at Wellesley no doubt resulted from intentional efforts faculty, residence hall staff, and others at the college made to awaken intellectual excitement, challenge assumptions, and foster new ways of understanding the world, both by structuring academic study and by establishing a climate and conveying a set of expectations. Other influences, particularly those connected with the Southern Club, seem to have been fortuitous. Had Clark Foreman not made a personal transformation of his own in the years following college, he could not have played a catalytic role in Virginia Durr's awakening.

This book takes up the question of what kinds of influence undergraduate education can have on students' development as ethical, committed, and engaged human beings and citizens. The undergraduate years are just one part of a lifelong developmental process, but especially if efforts are intentionally designed with these developmental outcomes in mind, colleges can establish some groundwork that students can later build on, shape the intellectual frameworks and habits of mind they bring to their adult experiences, change the way they understand the responsibilities that are central to their sense of self, and teach them to offer and demand evidence and justification for their moral and political positions and to develop wiser judgment in approaching situations and questions that represent potential turning points in their lives.

In a loose sense, undergraduate education at its best can resemble the preparations explorers make when preparing for expeditions into uncharted territories. Meriwether Lewis, for example, prior to his exploration of the North American continent with William Clark, collected a wide array of tools and learned how to use many that were new to him (chronometers, sextants, and other scientific instruments; medical equipment; and so on). With the help of some extraordinary teachers and mentors, including Thomas Jefferson, Albert Gallatin, Benjamin Rush, and others, he mastered knowledge that he would need (in geography, botany, natural history, astronomy, commerce, and American Indian culture) and learned scientific techniques that would allow him to use his explorations to expand the boundaries of that knowledge. Before assembling a team, he thought hard about what kind of men he needed and how he could maintain a cohesive corps. Lewis also collected the best existing maps, however incomplete they were, and out of his experience with those maps and integration of the disparate bodies of knowledge he had studied, his plans took shape (Ambrose, 1996). These preparations shifted somewhat the course of Lewis's journey and the route adjustments he would make in response to unexpected barriers and events. When he finished the preparations and set out, his direction was perhaps only slightly different than it would have been with less groundwork, but over many months of travel the slight initial shift in trajectory and the continuing, responsive alterations no doubt led to a route distinctly different from the one he would have taken without such extensive preparations. Moreover, the viability and scientific productivity of the expedition was critically dependent on what he had learned during the preparation phase.

Similarly, students may leave college with the trajectories of their lives shifted only slightly but with ways of approaching and responding to their subsequent experiences that magnify the shift over time, until much later it becomes clear that the gap between where they are and where they would have been without those influences is dramatic. The undergraduate experience has the potential to be this kind of *preexpedition* for millions of Americans, and we believe colleges will be most effective in this preparation if their efforts are self-conscious and intentional, not simply dependent on the fortuitous impact of the kind that Clark Foreman had on Virginia Durr.

College is the last stage of formal education for most Americans and the last formal education outside their field of specialization for those who pursue further study. Although informal education can continue throughout life—at work and through engagement with the media, the arts, and books—to a great extent experiences in college determine how inclined individuals will be to pursue this kind of ongoing learning and what intellectual and personal capacities they will bring to those engagements.

The Need for Undergraduate Moral and Civic Education

Although acknowledging the exceptional vitality of U.S. higher education, Ernest Boyer's report (1987) on the college experience also points to a number of things that diminish the quality of undergraduate education, preventing colleges from serving their students as well as they might. One issue that stands out in Boyer's investigation is the question of what the goals and purposes of higher education should be. Boyer's calls for greater attention to the moral and civic purposes of college have been widely quoted in the intervening fifteen years. In a chapter titled "From Competence to Commitment," he said:

> Throughout our study we were impressed that what today's college is teaching most successfully is competence—competence in meeting schedules, in gathering information, in responding well on tests, in mastering the details of a special field. . . . But technical skill, of whatever kind, leaves open essential questions: Education for what purpose? Competence to what end? At a time in life when values should be shaped and personal priorities sharply probed, what a tragedy it would be if the most deeply felt issues, the most haunting questions, the most creative moments were pushed to the fringes of our institutional life. What a monumental mistake it would be if students, during the undergraduate years, remained trapped within the organizational grooves and narrow routines to which the academic world sometimes seems excessively devoted [p. 283].

Through large-scale surveys of faculty and students and extended site visits at twenty-nine colleges and universities, Boyer and his colleagues concluded that by and large undergraduate education is not meeting the challenge of going beyond competence to commitment. The research team encountered a picture that seems quite at odds with our opening portrait of Virginia Durr's experience at a small, liberal arts college for women in the 1920s. The report points to conflicting priorities and competing interests, confusion about mission and goals, disciplinary fragmentation, a narrow vocationalism, a great separation between academic and social life on campus, and a disturbing gap between the college and the larger world. These trends and several others impede the efforts of faculty and administrative leaders who see the importance of higher education's civic mission and want to make the undergraduate years a pivotal time for moral and civic development.

It is a good time to revisit this question of the public purposes of higher education. The need is perhaps even greater now than it was at the time of the Boyer report a decade and a half ago. Global interdependence is ever more striking and insistent. Old social problems persist, and new ones are emerging. The country's increasing racial and ethnic diversity has brought tensions and raised dilemmas as well as enriched its already kaleidoscopic culture. And the complexity of the contemporary social, economic, and political worlds is accelerating at an alarming pace. If today's college graduates are to be positive forces in this world, they need not only to possess knowledge and intellectual capacities but also to see themselves as members of a community, as individuals with a responsibility to contribute to their communities. They must be willing to act for the common good and capable of doing so effectively. If a college education is to support the kind of learning graduates need to be involved and responsible citizens, its goals must go beyond the development of intellectual and technical skills and beginning mastery of a scholarly domain. They should include the competence to act in the world and the judgment to do so wisely. A full account of competence, including occupational competence, must include the abilities to exercise considered judgment, appreciate ends as well as means, and understand the broad implications and consequences of one's actions and choices. Education is not complete until students not only have acquired knowledge but can act on that knowledge in the world.

There is evidence that this kind of civic commitment has waned in recent decades. A number of social commentators have documented the excessive individualism of contemporary U.S. culture and its negative implications for this society (Bellah, Madsen, Sullivan, Swidler, & Tipton, 1991; Putnam, 1995). The consequences of this cultural climate include a growing sense that Americans are not responsible for or accountable to each other; a decline in civility, mutual respect, and tolerance; and the preeminence of self-interest and individual preference over concern for the common good. Goals of personal advancement and gratification too often take precedence over social, moral, or spiritual meaning. Although this emphasis on individual success has some social benefits, it can also entail high social costs by promoting a worldview in which there is no basis for enduring commitment beyond the self. Currently, the most visible alternative to this focus on self-interest is a kind of orthodox and intolerant moralism. Ironically, each of these opposing perspectives contributes to the same result: a polarized and fragmented society, whose members have little sense of being united by participation in a common enterprise.

Many commentators have also chronicled a widespread lack of trust in and respect for U.S. democratic processes and an overall decline in civic and political participation (Putnam, 2000). Demographic data indicate that political disaffection is especially pronounced among youths and young adults, including college students. Americans growing up in recent decades vote less often than their elders and show lower levels of social trust and knowledge of politics (Bennett & Rademacher, 1997; Putnam, 1995). In fact, voting among young people in the 2000 presidential election was at a record low even though overall turnout was up slightly from

1996. This mounting political apathy bodes ill for the future of U.S. democracy unless these generations of young people come to see both the value of and necessity for civic engagement and political participation.

Tempering somewhat this pronounced decline in young people's political engagement is their high level of participation in community service and other volunteer work. A study by the Panetta Institute (2000), for example, indicates that nearly three-quarters of college students (73 percent) have done volunteer work in the past two years, and most (62 percent) more than once. These students understand that their communities face real needs that they can help meet. But although undergraduates are increasingly involved in direct service activities, this involvement does not seem to foster broader or deeper forms of civic or political engagement among them (Gray et al., 1999; Mason & Nelson, 2000; Sax, Astin, Korn, & Mahoney, 1999). Too often students fail to understand that if they want not only to help a community kitchen feed people but also to help eliminate the need for that kitchen, they must work to change public policy and that strong engagement in one's community and in politics in one form or another is the means for affecting public policy.

Higher education has the potential to be a powerful influence in reinvigorating the democratic spirit in America. Virtually all civic, political, and professional leaders are graduates of higher education institutions, and the general public is attending college in ever higher numbers. Over fifteen million students are now enrolled in higher education. About 40 percent are in community colleges, and unlike students in earlier eras, most are commuting students, many with jobs and families. This extensive reach places colleges and universities in a strong position to help reshape broader culture. Although higher education reflects the values of the larger society in many ways, colleges and universities are not simply extensions of society, nor are they helpless in the face of social constraints. Rather they have the potential to act intentionally in fostering the moral and civic learning of their students, as we have frequently observed during the course of our work on this book.

Explorations in Undergraduate Moral and Civic Education Today

Although we see many of the same problems in colleges and universities today that Boyer reported in his study conducted more than fifteen years ago, we also see something that Boyer did not report: a number of institutions that have made their students' moral and civic development a high priority and have created a wealth of curricular and extracurricular programs to stimulate and support that development. This is a good time to revisit the issue of higher education's role in educating citizens not only because the problems in the world are great but also because educators and policymakers can now learn some important lessons from a close look at the efforts of those committed institutions.

In conducting the research for this book, we reviewed the practices of moral and civic education at many colleges and universities around the country and made in-depth visits to twelve: Alverno College; the College of St. Catherine; California State University, Monterey Bay; Duke University; Kapiʻolani Community College; Messiah College; Portland State University; Spelman College; Turtle Mountain Community College; Tusculum College; the United States Air Force Academy; and the University of Notre Dame. These explorations have shown us that an extraordinarily diverse range of colleges and universities take the moral and civic education of their students very seriously. These schools include every category of higher education institution—community colleges, four-year colleges, comprehensive universities, and universities with graduate and professional programs. Some are residential, others are nonresidential; some are public, others are private; some are large, others are small; some are religiously affiliated; some are military academies; some are single sex; and some are primarily for members of a minority group. These and others are represented among the institutions that treat their students' moral and civic development as central to their mission, although each one understands its specific goals somewhat differently and concerns itself with different aspects of this broad domain.

For a few U.S. colleges and universities, this commitment manifests itself as an intentional and holistic approach to moral and civic as well as academic education, an approach that shapes many or most aspects of students' college experience. In calling this approach intentional, we mean that these institutions are explicit about their goals and actively plan strategies to achieve them. By holistic, we mean that the approach addresses many different aspects of students' moral and civic development, and it does so through many different sites in the academic and nonacademic life of the campus, with significant efforts to connect those sites. These holistic, intentional efforts are of special interest because they illustrate the power of a serious institutional commitment to moral and civic education. A close look at these committed campuses shows that if an institution and its leadership adopt a comprehensive approach to moral and civic learning and seek to implement it with a high degree of intentionality, the results can be transformative for students and for the institution. We highlight institutions that take these intentional and holistic approaches not because this is the only or most prevalent option for campuses interested in these issues but because we believe that supporting students' moral and civic development is best achieved through the cumulative, interactive effects of numerous curricular and extracurricular programs in an environment of sustained institutional commitment to a set of overarching goals. The insights and approaches of these institutions are portfolios of good practices from which other campuses can draw, even if they begin by adopting just one or two courses or programs.

In the following chapters we describe the twelve schools we visited in greater detail than the many others whose work we reviewed in less depth. We spent several days at each of these twelve *case study* schools, interviewing administrators, faculty, and students; conducting focus groups; sitting in on classes; and observing a wide range of programs. Following the visits, we prepared a detailed case write-up on each institution, which was reviewed for accuracy by individuals at that campus. Campus representatives later reviewed descriptions of their programs in a manuscript draft of this book, suggesting corrections where needed. (Of course programs do change over time, so these reviews cannot guarantee that our accounts are completely up to date at the present time.) These twelve institutions are not flawless, and we will point out not only their successes but also some of the areas in which they are still struggling to find the right approach. They are also not necessarily the best exemplars of moral and civic education in the country. We did not conduct an exhaustive review of all possible candidates. Certainly they are not the only institutions doing notable work in this area. We chose these particular institutions in part because of the valuable work they are doing and also because we wanted a group that was diverse in mission and type, covering a broad geographical range.

In addition to institutions that implement moral and civic education holistically, there are many others with a few courses or specific programs that address students' moral and civic development. These colleges and universities focus their efforts on programs or activities that are powerful experiences for some students but do not reach all undergraduates. These targeted programs may take such forms as academic centers and institutes, freshman seminars, and senior capstone courses. Throughout this book our emphasis is on good practices in both the comprehensive and the targeted approaches to moral and civic learning in higher education and the challenges that must be overcome to succeed in those practices.

Ideals and Goals of Moral and Civic Education

Before going further we need to address the question: What do we mean by moral and civic education? What is it that we are calling for? Our answer takes us immediately into the perennially thorny issue of whether colleges ought to stand for particular moral values or ideals or call only for clarity and consistency of moral beliefs. We have taken the former position, that colleges and universities ought to educate for substantive values, ideals, and standards, at least in broad terms, and should not be content with what is sometimes referred to as *values clarification*. We are convinced that it is not possible to create a value-neutral environment, so it is preferable for colleges and universities to examine the values they stand for and make conscious and deliberate choices about what they convey to students. More important, we believe that there are some basic moral principles, ideals, and virtues that can form a common ground to guide institutions of higher education in their work, including the work of educating citizens in a democracy.

On the first point, educational institutions have never been and cannot be value neutral. For decades educators have recognized the power of the "hidden curriculum" in schools and the moral messages it carries. The hidden curriculum consists of the (largely unexamined) practices with which the school and its teachers operate, assigning grades and other rewards and managing their relationships with their students and the students' relationships with each other (Fenstermacher, 1990; Jackson, 1968; Kohlberg, 1971). Although much of the research on the hidden curriculum has examined elementary and secondary education, the concept applies equally to higher education. If college students see faculty rewarded for pursuing their own professional prestige rather than for caring for others or the institution, if they are subjected to competitive, zero-sum climates in which one student's success contributes to another's failure, if they are confronted with institutional hypocrisy, those practices convey moral messages that can contribute to students' cynicism and self-interestedness. Conversely, students can learn positive moral lessons when they see faculty who approach their scholarship with integrity and who are scrupulously honest and fair, caring with students and respectful of colleagues, and committed to the institution or the larger community.

Academic disciplines also embody values that shape students' perspectives and frames of reference, even though these assumptions are often unexamined and thus invisible. The preponderance of recent research in economics and in political science, for example, builds on a model of *rational choice,* which is seldom subjected to critical analysis in the teaching of these disciplines. This model of human behavior assumes that individuals will always seek to maximize their perceived interests and that social phenomena represent the aggregate of individuals employing this self-interested strategy. A similar perspective is fostered by research and theory in other fields, such as sociobiology and some approaches in psychology, which also assume a self-interested or mechanistic view of human nature. An unquestioning reliance on these models of human behavior can result in the *normalization of self-interestedness,* contributing to a belief that individuals are always fundamentally motivated by self-interest, that altruism and genuine concern for others' welfare are illusory, and that failing to act strategically to achieve one's own self-interested goals would be foolish.

In addition to values expressed through teaching, student-faculty relationships, and institutional norms and practices, values from the outside world permeate college campuses. Messages of instrumental individualism and materialism are becoming more and more prevalent in the broader institutional and peer cultures on many campuses. The commercialization of higher education, including corporate sponsorship of faculty and student research, corporate underwriting of programs, advertising on Web sites, and exclusive "pouring rights" given to soda companies at sports and other events, can provide important financial benefits but also reinforces themes of materialism pervasive in the general culture. By default, some powerful values are thrust on young people by outside sources, particularly advertising. Few would deny the influence of commercial interests represented by television, film, music, and other media on the peer culture and informal learning contexts of the campus. To the extent that higher education is influenced by broader cultural trends, it is influenced by those values as well.

In these and many other ways, educational institutions convey values and moral messages to their students. This is unavoidable. Given this reality, we believe it is preferable for colleges and universities to stand for values that are fundamental to their highest sense of purpose, rather than taking "a default position of instrumental individualism in which expertise and skill appear as simply neutral tools to be appropriated by successful competitors in the service of their particular ends," as William Sullivan (1999, p. 11) has described the prevailing ethos in higher education.

The Issue of Determining Goals and Means

How can we identify common values that constitute a foundation for moral and civic learning in U.S. institutions of higher education while still recognizing that those shared values often come into conflict with each other and that different individuals and subcultures may create different hierarchies among these values? Few would dispute that colleges' educational and scholarly missions entail a core set of values, such as intellectual integrity, concern for truth, and academic freedom. By colleges' very nature it is also important for them to foster values such as mutual respect, open-mindedness, the willingness to listen to and take seriously the ideas of others, procedural fairness, and public discussion of contested issues. The academic enterprise would be seriously compromised if these values ceased to guide scholarship, teaching, and learning, however imperfect that guidance may be in practice.

Principles and ideals that have a place in a common core of values can also be derived from educational institutions' obligation to educate students for responsible democratic citizenship. Most mission statements of both public and private colleges and universities explicitly refer to an institution's responsibility to educate for leadership and contributions to society. We show in the next chapter that this conception of higher education dates back to the founding of this country. Even institutions that do not make this part of their mission a central priority acknowledge some responsibility for it. Recognition of the obligation to prepare citizens for participation in a democratic system implies that certain values, both moral and civic, ought to be represented in these institutions' educational goals and practices. Some of these values are the same as those entailed in the academic enterprise itself; some go beyond that sphere. These values include mutual respect and tolerance, concern for both the rights and the welfare of individuals and the community, recognition that each individual is part of the larger social fabric, critical self-reflectiveness, and a commitment to civil and rational discourse and procedural impartiality (Galston, 1991; Gutmann, 1987; Macedo, 2000).

Educational philosopher Eamonn Callan (1997) argues that a liberal democracy based on free and equal citizenship requires not only certain social rules and political institutions, such as legal protections for free speech, but also moral and civic education grounded in democratic ideals. These ideals include "a lively interest in the question of what life is truly and not just seemingly good, as well as a willingness both to share one's answer with others and to heed the many opposing answers they might give; an active commitment to the good of the polity, as well as . . . competence in judgment regarding how that good should be advanced; a respect for fellow citizens and a sense of common fate with them that goes beyond the tribalisms of ethnicity and religion yet is alive to the significance these will have in many people's lives" (p. 3).

Beyond this generic set of core values that derive from the intellectual and civic purposes of higher education, some private colleges and even a few public ones stand for more specific moral, cultural, or religious values. Such institutions' particular missions—and the implications of these missions for the educational programs—should be made clear to prospective students and faculty. The most obvious examples of these highly specific values are found in religiously affiliated schools that offer faith-based education. Among public institutions, military academies are mandated to educate military officers, so their values are defined with reference to this goal. Other public colleges established to serve particular populations, such as American Indian colleges, also often explicitly acknowledge special values, such as traditional tribal values, in their curricula and programs.

When the values on which there is broad consensus within an institution are taken seriously, they constitute strong guiding principles for programs of moral and civic development in higher education. Even so, they leave open to debate the principles that should be given priority when values conflict as well as the ways in which individuals might apply the principles to particular situations. Especially in institutions that stand for a commitment to rational public discourse, as higher education must, the most difficult questions of conflicting values can and should be left to public debate and individual discernment. Moral and civic education provides the tools for these discussions and judgments. This means that institutions do not need to begin with agreement on the most difficult and controversial cases of conflict between values. And this openness is what makes it possible to reach a consensus on an initial set of core values. Because a willingness to engage in reasoned discourse and commitments to honesty, fairness, and respect for persons are among the ideals all colleges and universities should uphold, these values should help guide the community toward resolution of the more difficult questions. Colleges and universities should encourage and facilitate the development of students' capacities to examine complex situations in which competing values are at stake, to employ both substantive knowledge and moral reasoning to evaluate the problems and values involved, to develop their own judgments about these issues in respectful dialogue with others, and then to act on their judgments.

We recognize the difficulties and potential pitfalls educators face when discussing moral and civic values in a society as strongly pluralist as this one, in which tolerance and respect for differences are themselves held as fundamental values. Within any given cultural tradition and certainly across traditions, there are deep disagreements about many moral, civic, political, and religious issues. But even as educators appreciate the depths of these differences, it is important that they distinguish between *moral pluralism* and *moral relativism*. A pluralistic view of morality assumes there are two or more incommensurable moral frameworks that are justifiable. This does not mean that *any* possible moral framework is justifiable, however, only that there are multiple valid moral frameworks that cannot be reduced to a single system. In contrast, moral relativism holds that there is no basis for distinguishing among moral positions at all, that no position can be considered any more or less valid than another.

Even in anthropological research that documents striking cultural differences in moral values, there are boundaries around the range of what is seen to count as an ultimate moral good, and even very different moral perspectives include (though they do not stress) each other's values (Shweder, 1996). Differences in moral frames of reference are best understood as variations in the ways widely shared base values, such as freedom and loyalty, are ordered when they conflict and variations in the salience of values in practice. Even anthropologists who believe there is fundamental moral heterogeneity across cultures generally do not believe in extreme and unqualified cultural relativism. Very different and even fundamentally incommensurate moral perspectives still build on a base set of moral goods or virtues that human beings have in common. Presumably these commonalities will be stronger within a single country, even a culturally heterogeneous and pluralistic country such as the United States.

Educational institutions can respect diversity of opinion on particular ethical questions and avoid both illegitimate indoctrination and moral relativism if they are explicit about their commitment to the moral and civic values that are fundamental to a democracy, at the same time being careful not to foreclose open-minded consideration of multiple solutions to moral dilemmas in which fundamental values conflict.

The Salience of the Moral: Integrity and Engagement

Throughout this discussion we have referred to both *moral* and *civic* values, development, and education. We do so to underscore the point that the moral and the civic are inseparable. Because we understand the term *morality* to describe prescriptive judgments about how one ought to act in relation to other people, it follows that many core democratic principles, including tolerance and respect, impartiality, and concern for both the rights of the individual and the welfare of the group, are grounded in moral principles. Just political systems require citizens with "the capacity for moral reciprocity—the predisposition to create and abide by fair rules of cooperation" (Callan, 1997, p. 21). The problems that confront civically engaged citizens always include strong moral themes. These include fair access to resources such as housing, the obligation to consider future generations in making environmental policy, and the need to take into account the conflicting claims of multiple stakeholders in community decision making. No issue involving these themes can be adequately resolved without a consideration of moral questions and values. A person can become civically and politically active without good judgment and a strong moral compass, but it is hardly wise to promote that kind of involvement. Because civic responsibility is inescapably threaded with moral values, we believe that higher education should aspire to foster both moral and civic maturity and should confront educationally the many links between them.

If civic responsibility implies and includes moral responsibility, as we believe, then why not make our language in this book simpler by dropping the term *moral* because it is in some sense redundant? We were urged to do this by a distinguished philosopher of education and seriously considered it. In the end, though, we decided to retain the dual term *moral and civic,* along with whatever redundancy it may carry, in order to emphasize throughout this book the necessary connection between the moral and the civic. This is also our response to some quite visible civic educators who attempt to segregate civic from moral education, hoping to avoid controversy by doing so.

One key to legitimacy for moral and civic education is that it not indoctrinate. It must not "restrict rational deliberation of competing conceptions of the good life and the good society" (Gutmann, 1987, p. 44). We believe that colleges can foster core academic and democratic values and at the same time avoid indoctrination. But some skeptics have expressed the concern that however laudable its goals, moral and civic education is bound to indoctrinate in practice and therefore cannot be justified.

Although the institutions we studied take very different approaches to moral and civic learning, every one shares a central concern for developing student inclinations and capacities related to open inquiry and genuine debate. These include openness to reason, effective communication, tolerance of perspectives different from one's own, clarity of thought, critical thinking, and the capacity to conduct moral discourse across points of view. In these institutions the central pedagogies and other programs intended to foster moral and civic responsibility are consciously noncoercive (with the exception of honor codes, which require adherence to standards of honesty). In part because students are encouraged to think independently, those we observed did not appear reluctant to resist if they thought a faculty member or another student was trying to impose his or her views. In our visits to even the most specialized institutions, we were surprised by the consistency with which faculty took care to ensure that multiple points of view were heard, and encouraged students to question and think through the assumptions in the dominant institutional culture. Of course there may be abuses of these principles of noncoercion and open discussion by individual faculty or institutions, but this kind of abuse can occur whether or not the development of students' moral and civic responsibility is an explicit institutional goal. Urging institutions of higher education to be explicit and reflective in these efforts, to open their educational practices to public view, and to join national conversations about these practices with a diverse range of other institutions is more likely to minimize the abuses of power critics fear than is attempting to run a "value-free" institution. If pursued thoughtfully, an approach that brings civic and moral issues into public debate and discussion should make it possible to use words such as *morality, character, patriotism,* and *social justice* in ways that are not hidden codes for any particular agenda or ideology. This should open up communication about what these words mean and what their implications are for difficult contemporary social issues.

The irony in the well-intentioned fear that moral and civic education might impose arbitrary values on students is that achieving the values-based goals of liberal education is students' best *protection* against indoctrination, and it can continue to protect them throughout their lives. Helping students develop the capacity for critical thinking and the habit of using it, teaching them to be open-minded and interested in pursuing ideas, requiring them to back up their claims and to expect others to do the same, and encouraging them to be knowledgeable and accustomed to thinking about moral, civic, and political issues will put them in a strong posture to think independently about their positions and commitments. The more they have thought about these issues and learned to argue them through, the less susceptible they will be to indoctrination.

Goals for Student Learning

If moral and civic education is based in the kinds of fundamental values we have discussed here, what does that imply about its goals for students? In general terms, we believe that a morally and civically responsible individual recognizes himself or herself as a member of a larger social fabric and therefore considers social problems to be at least partly his or her own; such an individual is willing to see the moral and civic dimensions of issues, to make and justify informed moral and civic judgments, and to take action when appropriate. A fully developed individual must have the ability to think clearly and in an appropriately complex and sophisticated way about moral and civic issues; he or she must possess the moral commitment and sense of personal responsibility to act, which may include having moral emotions such as empathy and concern for others; moral and civic values, interests, and habits; and knowledge and experience in the relevant domains of life. We are concerned with the development of the whole person, as an accountable individual and engaged participant in society—local, state, national, and global. Responsibility includes viewing oneself as a member of a shared social structure and as a fair target of evaluative attitudes, such as praise and blame. Virtues such as honesty, trustworthiness, fairness, and respect are essential to personal integrity, fostering fair dealing and concern for the ways one's actions affect others. Social conscience, compassion and commitment to the welfare of those outside one's immediate sphere, is an important component of moral and civic development that goes beyond the level of personal integrity. Partially overlapping these two dimensions of personal integrity and social conscience is a specifically civic component: coming to understand how a community operates, the problems it faces, and the richness of its diversity and also developing a willingness to commit time and energy to enhance community life and work collectively to resolve community concerns. Finally, constructive political engagement, defined in terms of democratic processes, is a particular subset of civic responsibility that has been the focus of substantial concern in recent years. Although there is overlap, we believe it is important to distinguish the political domain from the nonpolitical civic domain, because they can be independent of one another in terms of both motivation for and modes of involvement.

Political engagement cannot always be sharply distinguished from other forms of civic participation because it exists on a continuum with apolitical forms of civic engagement. But making this distinction is important for understanding what it means to educate citizens. It is also important for identifying some of the strengths and weaknesses in moral and civic engagement in U.S. undergraduate education. We do not want to define political engagement as simply voting in national elections or joining political parties, because that excludes forms of participation that may have appeal for today's college students, particularly activities related to direct participation rather than electoral politics. In an effort to find a middle ground between an overly narrow and an overly inclusive conception, we define *political engagement* as including activities intended to influence social and political institutions, beliefs, and practices and to affect processes and policies relating to community welfare, whether that community is local, state, national, or international. Political engagement may include working informally with others to solve a community problem; serving in neighborhood organizations, political interest groups, or political organizations; participating in public forums on social issues, discussing political issues with family and friends, and trying to influence others' political opinions; working on a campaign for a candidate or issue; writing letters, signing petitions, and participating in other forms of policy advocacy and lobbying; raising public awareness about social issues and mobilizing others to get involved or take action; attending rallies and protests and participating in boycotts; and of course voting in local or national elections.

Even in this relatively broad definition of political engagement, not all forms of civic involvement count as political. Political involvement does not include some kinds of direct service volunteer work, such as tutoring in after-school programs, and it does not include social activities such as bowling leagues or book clubs, personal commitments such as recycling, and other endeavors not connected to concerns for policy questions (regarding animal treatment or environmental health, for example) or root causes of social problems (such as educational inequity) and not intended to result in broad social or institutional change.

Encouraging political engagement directly related to public policy is particularly important, because some of the most acute concerns for U.S. democracy relate to distrust of government and lack of interest in governmental affairs, especially among young people. To reconnect college students with political affairs and traditional forms of political involvement, faculty and program advisers need to help students see the links between their direct service activities, personal commitments, and lifestyle choices on the one hand and related institutional and policy questions on the other. In doing so, it is important that they build bridges to students' own conceptions of appropriate political analysis and action, which for many students are focused on grassroots activities and related activities rather than mainstream electoral politics, about which they remain skeptical. Although some institutions of higher education are seeking ways to stimulate political engagement as well as other kinds of civic participation and leadership, we have found that this aspect of civic responsibility is least attended to in higher education, even among schools with strong commitments to moral and civic learning.

The kind of moral and civic maturity we have outlined here entails a wide array of capacities. We have found it useful to group these capacities into three broad categories. The first is moral and civic understanding, which includes dimensions such as interpretation, judgment, and knowledge. The second category is moral and civic motivation and includes values, interests, emotions such as empathy and hope, sense of efficacy, and moral and civic identity. Finally, some core skills are essential for carrying out moral and civic responsibility by applying core knowledge and virtues and transforming informed judgments into action. Given these necessary capacities, moral and civic maturity requires competence in a wide range of practical areas, including moral and political discourse and other forms of communication, interpersonal relationships, and civic and political engagement. Among the skills needed for the latter, for example, are the ability to lead, to build a consensus, and to move a group forward under conditions of mutual respect. Through a diversity of strategies, under-graduate moral and civic education can support the development of capaci-ties and skills in all the essential areas.

The Integration of Moral and Civic Learning with Academic Learning

We are convinced that taking moral and civic outcomes seriously has the potential to simultaneously strengthen and enrich nearly all other educa-tional goals. In fact, there is considerable evidence that both moral and civic learning and academic learning more generally are at their most pow-erful when creatively combined. The civic education pedagogy that has been most subjected to empirical research is service learning (which links disciplinary study and community service with structured reflection), and the results of that research make it clear that service learning does enhance academic performance. In an evaluation of a large number of service learning programs, Alexander Astin and his colleagues found significant positive effects on grade point average, writing skills, and critical think-ing skills, as well as on commitment to community service, self-efficacy, and leadership ability (Astin, Sax, Ikeda, & Yee, 2000). There is also a body of research indicating that students' academic performance and their self-assessment of their own learning and motivation are increased through participation in high-quality service-learning programs, especially those that involve challenging service work that is well-integrated with the course material and is accompanied by opportunities for structured reflection on their service experience (Eyler & Giles, 1999).

Another part of the value of broadening the goals of higher education is that linking academic material to students' lives and personal concerns and passions will lead to deeper understanding and more memorable learning. Both cognitive scientists (Bransford & Stein, 1993) and schol-ars in the experiential learning tradition, going all the way back to Dewey (1916) and Whitehead (1929), have pointed out that much of the knowl-edge acquired through decontextualized classroom instruction may be use-less because students are likely to be unable to transfer the knowledge and principles to new problems. Most contemporary educational theorists agree that the "active construction of knowledge" is essential in order to achieve the kind of deep understanding that is required for application and transfer of knowledge (Shulman, 1997). In order to address this challenge directly, many curricular programs designed to foster moral and civic responsibility incorporate problem-based learning, service learning, and other *pedagogies of engagement* in their efforts to involve students more deeply and fully with the issues and support more lasting student learning. In doing so, they enhance academic learning as well as moral and civic responsibility.

Translating the Vision into Action

We have laid out in this chapter our ideals for the responsible and engaged citizen and will go on in later chapters to show how undergraduate education at some colleges and universities aspires toward these ideals. We know that despite the best efforts of these institutions and their committed administrators, faculty, and staff most students will not emerge transformed and complete. But this is not really the goal of moral and civic learning in college. Rather, the goal is to start students on, or move them further along on, a route that provides them with the understanding, motivation, and skills they will need to meet the challenges of engaged citizenship. We have seen that it is possible for an undergraduate education to act as a powerful preexpedition, equipping students with critical tools and skills, clearing away some of their central confusions, shifting them toward more constructive habits of heart and mind, providing them with new lenses for refracting the many problems and dilemmas they will confront, raising questions about their unexamined assumptions, and connecting them with others who can inspire them and become indelible images of the kind of person they want to become. The full outcome may not be evident until many years later, but their college years may shift these students' direction just enough to make a dramatic difference over the course of their lives as experiences accumulate and the individual approaches each one just a little bit differently than he or she would have otherwise. This is what happened for Virginia Durr. The potential is there for a similar impact on both those who are older, part-time, working students—now about half of all undergraduates—and those who enter college directly after high school.

To translate this vision for moral and civic learning into effective educational programs, educators must attend to many questions. What are the essential elements of moral and civic character for Americans in the twenty-first century? What specific dimensions of understanding, motivation, and skills contribute to those elements (recognizing that there may be a range of ways to be a good citizen)? What contribution can higher education make toward developing these qualities in sustained and effective ways? What are the problems confronting colleges and universities that make moral and civic education a priority, and what are the best strategies to help overcome these problems? These are the questions we have wrestled with in writing this book. They are issues at the heart of democracy's future in America, and we encourage others to join this conversation.

2

THE BROADER
UNDERGRADUATE CONTEXT

IN CHAPTER ONE we articulated what we understand to be the moral and civic goals of undergraduate education and some reasons for pursuing them. This chapter puts those goals in a broader perspective, both historically and with reference to the wider context of contemporary undergraduate education. Framing the endeavor this way brings into focus a number of challenges confronting those who wish to strengthen moral and civic education for today's undergraduates. A scan of the historical and contemporary issues in higher education also points to important allies, whose ongoing work, to the extent that it succeeds, will help mitigate these impediments and improve the conditions for undergraduate moral and civic education. These allies are the faculty and administrators who are pressing for more searching and systematic attention to undergraduate student learning, especially those who conceive the goals of that learning in terms of a contemporary understanding of the traditions of liberal education. Moral and civic development has always been central to the goals of liberal education. In fact we believe that the movement to strengthen undergraduate moral and civic education is best understood as an important part of broader efforts to revitalize liberal education, which many commentators have suggested has lost its way in the era since World War II (Orrill, 1997).

We say this recognizing fully that no single definition of liberal education will satisfy all. There is widespread agreement, however, about the general goal of this education: the preparation of students for lives that provide personal satisfaction and promote the common good. A liberal education aspires to expand students' horizons, developing their intellectual and moral capacities and judgments. As Louis Menand (1997) has written, "curiosity, sympathy, a sense of principle, and independence of mind are the qualities we want liberally educated people to have" (p. 2).

The educational means to this goal, in terms of both content and pedagogy, have been variously interpreted. A major split in perspective is reflected in the work of Robert Hutchins, who focused on structured discussions of Western canonical texts, and John Dewey, who emphasized collaborative processes of problem solving (Ehrlich, 1997). Those sharing Dewey's view generally believe that liberal education means development of a broad set of skills and habits of mind, and they usually support distribution requirements (which require students to take a requisite number of courses in a number of disciplinary categories) together with in-depth exposure in one field as the way to gain those skills and habits. Those who adhere to Hutchins's view urge that liberal education should involve a core of content and precepts that transcends any particular discipline and is best reflected in great books. Hutchins and Dewey crossed swords half a century ago, but the debates in which they engaged continue.

There are many variations on their analyses and prescriptions, and the institutional boundaries of what counts as liberal education have also been subject to debate and significant revision over time. We will sidestep these controversies and use the term *liberal education* to refer to the full range of efforts that pursue some version of the overarching goal of preparing students for lives that provide personal satisfaction and promote the common good, regardless of particular approaches or institutional arrangements. Therefore our definition embraces the education offered not only by colleges or schools of liberal arts but also by community colleges and even programs of undergraduate professional or vocational education when they embody this aspiration.

Despite this broad conception of liberal education, the iconic image the term calls up is the small, residential college, as we reflected in the way we began this book, with a story drawn from a liberal arts college in the 1920s. Since that time, however, the United States has seen both dramatic changes and important continuities in undergraduate education and in the world for which that education is meant to prepare students. The goals of liberal education have been reconceived in contemporary terms, taking the needs of present—and expected future—realities into account. New formulations stress the abilities to function in a culturally diverse, globally interdependent, technologically sophisticated, and rapidly changing world. But there are important continuities as well, and twenty-first-century visions for liberal education share much with earlier formulations. The contemporary world still requires of individuals the time-honored abilities to bring multiple perspectives to bear on any given issue; to exercise sound judgment in professional, personal, and civic contexts; to be faithful to strong ethical principles; and to contribute to one's community and the world. And even some goals that may sound like relatively new ideas—such as the development of intellectual skills as well as mastery of subject matter and the improvement of capacities to frame and deal with unstructured problems that require insights drawn from several disciplines—have a long history in the espoused purposes of liberal education.

By the time Virginia Durr (whom we introduced in Chapter One) attended Wellesley College in the 1920s, higher education had already changed in profound ways since the previous century, and it has continued to change. Many of these changes have made the specific goals of liberal education, including moral and civic goals, harder to achieve. As American higher education has evolved from the eighteenth century to the present, moral and civic concerns have moved from its center, inherent in the very concept of a college education, to its margins, segregated from the rest of academic life. If these trends prevail, education for responsible citizenship could be squeezed out altogether, at least in some kinds of institutions. At the very least these shifts in the landscape of higher education have resulted in a contemporary context that presents serious impediments to advancing both moral and civic education and liberal education more broadly. These impediments include many of the characteristics of undergraduate education the Boyer (1987) report pointed out, as well as some others: the strong departmental focus of colleges and universities, faculty reward systems that place relatively little emphasis on teaching relative to research, the structure of the undergraduate curriculum, the separation between academic and student life, and accommodations to market forces resulting in the *commodification* of higher education.

In later chapters we concentrate on strategies that are being developed to reclaim the moral and civic agenda. In some sense these strategies can be seen as adaptations of or challenges to the barriers presented by widespread institutional arrangements shaping undergraduate teaching and learning. At least in some kinds of institutions, the faculty and administrators who do this kind of reclamation work are swimming against the tide. This is one reason that a holistic approach to moral and civic education, grounded in an institution's broader educational stance, is so beneficial to these efforts. It provides an institutional context in which many forces are pulling in the same direction rather than exerting resistance that has to be overcome.

The institutions whose approach we have called holistic and intentional reflect more congenial developments in higher education, ones that strengthen and support the agenda of liberal education, including its moral and civic goals. Educational reformers and innovators have continued to refine, adapt, and affirm the goals of undergraduate education and to create new ways to put them into practice. These include innovations in such areas as curriculum design, pedagogy, assessment, faculty roles, and faculty development. But these reformers swim against a powerful tide, so we consider now, in very broad terms, the origins and shape of that tide.

Moral and Civic Learning in Nineteenth-Century American Higher Education

The belief that there are essential moral and civic dimensions to knowledge and learning is deeply rooted in American intellectual and educational traditions. Educators of earlier periods considered knowledge, morality, and civic action to be thoroughly interconnected and believed that higher education should promote them as mutually reinforcing aspects of preparation for life. This is evident in the calls of prominent Revolutionary figures for education that would foster republican ideals and virtues necessary for supporting the new democratic experiment. Noah Webster (1788/1965) noted that education holds a special place in a republic and should be designed to teach young people "the principles of virtue and liberty; and inspire them with just and liberal ideas of government" (p. 45).

In the nineteenth century, moral and civic learning was closely connected to the religious concerns and assumptions that then dominated higher education. Many of the earliest U.S. colleges were designed as seminaries for training ministers. Most were tied to a religious denomination, and educational structure, culture, and curriculum were all threaded with moral and civic learning premised on religion. During this time most colleges prescribed for all students a uniform course of liberal arts studies that emphasized classical languages and literature and religious faith and instruction. Until the late 1800s, education in the liberal arts generally meant a fixed course of study in Latin, Greek, mathematics, elocution and rhetoric, the sciences (known as natural philosophy), and moral philosophy. Physical education was also an integral part of the curriculum (Bennett, 1997). Neither students nor faculty specialized, and few campuses had distinct departments. Typically, a single tutor or professor might teach

Latin and Greek literature, plus ethics, history, and moral philosophy. Pedagogical methods were also limited: lectures and recitation were the chief methods of instruction, with students frequently reciting texts from memory at the front of the class (Lucas, 1994).

A primary purpose of this standard liberal arts curriculum was to shape character, including moral and intellectual virtues. The classics that dominated the curriculum were understood not as ends in themselves but rather, following the convictions of ancient Rome and Athens, as means of moral and civic instruction as well as intellectual learning and mental discipline (Graff, 1987). A strong presumption prevailed that ethical training, often strongly religious, should be a major component of students' experience within and outside the classroom (Reuben, 1996). In contrast to the espoused democratic aspirations of higher education, U.S. colleges were designed for and limited to a relatively small number of white, male students who were members of an economic and social elite. Both education in the liberal arts and moral and civic education were widely understood as crucial preparation for the positions of social, economic, and political power and leadership that graduates would assume.

At the same time, it is important to acknowledge that from its beginnings higher education was distinctly more democratic in the United States than it was in England or elsewhere in Europe, where higher education remained a preserve of the wealthy and aristocratic for much longer. In the early 1800s, England, for example, had four institutions of higher education for a population of twenty-three million, whereas the state of Ohio alone, with a population of just three million, boasted more than thirty-five colleges and universities (Lucas, 1994). By 1910, the United States had nearly a thousand colleges and universities enrolling 300,000 students, whereas France had just sixteen universities with 40,000 students (Bok, 1986).

The powerful expansion of higher education in this country was driven partly by the moral and civic values embedded in the American understanding of higher education, including egalitarianism and a belief in the vital role of colleges in shaping citizens and leaders of the republic. These values, coupled with a variety of social and economic forces, pushed higher education to expand rapidly after the Civil War. Among these forces were greater industrialization, an influx of immigrants at every level of education, and the Morrill Federal Land Grant Act of 1862, which turned some 17,430,000 acres of public lands over to secular, state-run colleges "to promote the liberal and practical education of the industrial classes in the several pursuits and professions of life" (Rudolph, 1990, p. 249).

Moral and Civic Learning in the Modern University

By the early 1900s, the focus and structure of higher education had undergone a wholesale shift that involved opening opportunities to a much larger and more diverse audience, gradual secularization, greater emphasis on practical and vocational education, scientific instruction and investigation, and widespread adoption of the German university model, which stressed specialization, scholarly research, and academic freedom. This turn-of-the-century transformation entailed dramatic changes in faculty roles and qualifications, curriculum, educational goals, and epistemological or ideological assumptions. These changes have had profound and lasting effects on undergraduate education, including its capacity to educate for moral and civic development. A great deal has been written about the rise of the research university model of higher education in the twentieth-century United States and the eventual adoption of many of its key forms, conventions, and assumptions across the full range of institutional types (see, for example, Kimball, 1997; Lagemann, 1997). We will not attempt more than a brief reference to a few key points from that voluminous literature. But an understanding of the constraints on and opportunities for undergraduate moral and civic education today requires at least a glance at some of the critical changes that occurred and their power in the contemporary context.

Faculty

As the goals and systems of the modern university took hold in the early twentieth century, faculty were no longer understood to be preserving and transmitting received wisdom in a broad array of classical fields but rather were perceived to be creating new knowledge through research and scholarship in specialized domains and training students toward expertise in those domains. Research distinction and productivity became the most important criteria for evaluating faculty, greatly outweighing considerations such as teaching excellence in decisions about faculty hiring, advancement, and compensation (Cuban, 1999). Over the course of the twentieth century the central place of research productivity in faculty evaluation spread from research universities to master's level universities and undergraduate colleges.

From the German universities the U.S. system adopted an emphasis on not only the preeminence of specialized research but also the atmosphere of academic freedom, which was seen as essential to scientific progress. American faculty visiting German universities were impressed by the

Lehrfreiheit (freedom to teach what one wishes) and *Lernfreiheit* (freedom to study what one wishes), and both came to be deeply held values in U.S. higher education (Kimball, 1986, pp. 161–162). Disciplinary specialization was accompanied by a shift in faculty attention and loyalty from the educational enterprise and the institution to academic disciplines and departments. As Ellen Lagemann (1997) has pointed out, historical scholarship (Haskell, 1996) links strong disciplines with professional autonomy and academic freedom. Peer evaluations and critiques from within the discipline provide standards for evaluation and accountability and thus help justify the exemption from institutional regulation that comes with academic freedom (Lagemann, 1997).

The Curriculum

Over time, leaders of the new universities replaced the old standardized core curriculum that concentrated on classical learning and religious themes with a new model that combined specialization in a major field with breadth obtained through a sampling of courses in other disciplines. At the end of the nineteenth century, Harvard president Charles William Eliot championed the new elective, or *open inquiry,* model on civic grounds of a sort: he believed that students allowed earlier and more intense specialization would develop their particular talents to a high level, supporting a meritocracy in which the most able and best-trained men would rise to positions of power, responsibility, and wealth (Lagemann, 1997, pp. 30–31). Eliot also argued that introducing students to new fields of learning and allowing them greater flexibility would make the curriculum more exciting and engaging to them (Bennett, 1997). The efforts of leaders like Eliot, combined with student demand for more scientific and practical subject matter (Kimball, 1986, p. 154), led to great expansion of the fields considered to be worthy of study and to what Douglas Bennett (1997) has called the "disciplining of the curriculum" (p. 135).

Critics of the new curriculum argued for the maintenance of the classics as the only way to ensure the achievement of liberal education's goals (including prominently its moral and civic goals). The counterargument advanced on behalf of the new curriculum stressed the concept of *mental discipline,* which had become popular in the nineteenth-century understanding of the value of studying the classics but was now extended to the new subject matter areas as they were introduced. According to this view, learning in one subject trains the mind to learn in other areas, so it provided a rationale for specialization because one subject could serve as well as another for acquiring mental discipline. At the same time, leaders in the modern university continued to speak of moral and civic goals, and the new scientific focus of college education, particularly the creation of social science disciplines, was frequently supported by moral and civic justifications. Drawing on prevalent utopian ideas about science, educational reformers claimed that open inquiry and scientific methods not only were superior forms of intellectual training but also, when infused into teaching and learning, would promote personal ethics and habits of moral behavior and would serve as engines of social progress and civic improvement (Reuben, 1996). In conjunction with these changes, science and scientific inquiry emerged as the dominant model for learning in college, including moral and civic learning. Free, open, and scientific inquiry would promote intellectual and social progress. Many educators, like Harvard's Francis Peabody, used the mental discipline concept to argue that scientific pursuits were associated with personal virtue and had strong moral benefits for students: "The scientific habit of mind calls for perfect fidelity, transparent sincerity, and instinct for truth, an unflagging self-control; and these are quite as much moral qualities as intellectual gifts" (quoted in Reuben, 1996, p. 75).

Despite the considerable advantages of the new arrangements, the internal dynamics of specialized academic disciplines unintentionally created deep divisions in campuses, often isolating students and faculty into groups based on discipline, major, or school, with little opportunity for cross-disciplinary conversations. The elective system raised the question of how to achieve the broader, more integrative educational goals, including moral and civic goals, and how to ensure that some learning would be common to all students, which many educators still considered important. The shared core curriculum and distribution requirements became the two main strategies for ensuring common learning or breadth, and they represent alternative visions of the "general education" that is meant to balance specialization in the major. These two curricular approaches are still the primary answers to the perennial question of how to balance breadth and depth of learning, and each has important implications for moral and civic education.

The general education movement sought to strengthen the integrative and potentially interdisciplinary core of learning in the face of specialization. Among other things, it led to the widespread creation of required courses focused on Western civilization and on the great books of that civilization. An important milestone in the general education movement was the publication of Harvard's influential "Red Book," *General Education in a Free Society* (Harvard University, Committee on the Objectives of a General Education in a Free Society, 1945), which called for common academic experiences for undergraduates in response to increasing specialization and fractionation of the curriculum. The basic idea underlying the development of a strong core curriculum was that all students should be required to complete courses in each of the three main academic spheres—humanities, sciences, and social sciences. But the initial premise of general education also had strong moral and civic features. The Red Book (Harvard University, 1945) made the case for studying science and the texts of the Western humanist tradition in part by associating them with freedom and democracy. It suggested that philosophy courses, for example, should assume a civic role, with professors researching and teaching the place of human aspirations and ideals in the total scheme of things.

During the same period, many campuses began to create humanities-oriented interdisciplinary core courses, particularly Western civilization and great books courses. A primary goal of these courses, which were often required of all students, was to expose students to a common body of knowledge and set of skills designed around the great ideas of Western heritage, nourishing a common culture and sense of citizenship. An equally important purpose was to introduce students to the study and discussion of moral, social, and political issues related to American culture and ideals. U.S. engagement in war created a strong sense of the need for higher education to introduce students to principles and traditions considered crucial for a healthy democracy. Following models developed at Columbia, Stanford, and Harvard Universities and the University of Chicago, hundreds of campuses adopted similar great books and Western civilization core courses in the post–World War II period. The important benefits of this approach were that all students shared a common learning experience and brought the perspectives of several disciplines to bear on broad questions and issues. Most of these courses included some form of explicit attention to moral and civic issues.

The creation of these core courses also represented a problematic division of educational labor, however, one that exists at many institutions to this day. Because most of these courses were interdisciplinary, they typically remained outside the boundaries of departmental disciplines. In this division, the "real" intellectual work of college learning occurred in individual disciplines, whereas moral and civic learning took place in relatively marginalized Western civilization or comparable courses. These courses were also hard to sustain across new generations of teachers because they fell outside the expertise of discipline-based faculty and thus required faculty with a special interest in or commitment to this kind of integrative teaching (Bennett, 1997).

During roughly the same period that these courses were being adopted at many college campuses, a new model of science as morally neutral was contributing to intellectual divisions, including divisions between academic learning and moral and civic learning. This understanding of science emerged together with the logical positivist and emotivist movements in philosophy in the 1930s and 1940s. It led to a set of influential assertions that science is value free, morality is outside the realm of scientific knowledge, and ethical judgments are a matter of emotion, not intellect (Reuben, 1996).

This intellectual shift marked a crucial change for the work of American colleges and universities, and many disciplines in the social sciences and humanities as well as the natural sciences were essentially redefined in the postwar period. Knowledge and morality, which had been considered inextricable from the earliest days of U.S. higher education, came to be viewed as separate spheres consisting of research and objective knowledge on the one hand and character and ethics on the other. Both arenas remained important for higher education, but they were increasingly pursued as independent goals. Formalism emerged in many disciplines, such as philosophy, sociology, and political science, as they fostered a separation of method from substantive ethics; sought distance from civics as a sign of professional maturity; and increasingly became ends in themselves, focused on their own internal logic rather than the social usefulness of the knowledge imparted (Bender, 1997).

The segregation of moral and civic education from the main concerns of the disciplines put this aspect of undergraduate education very much at risk as curricular flexibility and specialization among both students and faculty continued to grow, as it did throughout the twentieth century. Eventually most general education programs that were not simply a loose collection of departmentally based courses were drastically cut back or dismantled. Required Western civilization and great books courses lost popularity, and those that remained were often remade into more standard history or literature courses. In the process, even those that added a multicultural dimension, as many did, often lost their explicit concern with civic education.

As intellectual learning and moral learning came more and more to be seen as separate spheres, college and university administrators began to turn to extracurricular programs and activities as the primary institutional locus for moral and civic education. In the process the connections that had existed between academic learning and moral and civic learning frayed even more. The site of moral and civic learning shifted away from coursework and the curriculum as colleges and universities designed special student life efforts, such as freshman orientation programs and the establishment of residence halls as a means for creating a moral and civic community for students (Reuben, 1996). As a result, much of the explicit attention to moral and civic learning on today's campuses is provided in extracurricular programs rather than in classrooms.

This arrangement makes it very difficult for students to integrate their intellectual and personal development, because student life and academic affairs are on opposite sides of an administrative divide. This divide has become increasingly deep since its first emergence when liberal education was redefined in the late nineteenth century, separating elements of undergraduate education that had previously been integrated. As it moved away from a holistic approach to liberal education, the new definition systematically excluded pursuits that are physical rather than mental, practical rather than speculative, oral rather than written, and sacred rather than secular (Bennett, 1997, pp. 139–140). Clearly some of these pursuits, such as debate, religious observance, and sports are now represented in student life rather than in the academic sphere.

Currents and Pressure Points in Contemporary Undergraduate Education

The history of U.S. higher education reveals the roots of a number of powerful challenges and barriers to undergraduate moral and civic education. Many of the characteristics of higher education that developed over the past fifty or sixty years are still firmly in place, and emerging trends are adding further complexity to the work of educating citizens even as they present new opportunities. These structural and institutional features of higher education help explain why it is so difficult to revive the centrality of moral and civic learning for undergraduates, and they point to contextual realities that need to be taken into account by those who are working to bring moral and civic educational goals back from the margins.

Educational Legacies and Their Implications for Moral and Civic Education

The existing patterns of faculty specialization, autonomy, and rewards continue to have strong impact on moral and civic learning in higher education, as does the relatively marginal and isolated place of this learning in modern curricula.

FACULTY SPECIALIZATION. In contemporary higher education, faculty interests and expertise are as specialized as ever, with many faculty having become specialists not only in a discipline but also in a particular subdiscipline or substantive research area. Institutional structures and reward systems continue to reinforce the strong allegiances faculty have to their disciplines and departments, and there is little incentive to invest in institution-wide activities such as curriculum reform or community building. Because their primary institutional loyalty is to their department and to students majoring in that department, faculty are generally less interested in teaching introductory and other general education courses that draw mostly nonmajors than they are in taking on upper-level courses. Moreover, general education courses offer faculty little intrinsic motivation, since those are usually broad survey courses and thus do not correspond with faculty members' interests and expertise.

In most institutions general education is still expected to be the primary means of achieving many of the learning goals of liberal education, including moral and civic development. That education is most often assumed to be provided by requiring students to take a designated number of courses in the humanities, social sciences, and natural sciences— or in some other set of disciplinary groupings—and introductory courses usually fulfill these requirements. However, the lack of faculty interest and investment in these courses makes the achievement of liberal education goals especially problematic. Special attention even to some subset of general education courses would contribute a great deal to these efforts, because some of these courses reach very large numbers of students. A recent study estimated that about 80 percent of total enrollments in undergraduate core curricula are concentrated in just twenty-five courses, such as introductory courses in history, political science, and sociology (Weigel, 2000).

FACULTY AUTONOMY. One of the defining features of American higher education, again a legacy of the research university model, is the extreme autonomy of faculty, who are generally considered to be the sole owners of the courses they teach. Although faculty may be asked to teach introductory or other general education courses by their departments, these courses are often assigned to the faculty in the department with the least clout or to adjuncts. Other than being required to teach some of these "service courses," faculty are usually free to teach whatever and however they like once a course is approved for inclusion in the curriculum.

The norm in most institutions of almost complete faculty autonomy with regard to teaching makes it very difficult to structure undergraduate education to embody cross-cutting learning goals or to ensure that courses connect with and build on each other systematically, supporting cumulative advancement in the development of complex intellectual capacities. If institutions want to ensure that students achieve specific skills and capacities, including those integral to their moral and civic development, it is important that faculty plan the kinds of assignments students will undertake to foster those skills and capacities. In order for this planning to happen, faculty need to take into account not only their own interests but also the stake the institution has in each course and in the student outcomes it is intended to produce (Schneider & Shoenberg, 1998).

FACULTY REWARDS. It is difficult for institutions to make this kind of demand on faculty. At most four-year institutions, research distinction and productivity continue to be seen as more important than teaching excellence, and mobility both within and across institutions depends largely on scholarly reputation. This means there is little incentive to invest heavily in learning new pedagogies or in teaching that is labor intensive, as moral and civic education often is. In recent decades the importance of research productivity for faculty advancement has grown even at liberal arts colleges and other institutions that used to place greater emphasis on teaching (Huber, 2002). The absence of commensurate rewards for time spent on innovative teaching is a problem even for faculty at institutions that acknowledge heavy teaching loads by imposing lower expectations for publishing. The course loads in these institutions make it very hard for faculty to give concentrated attention to creative teaching. In regional colleges and comprehensive universities such as the twenty-two campuses of the California State University, for example, faculty generally teach four or even five courses per semester.

Further compounding this problem is the fact that credit for teaching is calculated solely through the number of course units taught, and these units are defined simply as the hours per week the class meets. A course that meets three hours per week is counted as a three-unit course, regardless of the time a faculty member spends designing it, preparing for classes, working with students on special projects, facilitating service placements, or providing feedback on student work. Faculty are seldom given additional credit when they teach courses that use demanding pedagogies such as problem-based learning or service learning, no matter how important the course is thought to be or how well it is taught.

The troubling result is that faculty may have no institutional incentive to do more than the minimum in any course, no external motivation to improve their courses, to use labor-intensive teaching techniques, or to introduce creative student projects. As a result, teaching that requires taking additional time to prepare classes or projects or to work with students, as courses that include a focus on moral and civic learning frequently do, is too often seen as an "extra" that faculty simply cannot afford. The relative lack of attention to teaching begins early in the careers of faculty members. Regardless of where they will later teach, most are trained at research universities. Their graduate training focuses primarily on research expertise and depth of knowledge in their chosen field, and most graduate students receive little or no instruction in how to be an effective teacher. Doctoral candidates may teach sections of large courses, or occasionally separate courses, but usually with no prior instruction, little faculty guidance, and no study of either the way students learn or of teaching practices that foster more complex modes of thought. This problem is exacerbated by the narrow range of professional development they are most likely to pursue once they begin their careers—reading in their field and attending scholarly meetings around their areas of interest.

These problems are serious because curricular and pedagogical innovation requires significant faculty investment. In fact, given the formidable barriers, it is amazing that so many faculty at many different kinds of institutions do invest a great deal of time and energy in crafting powerful learning opportunities for their undergraduate students. In Chapter Seven we look at some of the things that motivate these dedicated teachers.

THE PLACE OF MORAL AND CIVIC LEARNING IN THE CURRICULUM. One of the most striking patterns in the history of undergraduate moral and civic education is its progressive segregation into narrower parts of the curriculum, and its near removal to the extracurricular sphere in some kinds of institutions. The results of these historical shifts are institutional structures and practices that are not well suited to the goals of liberal education, including moral and civic learning. In many colleges and universities, complex forms of learning that cut across disciplines, if they are intentionally pursued at all, are separated from the rest of the curriculum and located in general education. Because general education is most often structured as a set of distribution requirements, with a wide range of choices that can be used to fulfill each requirement, it seldom represents a common or coherent educational core, and the courses that meet the requirements are rarely designed to ensure the development of cross-disciplinary capacities such as complex problem solving, integrative thinking, or a sense of social responsibility.

Even when general education courses are well tailored to the goals of liberal education, including the moral and civic goals, an important opportunity is lost if study in the major does not also contribute to these goals. Most students focus almost exclusively on their major fields for a third to a half or more of their time as undergraduates. Because the major often represents preparation for students' future careers, it is especially important that students be well grounded in the moral and civic issues likely to arise in their chosen fields.

The disciplinary focus of the undergraduate curriculum also presents an obstacle to moral and civic education. Both distribution requirements and majors are defined in terms of discrete disciplinary categories, despite the interdisciplinary interests of many faculty, and few institutions provide structured ways for students to connect their learning across disciplines or even across courses within the same discipline. Because civic issues and moral questions in real-life contexts are inherently interdisciplinary, the disciplinary structure of the curriculum is not well suited to facilitate the kind of integrative thinking these complex problems require (Schneider & Shoenberg, 1998).

New Challenges

In addition to the ongoing challenges to effective moral and civic learning presented by the entrenched roles and practices of faculty and the placement of this learning in the curriculum, new challenges are arising as the demographics of the student body shift and as higher education institutions respond to market forces.

THE CHANGING STUDENT BODY. Growth in the size and diversity of the undergraduate population has been continuous since the nineteenth century, with several periods of rapid change due to external conditions or influential government policies such as the Morrill Act. During and after World War II, the expansion was dramatically accelerated by the passage of the GI Bill, which doubled the number of students attending college between 1938 and 1948. It was at this time that college students began to be representative of the nation as a whole. As the middle class expanded and college enrollments tripled between 1960 and 1980, undergraduate majors in professional and preprofessional fields such as business, education, journalism, and nursing were more likely to be offered, and in some cases, such as business, became very popular.

The challenge of educating a larger and more diverse student body is not really new; it has been going on in one form or another for two centuries. But the degree to which the current population of students differs from the populations of the past represents a new kind of challenge. The inclusiveness of contemporary higher education has increased higher education's opportunity to have a significant impact on the preparation of responsible and engaged citizens yet has also made the task more complicated. At the present time about four thousand colleges and universities serve some fifteen million undergraduate students across the country.[1] The diversity of this group is reflected in the diversity of institutions they attend. The largest share, some 40 percent, attend community colleges, almost all of which are public, and another 39 percent attend universities, many of which are public. Small baccalaureate colleges still have an important role in higher education, but only about 7 percent of students attend these colleges. The remaining 4 percent of students study at specialized institutions, most of which provide professional training (for these and related statistics, see The Carnegie Foundation for the Advancement of Teaching, 2000).

Not only have the numbers of college students greatly increased and the kinds of institutions they attend changed but student demographics have undergone dramatic shifts as well. Compared with students of any prior generation, undergraduates today are much more diverse in every dimension—age, race, ethnic background, and economic status. As just one example, in the year 2002, for the first time, more than half the students offered admission to Stanford University's incoming freshman class were minorities ("Most Admissions Letters Go to Minority Students," 2002). Today nearly two-thirds of all undergraduates are women (U.S. Census Bureau, 2000), compared to one-third in 1940 (U.S. Census Bureau, 1975). And less than 20 percent of undergraduates fit the traditional pattern of earlier eras, in which undergraduates were most likely to be full-time students, just graduated from high school, and attending private, residential institutions.

A near majority of undergraduates today do not come to college or university directly from high school, more than three out of four attend a public institution, and almost the same share are commuter students (U.S. Census Bureau, 2000). College students today tend to be older than their predecessors, many work part-time and are part-time students, many are married, and many are parents. Their first obligation is often to families and jobs, and their college education—including the campus that provides it—is necessarily a lower priority. Their educational goals are also different. Many do not view themselves primarily as members of a "community of learners" but rather as consumers who wish to get their training and credentials as easily, quickly, and cheaply as possible. This may mean attending two or three different institutions in the course of an undergraduate career, often over a six- or eight-year period.

The new profile of the undergraduate student body makes moral and civic education even more challenging than it used to be. It is much easier to design multifaceted, holistic programs of moral and civic education for a residential, four-year institution than for a student body that is commuting, attending school part-time, and connected with the institution for a shorter duration. Creating a palpable culture and some sense of community on campus for the latter group requires special attention, and we describe in later chapters some creative efforts to do this. A student profile of this sort also underscores the importance of integrating moral and civic concerns into the curriculum, because many of these students find it extremely difficult to make time for extracurricular activities. The challenge of serving transfer students is particularly difficult. These students make up an increasing share of the student body on many four-year campuses and merit special attention, including a coordination of effort between community colleges and four-year campuses.

Another change is the growing number of returning adults in the undergraduate population. Their presence contributes to some educators' reluctance to endorse goals of moral and civic development because they question whether it is possible to foster moral and civic growth in adulthood. As we discuss in Chapter Four, however, social science research does not support the common belief that moral character is fully established at a young age, let alone civic maturity. For individuals engaged in challenging experiences, development can continue throughout adulthood.

Some in the academy also believe that it is presumptuous to try to affect the moral and civic development of adults even if it is possible. This belief may be based on an image of moral and civic education that is closer to the nineteenth-century practice of didactic training in a specific set of rules or guidelines rather than on a clear understanding of contemporary moral and civic education, which consists of activities and goals that most people would consider appropriate for all adults, including adult college students: thinking clearly about challenging moral dilemmas, engaging in an intellectually serious way the moral issues that arise in academic disciplines, participating in service to the community, adhering to high ethical standards of honesty and mutual respect, and becoming knowledgeable about contemporary social, policy, and political issues.

The increased racial, ethnic, and religious diversity of the contemporary college population presents both opportunities and challenges for moral and civic education. The opportunities lie in the reality that learning to understand and respect people of different backgrounds and beliefs is a central dimension of being a responsible citizen, and a diverse student body provides a training ground for that understanding and respect. Mutual respect and the willingness to take others' ideas seriously become much more than abstract ideals when fellow students bring very different perspectives from one's own. We say more about these opportunities later in this chapter. At the same time, members of diverse student populations may exhibit deep cultural differences, and those differences may lead to clashes. Whether these occasions also become *teachable moments* in the moral and civic lives of students or are treated as dangerous or simply troublesome diversions from the educational enterprise often depends on institutional leadership, as we discuss in Chapter Eight. Either way, these clashes underscore the challenge of finding some basic common values around which to build educational programs and a cohesive campus culture.

A trend that has contributed to the decrease in attention to education's moral and civic goals is the widespread sense among students that they are in college solely to gain career skills and credentials. This phenomenon is not new. In fact the call for more practical subjects by students and state governments was a key factor in the expansion of the curriculum as far back as the second quarter of the nineteenth century (Kimball, 1986, p. 154). But as in the case of the changing demographics, the current preeminence of vocational aims seems to represent a real qualitative shift in that it characterizes not only returning adults and relatively low-income students at public universities but also undergraduates of traditional age who enroll at private institutions. The data are clear that the expectation of acquiring marketable skills is the overwhelming reason why students and their parents are willing to pay the escalating undergraduate tuition, even at small liberal arts colleges (Hersh, 1997). The great majority of undergraduates today select a major because they believe it will provide their surest route to high-paid employment, a practice that has made business the number one major in the country (National Center for Education Statistics, 1996). As a result, many undergraduates view general education requirements—the courses most often associated with moral and civic learning—as hurdles to get over on the way to preparing for that career.

Students' impatience to complete their professional or vocational training with as few distractions as possible can make it difficult to interest them in broader goals of intellectual and personal development. But we have seen that vocational preparation need not be in competition with or disconnected from other goals, including moral and civic learning. Institutions of higher education are well situated to encourage students to think about a vocation as something larger and potentially far richer than simple careerism. The special nature of colleges and universities as intellectual communities gives them the opportunity to embed the occupational goals of students in a broad and socially meaningful framework. Students can be encouraged to see that their preparation for a career is incomplete if it does not include the development of ethical and socially responsible professional practices and an understanding of the larger social and intellectual context that gives work deeper meaning.

HIGHER EDUCATION AS A COMPETITIVE MARKET. Unfortunately, colleges and universities too often respond to students' consumerist orientation not by helping them explore the deeper significance of work but by structuring curricula to meet market pressures. Fractionating forces in higher education are pressing campuses to cater to narrowly defined career needs with all the individualized attention of a boutique and all the mass delivery capability of an ATM machine. We spoke in Chapter One about the atmosphere of commercialization that characterizes many campuses. This commercialization is part of a broader phenomenon that represents yet another challenge for those wishing to revitalize higher education's public mission. Louis Menand (2001) has called the postwar decades, roughly from 1945 to 1975, the academy's Golden Age. Enrollments, public funding, and research support were expanding, and the distinction and value of higher education was largely unquestioned. In more recent decades the climate has shifted. The academy has faced tightening resources, escalating costs, and pressure to justify its utility, show results, and keep costs down. This has led to what some commentators have called the *audit culture,* which parallels movements in other domains to use market-based economic principles to reshape spheres of life that have long been the province of noneconomic institutions (Sullivan, 2001, p. 2). Higher education has become a competitive "industry," and it has adopted the strategies and language of the market to deal with this change.

One strategy adopted by virtually all institutions in the face of this pressure to control costs has been the employment of ever higher numbers of adjunct faculty. Nearly 40 percent of undergraduate credit hours are now taught by adjunct faculty (U.S. Census Bureau, 2000). Because they are often hired on a part-time or year-to-year contract, typically without benefits and frequently with little departmental support or interaction, many adjuncts find it difficult to devote extensive time to the courses they teach, to develop relationships with their students, or to influence them outside the classroom, or to develop relationships with colleagues. It is not surprising, then, that faculty in this category often see themselves as entrepreneurial individual contractors with only weak connections to particular institutions. These changes in faculty roles and faculty loyalties make it more difficult to create a sense of campus community around moral and civic learning.

Even aside from this externally driven audit culture, higher education has become more and more a competitive market. Competition for resources, including faculty with distinguished scholarly records, grants and other funding, and high-achieving students, has produced a climate in which resource enhancement and reputation building are treated as ends in themselves. Colleges and universities increasingly define their worth with reference to their relative position in status hierarchies that are most starkly embodied in the *U.S. News and World Report* rankings. Although there is a growing awareness of the incongruity between this stance and the fundamental educational and service missions of U.S. higher education (Astin, 1997, 2000; Sullivan, 2001), it is almost impossible for any institution to "disarm" unilaterally; so survival or at least maintenance of one's position in the pecking order is believed to depend on participation in this competitive, zero-sum game. Of course this competition for prestige is most acute at research universities and other selective institutions, but competition for resources is equally important at every level of the status hierarchy. When strategies for competing successfully are framed in terms of "satisfying the customer," they too contribute to the commodification of higher education.

This competition for resources is not an unmitigated ill. Raw, market-based strategies are not the only alternative for attracting enough students to survive economically, and we describe in later chapters how the struggle to survive has led some colleges to redefine themselves through distinctive approaches that make students' moral and civic development prominent among their educational goals. And competition for students has been one source of motivation for some institutions, such as Trinity College, the University of Pennsylvania, and the University of Southern California, to contribute to their local communities in an effort to make their locations in relatively low-income areas safer and thus more palatable to students and parents.

On the whole, however, the dual dangers of the audit culture and the competition for academic prestige are serious threats to higher education's capacity to educate citizens. Institutions built on gain rather than responsibility are not well aligned with the goals of liberal education, including its moral and civic goals (Sullivan, 2001). These threats undermine the motivation for innovative teaching, the creation of strong moral community and culture, and concerns with integration, meaning, and moral purpose. The extreme of this market-based approach can be seen in the many for-profit institutions that have sprung up to offer higher education focused exclusively on career goals, narrowly defined. Like those of other for-profit companies, their sponsors are focused on the bottom line and concerned with students' learning only to the extent that it contributes to that bottom line. Moral and civic learning usually has no place in this equation. Yet these commercial institutions are increasingly aggressive competitors to nonprofit colleges and universities. Their argument is that they can better offer what students want: an education that emphasizes career, vocational, and technical skills and excludes "extraneous" learning.

The growth of *distance learning* and courses on the Internet has accelerated this trend, and there is every reason to believe that "education.com" will expand rapidly in the decade ahead. That explosion could have significant effects on moral and civic learning at campuses throughout the country in ways that are difficult to predict. There is no inherent reason why that learning cannot occur via the Internet, but at this point it does not seem to be among the goals of the distance learning programs at for-profit universities.

Hopeful Developments

So far we have painted a rather gloomy and daunting picture of the broad institutional contexts of undergraduate moral and civic education. But this sketch is not yet complete, because it leaves out important developments that are much more congenial to that work. The problems that existing institutional arrangements present for liberal education are well known, and proponents of the liberal education tradition have not been passive in the face of these barriers.

We began this chapter by pointing out that the move to redefine and revitalize moral and civic education for undergraduates is not a discrete, isolated element of the higher education landscape. Rather it is an integral part of an emerging vision for liberal education that asks what abilities college graduates will need for successful, meaningful lives in the twenty-first century and how higher education institutions can best equip students with those critical abilities. As educators grapple with the question of how best to prepare students to engage productively with complex and changing realities, a rough consensus has emerged that students need not only knowledge and technical skills but also facility with many forms of communication and modes of inquiry, integrative capacities, reflective judgment, and cross-cultural competencies. This consensus includes a recognition that graduates need "the capacity and resolve to exercise leadership and responsibility in multiple spheres of life, both societal and vocational" (Schneider & Shoenberg, 1998, p. 7). That is, colleges and universities need to be educating citizens.

An important theme in this consensus is the belief that the growing racial, ethnic, and religious diversity of the United States and its college students and the increasingly evident globalism of the world present important opportunities, indeed imperatives, for undergraduate education. Educators in all kinds of institutions stress that in a world of multiple and conflicting perspectives, experiencing and learning from differences is a crucial part of the educational process. The movement toward incorporating a focus on cultural diversity has grown quickly, creating new impetus for engagement with moral and civic questions. In a recent Association of American Colleges and Universities study, 60 percent of four-year campuses reported that they require courses providing experience with cultural diversity, and another 8 percent reported working to develop these requirements. Many of these courses inevitably raise values questions and conflicts by addressing such topics as identity, cultural encounters and conflicts, pluralism, systemic bias, and the like (American Commitments Program, 1995). The University of Michigan, for example, now offers a course titled Intergroup Relations, Conflict, and Community that exposes students to the ways different groups have experienced American democracy. Olivet College, a small liberal arts campus in Michigan, has established the required course Self and Community, which helps students think and talk about issues of diversity. Olivet students report that taking the course makes it easier than before to reach out to students whose backgrounds differ from their own and to discuss issues of racial conflict (Humphreys, 2000).

Of course the racial and ethnic diversity in higher education as a whole is unevenly distributed. For various reasons having to do with location, cost, and religious affiliation, some institutions are extremely homogeneous, while others are very diverse. In fact many of the institutions that stress the importance of celebrating diversity and learning to communicate across cultural differences are colleges whose student bodies are not very diverse at all, and it can be difficult to teach about the values associated with diversity when there is little actual diversity on the campus. These colleges often use a wide range of cultural exchange and community service programs to help students gain experience working with people from backgrounds different from their own. These institutions also use affirmative action admissions policies to try to increase the diversity of their student bodies, in the conviction that a more diverse environment will benefit all the students. There is a great deal of empirical evidence to support this belief that developmental benefits accrue to students when they attend institutions with diverse student bodies, especially when those institutions highlight multiculturalism and encourage students from different ethnic groups to study and pursue extracurricular activities together (Antonio, 1998a, 1998b; Astin, 1993; Bowen & Bok, 1998; Hurtado, 2001).

Along with the redefinition (or reaffirmation) of the central goals of undergraduate education has come a strong sense that the traditional pedagogies of lecture and discussion are not sufficient to accomplish deep and lasting achievement of these goals. Despite the relative lack of institutional rewards for teaching innovation, faculty from all kinds of institutions have been developing teaching strategies that engage students actively in their own learning and provide experiences with complex capacities that go well beyond the absorption of new information. These strategies include project-based and problem-based learning, collaborative learning, service learning, and other forms of experiential learning. We explore the potential of these pedagogies of engagement for moral and civic development in Chapter Five. In part as an accompaniment to community-based pedagogies, many institutions are building stronger relationships with their local communities. For example, in 1999 the more than fifty college and university presidents attending a Campus Compact–sponsored Aspen Institute invitational conference issued a bold declaration of responsibility for enhancing their campuses' civic engagement and offered an assessment tool to measure success in this endeavor. More than 700 college and university presidents have endorsed this declaration. Efforts to recommit to the public purposes of higher education are beginning to press back against the strong forces of the market-based approach and commodification of higher education.

One of the most daunting challenges of this emerging vision of undergraduate education is the dual need to evaluate whether students are achieving the array of intellectual, moral, and civic understandings and abilities that represent the purposes and values of that education and to conduct this evaluation in ways that help students consolidate what they have achieved, correct misconceptions, and see clearly what remains to be accomplished. Creative efforts to meet this challenge are underway, but a great deal of work remains before assessment is successfully reshaped to be well aligned with a variety of learning goals and rich in the insights it yields to teachers and students yet also practical and efficient enough to be adopted on a large scale. We talk about some of the special challenges entailed in assessment of moral and civic learning in Chapter Nine.

It is obvious that the more engaging pedagogies and more authentic assessments being advocated require a greater investment of faculty time and attention. Educational leaders are well aware that these efforts are hampered by some of the traditions surrounding faculty roles and by higher education's reluctance to recognize, assess, and reward the considerable intellectual work entailed in curricular and pedagogical reform (Schneider & Shoenberg, 1998). National organizations such as the Association of American Colleges and Universities, the American Association for Higher Education, and others have mounted systematic efforts to confront these barriers. AAHE, for example, has worked for more than a decade to help campuses rethink faculty roles and rewards and to align reward systems with new developments in teaching and assessment. Many philanthropies, including the Hewlett Foundation, the Pew Charitable Trusts, the Mellon Foundation, the Atlantic Philanthropies, the Surdna Foundation, and the Walter and Elise Haas Foundation, have supported many reform initiatives. These have included experiments in the scholarship of teaching and learning, interdisciplinary faculty development, and programming around diversity.

Prominent among the public voices offering new frameworks and strategies for reordering faculty and institutional priorities have been the former president of The Carnegie Foundation for the Advancement of Teaching, Ernest Boyer, and his successor, Lee Shulman. Boyer's *Scholarship Reconsidered* (1990), which formulated a powerful rationale for broadening what counts as scholarship, has been widely read and influential, stimulating a national conversation about the "scholarships of teaching, application, and integration" in addition to the more familiar "scholarship of discovery." The follow-up to that report, Glassick, Huber, and Maeroff's *Scholarship Assessed* (1997), takes up the thorny question of evaluating excellence in the full range of scholarly modes, in the recognition that they cannot be appropriately rewarded if they are not assessed. These books have spawned a great deal of work further elaborating the implications of their ideas for the scholarships of teaching, application, and integration and for particular disciplines (Berberet, 1999; Diamond & Adam, 1995, 2000; Hutchings, 1998; Lynton, 1995). The impact on colleges and universities has been significant, and many have redefined faculty roles around a broader definition of scholarship (Glassick et al., 1997; O'Meara, 2000).

Current Carnegie Foundation president Lee Shulman and his colleagues have taken the conception of teaching as a form of scholarship a step further. Shulman has been concerned not only with the lack of recognition of the scholarly nature of good teaching but also with the absence of structures and practices that make it possible for faculty to build on each other's work, so that teaching becomes cumulative, as other forms of scholarship are. In this view the scholarship of teaching includes more than scholarly teaching that is steeped in knowledge, intellectually engaged, carefully planned, creatively interactive, and inspiring, as Boyer (1990) so eloquently described it. It also entails documenting, investigating, publicly sharing, and critiquing teaching practices and reflections on them. Programs to elaborate, operationalize, and institutionalize this approach are at the heart of the Carnegie Foundation's current mission.

Finally, we see a growing recognition that graduate students and faculty need expert help to develop as teachers. In response, teaching and learning centers have been established on many campuses, providing programs and individual feedback to help faculty and graduate teaching assistants improve their teaching. Many of these centers encourage and support modes of active learning, including problem-based, collaborative, and service learning, which are especially well suited to promoting moral and civic development. Although teaching and learning centers are a welcome step toward the enhancement of teaching, like faculty they too are hampered by their institutional contexts. Use of their services is almost always discretionary, and most institutions offer no incentives for taking advantage of them.

Important initiatives such as the Preparing Future Faculty Program, sponsored by the Council of Graduate Schools and the Association of American Colleges and Universities, have also begun to redefine the preparation of academic professionals to place more emphasis on their roles as teachers. Many are hopeful that over time these and related efforts, such as the Carnegie Foundation's new Initiative on the Doctorate, will have a significant impact on graduate education. In the meantime, however, universities are a long way from providing their graduate students and faculty with adequate preparation for teaching. The new initiatives are still operating on a small scale relative to the magnitude of the task. And so far these programs have focused primarily on helping faculty and graduate students learn how to be better teachers of a particular discipline. If they are to support broad as well as specialized learning goals, they will need to incorporate experience with curriculum design, multidisciplinary courses, teaching for complex outcomes that cut across disciplines, and integrating moral and civic learning into discipline-based courses.

Despite these limitations and powerful opposing forces, there is an active movement underway to place greater emphasis on and offer greater rewards for teaching and to add to the academic agenda a strong focus on *learning* as well as teaching. Surveys indicate that many faculty, especially those at doctoral universities, do perceive an increased emphasis on teaching at their institutions (Diamond & Adam, 1998). Similarly, in a 1997 Carnegie Foundation survey, almost half the faculty at research universities said that teaching counted more toward faculty advancement than it had five years earlier, and large minorities at virtually all other types of institutions said the same thing. However, even larger numbers reported that research demands have been rising (Huber, in press). It seems clear that policies for faculty advancement are being rewritten, new guidelines are making integrative and applied scholarship more acceptable, teaching is being given greater weight, and the scholarship of teaching and learning is beginning to gain credibility (Huber, in press). These are indeed hopeful developments for liberal education, including its moral and civic goals. However, these developments coexist with the impediments we outlined earlier in this chapter, and many faculty still perceive a disconnect between the new policies and the actual practices of tenure, promotion, and compensation. Furthermore, when emphasis on teaching is increased as the importance of scholarly productivity is also going up, the pressures on faculty can become overwhelming.

The efforts to slowly shift some of the entrenched practices and structures that work against the new vision of what is possible for undergraduate education are a hopeful backdrop to the grassroots work on moral and civic education chronicled in this book. At this point, however, inhospitable structures and practices are still visible at most institutions. We believe it is important for those who care about the goals and value of liberal education (presumably a very large group when liberal education is broadly defined) to join with those who are paying special attention to the moral and civic components of those goals, so all can collectively throw their weight behind these hopeful developments. The new developments are gathering strength but so are the opposing trends of commodification, specialization, and institutional competition, so it is not a time to be complacent.

Despite the long-term importance of institutional change, we do not believe that the advancement of moral and civic education requires radical changes in these structural barriers before it can proceed. Clearly this work is viable even in the current conditions. But a full flourishing of student learning that will truly serve both graduates and their society requires attention to these patterns, which Carol Schneider, president of the Association of American Colleges and Universities, calls "habits hard to break" (Schneider & Shoenberg, 1998). With key educational leaders and organizations attacking some of the habits and barriers directly and committed teachers and visionary administrators personally taking up the charge at the campus level, it should be possible to progress toward more effective education for the citizens of the future.

NOTE

1. Only a subset of small baccalaureate colleges focuses primarily on liberal arts education. Such liberal arts institutions used to be a dominant force in U.S. culture as well as U.S. higher education, but today less than 2.5 percent of all undergraduates attend them.

3

WHEN EDUCATING
CITIZENS IS A PRIORITY

UNDERGRADUATE MORAL and civic education is not an institutional priority on most campuses. This is hardly surprising, given the dominant patterns of U.S. higher education, which we sketched in Chapter Two. However, a few colleges and universities are building moral and civic education into the heart of their undergraduates' learning. They make a conscious effort to reach all of their students and use multifaceted approaches to address the full range of dimensions that constitute moral and civic development. Institutions that do this can be found in every category of higher education, from small religious colleges to public urban universities and colleges, elite private universities, military academies, and community colleges. We have documented the work of twelve such institutions: Alverno College; California State University, Monterey Bay; the College of St. Catherine; Duke University; Kapiʻolani Community College; Messiah College; Portland State University; Spelman College; Turtle Mountain Community College; Tusculum College; the United States Air Force Academy; and the University of Notre Dame.

These colleges and universities differ from each other along many dimensions. We selected them for precisely this reason. We wanted to explore a wide variety of institutions that bring a high degree of institutional intentionality to enhancing the moral and civic responsibility of their students. Taken as a group, these twelve institutions convince us that it is possible to create powerful programs of moral and civic education for the diverse student population of U.S. college students in the twenty-first century.

The holistic approach these twelve campuses share is in each case an intentional effort by campus leaders, including the president and other top administrators and key faculty and staff. The upper levels of the administration in both academic and student affairs explicitly endorse the importance of moral and civic educational goals and allocate resources to programs designed to promote them. This commitment is part of a broader set of institutional priorities at these institutions, exemplifying the whole range of what we have called hopeful developments (Chapter Two). These institutions' attention to clarity of learning outcomes, the importance of teaching, curricular reform, and new approaches to assessment has created environments that are especially conducive to the development of holistic and intentional programs of undergraduate moral and civic education.[1]

The moral and civic education programs on these twelve campuses share a number of general features despite the diversity of institutional types:

1. In Chapters One and Two we stressed the importance of integrating moral and civic education into the curriculum rather than allowing it to be distanced from the academic mission of the college. This integration, which was a criterion for selection as one of our case study schools, acknowledges the central place of the intellectual dimensions of moral and civic development and connects general capacities for sophisticated and analytical judgment with substantive issues of real moral and social significance. At most of the twelve case study campuses, this integration takes place in both interdisciplinary general education courses and courses in a large cross section of disciplines. The consideration of moral or civic issues in coursework is often tied to efforts to foster critical thinking and effective communication, because these abilities are widely recognized as important features of civil discourse.

2. All the programs provide ways to go beyond the intellectual realm to action, both inside and outside the curriculum. They understand the importance of students' grappling with complex and messy real-life contexts and recognize that the skills of persuasion, negotiation, compromise, and interpersonal and cultural sensitivity can be learned differently in these settings than in the classroom. The institutions see that this work, if well designed, can heighten students' sense of efficacy and lead them to redefine their personal identity, making a sense of themselves as citizens and ethically responsible individuals central to that identity.

3. Issues of diversity and multiculturalism are closely linked to moral and civic education on these campuses. Most of the twelve institutions face challenges in this area, either with attracting a diverse student body or

faculty or with promoting full integration of the student body, and a few are notable for their lack of racial, religious, or socioeconomic diversity. Even so, they are committed to educating their students to function well in a diverse society, and they recognize the implications of this endeavor for the strength of the society's civic and democratic ideals. Developing in students an increased understanding of cultural traditions other than their own and promoting respectful engagement across differences are central goals for both academic programs and student affairs. Often these goals are incorporated into the core curriculum, and they are almost always central to community service and service learning experiences. In many cases, efforts to foster mutual respect across racial, ethnic, religious, and other differences are joined with efforts to develop a global perspective on social issues. The conviction that students must be educated for participation in a pluralist and multicultural society and a world that extends beyond the boundaries of the United States was present on every campus.

4. Finally, these institutions attempt to create a campuswide culture that calls attention to and validates certain shared values, providing a unifying and reinforcing context for the programs. They use a fascinating array of tools to accomplish this, some of which we describe later in this chapter.

These campuses also face some common dilemmas and challenges. Some are strategic: how to reach the largest number of students, how to integrate moral and civic education with academic learning in a way that enriches both, and how to know whether a program is working. Some challenges are practical. Developing, funding, staffing, and maintaining such ambitious programs is very demanding. Mounting programs of this sort is institutionally difficult, given the many other pressures colleges and universities are facing. Limited resources make it hard for most places to support the team teaching that interdisciplinary courses require, and faculty often see an elaborated core curriculum as draining resources from the disciplinary departments. Generally, this kind of work is labor intensive, and faculty time is a scarce resource on all campuses. And some of the challenges are philosophical, requiring institutions to answer questions like these: To what extent should we stand for particular values, and to what extent should we simply help students think through their own values and beliefs? How do we distinguish between those values we can endorse as an institution and those that must be left to individual judgment? How should we balance our institutional responsibilities to our local community with our responsibilities to our students' learning?

Definitions of Moral and Civic Responsibility

A close look at the campuses where this work is taking place reveals both strong commonalities and striking differences in what moral and civic development and education means at each one. We also briefly introduce each of the case study schools as we indicate its place in the mosaic of shared and distinctive definitions.

On almost all twelve of the campuses, moral and civic development is defined to include students' understanding of ethical and social issues, consideration of multiple perspectives on these issues, willingness to take responsibility for their own actions, commitment to contribute to society, and appreciation of cultural pluralism and global interdependence. Yet the case study institutions also bring a distinctive quality to their vision of these goals. These special "takes" on moral and civic education are in some ways unique to each campus, but they can also be characterized by some cross-cutting themes. For some institutions, connections with and service to particular communities are central to institutional identity. For others, a special focus on distinctive core values or virtues is essential. For yet others, the pursuit of social justice is a defining feature.

Most of the twelve institutions reflect two or all three of these themes, and the complex mix on virtually every campus makes grouping institutions by theme somewhat arbitrary. For example, California State University, Monterey Bay, is particularly concerned with social justice, but it is also closely linked with its surrounding community, and community engagement is central to its conception of moral and civic learning. Similar caveats could be expressed about each of the thematic identifications that follow. Even so, for many of these schools one theme is especially salient. These themes do not capture any school's approach perfectly, but they help illustrate the range of approaches that can be taken to the same broad goal of enhancing the moral and civic responsibility of undergraduates.

Our thumbnail sketches of the case study schools begin with three that show some commonalities in moral and civic learning outcomes that cut across most of the twelve. Alverno College, Tusculum College, and Duke University illustrate the ways these widely shared learning outcomes or competencies are operationalized on three very different campuses. Next we turn to illustrations of the thematic approaches, beginning with three campuses that represent the salience of community connections, though in distinct ways: Portland State University, Spelman College, and Kapi'olani Community College. The United States Air Force Academy, Turtle Mountain Community College, and Messiah College are equally diverse in the ways they illustrate the moral and civic virtue approach. Finally, California State University, Monterey Bay; the University of Notre Dame; and the College of St. Catherine represent different instantiations of the social justice, or systemic social responsibility, approach.

Moral and Civic Competencies

At least half of the twelve schools are very explicit about what they mean by moral and civic development, and these definitions have a lot in common. Many of these campuses have adopted some version of an outcomes-based approach to undergraduate education, so the moral and civic competencies they expect students to master are well known to both faculty and students. Although far from identical from one campus to the next, the lists of requisite competencies share a number of elements. Not surprisingly, they always include some student learning outcomes that are central to higher education in general and also play an important role in moral and civic maturity, such as critical and integrative thinking, communication, and problem solving. Other common elements include various versions of these capacities:

- Self-understanding or self-knowledge; understanding of the relationship between the self and the community
- Awareness of and willingness to take responsibility for the consequences of one's actions for others and society
- Informed and responsible involvement with relevant communities
- Pluralism; cultural awareness and respect; ability to understand the values of one's own and other cultures
- Appreciation of the global dimensions of many issues

Alverno College

Alverno College is a small Roman Catholic college for women in Milwaukee, Wisconsin. Founded in 1887, it has been a leader since the 1960s in spelling out the competencies that its students should have when they graduate and in defining and assessing those competencies. Alverno draws both traditional aged and older students from a variety of backgrounds—about 1,000 in its Weekday College and 800 in its Weekend College. It expects its graduates to be engaged and responsible citizens, and much of its education is explicitly focused on those goals. Alverno's abilities-based approach "makes explicit the expectation that students should be able to do something with what they know."

The curriculum is constantly being reshaped and refined, and Alverno has been unique in publishing an extensive literature on that curriculum (see, for example, Mentkowski & Associates, 2000). The curriculum is designed to foster mastery of eight abilities, titled Valuing in Decision Making, Social Interaction, Global Perspective, and Effective Citizenship. All eight abilities are introduced during the first year, and each ability is divided into six levels. All students must demonstrate mastery at the fourth level or higher on all eight before graduation; an additional two levels are set for abilities relating to a student's major. Many of the academic programs have a strong focus on moral and civic responsibility. One major, for example, is community leadership and development and another is experiential learning and community development.

No less important than the articulation of competencies is the attention to assessment at Alverno. In both individual course assessments and integrative assessments, the latter focusing on learning from multiple courses, the college elicits samples of performance representing expected learning outcomes. A large cadre of trained community volunteers serve as external assessors along with the faculty and staff, and Alverno seeks a virtually continuous process of feedback for its students. It has developed a *diagnostic digital portfolio,* which maintains a record of the outcomes of each student's assessments and other examples of their learning to be used by the student, the faculty, and prospective employers.

Tusculum College

Tusculum College, a small liberal arts college in Tennessee, was on the brink of closing when, in 1989, its president and faculty decided to create an educational model that is centrally concerned with building better citizens. A key element of the college's new identity is a competency program quite similar to Alverno's. Students must demonstrate nine competencies, titled, for example, Self-Knowledge: The Examined Life, Civility, and Ethics of Social Responsibility.

Along with the competency program, Tusculum has instituted a required Commons Curriculum, which includes courses like Our Lives in Community and Citizenship and Social Change: Theory and Practice, and has put in place a strong program of service learning, along with a community governance structure in which students and faculty participate in decisions that previously were made by the administration. Tusculum's mission statement speaks of graduating young men and women who possess "a spirit of civic-mindedness" and who are "actively committed to responsible participation in the communities in which they live." An unusual feature of Tusculum's curriculum is its exclusive focus on one course at a time. Each course in this *focused calendar* meets every day for three and a half weeks. Each academic year contains eight of these blocks.

Both similarities and subtle differences are revealed when we compare the ways Alverno and Tusculum articulate what counts as achievement of the competencies each requires. To take one example, Alverno's definition of Effective Citizenship proceeds through six levels, moving from, at the first two levels, students' abilities to assess their knowledge and skills for dealing with local issues and analyze community issues and develop strategies for informed response to, at the fourth level, their abilities actually to apply their developing citizenship skills in a community setting to, at the highest levels, students' more advanced leadership capacities in their majors or areas of specialization.

Tusculum's Ethics of Social Responsibility competency is divided into four subcategories: Individual and Community, Public and Private Life, Diversity and the Common Good, and Civic Responsibility and Social Change. Although these do not correspond directly to Alverno's abilities, they bear a strong family resemblance. The Civic Responsibility competency, for example, is defined for three levels, moving from understanding the basic processes of social change in a democratic system through understanding the complexity of social change and the responsibility of citizens as agents of change to actual participation in the community as a citizen, recognizing and addressing ethical issues that may arise in connection with that participation. Almost all the campuses we visited shared some version of this goal of educating students to take responsibility for improving their communities and even contribute to social change more broadly in an informed, thoughtful, and effective way.

Another goal of moral and civic education at most of the schools we visited concerns moral or ethical values. Alverno lays out levels that describe students' increasing capacity to infer, analyze, and apply moral values; Tusculum describes a similar sequence in which students become better able to articulate their own ethical values and to use ethical values different from their own to gain perspective on and possibly transform their beliefs.

Duke University

Duke University also makes explicit its goals for students' development, but it does so through the articulation of goals for its general education curriculum rather than through an outcomes-based approach. Duke is a private research university located in Durham, North Carolina, with 6,300 undergraduates. Under the leadership of its president, Nannerl Keohane, the university recently completed a major revision of its entire general education program. The new Curriculum 2000 includes two required Ethical Inquiry courses as well as a first-year writing program that has a strong emphasis on ethics. An important institutional spark plug for the focus on moral and civic concerns is the Kenan Institute for Ethics, which has as an affiliate a national organization promoting honor codes on campuses throughout the country—the Center for Academic Integrity. Not surprisingly, Duke itself has an honor code that is taken very seriously.

The rationale for the Ethical Inquiry requirement reveals Duke's conception of moral and civic development: "Undergraduate education is a formative period for engaging in critical analysis of ethical questions arising from the world in which we live. Students need to be able to assess critically the consequences of actions, both individual and social, and to sharpen their understanding of the ethical and political implications of public and personal decision-making. Thus, students need to develop and apply skills in ethical reasoning and to gain an understanding of a variety of ways in which ethical and political issues and values frame and shape human conduct and ways of life." The objectives of Ethical Inquiry include enabling students to develop the capacity for discernment and for making choices about diverse systems of values and competing courses of action; a critical understanding of diverse meanings of justice, goodness, and virtue; and the capacity to articulate ethical questions, to assess competing claims and approaches to ethical thought, and to engage in careful and critical reflection about individual and social behavior, institutions, and ways of life.

As different as Duke is from Alverno and Tusculum and other small colleges we visited, this understanding of moral growth is not radically different from the understandings we saw at the other schools. We also found that almost all the case study schools share most of the same concerns, even though some spell them out more and some less explicitly and even though emphases and specific meanings differ from one campus to the next and the various goals are often organized differently by each school when they are presented and operationalized. Having looked at these common features of moral and civic education, we turn now to the three thematic approaches, which weave in various configurations through all twelve of the case study schools.

Community Connections Approach

Connections with and service to particular communities are integral to education at some of the case study institutions. The very different characters of these communities underscore the distinctiveness of each campus's definition of moral and civic education even within the same thematic cluster. Mission and location are often linked in these distinctive understandings of community connections.

Portland State University

Portland State University (PSU) is a large, urban public university, with more than 20,000 students. Most of its students come from the Portland area and expect to remain there after graduation. As we entered the campus, we were struck by the motto on a bridge connecting two buildings: "Let Knowledge Serve the City." The university has many programs in place that make that motto (which was initiated by students) a reality for faculty, administration, staff, and students. Service to the community and community partnerships are key elements of curricular and extracurricular activities and also provide the focus for much faculty research. Under the leadership of former president Judith Ramaley and former provost Michael Reardon, the university recast its entire general education program to emphasize four goals, including ethical issues and social responsibility. That program, called University Studies, is structured to emphasize civic involvement, starting with freshman seminars and continuing through senior capstone experiences.

Most colleges and universities maintain ties with their surrounding communities, if only to minimize the tensions that inevitably arise between town and gown. Portland State University goes further than most campuses, in that community involvement is inherent in its very definition of undergraduate learning. More important than the symbolism of the motto on the bridge, the standards for evaluating faculty members for tenure, promotion, and compensation explicitly include "the scholarship of community outreach." The term *community* does not mean only the Portland area, but the standards for faculty advancement state that "[t]he setting of Portland State University affords faculty many opportunities to make their expertise useful to the community outside the University." The standards make clear that community outreach is relevant only to the extent that it involves scholarly activities, as defined by the broad conception of scholarship that Ernest Boyer (1990) urged in *Scholarship Reconsidered*. PSU is also a leader in promoting teaching and research that relates directly to the Greater Portland Metropolitan Region. Community service learning courses are part of the civic involvement emphasized in the University Studies curriculum.

The goals of the freshman-level segment of University Studies reveal PSU's distinctive emphasis on connecting with the community, and at the same time they map quite closely onto the goals and outcomes evident on the other campuses: for example, "The student will understand the impact of individual and collective choices in society, e.g., through awareness of political and social phenomena." "The student will become aware of the consequences of his or her actions on others." "The student will realize the value and importance of service to the community." "The student will participate in a learning community . . . through group projects and collaborative work in both peer mentor sessions and large classes. The student will also develop connections with faculty, the university community, and the surrounding metropolitan area."

Spelman College

The mission statement of Spelman College articulates goals that reflect the same general understanding of moral and civic development that we saw on most other campuses. The college purposes to "develop the intellectual, ethical, and leadership potential of all its students" and to "empower the total person, who appreciates the many cultures of the world and commits to positive social change." At Spelman, just as at Portland State, the distinctive understanding of these goals features community connections.

Spelman College connects primarily with two communities. One is the relatively poor, black section of Atlanta in which the college is located, which includes the neighborhood in which Martin Luther King Jr. was born and grew up and in which the famous Ebenezer Baptist Church, which played such a critical role in the civil rights movement, is located. The other, perhaps even more central to Spelman's special understanding of moral and civic responsibility, is the broader community of African Americans, especially African American women.

As one of only two historically black colleges for women (the other is Bennett College, in Greensboro, North Carolina), Spelman's sense of mission is closely linked to its history, the student population it serves, and its role as a prominent institution in black society. Although in many ways Spelman (with 2,065 students) is quite similar to other small liberal arts colleges, its identity as an institution dedicated to preparing African American women for excellence and leadership distinguishes it from virtually every other educational institution in the country. As students and visitors enter the campus gates, they see a small commemorative plaque that reads "Spelman College, Women Who Serve," a phrase that acts as an unofficial motto for the college. Spelman's mission statement echoes the same theme. Leadership, service, and commitment to the improvement of the local community, the larger black community, and the country have been at the core of Spelman's educational mission since the college's inception, although students' service and leadership have taken different shapes in different eras. Spelman has worked in recent years to translate its larger mission and purpose into a set of institutional goals and a list of skills and areas of knowledge that Spelman students should be able to demonstrate by the time they leave. These goals are explained in the student handbook, which every student receives at the beginning of her studies. The institutional goals include educating black women leaders; promoting intellectual, cultural, ethical, and spiritual development; and nurturing pride, hope, and strength of character. In the personal development area, goals include the abilities to apply ethical values as a guide to behavior, demonstrate cultural sensitivity and understanding, serve the community to bring about positive social change, and exercise leadership in community and other organizations.

Spelman works to accomplish these goals through many different means, including a yearlong freshman orientation program, a required multidisciplinary course in the first year, a required sophomore assembly program, courses in many academic departments that incorporate moral and civic goals, and many clubs and other extracurricular programs, which are coordinated through the Johnetta B. Cole Center for Community Service and Community Building. The center's name honors a charismatic former (1987–1997) president of Spelman who brought to the college a heightened concern for moral and civic issues. The dual definition of community is evident in both the required and elective courses. All students must take The African Diaspora and the World, a two-semester, writing-intensive course that explores the relationship of the African diaspora to other cultures and to major historical, philosophical, artistic, and scientific developments in the world. The course Urban Education, which is required of all education majors, includes field placements in which students work to revitalize the local community and its schools. As one faculty member told us, "when the community's problems are right there across the street from you, you can't just turn a blind eye to them [but must confront them in the classroom]." About 75 percent of the department's graduates remain in the Atlanta community to teach, which helps cement strong ties between Spelman and the local schools.

The artificiality of identifying each of the twelve campuses with one prototypical approach to conceptualizing moral and civic development is evident on many campuses, and it takes an interesting form at Spelman College. We have characterized community service and engagement as the central thrust of Spelman's distinctive definition of moral and civic development, but social justice forms a strong subtheme. These approaches are not mutually exclusive, but there is some tension between the two at Spelman, with faculty who favor a more thoroughgoing social justice approach challenging what they see as the more traditional service emphasis on campus. Social and racial justice are central commitments for many Spelman faculty, and many of them bring those issues explicitly into their courses. Some of the more politically oriented faculty are critical of Spelman's "fairly predictable nineteenth-century notion of race-based self-help," with a strong emphasis on the idea of "lift as you climb." They argue that Spelman should work harder to help students understand the root causes of the social problems they are engaged with, become active in addressing those causes on a policy and political level, and question some of the assumptions about the importance of individual advancement that are implicit in Spelman's goal of preparing students for leadership positions in business and other private sector careers.

Kapi'olani Community College

Like the missions of virtually all community colleges, the mission of Kapi'olani Community College is built around strong connections with the local community. In this case the local community is Honolulu, which gives Kapi'olani a distinctive character. This two-year college serves a student population of 7,200 in which there is no single ethnic majority, and many of these students are recent immigrants for whom English is a second language. The campus uses an outcomes-based approach to education that articulates some of the same goals that other campuses promote. Among several goals that represent moral and civic learning are these two: graduates should be able to "examine critically and appreciate the values and beliefs of their own cultures as well as those of other cultures; and demonstrate an understanding of ethical, civic, and social issues relevant to Hawaii's and the world's past, present, and future."

Kapi'olani's approach to education is revealed in two of the college's six *across the curriculum emphases*, which help shape many courses at the college. The first is an emphasis on service learning, through which a great many faculty and students develop sustained involvement with the local community. As at Portland State, faculty involvement in the local community is an important criterion of promotion and tenure, and service learning is very well developed. The second is a focus on Hawaiian and Asian-Pacific values, which underscores the complexity of the area's intersecting traditions. Nearly half of the Kapi'olani faculty incorporate a

Hawaiian and Asian-Pacific emphasis into their teaching, and the campus as a whole is infused with a strong Hawaiian identity.

Campus leaders see the incorporation of values, ethics, and service into the curriculum as an organic, bottom-up process triggered and fostered to a large extent by the involvement of the institution with the community. Carole Hoshiko, dean of Business, Food Service and Hospitality Education, and Community Programs, said that many of the faculty in these areas consider it natural to incorporate various aspects of moral and civic learning into their courses, including service learning. This was evident, for example, in the food services program, where many faculty had already established close community partnerships and often encouraged students to volunteer and help coordinate events with these community partners. Faculty are enthusiastic about the strong presence of Hawaiian values in the food service curriculum, partly because they recognize that what sets Kapi'olani apart from similar programs in other parts of the country is the rich heritage of cultural traditions found in Hawaii. As a result, placing greater emphasis on these values and traditions, such as the "aloha spirit" of welcoming and generosity, was a win-win decision for students and faculty: not only is it a powerful teaching tool and a means of helping students reflect more meaningfully on their studies and work but it makes students more marketable when they look for jobs. Kapi'olani's culinary program often provides food services free of charge for events put on by local service organizations, so the connections with the community are strong.

Moral and Civic Virtue Approach

Of course all twelve of the case study campuses concern themselves with virtues in that academic integrity, respectfulness and concern for others, responsible citizenship, and willingness to be held accountable are virtues, but on some campuses an emphasis on personal virtues and values, rather than community involvement or social justice, plays an especially central role in the institution's understanding of moral and civic education. This emphasis takes very different forms at the Air Force Academy, Turtle Mountain Community College, and Messiah College.

United States Air Force Academy

The virtues approach is most clearly illustrated by the United States Air Force Academy, a coeducational public institution for the education of future Air Force officers. The academy, located in Colorado Springs, Colorado, is one of only a small handful of colleges and universities that refer to the goal of their moral education as character development. The institutional commitment to character is well articulated, broadly infuses the campus culture, and has significant resources behind it.

With the support of the academy superintendent (president), the academy's Center for Character Development coordinates a number of programs that reach all the cadets. The center uses the language of virtues to define the character development outcomes these programs are meant to foster: forthright integrity, selflessness, commitment to excellence, respect for human dignity, decisiveness, responsibility, self-discipline and courage, and appreciation of spirituality.

An explicit focus on developing good moral habits underlies the academy's strict honor code: "We will not lie, cheat, or steal, nor tolerate among us anyone who does." Absolute honesty is seen as indispensable for military officers, so there is little tolerance of infractions. Cadets are held strictly accountable not only for their own compliance but for confronting and, if necessary, reporting the violations of others. Although there is some resistance to what is known as the "toleration clause," many cadets see a purpose in it, commenting that the requirement to report others makes them press their friends to behave so they will not be put in the awkward position of having to choose between turning in their friends or violating the code themselves. Both cadets and faculty justify the requirement to report others by suggesting that in combat it would create a serious problem if officers covered up unlawful behavior of their peers, placing their loyalty with their friends rather than with the combat unit and the Air Force as a whole.

Also central to the academy's understanding of character and honor are three core values: "Integrity first, service before self, and excellence in all we do." Like the academy honor code, these values are understood with reference to the responsibilities of military officers. Service before self implies, for example, that an honorable officer will not create advantages for himself at the expense of his troops or save himself while leaving them in harm's way. Along with the honor code, these values are enshrined on many campus walls, and awareness of their importance is woven into the daily lives of cadets, faculty, and staff.

Many cadets participate in community service, including tutoring and serving as mentors for at-risk local youth, and there are some service-learning courses at the academy, but community involvement is much less central to the academy's definition of moral and civic development than it is to most other campuses' definitions. At the Air Force Academy, service is more likely to be understood as *military* service to the country and its citizens. Questions of social justice are notably absent from most discussions of ethics and social responsibility at the academy. This was not true of the other campuses where a focus on personal virtues was primary.

Turtle Mountain Community College

The core values of Turtle Mountain Community College are drawn from teachings of the Chippewa tribe. The explicit focus is ethnic, as at Kapiʻolani Community College, although what this means differs dramatically at the two campuses. Instead of overlooking Oahu's Diamond Head beach, Turtle Mountain Community College (with 650 students) is huddled up against the Canadian border, two hours' drive from the nearest city (Minot, North Dakota, with a population of about 36,500) and sited on the Chippewa Indian reservation that bears its name. The entire campus is housed in a new building that is a physical representation of tribal culture in both its overall design and its details. The college mission statement stipulates that the culture of the Turtle Mountain Band of Chippewa be brought to bear throughout the curriculum. Faculty are asked to infuse the culture into every course offered, and this has been achieved in most courses.

The core values of Turtle Mountain College are written on columns at the building's entrance: humility is to know yourself as a sacred part of creation; to know love is to know knowledge; to know creation is to have respect; bravery is to face the foe with integrity; honesty in facing a situation is to be honorable; to cherish knowledge is to know wisdom; and truth is to know all these things. These teachings cannot be traced to a single source and are not found together in sacred texts. Rather they are distillations of core tribal values as interpreted by the college. The teachings are not as sharp edged as those in the Air Force Academy's Honor Code, and members of the faculty and administration disagree about details of tribal culture and the application of the teachings in specific circumstances. But they are united in a commitment to the common good of the tribal community and to helping students search for meaning in their personal and professional lives that is related to the well-being of the community. Because only fragmented sources are available for re-creating tribal culture, the whole college is engaged in multiple searches for that culture, and in that process students, faculty, and staff significantly enhance the culture as well. Further, because there are many strands to tribal culture, and many more strands to Native American culture generally, recognition and celebration of diversity are key parts of Turtle Mountain's approach.

Messiah College

Messiah is a small college in rural Western Pennsylvania founded by the Brethren in Christ, a Protestant denomination closely related to the Mennonites. Its mission is "to educate men and women toward maturity of intellect, character, and Christian faith in preparation for lives of service, leadership, and reconciliation in church and society." Many aspects of institutional policy, classroom practice, and campus life support this mission, and it is key to Messiah's particular inflection of education for moral and civic responsibility. Christian moral and spiritual dimensions are integrated into the curriculum, and general education requirements include an ethics course, several courses focused on Christian faith, and several more courses in the area of social responsibility. Students are also required to complete a capstone course that integrates faith, values, and service in their major area of study. Messiah's core values are woven into much of the extracurricular lives of students as well.

Messiah's *foundational values* help specify what lives of service, leadership, and reconciliation are all about. They refer to a worldview that joins revelation with rational inquiry and that emphasizes the importance of valuing each person and protecting each other's freedom while encouraging responsible living; the significance of community and the community's need for humane rules; the importance of joining discipline and creativity; the love of God in service to others; and the imperative to work for justice wherever injustice prevails. To help students develop lives that express these values, Messiah College has formulated seven educational objectives, each with several parts. These objectives include a reasoned, mature Christian faith and self-understanding; the expression of Christian values in responsible decisions and actions; participation in organizations that are working for the common good; and good stewardship of economic and natural resources.

All members of the community are expected to abide by the Community Covenant, pledging to work together to create the conditions in which the mission, foundational values, and educational objectives can be achieved. The covenant would no doubt seem unacceptably constraining to faculty and students in secular institutions, but members of the Messiah community enter with full knowledge of these guidelines, and only a few consider them an intrusion on their privacy or autonomy. Even these few are willing to accept the constraints for the sake of maintaining a strong community. The covenant includes four pledges, two of which illustrate especially well the institution's focus on virtues as the core of moral and civic development. The first refers to the community's commitment to express Christian values in responsible decisions and actions in many aspects of life, including use of language, leisure time and entertainment options, and personal appearance. The second refers to the belief, based in scripture, that the community members' lives should be characterized by love, joy, peace, patience, kindness, goodness, faithfulness, gentleness, and self-control. This pledge goes on to say: "We are to use our gifts in doing such things as serving, teaching, encouraging, giving, leading, and showing mercy. Although wrong attitudes such as greed, jealousy, pride, lust, prejudice, and fractiousness are harder to detect than wrong behaviors, both are prohibited as sinful and destructive of community life and of the body of Christ."

Unlike the approach of the Air Force Academy, Messiah's approach to moral and civic education places significant emphasis on both community service and justice. But unlike secular and even some Roman Catholic campuses where these concerns were central, Messiah understands both service and justice in distinctly Christian terms and frames them with reference to personal virtues of generosity and goodness. Service at Messiah is seen in "a faith light," informed by the Brethren in Christ tradition, and places strong emphasis on the question, "What would Jesus do?"

Social Justice Approach

Faculty on many of the case study campuses spoke of their desire to promote greater social justice in the United States and the world and their hope that they could educate their students to understand, care about, and work toward social justice. By "promoting social justice" they generally mean contributing to social change and public policies that will increase gender and racial equality, end discrimination of various kinds, and reduce the stark income inequalities that characterize this country and most of the world. The term *social justice* has left-of-center political connotations for many people. On some campuses this perception was borne out, but on other campuses it was less true. We believe that the theme of social justice can be consistent with a wide range of political perspectives. However, because of the associations many people have with the language of social justice, a term such as *systemic social responsibility* may carry less ideological baggage. We will use these terms interchangeably.

On the twelve campuses we studied, as on virtually all college campuses in this country, the administration avoids taking stands on questions of public policy or social justice except in the broadest terms. Most presidents and administrative leaders worry that if they comment on matters of public policy that do not directly affect their campuses, their comments may be viewed as representing institutional rather than personal views and that this could jeopardize their schools' nonprofit status and support for their efforts to gain legislative or other action on matters that do affect them directly. Leaders of public institutions, responsible to state governors and legislatures, are especially wary in this realm, but presidents of private colleges and universities also work hard to maintain a neutral stance on most issues out of respect for the diverse views of their faculty, students, alumni and alumnae, trustees, and key benefactors. Despite this reticence among upper-level administrators, social justice is a concern for faculty and students at many colleges and universities. On some of our case study campuses it was a strongly unifying theme, well integrated into the students' learning experiences.

California State University, Monterey Bay

California State University, Monterey Bay (CSUMB), is a new campus of the California State University system, having opened its doors to students in 1995. Unlike most other CSU campuses, CSUMB is residential and quite small, at least for now, with about 2,000 students but expected to grow to 20,000. Built on a former Army base, the campus is located in a beautiful section of the mid-California coast, notable for its agriculture as well as tourism.

A concern for social justice has been a central part of CSUMB's identity since its founding. The founding administration and faculty began by creating a *vision statement,* which remains a powerful guiding force in everything the university does, serving as a touchstone for decision making and a template for·shaping curricular and cocurricular life. The statement declares that "the campus will be distinctive in serving the diverse people of California, especially the working class and historically undereducated and low income population." The vision statement is posted on walls throughout the campus and signed by all new faculty and staff. Faculty discussions of curricular and other matters frequently refer to it as the central and guiding text. We sat in on a number of curricular reviews and often heard such remarks as, "Is this approach consistent with the vision statement?" "Does that requirement further a goal of the vision statement?" Faculty are passionate about their personal commitments to social justice, and despite their heavy workloads, they are delighted to be working in an institution that encourages such zeal.

Like the curricula of a number of the case study campuses, CSUMB's curriculum uses an outcomes-based approach, and the abilities students must develop, known as *university learning requirements* (ULRs), are reminiscent of those at the other campuses. The university-wide requirements related to moral and civic learning are titled Ethics, Democratic Participation, Community Participation, Culture and Equity, and U.S. Histories. Additional requirements are Language, Math Communication, Science, Technology and Information, English Communication, Literature and Popular Culture, Creative and Artistic Expression, and Vibrancy. Departments structure the requirements for majors around additional competencies, many of which obviously reflect moral and civic concerns. A closer look at the requirements reveals the particular social justice slant that characterizes CSUMB's approach to moral and civic education. The guidelines for the culture and equity requirement, for example, state that along with achieving two other outcomes, students should be able to "analyze and describe the concepts of power relations, equity, and social justice and find examples of each concept in the U.S. society and other societies"; "analyze historical and contemporary crosscultural scenarios of discrimination, inequity, and social injustice"; and "describe and plan personal and institutional strategies/processes to promote equity and social justice." A review of this and other ULRs also reveals a liberal bent, but the students at CSUMB are a diverse lot politically, and faculty say that they are careful to respect that diversity. In addition, the risk that the strong focus on a politically liberal or progressive conception of social justice might suppress dissenting opinions is mitigated by the central role played by the concept of *ethical communication,* another strong norm on campus.

Due to the influential work of Josina Makau, a faculty member and dean who played a leadership role in developing CSUMB's approach to moral and civic education, the concept of ethical communication has widespread currency on campus, both as a goal and as a mechanism for development. Ethical communication describes exchanges characterized by individuals' cooperative, responsible attempts to understand each other's points of view, with "open-heartedness" and with a nonmanipulative intent, as opposed to efforts to win the argument or gain control over others, subjugating alternative points of view. Though recognizing that ethical communication is an ideal that real behavior can only approximate, faculty and staff are conscious of their responsibility to model compassionate and respectful communication, even during disagreements. Conscious efforts to practice ethical communication are evident in classroom discussions, administrative meetings, and public discourse on the campus.

University of Notre Dame

An interesting variant of the social justice (or systemic social responsibility) approach deriving from the Catholic social justice tradition was evident on several Roman Catholic campuses we visited. The University of

Notre Dame is a large Catholic university in South Bend, Indiana, with 7,800 undergraduates, about 85 percent of whom are Catholic. The mission statement is one of many documents that reveal Notre Dame's concern for social justice: "[The university] seeks to cultivate in its students not only an appreciation for the great achievements of human beings but also a disciplined sensibility to the poverty, injustice, and oppression that burden the lives of so many. The aim is to create a sense of human solidarity and concern for the common good that will bear fruit as learning becomes service to justice."

Notre Dame is very much a residential campus, and the residence halls are important sites for moral and civic education. Residence hall leaders, known as rectors, create programming as well as informal exchanges around the themes of social justice and service. For example, it is not unusual for over a thousand students in a given year to participate through their residences in the Christmas in April program.

Notre Dame also has a number of programs that help its students prepare for the tensions they will face between their desire for career success and their concern for social change. At graduation many students wear green ribbons to signify that they have signed a pledge, sponsored by the Peace Studies Department, to "investigate and take into account the social and environmental consequences of any job [they] consider, thereby striving to create a just, peaceful, and nonviolent world." Notre Dame's Alliance for Catholic Education places about eighty graduates a year in teaching positions in low-income schools in the South. The teachers live in community with one another and have mentors and regular seminars, participating in an intensive program over two summers that leads to a master's degree in education. Notre Dame's Center for Social Concerns is the organizational embodiment of the concern for social justice. Father Don McNeill, director of the center from its founding, views Catholic doctrine as requiring a deep commitment to social justice through active engagement in moral and civic concerns. The center has been an important catalyst for stimulating and sustaining that commitment at Notre Dame, as we will describe later in this chapter.

The College of St. Catherine

The College of St. Catherine, informally known as St. Kate's, is the largest Catholic women's college in the country. It comprises two campuses, one located in St. Paul, Minnesota, the other in Minneapolis. The missions, structures, and student bodies of the two are quite different, but both are committed to preparing students for lives of personal and civic responsibility. The Minneapolis campus offers two-year associate of arts degrees as well as two-year degrees and several graduate programs in a number of health care and human services fields. Although this campus is coeducational, the majority of its students are women. The St. Paul campus is a four-year, primarily residential, college for women that offers a bachelor's degree in liberal arts as well as professional programs in business, health care, and human services. Although neither campus has a predominantly Catholic student body, the college is influenced by its Roman Catholic heritage, especially the special heritage of the founding order of nuns, the Sisters of St. Joseph of Carondelet. The sisters of this order are known for their strength, independence, concern for the disadvantaged, and social activism, and these qualities set the tone for both campuses of the college.

The college works hard to balance its desire to honor its origins while also ensuring religious and intellectual openness. This commitment is expressed in its "Roman Catholic Identity Statement," which stresses critical inquiry about religious questions, the nondogmatic and ecumenical nature of the college's approach to spirituality, and the Roman Catholic Church's long tradition of commitment to the poor. It goes on: "Drawing on these traditions, we seek to promote, through our student services, campus ministry, administration, faculty and staff, a common search for wisdom and the integration of our daily lives and work with our spirituality. Without being exclusive of other ecclesiastical and spiritual traditions, we will continue to ask ourselves how this Catholic heritage enhances the people we serve and the well being of the planet."

A passion for social justice and community activism is evident in the curriculum, the campus culture, and the relationship of both St. Kate's campuses to their local communities. For example, the Minneapolis campus program Access and Success encourages low-income women, including those on welfare, to train in nursing, physical therapy, and other health care fields. Each year this program provides three hundred single-parent students with a wide range of financial and academic support, including help with child care, low-cost housing, and mentoring programs to make sure they succeed in their studies. One of the programs that Access and Success sponsors is Mother to Mother, in which single mothers in the college reach out to single mothers in local high schools, urging them to continue their education as a way out of poverty and dependence on public assistance. Several years ago the Minneapolis campus adopted a new curriculum that emphasizes not only academic preparedness but also diversity, ethics, and spirituality. Many faculty members at St. Kate's, including those teaching preprofessional courses and those teaching general education courses, have incorporated these three elements into their courses.

On the St. Paul campus the centerpiece of the core curriculum is a pair of interdisciplinary bookend courses, one taken in the first year (The Reflective Woman), the other a senior capstone (The Global Search for Justice). The Reflective Woman is intended to help students develop frameworks for thinking about the way their values and lives can be informed by a range of moral, spiritual, and intellectual traditions. The Global Search for Justice is a multidisciplinary seminar that addresses global issues of peace, meaningful work, and social justice, with the intention of helping students to "develop the discipline and consciousness needed to change oppressive systemic conditions and reshape their world."

Integrating the Three Thematic Approaches

In order to create approaches to moral and civic education that are well suited to the institution's particular mission, history, constituencies, and institutional strengths, it is appropriate for colleges and universities to specialize to some extent in the relative emphasis they place on these three ways of framing moral and civic education. Naturally, each of the three will not be equally salient in most cases. Even so, the three emphases can also be understood to represent different aspects of a full picture of what moral and civic education should be. Despite the value of unique adaptations, we believe that moral and civic education is incomplete if it does not somehow take account of all three: virtues and character, systemic social responsibility, and engagement with and response to communities of various sorts.

An overly strong focus on building students' character or virtues runs the risk of limiting students' development to private, personal domains of interaction and failing to prepare them adequately for their roles as active and engaged citizens. It may also miss opportunities to build on the strengths of the community and systemic approaches to deepen some aspects of students' character development, such as open-mindedness or moral courage.

An emphasis on systemic social responsibility or social justice that does not include sufficient attention to moral virtue is especially vulnerable to the illegitimate imposition of a political party line or to students' use of morally questionable means to pursue the ends of social justice about which they have passionate convictions. Harry Boyte (2001) calls attention to the fact that many young people first become involved in political action by participating in canvassing campaigns. One drawback of this kind of involvement as an educational experience is that it often involves a deliberate polarization of issues and demonization of the opposition. When these portrayals of issues and members of the opposition are less than honest, the experience teaches unsavory moral lessons. If the educational goal is to prepare activists with integrity, explicit attention to virtue is essential.

Likewise, community involvement without virtue or systemic social responsibility is subject to a number of problems. If community service does not include some attention to the systemic implications of the problems it addresses, it is needlessly limiting students' learning and the good they can do as engaged citizens. It was concerns of this kind that impelled some faculty at Spelman to broaden that college's approach to emphasize social justice as well as service to the community. And if community involvement does not include careful attention to ethical concerns, it can actually do harm rather than good to both the students and the community partners. Finally, virtue-based and systemic approaches can both be abstract and disengaged unless they are connected with some kind of community-based action, whether that community is on the campus, in the surrounding area, national, or international.

When we recommend that institutions find a way to incorporate some version of the three approaches—virtue or character, community connections, and systemic social responsibility, or social justice—we do not mean that institutions' approaches to moral and civic education should be homogenized. Each school can still have its own special quality. One approach can still be primary if that makes for the most powerful and natural connections with the institution's history and mission. These considerations about breadth of focus are most pertinent when thinking about balance across programs at the institutional level, but they also apply to some extent within courses and programs. Some courses or programs will focus much more intensively on one approach than on the others, but even in these cases a focus on one should not clash with or undermine the others. Faculty and program leaders may be called on to put the goals of one approach into the context of the others if a clash emerges. A faculty member at one campus we visited told of a student volunteering at a soup kitchen who very much enjoyed the experience and felt that it had made him a better person. Without thinking through the implications of his statement, he said, "I hope it is still around when my children are in college, so they can work here too." This kind of comment provides a teachable moment in which to place the community connections perspective in juxtaposition with a focus on systemic social change.

How They Do It: Leadership

The twelve colleges and universities we have described here approach the moral and civic development of their students with an unusual degree of commitment, perseverance, and creativity. They have also created institutional structures and climates that support the wider range of undergraduate learning goals of which moral and civic development is an integral part. What makes this possible? What led them to make this kind of sustained commitment? As with any thoroughgoing institutional focus and commitment, strong leadership is essential to the success of this kind of effort. Presidential support for the agenda is critical, and in some cases it has been a visionary president who led the development of a campuswide program of moral and civic education. In other cases the most powerful impetus has come from faculty who worked together to build the programs. In yet another model a strong and integrative center for moral and civic education has taken the lead, developing implementations in collaboration with interested members of the administration and faculty. In most cases at least two of these forms of leadership are operating in a dynamic interaction.

Presidential Leadership

Presidential leadership played a key role in the development of moral and civic education at many of the case study institutions. The presidents who play this pivotal role share a belief in the potential for higher education to shape graduates who will be as interested in what they can contribute to the common good as in their own personal advancement. These administrators also believe that making moral and civic education a central part of the school's identity is good for the institution itself. In some cases an expanded program of moral and civic education was initiated as part of a strategy for dealing with a problem—insufficient sense of community on campus, low rates of student retention, or even threats to the institution's survival. In virtually every case, this program provides a distinctive character to higher education at that institution relative to its peers, and that distinctiveness is seen as advantageous for some aspects of institutional advancement.

In each case presidential leadership required enlisting the enthusiastic participation of others in the administration and enough faculty to ensure thoughtful development and effective implementation of the program. In every case in which the president was said to be especially influential in supporting moral and civic education, the president worked collaboratively with a strong and carefully selected administrative team. Turtle Mountain, Alverno, Portland State, and Duke are clear illustrations of this approach. Because all twelve case study institutions determined that moral and civic issues should be integrated into the curriculum as well as into cocurricular experiences, all the presidential leaders had to set in motion a curriculum revision that made moral and civic education an important goal of student learning. This entailed some specification of what that learning is, with one notable result of that process being the distinctive definitions of moral and civic maturity reviewed earlier in this chapter.

TURTLE MOUNTAIN COMMUNITY COLLEGE. Gerald "Carty" Monette has been associated with Turtle Mountain Community College since its founding in 1972 and its president since 1978. The college's success is due in large part to the continuity of his visionary and charismatic leadership. President Monette was instrumental in establishing the college, which was a politically complex undertaking. Founding a college on the reservation required the backing of the Chippewa tribal government, which was skeptical about the project from its inception. Carty Monette believed that a central rationale for establishing a college on the reservation was that this school could revitalize the cultural heritage of the Turtle Mountain Band of Chippewa and integrate that heritage into students' academic and vocational learning. He saw to it that this goal, which is built into the college mission statement, became a real force in shaping the college's programs.

From the outset Monette and his colleagues had to deal with almost overwhelming challenges. The students at Turtle Mountain are underprepared academically and too poor to pay tuition or even buy their own books, so all revenue must be raised from other sources. The political complexities of the college's relationship to the reservation and to the federal Bureau of Indian Affairs are ongoing and need to be continually managed. And the curriculum must evolve over time to be responsive to the needs of the reservation. It was not until the mid-1980s that Monette was able to hire an academic dean. Carol Davis came in that role in 1989, and subsequently became vice president for academic affairs.

Throughout all this, President Monette and his colleagues have always maintained the strong focus on Chippewa values and culture and on service to the local community, even as the college has evolved to meet the changing needs of the student body. The collaborative work style that characterized the founding years continues as well, maintaining what the president calls "the feeling of doing things together at the college like in the beginning." Although the institutional architecture of the college is very much his doing, he works so collaboratively with his senior staff that he says any of the six could take over as president. He also works closely with presidents of other tribal colleges, playing a leadership role in the American Indian Higher Education Consortium, of which Turtle Mountain was one of six founding members.

Until 1999, the college was located in a collection of inadequate wooden buildings. Under President Monette's leadership, the college raised the $12 million needed to build the handsome new facility in which it is now housed. In designing the new building, the senior administration of the college made sure that it dramatically represents the Chippewa values and culture that are such an integral part of Turtle Mountain's educational mission.

ALVERNO COLLEGE. Turtle Mountain Community College clearly benefited from the exceptional length of Carty Monette's presidency, and we saw the value of continuity in leadership on a few other campuses as well, most notably Alverno College. Sister Joel Read, who has been president of Alverno since 1968, has been a major force behind the transformation of the college from early in her long presidency. In the early 1970s, Alverno faced a crisis of survival, with declining enrollments and revenue. The college also struggled with the difficult challenge of educating a wide range of students, including many first-generation college students. From the beginning, Read believed that a new kind of institution was possible, one that would better serve the needs of Alverno's student body. Toward this end she and the faculty worked closely to create Alverno's abilities-based approach, in which the curriculum is structured to ensure the development of key abilities and students receive a great deal of feedback on their developmental progress instead of grades. Alverno's abilities-based program reflects the fact that Read and the faculty consider moral and civic capacities to be as important as the more strictly academic outcomes. As Read told us, all students need to think about "who they are and what roles they are going to play in the world." Read notes that Alverno was a lone pioneer when it first started the abilities-based program but is now a beacon for educators interested in outcomes-based approaches and creative modes of assessment. (For more on the history of the change process at Alverno College, see Read & Sharkey, 1985.)

PORTLAND STATE UNIVERSITY. Of course, relatively few colleges and universities benefit from the kind of continuity in leadership that Alverno and Turtle Mountain have enjoyed, so if programs of moral and civic education are going to remain in place long term, they must be able to weather changes in administrations. Portland State University is a case in point. Judith Ramaley, the powerful and creative leader who spurred the creation of University Studies at PSU, left the university after eight years to become president of the University of Vermont. Although the changes she and her colleagues had put in motion were well underway by that time, they were by no means complete and could have been vulnerable to a presidential transition. The current president, Daniel Bernstine, is maintaining most of the changes President Ramaley put in place and appears to share her vision of PSU as integrally connected with the local community. As he said, "My vision is of a university so thoroughly engaged with its community that people throughout the region refer to it as 'our university.'" Nevertheless, President Bernstine seemed to us less personally interested in undergraduate moral and civic education than Ramaley was. University Studies, community-based learning, and related initiatives are moving forward in part because Ramaley engaged the faculty so deeply in shaping these initiatives. The work of these committed faculty gives the efforts continuity despite the shift in administrative leadership.

Following a pattern we saw at several of the case study institutions, the transformation envisioned by President Ramaley was in part a response to a serious challenge facing the university. In the early 1990s, Oregon severely cut public funding for higher education, and PSU's student retention and graduation rates were low, even relative to other nonresidential, urban universities. These pressures added urgency to the question of how PSU could best serve its students and ensure their success and better graduation rates. A comprehensive, new educational approach for PSU would also have the advantage of giving it a clear and distinctive identity relative to the University of Oregon and Oregon State University.

Ramaley's vision for PSU drew on the civic mission of the university that had been present from its founding as a campus that catered to returning veterans and other adults at the end of World War II. Ramaley believed that the university could draw on its history even as it rewrote its mission statement and rethought its relationships with the community, its curriculum, the nature of faculty work, and the criteria for faculty advancement. Her conception of the new general education curriculum was inspired by her conviction that key educational experiences concern not only the content students learn, which is important, but also their reflection on what they learn and their integration, interpretation, and application of what they learn—that is, not only what they do but how they think about what they do, how they explore its impact and implications. She worked closely with then-provost Michael Reardon on this effort and got the faculty deeply involved so that it became very much an "authentically faculty-guided effort." In addition to investing financial resources in the work, President Ramaley's role in the transformation consisted largely of "giving voice and expression to the ideas, telling stories, recognizing the people who were doing the work, and holding them up as models to be admired—'loving the stuffin' out of them,' as I used to say."

DUKE UNIVERSITY. Research universities are notoriously difficult to lead with the integrative force that Presidents Monette, Read, and Ramaley brought to their institutions, and one might argue that a research-intensive environment works best without that kind of direction. Highly selective, research-oriented universities are almost always characterized by the patterns we identified as impediments to moral and civic education in Chapter Two: a specialized and extremely autonomous faculty, an emphasis on research productivity at the expense of teaching, and the absence of a curriculum that supports the development of integrative capacities and other cross-cutting learning goals. It is therefore not surprising that we identified very few institutions of this type that pursue undergraduate moral and civic education with real cohesion and intentionality.

Nan Keohane, president of Duke University since 1994, is exceptional among her peers in that she has been able to establish this cohesion and intentionality in a secular, research-oriented university. Keohane came to Duke from the presidency of Wellesley College, bringing with her a long-standing interest in and commitment to gender equality and other aspects of social justice, a great deal of experience with liberal arts education, and a deep appreciation of the importance of building a strong campus community. She began by creating a strong senior administrative team that shared her commitment to moral and civic development as an important part of undergraduate education. Over the next few years the administrative team worked with faculty committees and others to write the mission statement for the Ethical Inquiry requirement that we quoted from earlier in this chapter, completely revamp the general education curriculum to create Curriculum 2000, strengthen the university's relationship with the local community, make important changes in student life, establish the Kenan Institute for Ethics, and bring the Center for Academic Integrity to the Duke campus.

Provost Peter Lange and dean of the Faculty of Arts and Sciences William Chafe, together with Robert Thompson, the dean of Trinity College of Arts and Sciences (the undergraduate school), took the lead in reshaping the curriculum. According to Lange, the discussions of the Curriculum Review Committee were "shaped by a vision of what a Duke graduate in the next century should carry into life beyond college." Ethics came up early in these discussions, and although there was general agreement that ethics must somehow be a part of Curriculum 2000, the committee struggled with a number of difficult questions before settling on the Ethical Inquiry approach. The members talked at length about how to avoid imposing particular ethical views, why ethics should take priority over some alternative emphases that seemed important, and whether they were overemphasizing personal ethics or individual morality at the expense of a more social or political perspective. After a series of extended discussions and numerous revisions, they put forth the rationale that we quoted earlier, which refers to the undergraduate years as a "formative period for engaging in critical analysis of ethical questions" and students' need to "assess critically the consequences of actions, both individual and social, and to sharpen their understanding of the ethical and political implications of public and personal decision-making."

In their thinking about how the new curriculum could best support moral and civic engagement, the committee members felt it was important to link the curriculum and the campus culture by establishing multiple sites through which students would engage in service and think about their civic responsibilities. They wanted to provide numerous opportunities for students to develop their own moral values and to assume leadership positions through which they could test, refine, and extend those values. Committee members saw the two-course Ethical Inquiry requirement as a "moral primer," complementing cocurricular programs and enabling students to think about their own ethical systems and choices, rather than inculcating a specific ethical code.

A number of steps were also taken to accomplish the important goal of increasing the sense of community on campus, thus creating on this large campus a "community of communities," as Nan Keohane describes it. One key change was to bring all the freshmen together into one group of dorms to give them a stronger sense of community with each other at the outset of their college lives.

Leadership from Centers and Institutes

Centers and institutes play critical roles for moral and civic education at several of the twelve case study schools. Three that stand out are the Kenan Institute for Ethics at Duke University, the Center for Character Development at the U.S. Air Force Academy, and the Center for Social Concerns at the University of Notre Dame. These entities are well supported by the campuses' upper administration, have significant resources to work with, and perhaps most importantly have had especially strong, creative, and dedicated leadership over a sustained period of time.

KENAN INSTITUTE FOR ETHICS, DUKE UNIVERSITY. The establishment of the Kenan Institute for Ethics was another very important step in creating an institution-wide commitment to moral and civic education at Duke University. The institute was begun in 1995 as a five-year, grant-funded program and was endowed as a center in 2000 with a $10 million gift from the William R. Kenan Jr. Fund for Ethics. The institute not only became a central catalyst and energy source for continuing development of the moral and civic focus at Duke but also made the university a national leader on these dimensions of education.

Professor Elizabeth Kiss, the institute's first director, explains that its mandate is to "reach broadly through the university and beyond, providing not only formal teaching but occasions for ethical practice, not only reasonable intellectual constructs but opportunities for commitment, not only the transmission of received principles but also the encouragement of ethical innovation in the face of new moral challenges posed by a rapidly changing environment." To a remarkable degree this mandate is being met, in large measure because of Kiss's leadership, the support of the administration and faculty, and the enthusiasm of students.

The institute has significantly expanded the infusion of ethics across the curriculum through course development and evaluation; support for service learning; incorporation of ethical discourse into Duke's First-Year Writing Program; and provision of the Kenan Instructorship in Ethics, a fellowship awarded to a graduate student to develop and teach an undergraduate course with substantial ethical focus. The institute also works to bring a focus on ethics to campus life through its affiliation with the Center for Academic Integrity and workshops for campus groups. The institute has become visible on the national level due in part to its biennial conference, Moral Education in a Diverse Society, which has been cosponsored by North Carolina Central University, Shaw University, and North Carolina State University. This conference brings together educators and researchers from schools, colleges, and universities across the country to discuss the means and ends of K–12 and postsecondary moral education.

CENTER FOR CHARACTER DEVELOPMENT, UNITED STATES AIR FORCE ACADEMY. One challenge for the Center for Character Development at the Air Force Academy is the frequent turnover in professional staff that results from the Air Force policy of transferring officers to new posts every few years. Center director Mark Hyatt must live with this reality, providing strong leadership and training for new staff members. When it came time for him to move on after his initial term as director, Colonel Hyatt chose instead to stay on as director, passing up any possibility of advancement in rank in order to provide more sustained leadership for the center. The Center for Character Development was created in 1993 and is perhaps even more critical to moral education at the academy than the Kenan Institute is at Duke, because virtually all of the institution's moral education is operationally coordinated through the center. An autonomous Character Development Commission, appointed by the academy superintendent, is concerned with policy in this matter, but the commission does not operate any programs directly. Instead, the superintendent and his appointed commission in essence delegate responsibility for the cadets' moral education to the center. This contrasts with the practice at both Duke and Notre Dame, where the centers are important parts of a broader set of strategies and where the presidents and others in the administration are themselves directly involved in shaping the institutions' approaches to moral and civic education.

The critical leadership role of the Center for Character Development gives it a broad mandate, and its work encompasses several programs. The Honor Program educates cadets about the meaning of honor and administers the honor code. The Human Relations Program deals with issues of diversity, "promoting the understanding of how cultural, ethnic, gender, racial, and religious differences affect the quality of life for various cadet groups." The Character/Ethics Program runs workshops for faculty, coaches, staff, and cadet leaders to help them learn how to foster cadets' character development, especially outside of class; brings to campus Air Force leaders who are carefully chosen to represent honor, integrity, and moral courage; organizes an annual national conference on character and leadership; and oversees community service activities. The Curriculum and Research Program develops curriculum materials, conducts program assessments, and oversees the development of ethics across the curriculum. In all these areas the center provides leadership, oversight, and support.

CENTER FOR SOCIAL CONCERNS, UNIVERSITY OF NOTRE DAME. With much of the impetus coming from students, the Center for Social Concerns was established in 1983 at the University of Notre Dame to integrate a number of disparate campus programs that promoted experiential learning and volunteer service. The center is at the heart of service and social awareness at Notre Dame, especially for students but for many faculty and staff as well. Although it reports directly to the Office of the Provost, the center is affiliated with the Institute for Church Life, and spiritual development is a key mission, along with moral and civic development.

The center works with about fifty faculty members who teach service-learning courses. Among other things, it funds nine staff members to work full time in local social service agencies, acting as support for the students who volunteer there in connection with their service-learning courses. In recent years the number of service-learning courses sponsored through the center has increased substantially, and now about 40 percent of all graduates (about 75 percent of arts and letters graduates) have taken at least one service-learning course, most of which are sponsored through the center or in collaboration with it. In addition about forty student groups are linked to the center.

Even with its growth over the past several years the center is still struggling to maintain an adequate level of support for its work. Unlike the Kenan Institute it is only partially endowed (covering only about a third of its overall budget in this way), and unlike the Air Force Academy's Center for Character Development, the Center for Social Concerns is not linked to all of its school's life. Yet the "public television syndrome" is nevertheless at work in the minds of some on campus. Some faculty say, in effect, "The center takes care of community service, so I don't need to think about it." The university's research-focused reward structure for faculty still makes it a challenge to involve faculty in the center's work, and departments often actively discourage nontenured faculty from such involvement.

Despite these obstacles the center plays a critical leadership role in moral and civic education at Notre Dame, shaping the meaning of that education by grounding it in the Catholic social justice tradition and forever prodding the campus to move forward on this important agenda. Especially in the absence of an endowment, the powerful, long-term leadership of Father McNeill has been important to the center's vital presence on campus. We saw in all three of the institutions just discussed that campus leadership from centers and their directors can be as significant as presidential leadership in sustaining and developing moral and civic education.

Faculty Leadership

On some of the campuses we studied, the critical leadership that placed moral and civic education squarely on the institution's agenda came from faculty. Even when presidential or center leadership played an important role, faculty leadership was absolutely essential to the implementation of curricular and even some cocurricular efforts. Faculty leadership was important on many campuses; we will describe two on which it played an especially pivotal role.

KAPIʻOLANI COMMUNITY COLLEGE. The leadership of a small group of faculty has been instrumental in infusing Kapiʻolani with service learning and an explicit focus on values. A major force in the development of the service-learning emphasis has been the strong leadership of Robert Franco. Franco is a professor of anthropology as well as co-coordinator of service learning at Kapiʻolani and draws on his background in cultural anthropology in his approach to service learning. Early on, he and the academic leadership of the college saw service learning as particularly well suited to the mission of community colleges, despite the resource challenges these colleges face in trying to create and maintain such programs. It is so suitable partly because of the great diversity of community college students in experience, interests, social class, race, ethnicity, age, life situation, and religion.

Professor Franco explains the school's decision to add a strong service learning emphasis as having been largely the result of a belief in its academic value. He and others at Kapiʻolani saw service learning as "a powerful new pedagogy to improve the academic performance of an extremely diverse traditional and nontraditional Native Hawaiian and Pacific, Asian, and Euro-American student population." As a pedagogical tool service learning can help students learn experientially some competencies they need in order to be successful academically and in their lives. These include critical-thinking, time management, decision-making, problem-solving, and communication skills. Franco and others who promoted service learning at Kapiʻolani believed that in addition to its academic benefits, service learning would help students develop civic responsibility and respect for diversity and would create a more powerful relationship between the college and the community it serves through the new partnerships this learning fostered (Franco, 1999). Franco has become a spokesman for service learning throughout the University of Hawaii system and nationally, bringing visibility to Kapiʻolani and tying it strongly into a national agenda of pedagogical and curricular reform. His work has been very much appreciated and supported by members of the senior administration at Kapiʻolani and the University of Hawaii, and this has been key in ensuring that there is institutional infrastructure underlying the effort. Because many of the other Kapiʻolani faculty, especially those who are themselves native Hawaiian, are committed to bringing Hawaiian and Asian-Pacific values onto the campus in both curricular and extracurricular programs, Franco has had a wealth of collaborators. It is Franco and these collaborators who have really made the transformation happen.

THE COLLEGE OF ST. CATHERINE. At the College of St. Catherine the impetus for incorporating a concern for moral and civic development into the undergraduate experience also came more from faculty and less from the administration than at many of the other twelve campuses. Although the influence of its Catholic heritage, and particularly the heritage of the Sisters of St. Joseph of Carondelet, has been present since its founding, some of the faculty have undertaken an "experiment in civic renewal" at the college over the past ten years, bringing moral and civic concerns into the classroom in a much more conscious and systematic way. These efforts at civic renewal on campus were made in response to a perception that the faculty were fragmented and isolated, notably along disciplinary lines, with attempts to work together proving unproductive, sometimes even uncivil (an illustration of the reach to other institutional types of some problematic features of the university model). Nan Kari, who was an associate professor in occupational therapy at St. Kate's for many years, was especially influential in the shape this work took and saw to it that the initiative had a strong civic focus. Professor Kari had long been interested in civic engagement, having worked with Harry Boyte before coming to the College of St. Catherine in a program to engage youths in what Kari and Boyte call *public work*. The program, Public Achievement, has become a national model for youths' civic engagement, and Kari published widely on the public work perspective on citizenship throughout her tenure at St. Kate's. She continues to work with the college and on civic education more broadly from her new position as codirector of the Jane Addams School for Democracy and coordinator of the West Side Leadership Institute.

In 1991, with funding from the Bush Foundation, Kari and a number of other faculty formed a series of faculty study groups. Each faculty study group was a self-selected collection of faculty representing at least five disciplines who pursued a topic of mutual intellectual interest for a year and produced a public product at the end of the year. Over the course of three years, 60 percent of the college faculty participated in faculty study groups, which were seen as having a major impact on working relations among faculty and on the curriculum. One of these groups, the Citizen Politics Study Group, initiated a number of changes at St. Kate's, including the establishment of community meetings to promote the practice of public deliberation on campus. These meetings have continued into the present, discussing heated campus issues with broad participation and clear guidelines for discussion. The faculty study group process laid the foundation for a successful effort by a faculty committee to revise the general education curriculum in 1993. This resulted in the interdisciplinary bookend courses, The Reflective Woman and The Global Search for Justice, that we described earlier in this chapter.

In 1994, the Bush Foundation awarded the college another grant to implement a second phase of renewal. This led to the establishment of the Teaching-Learning Network, which links learning resources on both campuses in an effort to promote collaborative learning throughout the institution. One function of the network is to develop theory about collaborative work and learning tied to education for citizenship. At St. Kate's, as at many of the case study institutions, the strengthening of moral and civic education and the reform of other aspects of pedagogy and the curriculum were mutually reinforcing.

In all of these efforts—the strategies for building and maintaining a sense of community, the conscious infusion of social justice into a wide array of campus programs, and the dramatic revision of the curriculum—faculty took the lead. Although the administration has been supportive of the changes that have taken place over the past ten years, the real creative energy has come from faculty, as it has at Kapi'olani.

How They Do It: Campus Culture

Whether the leadership comes from the president and others in the upper levels of administration, from catalytic centers, or from interested faculty, a full-scale institutional commitment to moral and civic education involves creating a campus climate or culture that reinforces what students learn in curricular and extracurricular programs. Academic coursework has less impact when students walk out of the classroom into a setting that does not support the new interests and commitments they have begun to develop. Shaping the right kind of campus culture is a key element in creating an overarching sense of commitment that goes beyond specific programs and makes the institution's commitment to its students' moral and civic education a holistic effort.

Our story in Chapter One about Virginia Durr's experience at Wellesley College illustrates how powerful a holistic commitment can be. Wellesley's insistence on racial integration in its dining rooms ultimately had a life-changing impact on Virginia, making her receptive to later influences that eventually led her to become a civil rights activist. Rules like this, along with less formal norms for student behavior and for the multitude of practices and routines that characterize life at college, are powerful sources of socialization. By *socialization* we do not mean simply the internalization of static cultural messages but rather habitual participation in practices, routines, and communal events that are the basis of shared culture (Corsaro, 1997). The habitual, taken-for-granted character of routines gives them the power to shape the frameworks through which future experiences are interpreted.

This is not a simple matter, because culture, even within a single institution, is seldom homogeneous, integrated, or stable. College students experience one or more peer cultures, which may intersect to various degrees with the broader American youth culture and which may be consistent or in conflict with one or more institutional cultures (representing, for example, the norms of academic life or the norms of sports teams or of other extracurricular groups or settings). Students may choose among available residences and student organizations according to their reputations for embodying a particular subculture (artistic, athletic, hard partying, and so on), and this self-selection contributes to the survival of those subcultures. Many institutions are also quite demographically heterogeneous, and the different ethnic and religious groups form clusters with their own distinct climates. Students who live off campus experience the multiple environments of their home neighborhood and of the college campus and often the environment of a work setting as well. And of course everyone is subject to the various cultural currents in contemporary U.S. society, because campuses can never be ivory towers.

To add to the complexity, neither students nor faculty are passive recipients of enculturation—people understand the same cultural artifacts and practices differently, pay attention to different things, and sometimes take a critical look at the institutional culture, raising questions about features that others take for granted. Even when members of a campus community participate in a shared cultural practice, that practice can have different, sometimes conflicting, meanings for different people. Students, faculty, and administrators all have the capacity to reflect on, critique, take action on, and possibly make a difference in the cultures in which they participate. Especially for students who come to college directly from high school, one of the most dramatic experiences of their undergraduate years is having their eyes opened to the ways in which they have been living according to particular cultural assumptions, norms, or scripts without being aware of it. In college they encounter students, faculty, and staff who do not share their assumptions, so they begin to notice and question those assumptions and see them in the context of a wider range of possibilities. Even many older students may not be accustomed to reflecting on the cultural norms they have taken for granted and may come to see their various contexts in a new way.

Moral and civic education programs almost always include among their educational goals an increased awareness of a variety of cultural frameworks and the place of one's own values and beliefs in that expanded range. At Tusculum College, for example, to demonstrate the competency of Self-Knowledge: The Examined Life, students must exhibit competence in five areas, one of which involves possessing an awareness of the roles their key life events, family backgrounds, and cultural contexts have had in shaping their values and outlook and having the ability to locate their own history in a broader cultural context and to use that history as an instrument for reciprocal understanding of other individuals, communities, and cultures. Other campuses echo this goal of helping students develop a more nuanced perspective on themselves and their own culture as well as better knowledge of and respect for other cultures. Service-learning courses are especially well suited to heightening cultural awareness because they often place students in communities that are very different from any they have experienced before and follow the service experiences with reflections on the encounters through structured discussions with professors and fellow students.

This growing cultural awareness can build tolerance and understanding, help free students from constraining assumptions that may not stand up to scrutiny, and stimulate them to become more consciously active in evaluating, critiquing, and choosing the values and practices they believe in and want to live by. That is, it can make them more thoughtful about themselves and the settings in which they live. At the same time, it may lead them to jettison some values and beliefs prematurely, leading to alienation, confusion, and unsophisticated versions of cultural and moral relativism. Lack of a strong sense that their institution really stands for some shared values may even cause students to cede more power to the consumer culture and instrumentalism that are such strong themes in contemporary U.S. culture.

The twelve case study institutions each create a vibrant sense of mission and a palpable and distinctive culture in many ways, some quite conscious, others no doubt less so. In visiting these twelve campuses we were almost always struck by the physical symbols of the mission and culture. On many campuses we heard the same stories over and over—stories relating to an institution's founding or transformation, stories about heroes, and stories of transgression against cherished norms and about areas where the boundaries of "right behavior" were contested, sometimes along the fault lines of power relationships. On some campuses a few simple ideas were a shared focus across levels and groups. Sometimes shared ideologies or philosophies were part of the cultural fabric. All the institutions had rituals that carried meaning, and sometimes (though by no means always) this meaning had become a subject of public discussion. We also saw many explicit as well as implicit strategies for socializing new students and faculty into the campus community.

Physical Features of the Campus

For some of the institutions we visited, it is almost impossible to describe their distinctive approaches to moral and civic education without mentioning certain features of their architecture, decor, landscaping, or other aspects of their settings. We have already mentioned that the building in which Turtle Mountain Community College is housed was designed to reflect the college's commitment to Native American values. The 105,000-square-foot building is designed in the abstracted shape of a thunderbird, and an interpretive trail encircles it. All the design elements—even the railings—reflect the college's efforts to integrate tribal culture into the education of its students. From a distance a large skylight behind the entrance gives the impression of a turtle's back. In front of the entrance is a circle of seven columns, each of which has one of the seven "teachings" of the Chippewa Band that are central to the Ojibway heritage: Wisdom, Love, Respect, Bravery, Honesty, Humility, and Truth. The brickwork on the exterior represents the hills, and throughout the entire building the colors and designs are symbols of the tribe's heritage. In the main common area inside, the floor incorporates a medicine wheel in traditional colors: yellow represents the east, white the south, red and black the west and north. The red tiles that surround the medicine wheel and separate the directions symbolize the blood of the Chippewa that was shed to preserve the homeland for generations to come. The campus plans an interpretive center—to be used as a teaching and meditation center—and a number of other features to enhance the campus's relation to tribal heritage as well as its beauty.

Almost every point on the campus of Kapi'olani Community College provides a view of the historic landmark of Diamond Head Crater at Mount Le'ahi on the island of Oahu, and of the ocean beyond, underscoring that this is an island culture, a fact that has many implications and ramifications. This facility of twenty buildings was built de novo when the college moved to its present site from a nondescript urban campus in the 1980s. The move provided a rare opportunity to plan the complete facility, weaving Hawaiian themes throughout. With input from students, the decision was made to name each building for an indigenous plant with a metaphorical significance connected to the function of the building. For example, the library is the Lama Building. *Lama* is the candlenut, once used by native Hawaiians to light the night sky; on the library the name refers to the capacity of knowledge to illuminate the darkness. The campus center building, which houses the cafeteria, clubs, bookstore, and lounges, is called Olona, after the plant used by native Hawaiians as a binding cord. The purpose of the building is to bind people together through community and mutual understanding. The landscaping for many of the buildings includes their namesake plant, and a large garden near the entrance to the campus includes a wide array of native Hawaiian vegetation. Developing and caring for the garden is part of a service-learning project for Kapiʻolani's ethnobotany students.

We have already mentioned the signs greeting visitors to Portland State University and Spelman College ("Let Knowledge Serve the City" and "Women Who Serve"). These are reminders of messages that are reinforced in many different ways throughout these institutions' programs, and they gain their significance from that reinforcement, because the artifacts themselves may not be noticed by students and faculty who pass them every day. At CSUMB and the Air Force Academy, the values posted on the walls are impossible to ignore. Both faculty and students refer to and even point to them often.

Stories

The occasion of researchers visiting a campus in order to understand and describe some of its practices is bound to call up stories, even when the visitors do not ask for them directly. Sometimes the same story comes up over and over from different groups and seems to represent something iconic about the institution. Stories about Sister Antonia, the founder of the College of St. Catherine, are told and retold by both faculty and students. The two favorite stories concern incidents in which Sister Antonia defied secular and church authority to realize a more ambitious plan for the college. One of these stories tells of her resistance to an effort by the city to build a major road through the center of campus, thus disrupting the St. Kate's community. Sister Antonia responded to the threat by siting a new science building in the path of the proposed road, stopping the road and maintaining the integrity of the campus. The other story describes the events after Sister Antonia was given permission by the bishop to build a modest chapel on campus. While the bishop was abroad for an extended period, Sister Antonia began construction of a much larger and more imposing chapel than he had authorized, and the chapel stands today as a symbol of the founder's resistance to the male hierarchy of the Roman Catholic Church. These stories are told with pride and a sense that the women of the College of St. Catherine today aspire to the same kind of courage and independence.

Founding stories and hero stories like these are important on several campuses. Because Turtle Mountain Community College and CSUMB were established so recently, many people involved in the founding are still part of those communities, and their stories are known firsthand, unlike the stories about Sister Antonia. These stories revolve around what the founders believed in and were trying to do, highlighting for more recent arrivals the special missions of these institutions. The Air Force Academy makes a conscious effort to incorporate heroes into its education for character. The Falcon Forum regularly brings Air Force officers who represent exceptional courage and integrity to the campus as speakers. They tell their own stories and engage with the cadets in discussions of why they acted as they did. A recent conference sponsored by the Center for Character Development was titled Hymns, Heroes, and Hardiness and explored the inspirational power of both hero stories and music.

At Tusculum College the story told most often is about institutional transformation and salvation. The story is so well known that it is commonly referred to simply as the story of the "side porch conversations." In 1989, Robert Knott became president of Tusculum. With a $3.5 million deficit and the school's very survival at stake, the new president "led the faculty in what some called a 'Civic Arts Revolution' by issuing the challenge that education should be about building better citizens" ("Start of Art?" 1996, p. 4). Knott and the faculty began to meet weekly on the side porch of the president's house to talk about selected readings from Plato, Cicero, Aristotle, and others and the relevance of their ideas for a new vision of undergraduate education at the college. These meetings yielded a set of radical proposals for change, unanimously endorsed by the faculty, that Knott then took to the board of trustees. The key elements of the new vision were the interdisciplinary Commons Curriculum, the focused calendar, the outcomes-based competency program, and a philosophy that "concentrated on the arts of practical wisdom" ("Start of Art?" p. 4). In the fall of 1991, Tusculum College was reborn, having at least the initial phases of all these innovations in place. In addition to enshrining the civic arts focus as the school's savior, the story reveals the faculty's reverence for President Knott's strong and collaborative leadership and the whole-hearted support for the plan among faculty.

We heard more than one story of transgression against shared values and collective response to the violation. At California State University, Monterey Bay, an incident that had happened a year prior to our visit was the subject of a story that was told often to illustrate some of the tensions on campus and a response to those tensions that was a source of great pride. As happens on many college campuses, CSUMB had experienced an incident in which hate speech was widely disseminated via e-mail. The students themselves organized a response, holding a rally that drew most of the campus, featuring speakers from many races and ethnicities, all speaking with both passion and civility. The goal was to give the hate speech perpetrators and any sympathizers they might have a clear message: "We can't stop you from saying this kind of thing, but we want you to know that we don't think it is funny or cool. It is contrary to everything we believe in, and you who find this amusing are in the minority here."

Not every story constitutes a straightforward endorsement of the received institutional values. Some represent efforts to shift the institutional culture. We have already referred to the tension at Spelman College between the traditional service orientation and a more politically charged emphasis on education for social justice. A symbol of the former in the minds of its critics is the newly revised *Decorum Guide,* which offers both suggestions and rules to ensure student conduct that is polished, dignified, and in good taste. The guide suggests, for example, that students wear dresses with "near the knee" hemlines when attending church and use "basic, professional" messages on home answering machines. Although acknowledging that teaching this kind of social convention can be useful, some faculty and students feel the strong emphasis on decorum is misplaced. In an effort to link students with a more activist side of Spelman's history and identity, they are creating occasions to tell vivid stories of Spelman students' participation in the civil rights struggles of the 1950s and 1960s. These stories are told in public lectures and films and through student and faculty participation in a reenactment of the historic march from Selma to Montgomery, Alabama.

Shared Ideas, Philosophies, and Ideologies

Of course all these stories embody ideas, but sometimes the ideas themselves, in a more abstract form, provide a reference point for institutional norms. We have mentioned several of these ideas already. One is the concept of honor at the Air Force Academy, which serves as a focus for disciplinary structures, formal programming, and "ground-level" conversations about aspirations and transgressions. The question "What would Jesus do?" serves a similar guiding role at Messiah College. CSUMB's concept of ethical communication is a third.

Josina Makau, through whose leadership the concept of ethical (also termed *invitational*) communication has gained currency at CSUMB, is dean of Communications and Creative Technologies. Professor Makau's training is in rhetoric, which informs the way she has shaped the university's approach to the field of communications. Drawing on the work of Seyla Benhabib, she has written about ethical communication in her own scholarship and has helped infuse those ideas into the university's goals for student learning. What is more unusual is the degree to which Makau has used ideas based in her scholarship and teaching to affect the way routine communication on campus is understood and practiced. As she said when we met with her: "We believe that . . . to solve problems together, cross cultural boundaries effectively, be peacemakers and live in harmony, to be able to do that one needs to have a very strong will and capacity to understand—meaning that in the fullest sense of the word—so that when we communicate on this campus, our aspiration is not to win but to truly understand." The frequency with which other faculty, administrators, and students referred to these ideas suggests that they have taken hold and become part of the institution's understanding of itself.

We were also interested to see the limits of the ethical communication approach when it came up against CSUMB's strong norms of multiculturalism and social justice for people of color. When the president removed a Mexican American woman from her position as his assistant and transferred her to another position because he thought that she was unable to meet the needs of the original position, the action was widely labeled as racist, and there were calls from within the campus for the president to resign. Eventually, most on the campus seem to have decided that the issue had been beaten to death and that they should move on to other campus concerns, but it still rankles some. There are differences of opinion regarding the extent to which the discourse that took place around this volatile issue can be characterized as ethical communication (with sincere efforts on both sides to "respond with a genuinely open heart"), but at least some members of the community believe that one norm (multiculturalism) trumped another (ethical communication), perhaps unnecessarily. Of course the fact that two strong norms can come into conflict is consistent with both operating when they do not conflict, but this incident does give some indication of the relative power of these two norms at CSUMB and the challenges of maintaining an ideal under conditions of great and deeply felt disagreement.

Rituals

We have already described the privileged place of the vision statement at CSUMB. The statement serves as a guiding idea and a physical reminder of the institution's values. It is also the basis for a dramatic ritual in the community. In a ceremony each fall, new faculty and staff members are welcomed to the campus on a platform where the backdrop is a giant blow-up of the vision statement. As new members are introduced they actually sign the screen as a symbol of their commitment to support the values and culture of the campus. This practice may sound potentially coercive, but we did not encounter anyone who described it as intrusive or heavy-handed. Whether or not some feel that way, there is no denying that the practice underscores the continuing importance of the founders' vision of education at this university.

When we arrived at Kapi'olani Community College, we were first greeted with leis in a garden courtyard (a sign of celebration and honor) and then Kawika Napoleon, one of Kapi'olani's native Hawaiian language faculty, sang an intensely emotional, traditional Hawaiian greeting. The college has revived this chant, which recounts the genealogy of Hawaiian leaders, and has it sung as a traditional greeting to important island visitors as an indication of the institution's special character. When we were there, the event attracted many students and faculty who happened to be passing by, and they paused to reflect on the spectacle on their way to work or class.

The campus's annual Asian Pacific Festival and Parade of Cultures engages even more of the Kapi'olani community. The festival is a four-day celebration of the community's Hawaiian, Pacific, and Asian past, present, and future. The festival, which has taken place every year since 1988, has come to represent the college's commitment to creating a multicultural learning environment that extends beyond classroom walls. What began as a modest, one-day event to promote respect for cultural differences has become an ambitious program filled with lectures, workshops, dances, debates, art exhibits, literature readings, and perhaps most important, the culminating Parade of Cultures. The festival is designed and implemented almost entirely by student clubs, and the student body chooses a different theme each year by vote. The festival is open to the wider community, and many local residents do attend.

Socialization Strategies

Orientation and faculty development materials for new Kapi'olani faculty are also filled with references to native Hawaiian phrases and metaphors. For example, the college's *Teaching Equitably* training materials, which include a video and workbook, connect their lessons to traditional Hawaiian sayings. One of these is *pa'a'ia iho i ka hoe uli i 'ole e ikai ke ko'a,* or "hold the steering paddle steady to keep from striking the rock," which points to the importance of consistency in teaching. A saying that urges faculty to make personal connections with students and create a cohesive classroom environment is *he waiwai nui ka lokahi,* or "unity is a precious possession." To stress the importance of collaborative learning, the materials introduce the idea of *ma ka hana ka 'ike,* or "in working one learns."

Faculty and staff at the Air Force Academy are introduced to their roles as moral educators very explicitly through the Air Force Character Education Seminar, a daylong workshop that all attend. The workshop prepares them to be socializers of cadets and provides an opportunity for them to talk with each other and with the staff of the Center for Character Education about what this means.

Of course every higher education institution has strategies for socializing new students as well as new faculty, and these strategies vary in the extent to which they invoke moral and civic values. A distinguishing feature of the twelve case study schools is the extent to which their orientations for first-year students socialize students into the moral and civic values of the campus rather than addressing only practical issues such as study skills and how the library system works. At the case study schools the explanation of honor codes and the role they play in the institution is often an important part of students' introduction to campus. On some campuses the ritual of signing the honor code is repeated each year, and all the honor codes are explicit in setting expectations for students. Clear and frequent endorsement of academic integrity is important because this central value of higher education is often experienced by students as conflicting with other values that are prized on campus, including loyalty among friends and a culture of individual advancement, and that are reflected in peer norms that tolerate cheating. We return to first-year orientation programs and honor codes in Chapter Eight, "Moral and Civic Learning Beyond the Classroom."

Perceptions of Hypocrisy

Faculty at several of the case study schools spoke of tensions around the question of institutional hypocrisy and the educational potential of these tensions if they are handled well. Students are notoriously sensitive to hypocrisy, and this can present both challenges and opportunities when conflicts arise between the institution's espoused values and its actions. At the Air Force Academy, for example, perceived discrepancies between community values and actions emerge because cadets are held to very high standards of honesty and yet there is sometimes pressure for the academy to present a "cleaned up" image to the public in order to prevent a local scandal from becoming public. Because their budgets are based on allocations of tax dollars, military academies are very vulnerable to public perception. Those concerned with the character development of cadets are aware of the corrosive effect of hypocrisy, and faculty are frequently reminded of the need for consistency between words and deeds.

The Air Force Academy is by no means alone, however, in experiencing tensions between institutional pressures and the moral and political standards held out for the campus community. CSUMB is built on a former military base, and some of the land on which the campus is built is contaminated with toxic wastes such as jet fuel, which are now being removed, and the campus has been designated a federal Superfund clean-up site. Because the substances are not considered a health threat, students are not told the campus is a Superfund site until they arrive. This policy has aroused significant opposition among students who believe this campus policy violates the university's espoused commitments to ethical communication and community participation. As one faculty member explained: "We have a community participation requirement and encourage students to be politically engaged, but we are not totally prepared for the consequences of students' actions, and that's challenging. . . . Students wanted to work on the Superfund issue as their project, and that's a serious predicament for the university because there is growing mobilization building to force the university to take some kind of action to tell prospective students about it. . . . So some of the university's goals boomerang back in their face—it might be a case of 'be careful what you wish for because you just might get it.'"

Colleges and universities that take students' moral and civic development seriously must pay close attention to these issues, which can undermine the sense of campus community. When students perceive their institution as preaching one thing and living another, they are likely to become cynical. But if it is handled well, communication about difficult institutional issues and conflicts in values can strengthen the community rather than engendering alienation.

Potential Risks of a Cohesive Campus Culture

Creating a strong moral and civic culture on campus carries both benefits and risks. On the one hand, when curricular or cocurricular programs are disconnected from the surrounding campus culture, they can meet powerful resistance that makes it difficult for students to live out the ideals they may develop in the context of those programs. On the other hand it is imperative that colleges and universities stand for intellectual and moral open-mindedness; cultures that are so powerful as to be coercive have no place in programs of moral and civic education. This issue is complicated by the fact that what counts as coercive is itself subject to debate, and what may appear coercive to an outside observer may not be experienced as coercive by insiders. The question also arises whether those who experience a culture as oppressive feel free to voice those concerns, because taboos on voicing them may be part of the problem. In our view the existence of a cohesive and powerful culture becomes problematic when students and faculty are discouraged from questioning the prevailing assumptions.

On many campuses this issue is addressed directly, but as in all communities, there are limits on the extent to which members of the community can opt out of the shared norms. At the Air Force Academy, cadets are encouraged to think about when they must obey the orders of their superiors and when an order is unlawful and must be disobeyed. At the same time, there is really no place for questioning the legitimacy of the honor code and the consequences of violating it. At Messiah College, students are encouraged and helped to think through religious doubts and questions they may have, but both students and faculty are bound by the Community Covenant whether they agree with all of its assumptions or not. Likewise, whether they like it or not, students at CSUMB will be exposed to many left-of-center messages, such as analyses of social issues that rely heavily on concepts such as group privilege and marginalization.

Making explicit and opening for public discussion the whole set of questions around culture, community, shared norms, and legitimate challenges to those norms can be extremely useful educationally, so providing forums in which to address these tensions directly may be the best solution to these difficult issues. The twelve campuses varied in the extent to which this happened, and in our view most could benefit by more attention to these questions. Reflecting on what the institution and its programs stand for and opening those issues to dissent and new ideas contribute to reducing hypocrisy and to keeping moral and civic education evolving, authentic, and alive. Clifford Geertz (1973) has spoken of human beings as suspended in webs of significance they themselves have spun and of culture as those webs. In commenting on this conception of culture, Carnegie Foundation president Lee Shulman (personal communication with A. Colby and T. Ehrlich, December 1999) said: "The notion that humans are suspended in webs of meaning, of course, suggests the metaphor of the spider, whose webs are both traps and freeways for locomotion. Webs both imprison and liberate. Thus with culture, it both locks its inhabitants-creators within its confines and offers them opportunities to transcend it. This is the paradox of human beings as simultaneously agent and product, active and passive, origin and pawn. Its sociological equivalent is Robert Merton's observation that we create our organizations and they, in turn, create us." These are important insights for colleges and universities to keep in mind as they attempt to remain true to their espoused values while continually rethinking the way these values are made concrete on campus through both programs and cultures.

NOTE

1. It is worth noting that five of the twelve schools we chose for this study (Alverno College, Duke University, Kapi'olani Community College, Portland State University, and the United States Air Force Academy) were also selected by the Association of American Colleges and Universities as leadership examples for its Greater Expectations initiative. The twenty-two Greater Expectations campuses were chosen because they illustrated a high degree of intentionality in articulating goals for students' overall learning and in aligning practices and policies with these goals.

4

THE MULTIPLE DIMENSIONS
OF MORAL AND
CIVIC DEVELOPMENT

BY THE TIME students arrive at college, a lot has happened to form their character, values, interests, understanding of moral issues, and attitudes toward civic life and politics. Some would argue that by the time people reach college, most important aspects of their moral and civic character are already permanently established, for better or worse. The research evidence on human development does not support this view, however. Studies have consistently shown that under the right circumstances, moral and civic development continues throughout adolescence and well into adulthood.

What is known about late adolescent and adult development that will help educators identify the key areas in which continued development is likely to occur? What do people at these stages in life still need? What are the opportunities for higher education to contribute to their further development? In this chapter we review research and theory that help to answer these questions. Because the research on moral and civic development is extensive and complex, however, we limit this review to the work that bears most directly on the question of higher education's role in fostering this development. Our review also places somewhat more emphasis on moral than on civic development, because more research has been conducted in the moral domain; nevertheless, many of the findings illuminate both moral and civic development because the two are related in a number of ways.

In previous chapters we talked about the value of holistic approaches to moral and civic education. Part of what we mean when we call an approach *holistic* is that it addresses the full range of important developmental dimensions and uses a full array of strategies to do so. In this chapter we draw on social science research and theory to articulate what we believe are the key developmental dimensions that higher education ought to support if students' moral and civic functioning is to reach its full potential. A clear understanding of these dimensions is critical to formulating both the goals and the strategies of moral and civic education. A consideration of the cognitive dimensions clarifies why moral and civic education works best when it is integrated with the curriculum, rather than being pursued only in extracurricular activities. Attention to moral and civic skills and practical expertise along with the motivational dimensions provides a framework for articulating the goals of a wide range of experiences outside the classroom. Recognizing the centrality of dimensions such as moral and civic identity and habits of moral interpretation helps explain why the campus cultures we described in Chapter Three are so important and how they affect students.

As we have discussed, different colleges and universities evolve different conceptions of moral and civic education, crafting approaches that are especially well suited to their missions, histories, and student bodies. This means that the particular content, shape, or meaning of the various dimensions we lay out here will be somewhat different depending upon the institution's distinctive approach. So, for example, central to moral and civic knowledge and understanding at Spelman College is an understanding of the African diaspora and the history of the civil rights movement, whereas at the United States Air Force Academy it is critical for cadets to develop an understanding of the principles underlying military law so they can judge whether or not orders they receive are lawful. But regardless of an institution's unique conception of moral and civic maturity or which of the three thematic approaches it draws on most heavily (community connections, moral and civic virtue, or systemic social responsibility), every institution that is intentionally pursuing undergraduate moral and civic education will benefit by establishing programs that connect with the same basic developmental opportunities.

Students' Moral and Civic Development on Entering College

Both students who come to college soon after high school and those who enter college later in their lives bring with them a lot of personal history. They have been affected by the cultures in which they grew up, many aspects

of their family environment, the schools they attended, their peer relationships, their participation in religious institutions, jobs they have held, their
community involvements, and their activities such as volunteer work, clubs,
or sports.

Patterns of habitual morality, at least roughly aligned with the norms of
the larger society, develop over time for most people as a result of growth
in understanding, sanctions for noncompliance, and experiences in families, schools, and peer groups. Although many are only partially compli-
ant, late adolescents know the rules of the main settings in which they
operate (school, home, peer situations, and the like), and most have developed habits of basic honesty, civility, and self-regulation. Most late adolescents have also come to understand that it is legitimate for others to hold
them accountable for their actions and choices. In addition to these basic
moral habits, by late adolescence most (though not all) people have the
capacity to think about moral dilemmas from the perspective of a member
of a moral community. They understand, at least in a simple way, the
shared norms and expectations about what it means, from the moral point
of view, to be a good friend, spouse, or parent, and they have an appreciation of the moral significance of interpersonal trust (Colby, Kohlberg,
Gibbs, & Lieberman, 1983). (In other words, as we discuss a little later,
most adolescents have reached at least Stage 3 in Lawrence Kohlberg's
sequence of moral judgment stages.)

Basic empathy develops very early in life and is reshaped during childhood and early adolescence by an increasing capacity to see situations
from another's point of view (Hoffman, 1981; Selman, 1980). Likewise,
a sense of fairness is present in early childhood, but young children are
unable to appreciate impartial criteria for fair distribution or the legitimacy of equity as opposed to strict equality (Damon, 1975). By the time
they reach late adolescence, most people understand basic principles of
impartiality and equity, even if they cannot apply them in complex situations or do not practice the distributive and procedural justice[1] of which
they are capable when impartial fairness conflicts with their self-interest.

In addition to these habits and cognitive capacities that develop in the
course of ordinary life, some high school graduates have achieved a good
basic understanding of U.S. history and government, although studies of
the effectiveness of high school civics courses reveal that all too few secondary school students achieve this understanding to any significant
degree (Dionne, 1991).[2] Many students also participate in volunteer work
in high school or belong to other organizations that have helped them
develop leadership and other civic skills.

Developmental Issues Entering Students Still Confront

In spite of the dramatic developmental changes that take place in the first eighteen years of life, many developmental issues remain only partially resolved for undergraduates, especially for the late adolescents or young adults who come to college soon after high school. Additional dimensions of moral and civic character continue to develop throughout life and so are open to further growth even for adults returning to college after a longer time out of school.

Although by age eighteen most people know the rules and follow them much of the time, even many adults are inconsistent in their moral practices, especially under pressure. (It is known, for example, that cheating in college is widespread, as is cheating on taxes and some other forms of dishonesty in adulthood.) Only a minority of adults achieve a deep understanding of the social system and a wise and sophisticated grasp of difficult moral and political issues. Recent years have also seen a decline in civic engagement, especially among younger cohorts (Putnam, 2000), and a great deal of evidence exists that younger Americans lack interest and trust in politics (Astin, Parrott, Korn, & Sax, 1997; Sax, 1999; Sax, Astin, Korn, & Mahoney, 1999). Although most late adolescents and adults have the capacity for both empathy and impartiality, few can claim to exhibit these consistently in the most challenging situations. By early adulthood most people have a sense of responsibility and accountability, but this capacity may be compromised by habits of self-deception and rationalization or may be applied only to immediate family and friends. Virtually everyone has moral weaknesses as well as strengths, so moral growth is a work in progress for all but the saintly few.

Research on human development reveals three major clusters of capacities that are critical to fully mature moral and civic functioning, and all three can continue to develop in adulthood under some circumstances. The first main area is moral and civic understanding. This includes the capacity to interpret, judge, acquire knowledge of, and understand complex issues and institutions, and a sophisticated grasp of ethical and democratic principles. The second major set of capacities has less to do with understanding what is right than with having the motivation to do the right thing. This cluster includes the individual's goals and values, interests, commitments, and convictions, and the ability to persevere in the face of challenges. It also includes a sense of efficacy and emotions such as compassion, hope, and inspiration. Closely related to these dimensions is the individual's identity, the sense of who she is and what kind of a person she wants to be. The third broad category is the domain of practice.

Fully effective citizenship requires a well-developed capacity for effective communication, including moral and political discourse; skills in political participation; the capacity to work effectively with people, including those who are very different from oneself; and the ability to organize other people for action. Political action, for example, is rarely a solitary activity. Both within and across these categories, the various underlying dimensions are only loosely linked together developmentally if they are linked at all. People may be advanced on some yet quite undeveloped on others. It is not unusual, for example, for a person to exhibit a sophisticated capacity for moral judgment without feeling at all politically efficacious. Likewise, there is no reason to assume that people who are highly caring and generous will understand the systemic dimensions of the issues they are dealing with on a person-to-person level.

Even though knowledge, judgment, values, identity, and skills may develop independently to some extent, at any given time they will operate as one system, intersecting and interconnecting in many ways. Of course knowledge and judgment play a critical role in moral and political discourse, and interpretation is very much influenced by values and interests and emotions such as hope and inspiration. For the sake of explication, we will treat these three clusters as more separate than they are in reality.

First-year college students exhibit a wide range of development in all three areas, not least because of the ranges of ages and life experiences that characterize college students in the contemporary United States. Students who enter college as adults may be more fully developed on many of these dimensions than younger students. Yet this is not necessarily true, because most studies show developmental variables to be more highly correlated with educational attainment than with age.

Moral and civic education is no doubt most effective when it addresses as many of these facets of development as possible; they cannot and should not be dealt with separately. Any one program or experience is likely to affect many of these dimensions, and changes in one dimension can contribute to changes in others. For example, the process of structured reflection in service-learning courses can be very important in deepening students' knowledge of the relevant issues on many levels, especially when reflection on social problems considers root causes and analyses of policies and other factors pertinent to the nature and extent of the problem. Moreover, this process can also enhance students' awareness of their characteristic habits of interpretation, including defensive strategies such as distortion and cultural biases and preconceptions. Well-designed reflection can also stimulate consideration of what kind of person the student is, wants to be, and fears being and can help him move toward being the kind of person he admires and wants to be. Finally, reflection can help students develop capacities for effective communication, through discussions and written assignments. Multiple desirable outcomes can be similarly traced for many other pedagogies and experiences both within and outside the classroom.

Moral Judgment, Moral Interpretation, and Knowledge

Supporting the development of moral and civic understanding lies at the heart of preparing students for responsible citizenship. Colleges and universities can help students learn to think more clearly about moral issues and understand social and political relationships, processes, and institutions in a more sophisticated way. Higher education can also influence the implicit frameworks of meaning within which students interpret the many complex and ambiguous situations they will inevitably confront. More mature moral and civic understanding also entails the acquisition of rich substantive knowledge, which provides the foundation for wise and effective judgment.

MORAL JUDGMENT. The ability to think clearly about difficult moral issues is important not only in the domain of personal morality but also in civic and political affairs, because the latter domain so often entails such issues as balancing the rights and welfare of individuals and groups. Fortunately, quite a lot is known about the development of moral judgment because this has been an active research area for several decades. The cognitive-developmental theories of moral judgment put forward by Jean Piaget (1932) and especially Lawrence Kohlberg (1969) were groundbreaking when they were introduced and have dominated the field ever since. These theories are based in a conception of the developing individual and the developmental process very different from the conception underlying the theories of morality that were most influential previously—behaviorism and psychoanalytic theory. Kohlberg spoke of "the child as moral philosopher," by which he meant that children are not the passive recipients of socialization but instead, through their social experiences, actively construct and reconstruct their understanding of moral concepts like justice, rights, equality, and welfare. This is even more obviously true for college students. Unlike behaviorist and psychoanalytic theories, this formulation does not view morality as externally imposed on people in order to subdue inevitable conflicts between their wants and needs and the interests of society. Nor is morality based solely on avoiding negative sanctions or emotions such as guilt and anxiety. Like Kohlberg, we believe individuals develop increasingly mature conceptions of morality through their active and positive participation in relationships with the social world, including adults, peers, cultural practices, and social institutions (for further discussion, see Turiel, 1997; Turiel, 2002).

This conception of morality and moral development emphasizes the importance of individuals' moral judgments and moral thinking, rather than viewing moral judgments as mere reflections of emotional dynamics or derivatives of externally imposed rewards and punishments. One of the most significant aspects of cognitive-developmental theory for understanding how higher education can promote moral and civic development is the insight that the way people *understand and think about* moral issues makes an important difference in their moral functioning. Clearly, it is not the only thing that matters, but it does matter.

This may seem obvious to many readers, especially to educators, but it is still disputed by some psychologists and philosophers (Haidt, 2001; Kagan, 1984; Noddings, 1984). Jonathan Haidt (2001), for example, refers to "the emotional dog and the rational tail," arguing that moral conduct is driven by moral emotions that are fundamentally nonrational. In his view (which is linked to biological and ethological theories of human behavior), what people offer as reasons for their behavior are in fact *post hoc* constructions, formulated after the fact to explain or justify automatic, emotionally based moral intuitions. This is not the place to articulate the rather complicated theoretical disputes surrounding the relationship between moral judgment, emotions, intuitions, and conduct. For our present purpose, it is sufficient to say that in contemporary theory and research, positions that begin from a cognitive perspective and those that are more fundamentally intuitionist have converged and that both sets of positions have begun to acknowledge the importance of both moral intuitions and moral judgments, although they conceive of the relationship between them somewhat differently. We say more about moral intuitions later in this chapter.

In response to research findings and critiques of various kinds, many features of cognitive-developmental theory have been questioned and revised, and moral judgment has been reconceived as only one component in a complex set of processes. Even so, Kohlberg's description (1969) of the increasing sophistication of people's capacity to think about difficult moral issues remains a useful tool for operationalizing what we mean by the intellectual side of moral growth. Kohlberg proposed that the underlying logic or structure of individuals' thinking about moral issues can be described independently of the content of their beliefs and that this logic becomes more sophisticated and functionally adequate as development proceeds.[3]

In Kohlberg's scheme, children begin (at Stage 1) by understanding morality in very simple terms that essentially label certain actions good or bad, right or wrong, and that assume that bad acts will be punished, almost by definition. At Stage 2, children become capable of grasping moral reciprocity, understanding the fairness of "doing for others if they have done for you." But reciprocity as the sole basis for morality, although an advance over Stage 1, is limited, because it assumes that each person is acting in his or her own self-interest. At Stage 3, individuals become capable of understanding the meaning and importance of mutual trust and the responsibility people have to maintain trust and loyalty. They begin to approach moral questions from the perspective of a member of a community rather than only in individual terms and also begin to comprehend the idea of shared norms for what it means to be a good friend or spouse. At Stage 4, this essentially interpersonal conception of morality is seen to be inadequate, and the idea of a social system that requires a considerable degree of legal consistency becomes available and important. Not until they reach the final stage (Stage 5) do people fully understand the complex interplay of the legal system with a recognition of fundamental human rights that are in some sense prior to that system in the social contract.

Although the transition from one moral judgment stage to the next involves a qualitative reorganization of thinking, later stages build on earlier understandings and incorporate some of the most important advances achieved at earlier stages. For example, once individuals become capable of understanding the importance of maintaining interpersonal trust and contractual agreements (first understood at Stage 3), this understanding will be incorporated into their evolving conceptions of human society and relationships as these develop further. Thus, once understood, the importance of maintaining trust and contractual relationships is not discarded, although it may later be reconceived in more sophisticated terms and subordinated to other considerations in some circumstances. Likewise, individuals at Stage 5 appreciate the importance of a well-functioning social system, but they also understand that justice sometimes requires considerations of human rights to override the value of social order. In essence, Stage 5 represents a substantive ideal of democratic constitutionalism, so it is not really content free even though individuals reasoning at that stage may disagree in their judgments about many particular moral dilemmas.

As individuals develop through the successive stages, their moral judgment moves from simple conceptions of morality grounded in unilateral authority and individual reciprocity to judgments grounded in shared social norms to an appreciation of a more complex social system to a perspective that is capable of evaluating the existing social system in relation to some more fundamental principles of justice. These shifts have important implications for people's understanding of and judgments about a whole range of important issues.

For example, when Candee (1975) asked a sample of college students to think about the Watergate scandal shortly after it took place, he found that only Stage 5 respondents were consistently clear that it was wrong for members of Nixon's Committee to Re-elect the President (CRP) to cover up their involvement in the Watergate break-in. For many Stage 3 and 4 respondents (as well as for the Watergate defendants themselves), loyalty to President Nixon and to their colleagues in the CRP or a concern for national security was sufficient to justify the initial violations of civil rights and the breaking of many laws in the subsequent cover-up. Only at Stage 5 does a clear understanding emerge that human rights constitute the foundation of a democracy and cannot be overridden by considerations such as those cited by the Watergate defendants. This then is one way in which achievement of a high level of moral development has important implications for civic development.

Some critics have argued that the conception of morality at the heart of Kohlberg's theory is too narrowly defined around justice and individual rights and fails to take account of other equally valid conceptions of morality, including those based on perspectives of divinity, community, or interpersonal care (Gilligan, 1982; Shweder, Mahapatra, & Miller, 1987). Cross-cultural research supports the argument that there are several kinds of broad ethical frameworks, each of which approaches moral questions in a different way and not all of which are captured by Kohlberg's scheme. However, we believe that Kohlberg's description of development within a framework of justice is particularly important both for connecting moral development with civic development and for thinking about the civic goals of U.S. higher education, because justice and human rights are central to the way the U.S. systems of politics and law should function. For this reason, Kohlberg's descriptions of the development of moral judgment and his emphasis on justice can be a useful way to frame the increasing maturity of thinking in the intersection of moral with political, civic, and legal issues.

RELATED DIMENSIONS OF SOCIAL COGNITION. Moral judgment is part of the broader domain of social cognition, which includes a number of other dimensions that have also been framed in cognitive-developmental terms. Investigators studying the development of individuals' understanding of friendship, interpersonal perspective taking, political understanding, and religious faith have all described trajectories of increasing maturity, which are said to emerge from individuals' attempts to interpret their experience as they interact with other people and social institutions. Although an individual's development can proceed at different rates in the different dimensions of social cognition, the basic patterns of developmental change within these dimensions show striking parallels. For example, James Fowler (1991a, 1991b, 1994) has described the increasing maturity or sophistication of religious faith in terms that are reminiscent of the general features of development in the moral and political arenas.

Studies of political understanding (Adelson & O'Neil, 1966; Helwig, 1995; Jankowski, 1992; Raaijmakers, Verbogt, & Vollebergh, 1998) have revealed roughly parallel developmental shifts toward increasingly subtle and complex conceptions of social and political institutions. Concepts such as civil liberties, methods of social control, and governance show regular patterns of elaboration as development proceeds. Political thinking has been described as moving from the personal or authoritarian toward greater comprehension of social structures and general principles. For example, younger adolescents are usually insensitive to individual liberties and opt for authoritarian solutions to political problems. At the same time, they are unable to achieve a differentiated view of the social order, and thus cannot grasp the legitimate claim of the community upon the citizen (Adelson & O'Neil, 1966).

What does all this mean? First, it is clear that social, moral, political, and religious development all have an important intellectual core. It is therefore impossible to divide moral and civic development sharply from intellectual or academic development because much of moral and civic development *is* intellectual. Second, this insight reinforces our central argument that moral, civic, and political development have important links. It also points to an essential compatibility between efforts to foster these intellectual aspects of moral and civic development and the academic endeavor more broadly.

MORAL INTERPRETATION. Even though the way people think about moral issues is important, this does not mean that morality is always conscious, rational, reflective, and deliberative. Although this is sometimes the case, often it is not. It is useful to distinguish between two kinds of moral process, *reflective morality* and *habitual* or *spontaneous morality* (Davidson & Youniss, 1991; Walker, 2000). In daily life, reflective morality, which involves careful evaluation and justification, comes into play relatively infrequently, when the right course of action is not obvious or when one's initial moral response is challenged and there is time to reflect. In contrast, most moral actions—the many unremarkable moral choices and actions that characterize daily life—are not preceded by conscious reflection but instead are immediate, seemingly intuitive responses. For example, most people do not have to stop and think before paying a blind newspaper seller. They do not consciously choose between paying and pretending to pay. This kind of routine honesty is taken for granted. As its name implies, habitual morality is based in repetition over time, not only behavioral repetition but also repetition of ingrained habits of interpreting, or "reading," moral situations.

One reason that moral interpretation is so important is that in real life moral dilemmas do not come neatly packaged like hypothetical dilemmas, which typically involve a given set of simple facts. Almost any real moral dilemma or question involves significant ambiguity, and interpretation of the situation may differ from one person to the next. Thus, in order to find meaning amid the moral ambiguity of real-life situations, people must develop habits of moral interpretation and intuition through which they perceive the everyday world. People with different habits of moral interpretation see the world in very different terms and are therefore presented with very different opportunities and imperatives for moral action. Through the aggregate of their moral choices in daily life, they actively shape their own moral reality (Walker, 2000).

But even habitual morality has important underlying cognitive elements. People's thinking processes rely on their capacity to recognize patterns in the environment, and this pattern recognition depends on cognitive schemas that derive from many sources. One source is the set of concepts and assumptions accrued through cognitive-moral development. Even though it seems clear that people do not think or argue through every moral situation in a way that mirrors the kinds of moral argumentation elicited in research interviews, different cognitive-moral frameworks (like Kohlberg's moral judgment stages) represent different sets of assumptions that help inform and shape individuals' reactions to the many small moral decisions of both habitual and reflective morality. In this sense, individuals' conceptual frameworks, including understandings associated with their developmental stage, provide patterns, or schemas, that shape moral interpretations. The way people understand fairness, for example, will be the grounds on which they react to perceived injustices. Concepts such as distributive justice, moral authority, trust, and accountability are central to morality, and the way they are understood plays an important part in shaping the individual's understanding of ambiguous moral situations.

However, the developmental aspects of individuals' implicit assumptions are only one source of the schemas that shape moral perceptions, interpretations, and actions. Individuals also learn what constitutes a meaningful pattern through interaction with their social environment. As they participate in cultural routines, they acquire habits of interpretation consistent with that culture. The various aspects of campus culture that we described in Chapter Three contribute to these habits of interpretation. If students confront daily reminders of the campus honor code, for example, they are likely to approach their studies with a heightened sensitivity to questions of academic integrity. The impact of the social context on habits and schemas is part of the broader issue of socialization of values, to which we will return later in this chapter.

Cognitive schemas can influence interpretations, judgments, and behavior without the conscious awareness of the actor, but it is also possible for individuals to reflect on their moral interpretations and discuss them with others. These processes can lead to moral growth. In the many brief moments of moral decision individuals encounter every day, they have the capacity to reflect, and they have some room to consciously settle on an interpretation, over time creating new habits of interpretation that can lead in a new direction. This process may involve considering and resolving several conflicting interpretations or questioning one's original interpretation after confronting an uneasy feeling that one's interpretation may be self-serving or biased in other ways. The capacity to override or change personal habits of interpretation is important, because by doing so one can actively shape future moral habits. In this view of moral development, people can grow morally by making an effort to become more aware of their own interpretive habits, acknowledging and trying to overcome their biases, and working to understand and take seriously others' interpretations (Walker, 2000).

DEVELOPMENT OF MORAL JUDGMENT AND INTERPRETATION DURING COLLEGE. What is known about the development of moral judgment and interpretation during college? First, many college students do experience moral growth. In part due to the availability of a measure that is fairly easy to use (James Rest's Defining Issues Test [DIT], see Rest, 1979), moral judgment as conceived by Kohlberg has been included in many studies of college student development (for a review of this literature, see Pascarella & Terenzini, 1991, pp. 335–368). Investigators have found consistently that attending college does increase students' scores on this measure, and many studies have found a significant correlation between years of higher education and scores on Kohlberg's Moral Judgment Interview as well as on the DIT.[4] This is true regardless of the students' age. Moral judgment stage is more likely to stop increasing at the end of formal education than at any particular age. In fact some studies have shown a small negative correlation of DIT scores with age (probably a cohort effect)[5] and a larger positive correlation of DIT with educational attainment (Pascarella & Terenzini, 1991).

Given the evidence that higher education contributes to higher levels of moral judgment, it may seem that colleges and universities do not need programs aimed specifically at fostering moral development. However, the research in this area makes it clear that there is significant room for educational improvement even with regard to moral judgment itself. Despite the positive impact of higher education on moral judgment stage, most college educated adults do not achieve the highest level of moral judgment. Most reason at Stage 4 or some combination of Stages 3 and 4 (Colby et al., 1983). Because a deep understanding of the U.S. Constitution and legal system requires a Stage 5 perspective, in which the social system is understood to be grounded in fundamental human rights, the failure of many citizens to achieve that developmental level raises questions about their capacity to fully appreciate the foundations of American democracy. A large body of research makes it clear that the experience of grappling with challenging moral issues in classroom discussions or in activities that require the resolution of conflicting opinions contributes significantly to the increasing maturity of individuals' moral judgment. This is especially true when the teacher draws attention to important distinctions, assumptions, and contradictions (see, for example, Blatt & Kohlberg, 1975). If these kinds of discussions were thoroughly integrated into the college curriculum, the maturity of students' thinking about moral issues would almost certainly be increased.

The college experience can also be a powerful opportunity for students to develop more reflective and mature habits of moral interpretation. Students bring their own characteristic habits of interpretation with them when they enter college, but their experiences in college have significant potential to reshape those habits. Much of the positive impact of programs that foster understanding across the diversity of a campus and its environment may reside in the power of those programs to make students aware for the first time of their previously unquestioned interpretive schemes, to bring biases to light, and to highlight the inherent ambiguity of moral situations that previously appeared clear-cut. This view of moral change also clarifies the significance of the reflection component that is known to be critical to the success of service-learning courses. Reflection on service activities often involves discussions in which students share with each other their interpretations of the common experience and written assignments in which they explore the ways in which the service experience changed their understanding of the people with whom they worked, the social issues their work confronted, and their relationship to those people and issues. This kind of activity is ideally suited for revealing alternative interpretations of common experiences and helping students see the personal significance of those alternative interpretations through self-examination.

In addition to using programs explicitly designed to foster moral and civic growth, colleges and universities can also transform students' interpretive frames, for better or worse, through traditional academic coursework. Faculty often talk of transforming student understanding through their teaching. Along with changes arising from substantive and theoretical disciplinary learning, this transformation can entail changes in students' frameworks of interpretation. For example, a powerful course can open students' eyes to global economic interdependence or the influence of opportunity structures on individual achievement. Some of these interpretive shifts may contribute to greater moral and civic responsibility, whereas others may have a negative effect. For example, some reductionist psychological theories and many economic models can lead students to see all behavior as motivated by self-interest, ignoring the complex and ambiguous reality of the economic, political, and moral worlds. Coming to rely on this kind of narrow frame when interpreting personal experience may affirm students' cynicism and lead them to rationalize self-serving behavior. Likewise an ethics or other moral philosophy course that does no more than critique one theory after another may lead students to believe that all ethical perspectives are seriously flawed and that therefore all ethical questions are matters of personal taste and opinion.

MORAL RELATIVISM. As students begin to question their unexamined assumptions and appreciate the multiplicity of interpretations inherent in any situation, they may conclude that there are no grounds for evaluating the relative validity of different, sometimes conflicting moral or intellectual interpretations. The *dualistic* thinking that characterizes many entering college students is familiar to most who have taught undergraduates. Incoming freshmen tend to want "the facts," "the answer," or "what is in the professor's head," not recognizing that there is no simple answer to most of the questions a course addresses. As they begin to understand the limits of this perspective, they enter a stage of *epistemological relativism,* in which they believe that because there is no one right answer, the various alternative solutions must be "just someone's opinion."

At least some degree of both epistemological and ethical relativism is part of the predictable developmental sequence that college students go through as they begin to grapple with uncertainty and question the simple absolutes they previously understood as the "right answers" to complex and subtle questions. William Perry (1968) and others (for example, Knefelkamp, 1974) trace a developmental pattern in which individuals shift gradually from seeing the world in polar terms of right versus wrong and good versus bad to seeing all knowledge and values as contextual and relative and then eventually to seeing that it is possible to orient oneself in a relativistic world through the development of commitment, which is experienced as an ongoing activity through which identity and responsibilities are affirmed. Empirical studies of college students' progression through this sequence reveal that many students move from the initial dualistic stage to the more relativistic positions during college, but very few reach the most advanced level—the stage of commitment (Knefelkamp, 1974; Perry, 1968).

In light of consistent findings that college students tend to leave behind absolutistic thinking but generally do not reach a full understanding of grounds for intellectual and moral conviction, it is not surprising that faculty report a great deal of epistemological and ethical relativism among their students. Although we are not aware of any systematic research on how widespread *moral* relativism is among college students (aside from the studies of Perry's stages, which do not distinguish between epistemological and ethical relativism), many faculty and other observers have noted its pervasiveness.

This relativism can take several forms, often combining elements of positions that are philosophically distinct. Faculty often report a pattern that combines a number of different views into a system that is internally inconsistent but nevertheless apparently quite widely held (see, for example, Ricks, 1999; Trosset, 1998). *Student moral relativism,* as Ricks (1999) has called it, includes elements of cultural relativism (moral standards are relative to culture), ethical subjectivism ("right" means "right for me"), moral skepticism (nothing can ever be *proven* in ethics, because people will still disagree), moral nihilism (there are no truths in ethics), and (surprisingly)[6] an overriding concern for moral tolerance and respect for others' views. This position may reflect an unwillingness to think hard about challenging ethical questions or at least a limited understanding of what should count as convincing evidence and argumentation in the moral domain, a related reluctance to have one's own views and actions subjected to serious scrutiny by others, and an inability to distinguish between making reasoned judgments about the moral legitimacy of actions or views on the one hand and being judgmental, intolerant, or disrespectful toward other individuals or cultural groups on the other.

Despite the concerns of some social commentators (Bennett, 1992; Bloom, 1987) that moral relativism leads to immoral behavior, there is no evidence that this is the case. The very inconsistency of the most widespread versions of relativism may protect against this, because students' normative positions on specific ethical questions often seem to be unaffected by their relativism on the level of meta-ethics. But even so, college students' relativism ought to be cause for concern among educators, because beliefs such as "everyone is entitled to his own opinion and there is no way to evaluate the validity of those opinions" prevent students from engaging fully in discussions of ethical issues, learning to articulate and effectively justify their views, and adopting new perspectives when presented with high-quality evidence and arguments. In essence, "the stakes drop out of ethical deliberation," and students are less likely to take it seriously (Trosset, 1998).

KNOWLEDGE. Even intellectually sophisticated reasoning and judgment cannot be powerful forces for effective action if they are abstract or disembodied. Being deeply knowledgeable about the issues is also essential. In addition to fostering clearer reasoning and more mature judgment, colleges can promote students' moral and civic learning by imparting broad and deep knowledge bearing on civic, political, and moral issues.

At a minimum, foundational knowledge in a range of fields provides support for moral and civic effectiveness. The need for an understanding of basic philosophical concepts, for example, is evident in the phenomenon of student moral relativism. Students often fail to distinguish between a moral principle of respect and tolerance and the challenges inherent in evaluating the relative validity of moral claims. Insofar as these are developmental issues, it may take time for students to work their way through them. But coursework and classroom discussions focusing directly on these issues can contribute a great deal to clarifying the intellectual issues involved. Developmental research indicates that without foundational knowledge of basic political concepts, it is difficult for individuals to assimilate new information about political issues (Stoker, 2000).

Likewise, students need to develop foundational knowledge of democratic principles and an understanding of complex social, legal, and political structures and institutions if they are to be fully prepared as engaged citizens. Research on the context specificity of expertise suggests that programs attempting to foster generic analytical capacities are insufficient preparation for effective action. Skills of critical thinking and problem solving developed in connection with one field are not readily transferred to a new field, so it is important for students to begin developing field-specific expertise.

Research on expertise in such disparate fields as chess (Chase & Simon, 1973), the analysis of business problems (for example, Selnes & Troye,

1989), and medical diagnosis (for example, Patel, Arocha, & Kaufman, 1994) makes it clear that novices and experts differ dramatically in their perceptions of and approaches to problems in their field, differences that are grounded in their experience with and in-depth knowledge of the particular domain. Expert knowledge is organized into higher-order schemas that permit the expert to recognize patterns that are invisible to novices, allowing the expert to approach complex situations in ways qualitatively different from the approach of the novice.

Students will be more effective at the time they graduate if colleges and universities have helped them begin developing expertise in their areas of civic interest, even though recognizing that few students will be true experts when they graduate. But expertise in the nonacademic world is not entirely analogous to expertise in the academic world. Advanced undergraduate study in some academic disciplines is sometimes said to educate students as if they all intended to become professors (see, for example, Menand, 1997). To the extent this is true, the knowledge and skills acquired in mastering even the major may have a fairly loose relationship to the knowledge and skills graduates will need in their later lives. This underscores the value of student engagement with well-structured internships, challenging volunteer programs, and other forms of complex practice that connect with academic learning but also address some abilities and knowledge grounded in action.

Motivation for Moral and Civic Responsibility

Clearly, understanding and judgment are essential elements of moral and civic maturity, but they are not sufficient to explain what makes a morally and civically effective person. Some people with very advanced levels of understanding fail to act on their understanding. These people may have the *capacity* for effective action while lacking the *motivation* to act. Like understanding, motivation is multifaceted and includes values and goals; identity, or sense of self; a sense of efficacy or empowerment; faith; and various aspects of moral emotion such as hope and optimism, as opposed to alienation and cynicism. Although the connection of higher education with moral and civic motivation may be less obvious than its connection with knowledge and understanding, colleges have great potential to contribute to students' development in this area as well.

VALUES AND GOALS. There is a large body of evidence that a college education alters students' values, goals, and attitudes. Some of these shifts clearly support increased moral and civic responsibility. Despite the pluralism of American values, there are some values that most people would agree colleges and universities ought to promote and support if they are committed to graduating engaged and responsible citizens. These values include respect and tolerance for others, including social minorities; respect for civil liberties and other key elements of U.S. democracy; and an interest in politics and in contributing to positive social change, however that is defined. Part of the value of higher education is that it does contribute to the development of these values.

Other attitude changes in college, such as increased tolerance of alternative life styles, would be evaluated differently by people with different views on social and political social issues. Some of these changes in college students' values depend on characteristics of the college attended and on students' entering characteristics, including gender, religiosity, and political views (both their own and their parents'). For example, shifts toward increased political liberalism appear to be greatest in highly selective institutions (Astin, 1977; Knox, Lindsay, & Kolb, 1988).

Even so, ever since the 1940s, when research on these questions began to emerge, students in most colleges and universities have shown some common shifts in their values, including increased sociopolitical tolerance, greater concern for civil rights and civil liberties, more egalitarian views of gender roles, declines in authoritarianism and dogmatism, and more secular religious attitudes. Higher education is also associated with a modest increase in knowledge of and interest in politics (for a review of this literature, see Pascarella & Terenzini, 1991, pp. 269–334). Longitudinal studies indicate that most of these changes in attitudes and values are maintained in the years after college (for example, Newcomb, Koenig, Flacks, & Warwick, 1967). Changes in some civic values and attitudes, along with documented increases in intellectual dispositions such as interest in and knowledge of cultural and intellectual issues, tolerance for ambiguity, flexibility of thought, rational and critical approaches to problem solving, and receptivity to further learning, are at the heart of American higher education's espoused mission. The importance of higher education lies as much in these outcomes as in subject matter knowledge and vocational preparation.

This research raises a question for us: if higher education is already doing a good job of encouraging these broadly supported values and attitudes, then why are we encouraging colleges and universities to pay special attention to moral and civic education? The answer is that despite the undisputed positive impact of higher education, there is still immense room for improvement. Some changes, though statistically significant, are small. For example, the impact of higher education on students' social conscience and humanitarian values appears to be very modest (Pascarella, Ethington, & Smart, 1988; Pascarella, Smart, & Braxton, 1986). In addition, some positive shifts during college are not maintained in the post-college years. Sax (1999) reports, for example, that the percentages of students who rate as very important helping others in need, participating in community action, and influencing the political structure show temporary increases over the four years of college, but almost all of these increases disappear in the five years after college graduation. Finally, as we noted in Chapter One, the rates of political participation among college educated Americans are higher than the rates among those without a college education, but only a third of the college educated follow public affairs regularly and less than two-thirds vote regularly in both national and local elections. Participation numbers are significantly lower for the youngest cohorts of college graduates.

When considering the impact of college on students' values and political participation, it is important to keep in mind that most colleges and universities have few programs that specifically address the moral and civic development of their students, and a great many students make it all the way through college without participating in any of those programs. If higher education can have positive effects on students' values and civic engagement, albeit fairly weak effects, without addressing these values directly, it is reasonable to believe that the impact will be striking when more intentional programs are put in place. In fact there is clear evidence that this is the case with regard to service learning, which we discuss further in Chapter Five.

The college environment is an extremely rich source of influences on students, and researchers do not yet know exactly what leads to the shifts in values that have been so consistently documented. Data on the differential impact of different kinds of institutions (more or less selective, religiously affiliated or not, and so on) suggest that campus culture plays an important role. For example, in Sax's study (1999) the experience factor that best predicted college students' increases in social activism (controlling for entering level of activism) was the degree of commitment to social activism among undergraduates overall at the students' college. In *Involving Colleges: Successful Approaches to Fostering Student Learning and Development Outside the Classroom,* George Kuh et al. (1991) point to the importance on college campuses of both cultural artifacts (history, traditions, language, heroes, sagas, physical settings, and symbols) that express unifying assumptions and democratic values, and policies that consistently follow from the institution's core mission and philosophy. Just as these involving colleges make it clear that they stand for particular values, they also work to maintain open dialogue with students and sensitivity to student concerns. At the twelve case study campuses we highlight in this book, we saw this same effort to establish a positive and unifying culture around some core values, balanced with opportunities for reflection on and critique of that culture. The settings, stories, rituals, and other practices that we described in Chapter Three are clear parallels to those that Kuh reports. Students' values and goals can also change as a result of the activities they seek out, the people they encounter in the course of those activities, and the new demands that are made on them as a consequence, as we discuss further in Chapter Eight. Among the most important of these activities for the development of humanitarian social concern and values are leadership programs (Kuh, Douglas, Lund, & Ramin-Gyurnek, 1994; Kuh, 1993) and community service (Youniss & Yates, 1997). Anne Colby and William Damon (1992) have discussed how participation in prosocial activities like these can lead to a gradual transformation in a person's moral values and goals.

By *transformation of goals* we mean a process in which development occurs as a result of the interaction of the goals, motives, values, and beliefs a person brings to a situation and the social influences she experiences once in that situation. People may enter situations in order to meet a particular set of goals, and then as they engage with the situation and the people in it, their goals may change. So, for example, students might initially choose to participate in a leadership training program in order to learn skills for career advancement but then become unexpectedly engaged in civic life in the process of cultivating leadership skills through work with community organizations, especially if they come in contact with inspiring and engaging moral and civic leaders.

Political scientist Richard Brody (personal communication with E. Beaumont, September 2001) has observed the same phenomenon in the development of political engagement. In his exploration of the question of how people become politically active, Brody distinguishes between *consummatory* and *instrumental* participation in organizations (see Sills, 1972, for Herbert McClosky's original discussion of these terms). Consummatory participation refers to organizational members' involvement in the activities of the group as an end in itself, for the sake of enjoyment. For example, many people join the Sierra Club in order to take part in the hikes and other outdoor activities the club offers. Instrumental participation in organizations refers to members' participation in collective political action through the organization in order to work toward a shared political goal. The Sierra Club is not only a recreational organization. It also pursues a political agenda relating to protection of the environment.

In an analysis that shows striking parallels with Colby and Damon's concept (1992) of transformation of goals, Brody describes consummatory organizational participation as an important opportunity for some participants to begin developing an interest in political affairs. When people participate in an organization like the Sierra Club for the sake of its recreational activities, for example, they are also exposed to the political issues and debates in which the club engages. At least some of these people will feel strongly either for or against the positions the club takes on political and policy matters. These individuals, even though previously politically inactive, may care enough about some of these issues to become active participants, trying to shape the club's positions and goals, helping the club pursue those goals, or even leaving the club because of disagreement with its political and policy positions and working against those positions from within a different forum.

Because of this process of transformation of goals, the undergraduate experiences that are most powerful are those that connect with and build on the interests, commitments, and concerns students bring to their college experience, such as care and concern for family and friends or an interest in volunteering and helping others on an individual level. These kinds of values are important and need to be nurtured; indeed, by themselves, they are insufficient and can coexist with insularity, lack of participation in the democratic process, and an inability to understand social issues from a broad, system-level perspective. However, effective opportunities for moral and civic learning in higher education can connect with the interests, values, and goals students bring to college and then engage students in experiences that broaden their goals and commitments.

MORAL AND CIVIC IDENTITY. Despite the acknowledged importance of fostering values such as social responsibility and concern for those less privileged than oneself, these values are sometimes only marginally evident in the lives of even those who strongly endorse them. Yet for other people, moral and political convictions are deep enough to compel action, and espoused values play powerful roles in their lives. A key to understanding the differential impact of values on action is personal *identity*, which includes moral, civic, and political identity. The question here is what place moral and civic values, goals, and feelings have in one's sense of self. Psychologists who study moral understanding and judgment are well aware that taken alone these capacities are inadequate to explain moral conduct. After describing the development of more mature moral judgment, theorists are still left with the question, Why do some people act on their moral understanding while others do not? Most explanations of the psychological constructs and processes that mediate moral judg-ment and action have converged on the important role of an individual's sense of moral identity. In this view, moral understanding acquires mo-tivational power through its integration into the structures of the self (Bergman, 2002).

Following Erik Erikson (1968), we understand identity to be one's core or essential self (those aspects without which the individual would see himself to be radically different). It follows that people will be motivated to act in ways that are consistent with this core self, to maintain a sense of consistency in regard to these essential features of his identity. When these essential features of the self include moral beliefs and convictions, there is strong internal pressure to maintain consistency with those beliefs. Of course sometimes people act morally simply in order to avoid negative consequences. Yet often people act morally even when sanctions are not involved. We believe these people behave morally because not to do so would be a violation of their core self; to do otherwise would be to betray their true self (Bergman, 2002).

The way that the core self is understood and experienced changes and develops over time. In fact the integration of moral convictions into one's core sense of self is one of the most important challenges of moral de-velopment. Damon and Hart (1988) traced the development of self-understanding from childhood through adolescence, finding that younger children tended to focus on physical characteristics, skills, and interests when asked to define and describe who they are. Study participants did not begin to include moral qualities such as honesty or loyalty in their self-definitions until they reached adolescence. Erikson's life-span theory (1968) also focuses on adolescence as a critical time for the development of identity. For Erikson, the development of a mature identity requires young people to question some of the fundamental beliefs they have pre-viously taken for granted and to come to their own resolutions of a num-ber of important questions about life choices and ideologies—to rethink what they believe in as well as what they plan to do in life. But like all of Erikson's developmental issues, or "crises," the issue of identity is not resolved once and for all in adolescence but rather is revisited over and over throughout life. The college years have long been understood as a time when students, especially although not exclusively students who come directly from high school, begin to question and redefine their core sense of who they are.

Despite some developmental patterns that seem to hold for most peo-ple, both adolescents and adults vary in the degree to which morality is central to their sense of self and in the content of that morality. In "The

Moral Self," John Dewey (1998) wrote, "The real moral question is what kind of self is being furthered or formed" (p. 346). The importance of "what kind of self is formed" may be seen in studies of people who are especially morally and civically committed. Daniel Hart and Suzanne Fegley (1995), for example, found that moral concerns were more likely to be central to the sense of self and the ideal self in highly altruistic adolescents than they were in adolescents from a comparison group of normal but not especially altruistic individuals. Similarly, Colby and Damon (1992) found that a close integration of self and morality formed the basis for the unwavering commitment to the common good exhibited by *moral exemplars* who had dedicated themselves for decades to fighting against poverty or for peace, civil rights, and other aspects of social justice. Moral behavior depends in part on moral understanding and reflection, but it also depends on how and to what extent individuals' moral concerns are important to their sense of themselves as persons.

Others have written about the development of political or civic identity in a way that parallels this conception of moral identity (for example, Flanagan & Sherrod, 1998; Verba, Schlozman, & Brady, 1995; Youniss & Yates, 1997). For example, Youniss and Yates (1997) present data showing that the long-term impact of youth service experience on later political and community involvement can best be explained by the contribution these service experiences make to the creation of an enduring sense of oneself as a politically engaged and socially concerned person. In their view, civic identity—which entails the establishment of individual and collective senses of social agency and responsibility for society and political-moral awareness—links certain kinds of social participation during adolescence and young adulthood with civic engagement by these same people later in adulthood.

This question of the development of a civic or political identity may help explain why some changes that take place during the college years last well beyond college whereas others do not. McAdam (1988) studied adults who as college students had spent a summer taking part in the 1964 Freedom Rides, which sought to integrate interstate bus lines in the South during the civil rights movement. This powerful and dangerous experience had a long-term impact on those who took part, and they followed quite different life trajectories than did others who had volunteered to participate but were unable to join the group in the end. The follow-up data showed that the Freedom Riders' lives were permanently altered by the experience, and many went on to be leaders in community organizing for social justice, the movement against the Vietnam War, the women's movement, and other efforts to promote social change. The Freedom Ride experience had changed their understanding, beliefs, and values in a number of ways and also seems to have changed the way they understand their own identities. McAdam explains one aspect of the difference between participants and the comparison group this way: "Having defined themselves as activist, a good many of the Mississippi veterans had a strong need to confirm that identity through [further] action" (p. 187). In a 1985 interview, one of the volunteers observed that "you learned too much [in Mississippi] to go back to what you were doing before . . . part of what you learned was that you were part of the struggle" (p. 188). In contrast, Linda Sax's longitudinal study of college students (1999) revealed that many who became more civically engaged during college, apparently as part of a peer culture that supported activism, did not remain engaged in the years after college. In the same study, Sax reports on one group of student volunteers who persisted in their volunteering after college and a larger group who did not. Although Sax did not report a measure of civic identity, one might surmise that only those whose increased volunteerism and activism persisted beyond college had come to view their activism as an essential part of who they were.

This interpretation that changes in personal identity play a crucial role in determining behavior is consistent with longitudinal studies of blood donors by Piliavin and Callero (1991). These authors distinguish between externally motivated blood donors whose initial donation is determined by strong social pressure and internally motivated donors who make a personal decision to give blood, without significant pressure by others. With repeated donations the internally motivated donors begin to cite community responsibility and moral obligation when asked to describe their motives for donating blood. Eventually, what the authors call *role-person mergers* begin to occur, in which the blood donor role is viewed as part of the self. In these cases the values become part of the donor's identity or self-concept, and social recognition is less important as a motivator than confirmation of the self and expression of values appropriate to the self-concept.

Identity is one of a number of psychological mechanisms through which culture can have a long-term impact on an individual's behavior. The stories, images, and routines that constitute the cultural context can be incorporated into participating individuals' sense of self, thus becoming a stable aspect of their orientation to themselves, other people, and the world (Newman, 1996). This can work for either good or ill, depending on the cultural messages that are internalized. A recognition of this process lies behind the requirement some colleges have adopted that asks students to trace the various contexts that have affected their sense of identity. On some of the campuses we studied, members of the campus community were also quite aware of the positive potential of this phenomenon. At the College of St. Catherine, for example, the oft-repeated stories of the courage and resourcefulness of the founding nuns were commonly translated into the message that "we here at St. Kate's are women of unusual strength and moral courage." The hope and expectation was that graduates would take with them a sense of self that includes these virtues.

A large body of research on moral and civic identity makes it clear that the place of moral and civic values in one's self-definition or essential self is a critical element in determining behavior. But this does not mean that people always behave in accordance with even their most deeply held values and beliefs. People vary not only in their self-definitions but also in the psychological strategies they use to protect themselves from internal contradictions. We have referred to the tendency to maintain a sense of internal consistency in the elements of the core self and the role this plays in motivating moral behavior. There is more than one way for individuals to achieve this sense of internal consistency around their moral beliefs. The first is a straightforward pattern of fidelity to one's beliefs and values. A consistent pattern of this kind of fidelity is generally what people are referring to when they describe someone as "a person of integrity." Other approaches to maintaining consistency involve strategies that justify making exceptions when it serves one's self-interest to do so. Prominent among these strategies are biased interpretations of the situation and other rationalizations (see, for example, Bandura, 1986). Almost everyone rationalizes at times, but part of what we mean by moral character is that a person of character will use this kind of defensive strategy only infrequently. Differences in the extents to which people live their espoused moral values lie partly in the extents to which they habitually use various strategies for avoiding the awareness of inconsistency.

Moral growth involves becoming aware of these self-serving tendencies in oneself and working toward reducing them. In her studies of moral interpretation, Janet Walker (2000) documents people's differential tendencies to become aware of their interpretive habits, to give weight to others' interpretations of conflict situations, and to acknowledge and try to reduce their own biases. People who make a consistent effort to be open-minded and take others' perspectives seriously are facilitating their own moral development, even though they may not consciously think of themselves as pursuing integrity or moral growth.

Usually moral development seems to proceed without a conscious effort at self-improvement. This does not mean, however, that efforts to be self-reflective and to grow morally cannot have an effect. Many psychologists

(Bergman, 2002; Blasi, 1995; Markus & Nurius, 1986; Walker, 2000) have written about people's capacity to use self-reflection as a means of playing an active role in their own development, consciously working to shape what kind of person they become. For example, Blasi (1995) has studied children's growing capacity to "bring their moral understanding to bear on their already existing motives" (p. 236), thus having desires about their own desires. This kind of reflexivity can bear on the question of what kind of person they are and want to be. In this way the concept of the moral self connects back with the concepts of moral understanding and interpretation we discussed earlier in this chapter.

What are the implications of this work for moral and civic education? Identity development takes place in part through identification with admired others (Bandura, 1977, 1986). Hazel Markus (Markus & Nurius, 1986) has described the interplay between people's actual and possible selves; the latter may be both the selves they hope to become and the selves they are afraid of becoming. Markus and Nurius (1986) argue that the self-construct is not singular but "a system of affective-cognitive structures (also called theories or schemas) about the self that lends structure and coherence to the individual's experiences" (p. 955). They present data suggesting that individuals can reflect on their possible selves, and they understand development as a process of acquiring and then either achieving or resisting certain possible selves. Experience with people who provide either positive or negative models can contribute to the construction of possible selves and eventually to the individual's actual self. Exposure to faculty members, residence life mentors, members of the community, and other students who represent an inspiring vision of personal ideals can play an important role in fostering the incorporation of moral and civic values into students' sense of who they want to be and eventually who they feel they are. Likewise, awareness of why they do not want to emulate some others with whom they have contact can be a motivating force as they seek to avoid a feared possible self.

Undergraduate programs that adopt an outcomes-based approach often have self-understanding and self-reflection among their goals, asking students to think about questions like, What kind of self should I aspire to be? as well as the perennial college student question, Who am I? If reflections on questions like these are to have a lasting impact on students' sense of self, they must be of more than theoretical or academic interest. This fruitful reflection can happen best when the questions are asked in the context of engagement with complex moral pursuits such as those provided by high-quality service learning, when students are engaged in this work with people who represent inspiring models with whom they can identify, and when the campus culture supports the development of habitual moral schemes that are consistent with important moral values. Both academic and cocurricular activities can contribute to students' awareness of and reflection on what is important to them and to their sense that they can play an active role in determining what kind of people they become. Pedagogies of active engagement can be especially powerful in making intellectual work in higher education significant to what kind of person the student wants to be. We say more about this in Chapter Five, "Pedagogical Strategies for Educating Citizens."

POLITICAL EFFICACY AND MORAL AND CIVIC EMOTIONS. Colleges and universities can also foster students' sense of efficacy. In order to be civically and politically engaged and active, people have to care about the issues and value this kind of contribution. But socially responsible values alone are not sufficient to motivate action. People also have to believe that it matters what they think and do civically and politically and that it is possible for them to make some difference. This belief is what we mean by having a sense of political efficacy. Much of the research on sense of efficacy has focused on personal efficacy or personal control, a sense that one has active agency in one's life, a significant degree of control over the shape and direction of one's life. Although personal and political efficacy are not independent of one other, they are only modestly correlated, and political efficacy is more predictive of political activity and civic engagement than is personal efficacy (see, for example, Bandura, 1997). Many people feel they have control over their personal lives but do not feel that anything they might do politically could have an impact. This pattern is no doubt connected with the cynicism about the political structure and process that has become more widespread in recent decades.

It also makes sense that political efficacy would be lower in disempowered groups, and research data indicate that this is the case (Bandura, 1997). Both lower socioeconomic groups and racial minorities (even in comparable socioeconomic groups) score lower on measures of political efficacy (Lake Snell Perry & Associates, Inc., 2002; Verba et al., 1995). Given some of the items on the scale (for example, "How much influence do you think someone like you can have over local government decisions?" and, "How much influence do you think someone like you can have over national government decisions?" Verba et al., p. 556), it is not surprising that many people, especially poor people and groups that have experienced discrimination, would not exhibit a strong sense of political efficacy. Yet U.S. and world history shows that ordinary people, including members of disempowered groups, can make a difference politically when they work together and believe there is hope for change. Offering that hope and galvanizing collective action around desired goals is the essence of leadership, and people can be transformed by inspiring leaders, coming to believe that they can make a difference. The question for higher education is how to foster in students a sense that individuals' civic and political actions matter.

Contemporary American young people are much more likely to do volunteer work in which they help others directly than they are to participate actively in politics (Youniss & Yates, 1997). Part of the explanation for this is their feeling that by working in battered women's shelters and neighborhood clean-up efforts they can make a noticeable difference, at least on a small, local scale. Community service of this sort has been shown to reduce alienation (Calabrese & Schumer, 1986) and increase the likelihood of further volunteering (Sax, 1999). Social scientists agree that a sense of political efficacy is a critically important support for political action. But having a strong sense of efficacy does not mean one believes that political action will always have an immediate impact. And it does not mean that one evaluates the likely impact of each act and proceeds only when chances for success are high. It is clear that politically engaged people often act even when it is very unlikely their actions will make any difference. As the author and former Czechoslovakian president Václav Havel has said: "When a person behaves in keeping with his conscience, when he tries to speak the truth and when he tries to behave as a citizen even under conditions where citizenship is degraded, it may not lead to anything, yet it might. But what surely will not lead to anything is when a person calculates whether it will lead to something or not" (quoted in Meadows, 1991, p. 48). Likewise, studies of people who have dedicated their lives to serving others and improving their communities have found that these extraordinary individuals rarely asked themselves whether they were making actual progress toward their goals (Colby & Damon, 1992). Especially when working to fight poverty, as many were, they would have become discouraged if they had focused on the question of how much progress they were making in relation to the magnitude of the remaining problem. A participant in the Colby and Damon (1992) study, for example, said that he knows he will never finish his antipoverty work but that he tried to put in motion processes that will have some effect over succeeding generations. He compared himself to the cathedral builders, chipping away at social problems the way stonemasons of the Middle Ages inched along in building cathedrals, knowing that the massive churches would not be finished for three or four hundred years.

Others have suggested that promoting students' political interest also requires imparting a sense of passion and even playfulness about politics.

Political scientist Wendy Rahn (2000) argues that what students really need to learn about politics is "a love of the game and a sense of sportsmanship." If they do that, the question of whether they are making a difference with each specific act is less central. And yet fostering a love of the game, which pushes the question of efficacy into the background, is no doubt one of the most effective ways to foster a sense of political efficacy.

This love of the game, which motivates people to pursue civic and political understanding and action for their own sake, is akin to Mihaly Csikszentmihalyi's concept of *flow*. Csikszentmihalyi (1990) describes flow as "the state in which people are so involved in an activity that nothing else seems to matter; the experience itself is so enjoyable that people will do it at great cost, for the sheer sake of doing it" (p. 4). This kind of joyful absorption or unself-conscious immersion in the activity can diminish one's anxieties over the immediate results that one is able to achieve, alleviating some of the frustrations that inevitably follow from taking on difficult (sometimes impossible) challenges. Satisfaction is gained as much from the attempt as from the end results. When one takes on great moral and political causes such as poverty or political reform, this immersion in the process of collective action can preserve one's spirits and determination. Thus love of the activity for its own sake, passion for the cause, and solidarity with others working toward the same goals can all sustain moral and civic commitment in the face of difficulties that would otherwise be very discouraging. An important question for educators, then, is how to help students achieve a sense of flow in their moral, political, and civic discussions and action.

Implicit in Havel's statement is also the idea that there are things people believe in deeply enough that they feel they have to act on them whether it will make an immediate difference or not. This commitment generally reflects a deep faith in something transcendent, often, though not always, a religious faith (Colby & Damon, 1992). The motivating power of moral and spiritual convictions based in religion points to the importance of campus-based religious organizations in the moral and civic development of students. Many students move away from organized religion during college, however; so it is also important to support the development of deep and transcendent moral convictions of a more secular nature. It is this kind of strong conviction (whether religious or not), along with the love of the game, that can sustain individuals in the crucible of life after college.

Moral emotions play an important role in motivating action (Haidt, 2001; Hoffman, 1981), and many programs of moral and civic education include efforts to elicit some kind of moral emotion, either negative or positive—outrage at injustice, disgust with hypocrisy, compassion for the poor, hope for peace, and inspiration through solidarity. Research indicates that the motivational impacts of negative emotions and of positive emotions can be quite different. It is important to be aware of this because many educators rely heavily on eliciting negative emotions as a means to rouse students from self-absorption. Out of concern for social justice, faculty often take a critical stance toward U.S. history, culture, and politics. The goal is to shock students out of their complacency and motivate them to act through a sense of outrage. The irony is that in many cases this critical approach, instead of solving the apathy problem, *contributes* to the growing sense of alienation and cynicism that students feel and finally to a lack of conviction that anything can be done about an injustice that seems so pervasive as to be unavoidable. The belief that corruption, exploitation, and greed are rampant (and perhaps even part of the human condition) can be used to justify a life of self-interest as well as a life dedicated to improving society.

A study of political advertising helps to illuminate this phenomenon. This experimental study (Rahn & Hirshorn, 1999) looked at the effect of arousing either positive or negative feelings about the state of the country and found that both positive and negative feelings can lead to more involvement in community and political action. That is, feeling either more outraged or more inspired and hopeful can lead to more engagement. But the investigators also found an interaction between emotion and sense of efficacy. Positive emotions (hopefulness or inspiration) led to greater interest and engagement among study participants who began with *either* a low or a high sense of political efficacy. In contrast, negative feelings like outrage mobilized those who began with high efficacy, but demobilized even more those who started with low levels of efficacy.

It is likely that the teachers who create a sense of outrage by focusing very heavily on abuses and injustice have higher political efficacy than their students, so it makes sense that the teachers would feel mobilized by vivid critiques of the status quo and would expect students to be mobilized as well. But students who begin with low levels of efficacy could actually be further immobilized by the apparent hopelessness of the situation. An emerging understanding of this dynamic is contributing to a growing consensus that what educators need now is an approach that combines an appreciation of the ideals of the U.S. democratic system—an understanding that democracy is unrealized but not unrealizable—with a realistic sense of where it has fallen short of the ideals (Gutmann, 1996; Rahn, 1992). Educators need to find ways to avoid naive, uncritical complacency and at the same time avoid cynicism. In practice this is difficult to achieve. But teachers at all levels need to ask themselves which is the greater challenge (and thus worth the greatest attention and effort)—to make students more realistic or to make them more idealistic (Gutmann, 1996)?

Civic and Political Skills or Expertise

We have said that if colleges and universities are to educate engaged citizens it is important for students to have a sense of political efficacy. But what about actually *being* efficacious as well as *feeling* efficacious? In addition to understanding and caring about justice, people need to develop the skills and expertise of civic and political practice if they are to be engaged and effective citizens.

Amy Gutmann (1996) offers the reminder that national boundaries though not morally salient are *politically* salient and that it is primarily through their empowerment as citizens of particular nations that individuals can further the cause of justice, either at home or abroad. She points out that in order to achieve full participation as citizens, people need to be educated to skills, understandings, and values that are particular to their own political system. "Our obligations as democratic citizens go beyond our duties as politically unorganized individuals, because our capacity to act effectively to further justice increases when we are empowered as citizens, and so therefore does our responsibility to act to further justice. Democratic citizens have institutional means at their disposal that solitary individuals or citizens of the world only, do not" (p. 71).

In order to take full advantage of these institutional means, people need to know a lot about how to negotiate their own political systems, and they need to learn the particular mechanisms afforded by the various political and social structures and institutions of their local and national communities. This involves knowing how things work, including, for example, which issues and actions are appropriate to address at which level of government. Prominent among the needed civic and political capacities are skills of deliberation, communication, and persuasion. Engaging in compelling moral discourse requires the abilities to make a strong case for something, ensure that others understand one's point of view, understand and evaluate others' arguments, compromise without abandoning one's convictions, and work toward consensus. These capacities go to the heart of moral and civic functioning because individuals' moral and political concepts are both developed and applied through discourse, communication, and argumentation. Individuals take positions in the context of social interactions or discourse, and this context helps to shape the way those positions are played out, modified, and reconstructed (Habermas, 1993; Turiel, 1997). Having these political and civic competencies not only makes effective action possible, it naturally leads to a greater *sense* of efficacy or empowerment and also leads people to see themselves as politically engaged and thus to be further motivated toward engagement (Lake Snell Perry & Associates, Inc., 2002). That is, the development of skills contributes to and interacts with the development of values, understanding, and self-concept. Kuh and colleagues (1991) report, for example, that participation in leadership activities during college is the single most important predictor of students' development of humanitarian social concern and values. The significance of developing these practical competencies is also evident in longitudinal research on civic engagement. In a comprehensive review, Kirlin (2000) found that involvement with organizations that teach adolescents how to participate in society by learning how to form and express opinions and organize people for action is the most powerful predictor of adult civic engagement.

Relationships Among the Developmental Dimensions

Clearly, moral and civic development is a complex, multifaceted phenomenon, implying the need to pay attention to many different aspects of student development. We have touched on a number of the key dimensions here, although by no means all that could have been included. Furthermore, within each broad area—moral, civic, and political understanding, motivation, and skills—are many layers of further complexity.

The critical role of moral and civic understanding, knowledge, and judgment makes for a very natural fit between moral and civic education and the academic goals of undergraduate education. Various domains of social cognition are important for moral and civic responsibility, most notably moral judgment, moral interpretation, and political understanding. Many college students are also grappling with issues of epistemology—What is true and how can you know?—as well as questions of ethical relativism. Sorting out these questions and reaching some personal resolution of them is one of many developmental tasks that can be appropriately and fruitfully addressed by higher education. In addition to gaining increased maturity in these cognitive capacities, students also need to develop and learn to apply knowledge in areas of particular concern to them or of critical importance for responsible citizenship. This is another reason that moral and civic education must be integrated into the curriculum and academic understanding must be linked with practical understanding of the issues in real-life contexts.

Of course, in order to be morally and civically engaged and responsible, students must not only achieve a sophisticated understanding of the issues but also be highly motivated to do something about them. This means their interests and values must reflect social and moral concerns, and these concerns and values must be central to their sense of who they are. It also means they need to be faithful to these moral dimensions of themselves, rather than achieving a false sense of integration through self-deception. They must have a sense of political efficacy, a sense that what they think and do civically and politically matters, and they also need long-term faith and hope to get them through the inevitable times when their well-intended actions do not seem to move them toward their goals.

Finally, college graduates need to be *competent* in their civic and political participation. This means they need to develop an understanding of the particular mechanisms that are likely to be effective in tackling different kinds of issues and to have the practical capacities and skills they need to use these mechanisms successfully. They need the abilities to communicate effectively and to organize and work with other people, both persuading and leading others and knowing how to compromise when necessary without abandoning their convictions.

For the purposes of explication we have treated these various dimensions of moral and civic development as more separate than they are. In reality, there are multiple and dynamic relationships among them such that they inextricably intersect with and influence each other in multiple feedback loops. For example, part of what gives a person a sense of efficacy is political knowledge and understanding. This sense of efficacy then contributes to shaping interests and values, which then serve to increase the individual's knowledge, which feeds back to increase the sense of efficacy. Emotions such as hope and cynicism are also connected with the sense of efficacy and these different feelings can lead to different patterns of behavior in response to classroom and real-world experiences. These different responses in turn influence many aspects of the individual's self-understanding. Likewise, moral and political understandings are created in part through discourse and simultaneously shape the discourse itself. At the same time, effective discourse is a practical skill that is essential to political and civic action. Values, interests, moral and political beliefs and convictions, characteristic habits of moral interpretation, and a sense of one's own competence and efficacy can all be part of one's identity or sense of self. When important aspects of these elements change, as they often do during college, it can result in a real transformation in the student's sense of who she is and what she stands for.

NOTES

1. *Distributive justice* refers to fairness in the distribution of goods or resources and includes concepts such as deservingness and equality or equity. *Procedural justice* refers to fairness in the way decisions are made and includes concepts such as impartiality and consistency.

2. Only 30 percent of twelfth graders, for example, scored at or above the proficient level on the National Assessment of Educational Progress (NAEP) 1998 Civics Assessment (Lutkus, Weiss, Campbell, Mazzeo, & Lazer, 1999).

3. Kohlberg's account of the developmental progression was empirically derived from responses to hypothetical moral dilemmas involving conflicts among issues such as the value of human life, interpersonal obligations, trust, law, and authority. The theory originally posited six stages, but only five are represented in the stage scoring system (see Colby & Kohlberg, 1987).

4. Kohlberg's Moral Judgment Interview (Colby & Kohlberg, 1987) involves asking respondents open-ended questions about a set of hypothetical moral dilemmas. Responses are then scored by comparing them with prototypical responses at the five moral judgment stages. This process yields a stage score that represents the respondent's dominant stage and a secondary stage if one is identified in the interview. In contrast, the Defining Issues Test asks respondents to rate and rank the importance of each of a number of considerations that might be taken into account in deciding what is right in a hypothetical moral dilemma. The DIT (Rest, 1979, 1986) does not yield a stage score but rather a continuous variable indicating the percentage of endorsed items that reflect Stage 5 thinking.

5. As higher education has become more widespread, each successive generation or birth cohort attains, on average, a higher level of education than the previous generation did. Thus, if at any one time a group of forty-year-olds is compared to a group of sixty-year-olds, for example, and the latter group is found to be less intellectually advanced, relative age is not the only possible explanation for the difference. Unless the research follows the same people over time, it is impossible to say whether older people score lower on cognitive tasks such as the DIT presents because their cognitive capacities are declining over time or because as a group they are less well educated than the younger group.

6. We say this is surprising because moral claims like "we must be tolerant of people who have beliefs different from ours" are inconsistent with the belief that when individuals or cultures hold different moral views there is no basis for arguing that one position is better than another. If this relativist perspective were valid, there would be no grounds for justifying the claim that one ought to be tolerant.

5

PEDAGOGICAL STRATEGIES FOR EDUCATING CITIZENS

ON THE GENERAL LEVEL the challenges of teaching for moral and civic development are the same as the challenges of any good teaching—to help students achieve deep understanding of difficult ideas, impart knowledge and skills they can really use, and reach them on an emotional level, exciting passion and fostering commitment. More particular challenges arise from the wide-ranging complexity of moral and civic development, its multiple dimensions, and the special dilemmas it presents.

The moral domain is full of ideas that are multilayered, subtle, and often confusing. Many of these ideas conflict with students' preconceptions, making them even harder to grasp. Students predictably find it very difficult to understand moral pluralism, for example, or the grounds for evaluating a moral claim. They often ask questions like these: If there is more than one valid moral framework, how can anyone claim that some principles and values are morally preferable to others? How can I be tolerant of others yet question their moral beliefs? How can a moral claim be anything other than someone's personal opinion?

Issues of altruism, self-interest, and human nature may also be confusing and raise similarly complex questions: Is there really such a thing as altruism? If people get personal satisfaction from helping others, doesn't that mean they are helping for selfish reasons? Doesn't social science show that all people are really out for themselves and that to pretend otherwise is hypocritical?

And civic life presents puzzles of its own: With rare, heroic exceptions, how can it matter whether any particular individual is politically active? Isn't it better for a few knowledgeable people to run things and for everyone else to stay out of it? Is it always best to question authority, as some bumper stickers recommend?

Teachers also confront the challenge of getting students to relinquish stereotypes and oversimplified explanations that may seem to work for them in rough and ready ways and so persist in the face of contrary evidence—poor people don't have enough drive and ambition; politicians are crooks; wars and other conflicts are caused by the actions of a few bad people.

Teaching knowledge and skills that students can really use is no easier. How can teachers help students understand history or democratic or ethical theory in their own terms but also ensure that what they learn is usable in practice—that they can bring these theoretical schemes, rooted in centuries of scholarship, to bear on the messy, emotionally charged, and immediately pressing ethical and political problems of contemporary life? How can teachers encourage personal connections with course material without sacrificing analytical distance? How can teachers ensure that students learn to practice reasoned and respectful discourse not only in the classroom but also in more complicated and heated situations?

If classroom teaching is to support the full range of moral and civic development, it must connect with students on the emotional level as well as the intellectual level. This raises additional challenges and dilemmas: How can students come to admire and be inspired by moral leaders past and present when they are all too aware that everyone has feet of clay? How can teachers help them become less cynical about politics when their skepticism so often seems warranted? How can teachers foster both open-mindedness and conviction? If students do begin to tackle complicated social problems, what can teachers do to help them maintain resilience and hope in the face of inevitable setbacks?

These challenges mirror problems for education generally, not just for moral and civic education. Research clearly shows that students have a lot of trouble fully understanding difficult concepts, often do not know how to use what they do learn, and perhaps because they are not using that learning, tend to forget what they once knew. The experience of recalling information for a final exam but being unable to remember it later is familiar to everyone. In fact many college graduates cannot even remember what college courses they took. And sometimes students appear to remember the concepts they learned, but when asked to explain them, they reveal fundamental and persistent misconceptions (Clement, 1982; Perkins & Simmons, 1988). Students are known to hold these *naive theories* not only before but also after instruction in every discipline, and these misconceptions continue to impede consolidated understanding. Students often learn interpretations that conflict with their naive theories, but they learn them in the narrow context of the classroom and on a superficial level. When they are asked to explain or are confronted with a comparable issue outside that narrow context, their original misconceptions emerge intact. They have not achieved any real understanding of the ideas they believe they have learned but instead have learned to use heuristics or rough strategies that work much of the time in the classroom but that do not confront and uproot their misconceptions (Perkins & Martin, 1986).

Howard Gardner's review of this research in *The Unschooled Mind* (1991) offers illustrations from virtually every discipline. Some of these misconceptions are directly relevant to moral and civic development. For example, students may learn in a history course that wars result from multiple and complex forces, but they revert to a simplistic "bad man" explanation when asked to explain a contemporary conflict. And college students who have studied economics offer incorrect explanations of market forces that are essentially identical to those of college students who have never taken an economics course. Many students also continue to hold internally inconsistent ethical views even after taking courses in ethics. This persistence of stereotypes, oversimplified explanations, and erroneous naive theories seriously undermines the value of academic learning for educating citizens. To make matters worse, students often have knowledge they can recall when prompted but they do not think to use it, or do not know how to use it, in new situations where it could be helpful (Bransford, Franks, Vye, & Sherwood, 1989; Perkins & Martin, 1986). In many cases students cannot apply what they know even in a slightly different context. The research on this lack of *transfer* of learning is often startling, calling into question the subsequent usefulness of much academic learning.

Conventional modes of instruction, especially listening to lectures and reading textbooks, are especially vulnerable to producing fragile and superficial understanding. As a result students forget much of what they have learned, are unable to use in a new context what they do remember, and retain fundamental misconceptions that are inconsistent with what they seemed to have learned (Bligh, 1972; Gardiner, 1994). This has been shown in both natural settings and in the laboratory (Bransford et al., 1989). Lecture courses often do not support deep and enduring understandings of ideas and are even less well suited to developing the range of problem-solving, communication, and interpersonal skills toward which moral and civic education (and liberal education more generally) aspire. And the development of the motivational dimensions of moral and civic maturity—dimensions like a sense of identity as a responsible and engaged person; a passion for social justice; sympathy with others, including those who are different from oneself; and an enduring sense of hope and empowerment—is often beyond even the aspirations of this kind of teaching.

Student-Centered Pedagogies

Although a majority of college and university faculty use primarily lectures and discussion in their teaching (indeed, 74 percent of college courses rely on lectures, according to a recent survey, Shedd, 2002), a growing number are adopting an array of other strategies, including service learning, experiential education, problem-based learning, and collaborative learning (Sax, Astin, Korn, & Gilmartin, 1999). Many of these strategies represent models for teaching that if used well can support deep understanding, usable knowledge and skills, and personal connection and meaning. The pedagogies in this expanded and varied repertoire share a commitment to student learning as the central criterion of good teaching and conceive of learning as a more active process than it was once thought to be.

Faculty using these approaches, which are often called *pedagogies of engagement,* typically address a wider range of goals and attempt to match learning experiences more closely with those goals than do faculty using traditional approaches. These pedagogies are classified and named somewhat differently by different writers, so any given list is unavoidably somewhat arbitrary. The pedagogies also tend to intersect with each other, so the categories are not mutually exclusive. In addition, most existing lists include a number of approaches that we do not address here, such as undergraduate research and teaching methods based in information technology. For the sake of simplicity and focus, we limit our discussion to four well-known approaches that are particularly appropriate to moral and civic education.

Service Learning

In the last decade, *service learning,* also called *community-based learning,* has emerged as the most widespread and closely studied of the various student-centered, or engaged, pedagogies. It has become one of the most popular ways to integrate moral and civic learning into academic coursework. In service learning, students participate in organized, sustained service activity that is related to their classroom learning and meets identified community needs. They then reflect on that experience through activities such as journal writing and class discussions, connecting the service experience with the substantive content of the course and with various dimensions of personal growth, including civic responsibility (Bringle & Hatcher, 1995). Faculty teaching these courses provide the larger intellectual and ethical context for students' service work, helping them connect scholarship with practice and articulating grounds for commitment and action (Zlotkowski, 1999).

Other Experiential Education

Service learning is a subset of the broader category of *experiential education,* which includes many different kinds of direct, hands-on activities that are meant to help students connect theory with practice and represent and experience theoretical concepts in practical, behavioral modes and real-life settings. Experiential education employs a wide range of pedagogies, including simulations, role playing, internships and other fieldwork, and action research (Moore, 2000). Students often receive direct supervision and feedback in the field settings, which generally require the students to address complex and open-ended problems and projects. Faculty help students put their experiences into practical, theoretical, and ethical contexts and integrate the fieldwork with the course's academic content, rethinking theories in light of applied experiences.

Problem-Based Learning

In *problem-based learning,* students' work, occurring either individually or in groups, is organized around studying, evaluating, and often proposing possible solutions for concrete, usually real-world problems (Barrows, 1980). At the college level, students generally work on rich, complex, and relatively unstructured problems. The teacher serves as a resource and guide, helping students find and integrate information from many sources and assisting in their efforts to bridge theory and practice and put knowledge to work in applied situations.

Collaborative Learning

In *collaborative learning* students work together in teams on projects, group investigations, and other activities aimed at teaching a wide range of skills and improving students' understanding of complex substantive issues (Kadel & Keehner, 1994). The groups take collective responsibility for working together on assignments, often creating both joint and individual products. Student groups organize their own efforts, negotiating roles and resolving conflicts themselves. When differences of opinion arise, group members have opportunities to compare and evaluate their ideas and approaches, allowing more complex understandings to emerge. In collaborative learning the locus of authority is shifted from the teacher to the group, and the teacher acts as a coach and resource.

Why Engaged Pedagogies Support Complex Learning

The research literature on the effectiveness of pedagogies of engagement is extensive; it is also complicated because their impact depends on the quality and conditions of their use and the specific outcomes chosen to be assessed. A review of that literature is beyond the scope of this book, but taken as a whole the research indicates that if used well these student-centered, or active, pedagogies can have a positive impact on many dimensions of moral and civic learning as well as on other aspects of academic achievement. Teaching methods that actively involve students in the learning process and provide them with opportunities for interaction with their peers as well as with faculty enhance students' content learning, critical thinking, transfer of learning to new situations, and such aspects of moral and civic development as a sense of social responsibility, tolerance, and nonauthoritarianism (McKeachie, Pintrich, Yi-Guang, & Smith, 1986; Pascarella & Terenzini, 1991; Pederson-Randall, 1999).

Principles of Learning

There are good reasons for these positive learning outcomes—these pedagogies embody powerful research and theory about the nature of learning that has emerged in recent years from the fields of education, developmental psychology, and cognitive science. This research presents a picture of the nature of learning that explains why these pedagogies are so important for promoting deep academic learning and effective moral and civic education. It also forms the basis for our confidence that including moral and civic goals in coursework does not require a trade-off with other academic goals. As Lee Shulman (1997) has said, if one understands the implications of this research for resolving the major difficulties people experience with liberal learning (forgetting or misunderstanding what they learn or being unable to use it), it becomes clear that the kinds of pedagogy we associate with moral and civic education, service learning for example, are not curricular extravagances but rather ways to strengthen the very heart of liberal education. Here (necessarily oversimplified) are some of the central ideas from this research literature:

1. Learning is an active, constructive process. In order to achieve real understanding, learners must actively struggle to work through and interpret ideas, look for patterns and meaning, and connect new ideas with what they already know (Greeno, Collins, & Resnick, 1996; Resnick, 1987).

2. Genuine and enduring learning occurs when students are interested in, even enthusiastic about, what they are learning, when they see it as important for their own present and future goals. In life outside the classroom, knowledge and skills are most often developed through efforts to make progress on tasks that need doing. Although almost any approach to teaching will stimulate interest and enthusiasm in some students, rich and authentic tasks (like those performed in real life) are more likely to be intrinsically interesting for most. This is important, because intrinsic motivation tends to support more sustained, self-motivated effort and therefore greater learning (Lepper & Green, 1978).

3. Thinking and learning are not only active but also social processes. In most work and other nonacademic settings, people are more likely to think and remember through interaction with other people than as a result of what they do alone. Working in a group can facilitate learning as participants work through the complexities of a task together, comparing and critiquing different perspectives and building on each other's proposed solutions (Newman, Griffin, & Cole, 1989).

4. Knowledge and skills are shaped in part by the particular contexts in which they are learned; they are qualitatively different as a result of different learning contexts (Brown, Collins, & Duguid, 1989; Lave, 1988). Few skills are truly generic and equally applicable across very different contexts. For this reason, transfer of knowledge and skills to very different contexts is difficult. Despite this difficulty, transfer is essential if knowledge and skills are to be usable.

5. There are two key ways to increase the likelihood that transfer will be successful. The first is to make the context in which skills and knowledge are learned more similar to the settings in which they will be used. This can raise problems for traditional modes of instruction, because classroom learning is in some sense *decontextualized* (Greeno et al., 1996). Traditional classrooms are of course contexts in themselves, but in most cases they are notably artificial, bearing little resemblance to the contexts in which educators hope the skills and knowledge can be used. The second way to support transfer of learning is to consciously, reflectively draw out principles that can guide and support that transfer, making them explicit and articulating their implications for the new situation or context (Brown, 1989; Salomon & Perkins, 1989). Therefore, genuine, usable

learning depends not only on activity but also on carefully guided reflection on that activity.

6. Thoughtful, aware (reflective) practice, accompanied by informative feedback, is essential to learning. Because knowledge and skills are context specific, it is not usually sufficient for students to practice a performance that is assumed to be analogous to, though is actually quite different from, the one they will ultimately need. Too often schools and colleges do not teach what they want their students to know, instead asking students to practice distant substitutes. So, for example, if teachers want students to understand an idea well enough that they can explain it, represent it in new ways, apply it in new situations, and connect it to their lives, then students need to practice doing these things and not simply recall the concept in an abstract form. Students are more likely to develop understanding when they practice understanding (Perkins, 1992).

7. Students have different profiles of ability. Some are most expert with language; others are most skilled at logical and quantitative thinking or spatial representation; still others are especially insightful in understanding themselves or in understanding and managing other people (Gardner, 1983). Broadening the array of skills, tasks, and modes of representation used in a course increases the likelihood that students with different strengths will be able to connect productively with the work. It also provides opportunities for students to progress in areas where they are not yet strong, expanding the range of their competencies.

8. The development of genuine understanding is supported by the capacity to represent an idea or skill in more than one modality and to move back and forth among different forms of knowing (Gardner, 1991). Thus learning benefits when courses provide experience with a wider array of modalities than those that usually dominate higher education (namely the linguistic and logical/mathematical).

Pedagogical Implications

The connections between these principles of learning and student-centered pedagogies of engagement are clear. All these pedagogies build on the premise that learning requires students to be active and emotionally engaged in their work. This can happen in the context of a lecture course if the lectures are provocative enough to engage students actively in seeking answers to puzzles the readings or lectures raise, stimulating them to reflect, make connections, and organize and draw conclusions from some body of knowledge. But too often the active reflection, interpretation, and connecting are done by the lecturer, not by the students, and being an observer to this process does not suffice (Finkel, 2000). The more student-centered pedagogies ask students to do this work, although they are not expected to do it alone, and expert guidance from the teacher supports and shapes productive inquiry.

Recognition of the importance of students' practicing what it is hoped they will learn is behind many teachers' commitment to an expanded pedagogical repertoire that includes collaborative learning, simulations, internships, service learning, and problem-based learning. These all provide direct (and directed) practice of a wide array of performances. All attempt to create authentic, intrinsically interesting tasks for students. Often they allow students to create or choose these tasks themselves, increasing their investment in the work. In addition, these varied pedagogies tend to offer many different modes of representation, providing more entry points to engagement and reinforcing learning through integration across different modalities. In addition to these shared characteristics of engaged pedagogies, each approach also capitalizes in particular ways on some aspects of what is currently known about learning.

Experiential learning, including service learning, centrally acknowledges the context specificity of learning, providing educational settings that are less artificial than the classroom and much closer to the contexts in which students will later perform. When these settings are explicitly civic, as they are in service learning and many internships and other field experiences, they provide stronger support for moral and civic development than most lectures or seminars can. Service learning and other field experiences place students in contexts that involve social and conceptual complexity and ambiguity and often elicit emotional responses as well as unexamined stereotypes and other assumptions. Because the field contexts are so dissimilar from the classroom, learning to operate in those contexts, confronting the stereotypes and other misconceptions they raise, and being called on to trace ideas and principles across academic and applied settings can be a very effective means of deepening and extending learning. Reflective writing and discussions are essential components of high-quality service learning and other forms of experiential education in part because they provide opportunities for students and faculty to extract principles that facilitate the transfer of learning to new contexts.

Of course the essence of problem-based learning is inquiry into rich, complex, and authentic problems of real concern to the students. This can have a dramatic impact on their motivation and emotional engagement with the work. If students need the knowledge and skills they are learning in order to address or solve some problem with which they are preoccupied, especially a problem that is closely connected with their own interests and concerns, they will not ask the familiar question, Why do I have to learn this? (Finkel, 2000). Problem-based learning is also invaluable in providing opportunities for students to practice and receive feedback on intellectual capacities such as integrative thinking that might otherwise only be hoped for as a side effect of academic study and not actually taught.

Collaborative learning builds directly on what research has shown about the facilitative effect of social processes. This is why it is valuable in supporting students' learning of the many subtle and difficult concepts that are inherent in the moral and civic domains. Equally important, collaborative learning provides experience with a wide array of interpersonal skills, many of which are critical to civic participation. Among other things, students can practice cooperation, persuasion, negotiation, compromise, and fair distribution of efforts and rewards. When teams are composed of students with complementary strengths, participants can learn how to build on diversity in working toward a common goal. When students from different backgrounds work together closely over a period of time, they can achieve the cross-cultural competencies that are best learned through relationships and practice.

It may seem that the principles of learning we have discussed here are more relevant for acquiring moral and civic understanding and skills than for developing the motivational dimensions of moral and civic maturity, but this is not true. If anything, the development of values and goals, moral and civic identity, and a sense of efficacy, hope, and compassion is even more dependent on active engagement, complex and authentic contexts, social exchange, regular practice, and informative feedback than is the development of more traditional dimensions of academic understanding. Compassion and outrage become much more intense when students develop personal connections with those who have experienced hardship or injustice. When students work closely with inspiring people, they can internalize new images of what they want to be like more deeply and vividly than they are likely to do through reading. Students develop a love of the game only by playing it. The more students take civic or political action, especially if they enjoy it, the more they will see themselves as the kind of people who can and want to act civically and politically. If they see that their actions can make a difference, their sense of efficacy is strengthened. Of course they also need ways to maintain their commitment during the many times when their actions do not seem to have much effect. By weaving service into academic coursework, faculty can help students develop lenses for interpreting inevitable obstacles and failures in a way that will support rather than undermine their stamina. This connection between ways of understanding and dimensions of motivation is typical of the multiple and dynamic connections among understanding, skills, and motivation that become particularly real and salient through active educational experiences.

The skill with which these diverse pedagogies are implemented is critically important because experiential, problem-based, and collaborative approaches to learning do not automatically inspire interest or provide the kind of feedback that is required for learning. They are often harder to do well than traditional lectures precisely because the teacher is not "in control" of many of the student experiences. Nor do they spontaneously yield ideas that build cumulatively or principles that can guide transfer of learning. For this reason teachers must play a very active role in guiding and facilitating students' learning even in these student-centered forms of teaching. Among other things, teachers must make their specific learning goals clear, not only in their own minds but also to the students.

We have been defining the pedagogies of engagement on a global level, examining general pedagogical categories. But faculty shape what they do and ask students to do on a more *micro* level, and there are wide variations in what each pedagogy may involve for a given course. In addition, the broad categories intersect in practice, so it is not unusual for a particular classroom strategy to employ a combination of collaborative, problem-based, *and* service learning and to be interdisciplinary as well.

All teaching, but especially teaching that takes full advantage of these more complex strategies, begins well before the teacher walks into the classroom and continues beyond the conclusion of the course. Teachers have an underlying, often implicit, conception of teaching and learning that guides the many choices they make. Selecting texts, planning student activities, designing and implementing assessments, all are important elements of teaching, as is shaping and guiding the work that students do, including reading, writing, classroom discussions and projects, simulations or field placements (if they are used), and test taking or other demonstrations of learning. For this reason, we use the term *pedagogy* to refer to all the things teachers do and ask their students to do to support students' learning. Teaching in this comprehensive sense can also include the things that teachers do to assess their own performance and the impact of their courses—reviews or evaluations of a course while it is ongoing and after it is over, involving student comments, student work, peer reviews, and other information. These reflections on course effectiveness may be quite informal or more systematic. Either way they can support teachers' capacity to learn from their own experience and, when they are shared, make it possible for teachers to learn from each other's experience. Writing about the teaching of elementary school mathematics, Maggie

Lampert (1985) proposed an image of teachers as managers of dilemmas. In any given course the teacher holds multiple, conflicting aims and must find ways to balance those aims as the course proceeds. We find this image equally appropriate to teaching for moral and civic responsibility at the college level.

Teaching Ethics

In this section, we discuss the many ways faculty grapple with the challenges and dilemmas of teaching students about ethics and ethical issues, a key arena of moral and civic learning. Ethics is not the only issue we could have chosen to consider in detail, though it is among the most important. Some of the most difficult challenges of teaching ethics include working to move students beyond moral relativism, supporting deep understanding of and personal connections with ethical concepts, teaching the skills of moral discourse, promoting the values and themes that are central to the institution's goals for moral and civic education, and supporting transfer of learning to contexts beyond the classroom.

Moving Beyond Moral Relativism

In the area of ethics one of the naive theories, or fundamental misconceptions, that surfaces over and over in college classrooms is student moral relativism. As we discussed in Chapter Four, this is the belief that no moral position is more valid than any other and that therefore (illogically) one should be tolerant of moral beliefs different from one's own (Ricks, 1999). Student moral relativism is connected with another phenomenon that is widely reported by faculty teaching all kinds of student populations—students' tendency to avoid engaging with moral disagreement. If any answer is as good as any other, why think hard about these questions, why make a serious effort to justify your position? A corollary is many students' reluctance to subject their own moral beliefs to serious scrutiny. Ironically, student moral relativism, which reflects humility and tolerance (as well as intellectual laziness in some cases), can get in the way of open-minded consideration of others' views. As Ricks (1999) puts it, "The phrase 'Well, it's all a matter of opinion anyway,' when uttered during a conversation about ethical topics, is usually a clear sign that the discussion, for all intents and purposes, is over" (p. 3).

A central dilemma for faculty who teach about ethical issues is how to help students see the problems with this kind of thinking without implying that there is one clearly right answer to hard ethical questions. This is not easy, and many teachers do not succeed in moving students beyond relativism. In fact, standard approaches to teaching ethics may inadvertently contribute to the problem. The two most common approaches to teaching ethics, which are often combined, are presentation and critique of the major ethical theories (deontology, utilitarianism, and virtue theory) and discussion of very difficult cases in which moral goods conflict and there is no consensus on how best to resolve the conflict.

Any responsible introduction to ethics must teach students about the major ethical theories that frame the field. And the kind of analytical thinking involved in working out the limitations of these theories lies at the heart of what it means to engage in philosophy. On the one hand, teaching this kind of analytical thinking is itself an important aim, because understanding the modes of inquiry that underlie different disciplines is a central goal of liberal education (Schneider & Shoenberg, 1998). On the other hand, if schools are to educate citizens, it is important for students to develop convictions—a place to stand morally even if only tentative and subject to change. Too heavy a focus on critical analysis gives students the impression that because each theory is flawed, the major ethical theories are all equally valid (or invalid), and none provides a useful basis for actual moral decisions.

The second standard approach, discussion of very difficult cases, can give the impression that ethics concerns only serious and ultimately irresolvable disagreements. Sharon Rowe (2001), who teaches introduction to moral philosophy at Kapi'olani Community College, points to these and other unfortunate consequences of this approach. In her experience the cases typically used are likely to concern issues that are unfamiliar to most students, making it hard for them to feel connected with the debate. Even more problematic is the fact that the cases tend to generate conversations that polarize quickly, with students becoming entrenched and defensive. Students who are more articulate or passionate dominate these discussions, and the others retreat. The dynamic is exacerbated by the cultural backgrounds of the students at Kapi'olani, because many students of Asian or Pacific Islander ancestry consider it rude to criticize others publicly.

Making Personal Connections

Like many other faculty perplexed by these dilemmas, Rowe has found it more useful to focus on issues that are personally relevant for her students, helping them explore more fully the ethical implications of those issues. Two topics she has found especially fruitful are lying and sexual behavior. Exploration of these familiar issues can help students see the relevance of the major theoretical perspectives for their lives. For example, Rowe asks students to engage in small-group discussions to address the potentially sensitive issue of sexual ethics and asks the groups to develop a "Sexual Ethic for the 21st Century" and give it a solid conceptual foundation. In the course of these discussions students are forced to confront the implications of moral relativism and the merits of a stronger ethical perspective.

Although there are clear advantages in connecting ethics teaching with students' personal experience, this strategy presents dilemmas of its own. Too strong a focus on everyday morality may lead students to conceive of ethics as concerned primarily with issues of private life and focused on people with whom they already have a relationship. An understanding of the moral dimensions of social and political issues will remain beyond their grasp (Beerbohm, 1999). This argues for using a variety of approaches, including strategies for extending issues of personal relevance and concern beyond the immediate, private sphere. One way to do this is to focus on a complex social problem that is familiar to students, such as poverty or racial justice, and to draw from multiple disciplines, using ethical analysis as a central theme. These problem-based ethics courses draw from applied fields of particular interest to the students and often require them to keep journals or participate in community service. A challenge in these courses is to ensure that they provide adequate theoretical grounding and require students to treat problems analytically through persuasive reasoning and argumentation. Otherwise they may teach students to formulate their own beliefs and debate with others but not to ground their views in reason and principle or to see why this grounding is important.

This kind of academic weakness is not unusual. Surveying the syllabi of ethics courses at many colleges and universities, we found that too often the courses ask students to read only brief secondary source summaries of moral philosophy rather than primary sources. Often these courses, especially those that aspire toward "values clarification," fail to provide experience with the rigorous argumentation that is so critical to ethical problem solving. Students are encouraged to clarify what they believe, but little attempt is made to ground this reflection in larger scholarly debates or to consider and debate the relative merits of other values and ethical perspectives.

Teaching Skills of Moral Discourse

Recognizing how important it is for students to learn and practice moral argumentation, many courses and programs focus directly on these skills. This is a central component of The Reflective Woman, for example, a course at the College of St. Catherine. This required, first-year course includes a lengthy section in which students participate in *structured controversies*. Collaborating in small groups, they work out both sides of a controversial topic, conducting research, writing position statements, debating, and switching positions at various points in the process. Using the experience of thinking through opposing viewpoints to refine their arguments, the groups then present their structured controversies to the class. After the presentations each student in the group writes a paper from her own viewpoint, supporting her position with a thorough consideration of contrary evidence and viewpoints. Students also reflect on the experience of conflict, any uncertainties about their own views, and the experience of being challenged by opposing views. Because all freshmen are participating in structured controversies at the same time, the residence halls are able to sponsor dialogues that connect with and support the process.

Teaching moral argumentation is also a central goal of Stanford University's Ethics in Society Program. Students practice these skills in introductory courses in ethics, political philosophy, and "the ethics of social (including governmental) decisions." In support of this goal a section on the program's Web site (www.stanford.edu/eis) outlines the basics of moral argumentation. This Web resource, titled *Arguing About Ethics,* offers guidelines on how to make a moral case and presents short excerpts from articles and books by distinguished (often contemporary) moral and political philosophers. The selections are meant to convey "a sense of the range and diversity of moral arguments—how they are made and what makes them compelling." They include brief excerpts from Ronald Dworkin, T. M. Scanlon, and Peter Singer on the value and nature of theorizing in moral and political philosophy and other respected thinkers commenting on "the essential tools of moral and political philosophy." The Web site also provides examples of different modes of moral argument, such as employing theory to explain confused intuitions; drawing upon material from the world, to supply an essay not just with empirical facts but also with reasons; preempting objections to one's position; giving reasons for one's intuitions that an argument is "implausible"; acknowledging agreement where it exists; considering alternative positions to common debates; and avoiding simple dichotomies. Of course students are not expected to learn these forms of argumentation simply from reading examples, but the site does provide useful reference material for courses in which students practice moral argumentation through a wide range of pedagogies.

"Distinctive Definitions" in the Teaching of Ethics

At some colleges the mission and special perspective of the institution may permeate the teaching of ethics—providing a *distinctive definition* of moral and civic responsibility, as described in Chapter Three. For example, Haverford College, which is strongly rooted in Quaker values, requires all students to take a course on ethics as social justice. The ethics requirement at Shaw University, a historically black college in North Carolina, places special emphasis on the ethics of influential African Americans such as Booker T. Washington, W.E.B. Du Bois, Malcolm X, and Martin Luther King Jr. At many religious colleges, ethical issues and theories are connected with theological and other religious issues. This can be valuable as long as these courses encourage open inquiry and debate, critical evaluation, and skills of analysis.

Most educators would agree that students need to develop clear convictions and a commitment to certain values, such as honesty, courage, and mutual respect, and also learn to think through subtle and ambiguous moral issues. Debates about the appropriate balance between these two goals emerge from the distinctive definition of moral and civic development at the United States Air Force Academy. The academy's task is to instill professional ethics within the military structure, which is characterized by a tension between obedience to legitimate authority and personal responsibility for ethical choices. Among other things, academy faculty are teaching a code of professional ethics. To some extent they are teaching a set of rules—making sure cadets understand what is right and why. Some express concern that this kind of clarity is rare in higher education. Faculty we met at the academy referred to a recent public television special in which a small group of students and professors talked about whether it would be acceptable to cheat on a five-page paper if students were given only a few days to write it when they were already overwhelmed with work. In the televised discussion, only two of the students and one professor thought that it was clearly wrong, a judgment very much at odds with the norms about cheating reflected in the academy's strict honor code.

Many faculty teaching ethics at the academy believe it is important for them to take clear positions on some of the ethical issues likely to arise in the cadets' later careers in the military, including corruption, such as overcharging for supplies or falsifying equipment maintenance records. They believe cadets need to learn the realities of the serious, even life-threatening situations that have resulted from cutting corners in a military context, even in cases where the violation seemed a fairly trivial matter when it occurred.

.

Because many of the faculty are military officers themselves and have witnessed unethical behavior and its impact at some point in their careers, they can incorporate vivid stories into their teaching and help cadets connect lessons from these examples with difficult situations they are already beginning to face. Others at the academy believe it is more important to prepare cadets to make autonomous judgments about situations in which there are no obvious right or wrong answers. "Officers need the courage to constructively dissent—they may well be called upon to do this," one professor told us. This alternative point of view is in part a different prediction about what challenges cadets are likely to face as Air Force officers and in part a pedagogical claim that students gain more from working through dilemmas themselves than from being shown the implications of rules they are being asked to follow.

Although the academy no doubt feels a stronger need to establish clear ethical norms than most liberal arts programs do, many introductory ethics courses would probably benefit from consideration of the many basic values and beliefs around which moral philosophers substantially agree. Introductory science courses typically begin by studying the many areas in which there is wide agreement before moving to controversies or unresolved cutting-edge issues. When a version of this approach is used in ethics courses, it can reduce students' confusion about moral relativism (Ricks, 1999).

Supporting Transfer of Learning Beyond the Classroom

Recognizing how difficult it is to transfer skills learned in a classroom setting to the more complicated and emotionally charged contexts of life, many faculty incorporate experiential approaches into the teaching of ethics. When students face difficult moral issues in personal or public life, it will be important for them to consider multiple points of view and alternative courses of action and to appreciate the moral complexity of the issues. Moreover, sometimes difficult moral dilemmas require an answer urgently when there is no clear consensus on how they ought to be resolved.

Simulations can help students learn to make judgments in the face of uncertainty as they will need to do many times in the future. At the College of St. Catherine, students in health care fields participate in a number of ethical simulations: for example, they might sit on the board of a fictitious insurance company, making decisions about whether to cover certain kinds of experimental medical treatment. Guest experts such as attorneys and health care managers provide background information and varying perspectives on the issues, and then students must decide whether, for example, a patient with Parkinson's disease should receive coverage for his experimental implant.

Service learning plays an important role at many colleges because it offers an effective way for students to engage the complexity of ethical issues in the press and ambiguity of actual situations. This reflects the understanding that context and content matter—that real moral dilemmas are not solved by learning and applying an abstract moral algorithm. Debra Satz (2001), director of the Ethics in Society Program at Stanford University at the time of our visit, speaks to this issue:

> As a political philosopher, and as the head of an interdisciplinary ethics program, I have frequently been struck by how ill equipped much moral and political philosophy is to deal with the "limits of the possible." By the limits of the possible, I have in mind the non-ideal aspects of our world: that people don't always do the right thing, that there can be very high costs to doing the right thing when others do not, that information is imperfect, resources are limited, interests are powerful, the best options may not be politically or materially feasible, and that collective action problems are everywhere. We need a moral and political philosophy that integrates theoretical reflection on values with practical knowledge about how the world sets limits on what we can do and what we can hope for.

Satz and others in this program believe that making ethical judgments within the limits of the possible, that is, within the constraints and practical complexities of real life, is qualitatively different from "doing" academic moral philosophy or even applied ethics, and that service learning plays a vitally important role by placing students in contexts that give them necessary experience with this kind of contextual thinking.

Pedagogical Strategies in Four Courses

Teaching for moral and civic responsibility along with other aspects of academic learning requires faculty to address many different areas of understanding and foster a variety of skills while maintaining a course's coherence and building learning cumulatively across varied topics and tasks. In powerful courses the whole is greater than the sum of the parts. In order to convey a sense of some of these "wholes," we devote the rest of this chapter to describing the teaching strategies that make up the fabric of four quite different courses, all of which centrally address moral and civic learning. One of these courses prepares students for learning and service in the community, and another attempts to deepen and extend a service experience students have just completed. A third incorporates service preparation, action, and reflection on the action into a single semester, and the last of the four combines the challenge of conducting a course with these phases condensed with another challenge—attempting to reach students who begin the course with skepticism about and alienation from politics and civic life.

The Ethics and Politics of Public Service

The Ethics and Politics of Public Service is a course that grew out of a faculty service-learning institute organized by Stanford University's Haas Center for Public Service. It reflects the participants' conviction, consistent with research findings, that community service and service learning are more likely to help the community and to support student learning when students are well prepared before they embark on the work. The course serves as a gateway for students who plan to participate in service activities or enroll in courses with service-learning components. Rob Reich, an assistant professor in the Department of Political Science who was a member of the group, developed and teaches the course, which is cross-listed in six additional departments or programs—Human Biology, American Studies, Ethics in Society, Urban Studies, Public Policy, and Comparative Studies in Race and Ethnicity.

Ethics and Politics, which is aimed primarily at freshmen and sophomores, has two overarching goals: to prepare students for responsible service and to integrate their service experiences with their academic life. Reich believes that in preparing to engage with the community, students need to understand the history of the relationship between Stanford University and the surrounding communities; learn about socioeconomic, demographic, and political changes in the San Francisco Bay Area; and become aware of experiences, perceptions, dilemmas, and challenges that Stanford students have encountered previously while engaged in community service.

Because an important goal is to expand students' appreciation of cultural differences and the very different perspectives they can entail, the course naturally raises some of the same issues of moral and cultural relativism that arise in ethics courses. The challenge for Reich is to help students develop a deep respect for diverse cultural understandings yet also appreciate the importance of fundamental human rights. He hopes that in the process they will come to see the value of ethical pluralism, which acknowledges legitimate differences in moral perspective without giving up the belief that there are boundaries around what is morally acceptable and valid grounds for evaluating moral claims. Among the other dilemmas that Reich must negotiate are how to instill humility without triggering paralysis and how to help students maintain a sense of efficacy even though they can expect only limited success in many of their service endeavors.

Ethics and Politics meets twice a week, generally with one class each week devoted to discussing broad philosophical questions raised in the assigned readings such as: What does it mean to "do service"? Would service be necessary in a just world? Can service do harm? The other meeting explores the same questions in connection with examples of actual service experiences, often through case studies written for the class by former course participants who have subsequently taken part in community service. During class, Reich alternates among small-group exercises; full-group discussions in which he actively questions, probes, and pushes the students; and *mini-lectures* in which he introduces or summarizes a set of issues. In addition to class participation and extensive reading, students write four papers exploring the history, dilemmas, and complexities of public service.

PHASE 1: TO HELL WITH GOOD INTENTIONS. The first several weeks of Ethics and Politics are designed to challenge the facile notion that service is automatically a good thing. The challenge begins with readings and discussions concerning various motives for doing service. Some students think only people who are motivated by altruism are "good" service providers, whereas others think that serving for self-interested reasons (for example, wanting to build a better résumé) is acceptable. Reich pushes students to recognize the prevalence of mixed motives and then asks the class to consider the sufficiency of thinking only about motives. Reich assigns several readings that illustrate how good intentions, even though a desirable starting point, may lead to bad consequences. Most provocative on this point is the well-known essay "To Hell with Good Intentions," by Ivan Illich (1968). In an address to a group of U.S. volunteers who were about to embark on a summer of service in Mexico, Illich tells his audience:

> You will not help anybody by your good intentions. . . . I am here to tell you, if possible to convince you, and hopefully, to stop you, from pretentiously imposing yourselves on Mexicans. . . . By definition, you cannot help being ultimately vacationing salesmen for the middle-class "American Way of Life," since that is really the only life you know. . . .

All you will do in a Mexican village is create disorder. . . . At worst, in your "community development" spirit you might create just enough problems to get someone shot after your vacation ends and you rush back to your middle-class neighborhoods [pp. 1–4].

This paradox of good intentions yielding harmful outcomes is further explored in Anne Fadiman's *The Spirit Catches You and You Fall Down: A Hmong Child, Her American Doctors, and the Collision of Two Cultures* (1997). An investigation of a true story, the book explores the treatment of Lia Lee, a young Hmong girl with epilepsy, by her Hmong parents and her American doctors. Although the child's parents did not want their daughter to suffer any pain during her epileptic seizures, they did not want her to be "cured" of the disease—as the Hmong believe people with epilepsy are closer to divinity, and consequently these individuals hold an exalted status in the community. Lia's American doctors, however, believed the severity of her seizures would result in long-term brain damage, and they wanted to treat her with medication. As the clash of views and cultures played out, the outcome for Lia was tragic, despite the good intentions on both sides. As Reich sees it: "The virtue of the book is that it portrays the motives, intentions, and actions of everyone involved—the parents, the community organizations, the doctors, the hospital administrators—from a sympathetic point of view. There's no villain in the book, yet the outcome is tragic."

Both Illich and Fadiman make clear to students that good intentions alone do not ensure a good outcome, that cultural differences can be too great to bridge, and that well-intentioned people can sometimes unknowingly do harm when they try to help. Readings like these might lead to a classroom full of disheartened moral relativists who have come to see community or public service as an irresponsible endeavor fraught with insurmountable perils. But these readings are only the beginning of the conversation, not the final word. Through the use of further readings, classroom discussions, and written assignments, Reich attempts to move students to a place where they are conscientious but also able to "embrace the ambiguity" that is inherent in public service. Ultimately, he wants students to see themselves as intentional, reflective service providers—even "interventionists":

I use [these readings] as a way to talk to about cultural differences in doing service work and to talk about good intentions. One lesson I try to draw out of [Fadiman's] book is what it would mean to be a cultural broker or interpreter and what kind of preparation or knowledge one needs to play that role. . . . Is [the students' role] as a service

provider or service agent simply to forward the interests of the organization they're working with, however they see it, or can you can be
interventionist and attempt to show [misguided individuals in the orga-
nization], tell them, explain to them, come into dialogue with them,
to say why you think what they're doing is wrong or inappropriate or
ineffective.

Questions concerning moral relativism inevitably emanate from these
discussions. Reich uses strategic probing and challenges to confront students who take relativistic or dogmatic positions, drawing out the implications of both. With thoughtful and difficult questions, he tries to bring
these students to an appreciation of the plurality of moral values and the
ways values can conflict as they do in *The Spirit Catches You and You
Fall Down*:

> If students are pressing a line of, "Well, you've got to respect cultural
> beliefs," I'll press back with, "Does the state have an interest here?"
> Or if people are saying, "The parents are going to kill Lia—if they
> don't do anything about her epilepsy, she's going to have seizures and
> die," I'll press more about parental interests. Ultimately, what I'm most
> interested in is trying to get an appreciation of how both perspectives
> need to be considered and of how values can conflict in a particular
> case, as they do in this one.

Reich would like his students to be able to take multiple perspectives
on a given issue and to form reasoned positions in the face of difficult ethical dilemmas. He is quick to challenge students who try to avoid the hard
work of making moral judgments by simply saying, "Well, the Hmong
parents have their culture and I have mine, and they're entitled to raise
their kid the way they want."

PHASE 2: THE HISTORICAL AND SOCIOCULTURAL CONTEXTS OF SER-
VICE. Describing the second phase of Ethics and Politics, Reich says:

> The goal is really to give Stanford students an understanding about
> some of the local conditions. . . . So, if they do any volunteer service
> they have some concrete knowledge about the history of the univer-
> sity and the community. The goal is to prevent the stereotype of your
> average sophomore who shows up at Stanford and thinks, "Oh, it'd
> be great to do some service work." He goes over and signs up for ten
> hours of tutoring in East Palo Alto; logs in the ten hours and comes
> back home; and thinks he's struck some blow for goodness in the
> world simply by having spent ten hours [tutoring], completely unaware

of the rafts of Stanford students who have gone over there for twenty
or thirty years and the ill-will that might exist for good reason: the
sense in which these tiny, episodic kinds of service are the least effective ones in terms of establishing an ongoing relationship and a real
sense of connection between Stanford and East Palo Alto, not to mention that they are unlikely to provide meaningful help to the students.

Service learning does not happen in a vacuum, so this part of the course
helps students understand the local context as well as the difficulties they
may face as they attempt to negotiate between two different worlds.
Among other things, students read Chuck Carlson's *Bled Dry by the Cutting Edge: A Short History of Silicon Valley,* and the U.S. Department of
Housing and Urban Development report *Gentrification Forces in East Palo
Alto* in order to better understand Bay Area demographic and socioeconomic conditions. Work during this three-week period addresses questions about privilege and the ways that being a student at an elite university
can be a kind of stigma in the eyes of some who are less privileged. The
sense of their own privilege and the magnitude of the gulf between them
and the people they would like to help is paralyzing for some students. One
young woman described how active she was in high school (she started a
human rights club, for example, and worked with the Red Cross) but then
said that since coming to Stanford she has not been very involved in service. She described feeling paralyzed by the Stanford name and struggling
with what it means to come from such an elite community. Through discussions of cases and other course readings, Reich tries to help students see
how they can maintain a sense of humility and realism about the complicated politics of their local situation without succumbing to this paralysis.

PHASE 3: "PUSHING THE PEANUT FORWARD." In the last week of Ethics
and Politics, students reflect on what they have learned and look forward
to applying it. Service learning is highlighted, as students discuss its meaning, what one should know in order to be successful in service-learning
courses, and specific courses offered at Stanford. Many of the students
will go on to take these courses together, and Reich encourages them to
see each other as resources, not only for information but also for support.
The group talks about how to survive the "moral quicksand" of public
service. Even though service is fraught with difficult moral questions,
Reich does not want students to be immobilized by the ethical dilemmas
they will face. He tells them they must "embrace ambiguity" and advises
them "to strive for moral *decency* rather than moral *perfection*." In discussing pieces by Robert Coles, bell hooks, and Parker Palmer, students

acknowledge the importance of being reflective about their engagement and willing to accept (even seek) constructive criticism.

The course ends on an inspiring note as students discuss "Pushing the Peanut Forward," a chapter from Peter Singer's book (1998) on Henry Spira and the animal rights movement. Spira reminds students that "it's crucial to take a long-term perspective. . . . And when a particular initiative causes much frustration, I keep looking at the big picture while pushing obstacles out of the way. . . . It's like this guy from the *New York Times* asked me what I'd like my epitaph to be. I said, 'He pushed the peanut forward.' I try to move things on a little" (p. 198).

Integrating Community and Classroom: Internship Reflection

Effective service learning requires not only preparation before the field placement but also reflection and integration during and after it. The next course we consider follows a service experience, helping students extend and deepen their learning. Most service-learning courses are more condensed than this one, integrating academic learning with a service experience and reflection on that experience within the span of a semester or in a few cases an academic year. In Duke University's Service Opportunities in Leadership (SOL) Program, these basic elements are addressed in three phases that take a full year to complete. In the spring, students take a preparatory half-credit course, Civic Participation/Community Leadership, in which they participate in a service project and explore the ways in which values conflicts in local communities can affect civic participation and public policy.

After completing this course, students participate in the second phase—summer internships in which they work on projects for community-based organizations in the United States, Central America, or South Africa. About half the students choose to conduct optional service-learning research projects in conjunction with their internships. These research projects are designed collaboratively with the agency in which the students are working so that they address a real need and result in reports or other products that are genuinely useful to the agency. Research outcomes might take the form of survey data, documentary articles, oral history interviews, feasibility studies and business plans, or program manuals. Some recent project titles have been "Micro-Enterprise Development: Business, Job Creation, and Community Building in the New South Africa," "Child Care and Education: Barriers to Self-Sufficiency for Participants in the Supportive Housing Program," and "Tradeswomen's Stories, Tradeswomen's Lives: Oral Histories of Women in Blue Collar Trades." In addition to teaching valuable research skills, these projects can significantly strengthen students' sense of civic and political efficacy, because they serve such important functions for the agencies.

Following their summer internships, SOL students begin the third phase of the program, the one-semester full-credit course Integrating Community and Classroom: Internship Reflection. This seminar, taught by Alma Blount, a lecturer in Public Policy Studies, grapples with a number of issues, including some of the same ones Rob Reich addressed with Stanford students. Like many courses that attempt to foster long-term commitment to public service, this course takes up the question of how to support students' sense of efficacy when the outcomes of their work are sure to be mixed, so that students maintain resilience and hope rather than becoming cynical in the face of the realities of civic and political life. The course also builds on the students' summer field experiences, connecting them with deeper substantive knowledge and careful thought about the systemic dimensions of the social problems students confronted. The course allows students to place their service and research experiences in the context of related research and policy analysis and to deepen their commitment to civic participation.

Each week for seven weeks students read a diverse collection of texts around a different theme, writing a reflective essay each week that explores the ideas in the readings and their meaning in light of each student's field experiences and ideas and the students' questions about the theme. These essays are meant to be a cumulative investigation, laying the groundwork for a final essay on service leadership. Subgroups of students share essays each week so that preparation for class discussion involves not only doing the course reading and writing an essay but also at least skimming the essays of several other students. This practice builds community among the student groups, enriches the discussion, and stimulates discussion of course-related issues outside the classroom. The themes around which the readings and essays are organized are carefully designed to touch on key issues in developing and sustaining responsible engagement and commitment. They illustrate the interconnectedness of intellectual understanding and motivational factors such as cynicism versus hope, the values making up one's moral compass, and personal models of inspiration. The theme for Week 3, for example, is Facing Realities. Readings include selections from Paul Rogat Loeb's *Soul of a Citizen: Living with Conviction in a Cynical Time* (1999) and the same Ivan Illich essay ("To Hell with Good Intentions") that Reich uses. Later weeks focus on the themes Perspectives and Principles; Integrity, Congruence, and the Inner Work of Leadership; and Mentors, Models, and the Search for a Compass of Values, for which students read and write about the life of a Nobel Peace Prize winner.

In addition to this intensive reading, writing, and discussion, each student investigates an issue relating to the internship experience—thus pursuing problem-based, inquiry learning that builds directly on the summer field placements. Students also create portfolios based on the investigation, using research, reflections, and other resources to illuminate and focus the issue. Although these investigations and portfolios are individual projects, students have regular, structured opportunities for peer learning in connection with the projects. Each is assigned to a small group that meets regularly to discuss the ongoing social issue investigations, offering suggestions and feedback and helping plan presentations to the class. Then students spend the last seven weeks of the course learning from each other as they take turns presenting their research to the full group. Two elements in the social issue investigation are an interview with an admired practitioner in the student's field of interest and a memo laying out policy or action recommendations. The memo must grapple with questions like these: "What are the underlying structures or systems that need to change in order to make serious progress on this issue? Who are the key players that need to be involved in the change process? What social policy options do you see? Which option seems most viable? Where do you locate yourself in these proposed actions?"

Alma Blount continues to refine what she calls the *pedagogy of service leadership* that underlies not only the course but the full SOL experience. Among other things, she is working with others at Duke to articulate the parameters of community-based research as a teaching strategy and to assess its impact on students. This systematic reflection on the pedagogies represented in the program feeds back into ongoing course development and provides a basis for national conversations with faculty at other institutions who are doing related work.

Ancients and Moderns: Democratic Theory and Practice

Sequences that connect one or more courses with service experiences over the course of a year, or even longer in some cases, offer students a powerful set of experiences, but these extended sequences are the exception rather than the rule. Most faculty who teach for moral and civic development take on the challenge of preparing students, facilitating their service or other action projects, and helping them reflect and build on those experiences within a single semester. A political science course at Providence College illustrates how rich and demanding this kind of teaching and learning can be. Rick Battistoni, professor of political science, is clear about the goals of his political theory course, Ancients and Moderns: Democratic Theory and Practice. He expects students to develop a beginning understanding of democratic theory as represented in ancient Athens, eighteenth-century Europe and the United States, and the United States today, reading contemporaneous critics of democratic practices in each of these times and places as well as historical accounts and theoretical analyses. In addition to introducing important disciplinary concepts and other substantive content, the course is meant to create a set of lenses, or conceptual frames, through which the students can interpret their own experiences and contemporary social and political issues; to provide experience applying those lenses or modes of analysis; and to help students develop a more examined and systematic sense of their own convictions about democracy and their own role in it.

Battistoni uses a wide array of strategies to accomplish these goals. He gives lectures periodically to provide an overview for each new section of the course. The course also requires extensive reading and discussion, with texts as wide ranging as Plato's *Republic*, Jean-Jacques Rousseau's *On the Social Contract*, selected writings of Thomas Jefferson, and Amy Gutmann and Dennis Thompson's *Democracy and Disagreement*. Because many aspects of the course concern the active use of theory and the relation of theory and practice, Battistoni stimulates students to begin thinking about the meaning of theory even before the course begins by articulating some of the key ideas in the syllabus:

> The course is about democracy, but it is also about *theory* (and, as a result of theorizing, ultimately about practice). Political theory, simply stated, is reflective discourse on the meaning of the political, delving underneath the surface of political practice to ask questions and understand the meaning of politics. In ancient Greek usage, *theoria* was a journey taken by statesmen (yes, as we all know, women were excluded from public life) or citizens to other places and cultures. The person making this journey would go study other governments, cultures, customs, and practices, and report back to leaders of the homeland. The "theorist" was thus a person who was able to examine these other cultures and abstract from his own experiences more general understandings and standards of political behavior and action. These could then be applied in criticizing, justifying, or amending institutions and practices in the home community. In this sense, then, political theory is both a critical and a creative activity, for each generation

to participate in a continuous tradition. And in this sense, we are all
theorists. So, I want you to read about theories and practices of democracy in these three periods, but with a view to your own theorizing
about democracy.

The strategic use of simulations provides an experiential connection with
the democratic process. The course opens, for example, with a simulation
in which half the students are asked to design and act out a thoroughly
undemocratic classroom and the other half to design and act out a perfectly democratic classroom. Predictably, the undemocratic group creates
a form of dictatorial structure, and in the ensuing discussions students indicate that their representation not only draws on textual and other depic-
tions of illegitimate authority systems but also represents an extreme
version of their own experiences in school. Interestingly, the democratic
group presentations tend to depict "inefficiency, disorder, even anarchy and
chaos." In the discussions that follow the simulation, students in both
groups indicate their lack of experience with democracy, and many express
"their feeling that 'real' democracy is a nice idea, but utterly unrealistic,
and at some level, undesirable" (Battistoni, 2000, p. 2). This introductory
simulation uncovers on the first day of class some unexamined assumptions about democracy that might not have surfaced in a more general discussion of democracy.

As the course goes on, Battistoni uses a number of devices to bring democratic practices into the way the course operates. In a sense he makes the
hidden curriculum visible and intentional, making the "medium part of the
message." Research indicates that this kind of approach can be an important part of civic education. In fact an extensive review of the political
socialization literature concluded that the most positive contribution a
teacher at any level can make to the acquisition of democratic values is to
foster democratic practices in the classroom and that this form of pedagogy
was more important than any particular curricular component (Ehman,
1980). However, partly because this approach is so unfamiliar to students,
it is sometimes difficult to introduce. Battistoni found, for example, that he
and the students had to work through together what it would mean for the
students to have some input into their grades for class participation. In Battistoni's mind, class participation includes more than how much or how
well students speak in class:

> If we interpret democratic class participation to mean active engage-
> ment in the classroom, this includes not only giving voice to one's
> thoughts and opinions, but also what Langston Hughes once called
> "listen[ing] eloquently." It might also include preparation for class or

discussions between students about course material outside of class. . . .
To the extent that our definition of class participation includes things
beyond the vocalizations that the faculty member can evaluate, then
the student should have input, not only as a power-sharing arrangement but also because the student is the only one positioned to evaluate these other things [Battistoni, 2000, p. 6].

Throughout the course, students keep an ongoing *theory journal,* in
which they respond to questions posed by Battistoni or derived from class
discussions, using the readings and discussions to evolve their own theories of democracy. This writing involves the active interrogation of the assigned texts, analysis of the texts' meaning in a cumulative and recursive
way, and connection with a developing sense of what the students themselves believe. The journal writing, on which students receive regular evaluation and feedback from Battistoni, results in a document of seventy to
one hundred typed pages by the end of the course.

Finally, the students choose between two kinds of large course projects.
The most popular option is the Democratic Theory in Action Project. Students are then grouped by project, and each group is instructed to organize itself democratically (whatever this means for the group), then create
and implement some "democratic action." The nature of the action is up
to the group, but it must exemplify the democratic ideals and theories the
students have read about and discussed. The group submits a narrative
report that summarizes the action in light of democratic theory and also
chronicles the process followed by the group and the group's reflections
on that process in light of democratic theory and principles. In addition,
each individual writes a paper explicating his own conclusions about
democracy and democratic theory in light of the experience of carrying
out the project. For one recent democratic action project, students chose
to address a perceived lack of democracy on the Providence College campus and sought to increase student input into decision making. The group
organized a forum that brought together representatives from the college's
major institutions (faculty senate, student congress, student affairs, and
academic administration) to discuss student influence in decision making.

Alternatively, students can choose a more research-oriented option in
which they study an organization of their choice from the standpoint of
democratic theory, ideals, and values and their own understanding of what
is at stake with respect to the governance and operation of this organization.
Students are expected to spend a significant amount of time participating in
the work of the organization and interviewing key informants. The students
write a *Democratic Organizational Biography* based on this research, using

democratic theory to analyze the particular patterns exhibited in the chosen organization. One student studied the Providence College Student Congress, another examined the democratic governance (or lack thereof) of her church, and a third chose to compare the practices and ideals of the college's Political Science Department.

For Rick Battistoni, as for Alma Blount, pedagogy extends beyond the end of the course. Each year Battistoni critically examines this course, assessing the quality of student work and considering student evaluations and comments. This assessment has led to important modifications and continual strengthening of the course. When he first introduced the Democratic Organizational Biography project, for example, Battistoni provided a list of organizations to be studied, and he found both the process and outcomes of the projects to be disappointing. Students were not really engaged, and unless they had had previous contact with the organization they studied, they had no stake in the outcome of their findings. When he gave students another choice for a major project (the democratic action project), so that writing the organizational biography was optional, and allowed students to choose organizations that matched their own interests, student engagement and the quality of the outcomes improved dramatically.

In addition to adjusting his teaching strategies, Battistoni also connected his teaching more broadly with his scholarship and used his classroom experiences as one source for "rethink[ing] the relationship between democratic theory, democratic pedagogy, and undemocratic power relations as they manifest themselves in higher education" (Battistoni, 2000, p. 4). He has shared his reflections on teaching democratic theory and practice with colleagues by presenting papers about the work at meetings of the American Political Science Association and at other conferences.

Social and Environmental History of California

The courses we have considered so far are all directed primarily toward students who bring a preexisting interest in community service or politics. Courses that build on these interests and develop them further can help sustain these students' commitment and increase its effectiveness. But undergraduate education also has the potential to awaken an interest in social issues in students who have not experienced that interest before, helping these students begin to see that they can and want to contribute to something beyond their immediate personal sphere.

Gerald Shenk, associate professor of history, and David Takacs, associate professor of earth systems science and policy, take on this challenge in their course Social and Environmental History of California, at California State University, Monterey Bay (CSUMB). The course is geared toward juniors and seniors, particularly natural and behavioral science majors, many of whom enroll in order to satisfy the CSUMB learning requirements in the areas of Democratic Participation and U.S. Histories as well as the state requirements in U.S. and California history. This multi-disciplinary course looks at the way the geography of California has shaped the evolution of the state's diverse cultures and how the choices people made have shaped the physical landscape. In a way that is reminiscent of Rick Battistoni's aspirations regarding political theory, Shenk and Takacs hope students will learn not only about history but also about how to use historical analysis and knowledge to illuminate contemporary issues and to clarify what they believe in and are prepared to act on. Shenk and Takacs want students to understand themselves as "historical beings in relationship to each other and to the Earth" and to "come to see history as a tool they can use to understand and shape the world they live in." "Our primary goal," they say in their syllabus, "is for students to use what they learn in our class to become historically informed, self-aware, ethical participants in the civic lives of their communities."

Shenk and Takacs use a wide array of strategies to accomplish this, including reading assignments, periodic short lectures, discussions in which the forty students in the course frequently break into small groups and then come back together, journal writing, research on historical issues, and ambitious projects that include action in the community. "Every minute is precious," and Shenk and Takacs must make hard choices between content and process. Their answer to this dilemma has been to teach for thematic understanding, usable skills, and personal growth rather than mastery of large bodies of content knowledge.

The centerpiece of the course is the Historically Informed Political Project (HIPP). Constituting 75 percent of students' final grade, the HIPP brings together history, ecology, personal values, and political action. Projects must address a California issue that has both environmental and social dimensions. Students conduct historical research as background to the project, articulate the values and assumptions they bring to it, and reflect on how those values and assumptions have changed as a result of engaging in the project. The project must involve at least ten hours of community work and lead to a set of policy recommendations informed by the historical research and community experience. Students can choose to work together on a joint project or do their work independently, but even those doing individual projects have many opportunities to work through with others the questions their projects raise. By centering on the HIPP, the course takes advantage of the pedagogical strengths of multidisciplinary, project-based, collaborative, and service learning. These projects are extremely challenging for students. CSUMB students are accustomed to doing service-related projects and reflecting on that service, but the HIPP demands in-depth historical research and extensive analysis, synthesis, and evaluation. Students must place their political projects in a larger social and environmental context and make policy recommendations based on what they learn through their research and political action.

WHAT IS POLITICS? Because they recognize how difficult the projects are, Shenk and Takacs organize course readings and activities to help students construct them one step at a time. The first important milestone in doing a HIPP is defining politics. Students write a one-page thought piece on the following questions: "What is politics?" "What counts as politics for you?" "Do you ever act politically?" This seemingly simple task initially proves more a stumbling block than a cornerstone in constructing a HIPP, because most of the students begin the course uninterested in or disgusted by politics. With few exceptions, students in the course describe politics in negative terms: for example, "a corrupt system driven by people pursuing their own self-interest." Few students have any desire to become politically active. As one student put it: "I don't do anything political because I see anyone who makes a living at doing politics, usually one in government or in a position of power, as a little kid who is just squabbling over getting more money or more power. I do not want to be any way a part of that mess . . . so I don't do anything."

In an effort to broaden and reframe the meaning of politics by connecting it with things the students do care about, Shenk and Takacs ask students to consider the 1960s slogan: "The personal is political." They suggest to students that "virtually everything you do has some kind of impact on others"—from the way you get to class to the toilet paper you buy. To illustrate this point, Shenk and Takacs have students read Frank Bardacke's *Good Liberals and Great Blue Herons* (1994) and then take them to the nearby town of Watsonville to meet with Bardacke and discuss his life and political commitments. A veteran of the civil rights, free speech, and antiwar movements of the 1960s, Bardacke's recent efforts have focused on land use and labor issues in Watsonville. Referring to an exchange that speaks to the perennial challenge of maintaining stamina in the face of hard political realities, Takacs recalls with fondness Bardacke's response to a student who asked how many of his political battles he has actually won. "I have never won," he answered. "Well," she replied, "then how can you go on?" His answer: "You have to find joy in the struggle." In this, he echoes our comment in Chapter Four that part of what students need to sustain a sense of efficacy is a love of the game.

The idea that politics can be defined more broadly than students initially thought and that many seemingly apolitical matters have political implications intrigues most students, and they come to enjoy discussing their conceptions of what counts as politics. In fact these discussions are among the most dynamic of the semester as students grapple with defining politics in ways that reflect their personal values and ask each other provocative questions: What forms of political participation are valid for you, and what aren't? What do you approve of others doing, and what don't you approve of? Is protesting or boycotting a valid a form of political participation? Is breaking the law?

CYCLES OF ACTION AND REFLECTION. Shenk and Takacs use the image of a triangle to help students think about the relationship between their definition of politics, their personal values, and the political action they would like to engage in for the HIPP. Students begin filling in the three points of this triangle and discussing them in class early in the course, and they repeat the exercise over and over as their historical and political understandings grow and their projects progress. This repeated exercise helps students learn to articulate, revise, and refine the values and other assumptions that inform their beliefs about their responsibilities as citizens, and allows them to see how the three points in the triangle connect to shape the political projects they are pursuing. The hope is that they will internalize habits of mind that involve careful reflection, followed by action, which is followed by a return to reflection on the action and possible changes in values and other assumptions as a result of the cycle of action and reflection.

As Shenk and Takacs describe it, the cycle consists of four steps: (1) reflection about oneself (that is, one's assumptions, beliefs, and values) in relation to one's world, in order to understand what is important to one; (2) exploration of various perspectives through study, research, and discussion with others on one or more of the issues identified as important; (3) action that is informed by one's understanding of oneself and by study, research, and discussion; and (4) further reflection about the whole process, and preparation to move through the cycle again.

Shenk and Takacs recognize the importance of students' practicing the skills and habits the course is intended to teach, so students engage in many cycles of action and reflection over the course of the semester. Although the HIPP itself can be viewed as one big cycle, it can also be seen as made up of several smaller cycles. For example, defining and redefining politics does not take place through a single discussion or journal entry. It begins with students setting out their own assumptions about politics. Then they read Bardacke's book, which "helps broaden students' conception of political work and gets them thinking about how they might act politically in the world in a way that is consistent with their values." Following those discussions, students begin to design a HIPP and contemplate taking action that reflects their current conceptions of politics. This leads to further reflection and a reexamination of the question of what politics is. The changes in understanding of and feelings toward politics can be striking for some students, although for others it is only the beginning of what Shenk and Takacs hope will be an ongoing broadening of perspective. As Shenk said: "I think all we can do is introduce the cycle to them. It clicks for some, and maybe for the others—in five, ten, or twenty years—it'll click. . . . A lot of students are not ready for this—they're not ready for deep introspection—and we can't require it. . . . You can't force it to be the deep kind of introspection you imagined people would go through that would cause great transformation."

The HIPPs for the year we visited focused on a wide range of topics, including improving the health of a river, establishing an alternative campus newspaper, and changing the logging practices of a major lumber company. A theme that emerged in several projects was the connection between economic booms (surrounding, for example, the gold rush, oil, aerospace, and, most recently, electronics and the Internet) and unforeseen environmental and social effects. Building on this theme and his longstanding love of surfing, one student, Charles Tilley, used his project to look at the extent to which natural surf breaks have been lost to development on the California coast near CSUMB. At a nearby beach in Santa Cruz, for example, the construction of a jetty has eroded the ocean floor that produced surfable waves. Tilley's project involved assessing the costs and likely effects of building an artificial reef at the site, which would improve the quality of waves. As he lobbied for the construction of the reef, Tilley learned a great deal about local and state laws and policies as well as relevant court cases elsewhere in California. The same theme—the unintended consequences of development—informed the HIPPs of three students whose collaborative project worked toward the passage of a local ballot initiative (Measure E) designed to control urban sprawl and its negative effects on the environment. These students identified a candidate (Bruce Delgado) who favored the initiative and who was running for a seat on the Marina City Council. Among other things, they created signs and went door-to-door campaigning for this initiative and this candidate.

On election day the students were delighted to learn that Measure E had been approved (54.2 percent of the vote) and that Delgado had won by seven votes.

It is noteworthy, however, that this project was the only one that tackled electoral politics. Although there is no doubt that the course helped students reconsider politics and find a way to think about politics that was consonant with their values, electoral politics was still viewed by most of them as "a real turn-off." In order to better understand this and other aspects of the course, Shenk and Takacs undertook a careful review of their teaching and the students' learning, which included systematic analysis of the HIPPs. They developed two taxonomies to describe the range of student outcomes, one consisting of ten ways in which students used history to inform their political projects, the other of eight ways in which students thought or acted politically. They found that students were able to use history in many different ways to inform their projects, including analyzing systems of power relationships, seeing themselves as both products of history and actors in history, and drawing parables or lessons from history. Students were most successful in identifying and using historical themes to inform their action projects. Analyses of the ways students thought and acted politically supported Takacs and Shenk's impression that students did develop politically in the course, even if many retained some of their skepticism toward electoral politics: "Our initial reading and subsequent analyses of the HIPPs confirms our impression that students did seem to become less afraid of politics, more sophisticated in their understanding of politics, more committed to political work, and more aware of the connections between themselves and their communities" (Takacs & Shenk, 2001, p. 6).

Building Moral and Civic Learning into the Curriculum

At California State University, Monterey Bay, graduation requirements press students who might otherwise not do so to take courses such as Social and Environmental History of California that broaden their perspectives on moral and civic issues. Takacs and Shenk's course thus highlights one of the central challenges of undergraduate moral and civic education—how to reach students who are not already inclined toward civic participation. CSUMB accomplished this by establishing a set of learning outcomes that all students must meet in order to graduate. Alverno and Tusculum Colleges also use variants of this outcomes-based or abilities-based approach. Other campuses we visited use different approaches. But all struggle with the same dilemmas: how to integrate moral and civic learning throughout the academic curriculum in ways that will strengthen both moral and civic learning and other aspects of intellectual and personal development, how to ensure that work in academic majors and electives as well as in general education will contribute to moral and civic development, and how to reach the widest possible group of students. In the next chapter, we describe a number of different designs for the undergraduate curriculum that represent a range of solutions to these dilemmas.

6

WEAVING MORAL AND CIVIC LEARNING INTO THE CURRICULUM

AMONG THE UNDERGRADUATES at every college and university are some who look for ways to contribute to something larger than themselves, who are inspired by moral ideals or passionate about social or political issues. They are primed to take advantage of the many ways a college education can deepen their convictions and bring them to a higher level of intellectual and practical sophistication and competence. Even so, not all of these students find their way to the right developmental experiences; for some the inspiration will fade during college, giving way to narrower, more self-interested concerns so their earlier passion becomes only a memory. Other students come to college less interested in questions of personal integrity or social responsibility. They may have done some volunteer work and found it discouraging or unexciting; they may find politics confusing or even repellent. In our view, reaching this group of students—awakening in them broader concerns and giving them a sense that they can grasp and contribute to the complicated realities of civic and political life—is at least as important as reaching those who are more immediately receptive.

Weaving moral and civic issues into the curriculum is schools' best hope of connecting with the hard-to-reach students and making sure that students already on an inspired path will not lose their way. Extracurricular life is rich with sites of moral and civic engagement. Its impact on students can be transformative. But on many campuses it is difficult or impossible to structure extracurricular programs that will touch all students. We talked in Chapter Three about the encompassing nature of campus cultures. Surely *they* reach everyone. But what is salient in the culture and the meaning it conveys are not determined solely by what is objectively "out there." The lenses through which students notice and interpret their cultural contexts are also critical to what is seen, and these lenses are shaped by many things, including the intellectual frameworks students develop through their coursework.

Even aside from its capacity to reach all students, the curriculum is central to educating college students as citizens because so many key dimensions of moral and civic maturity are fundamentally cognitive or intellectual—rooted in understanding, interpretation, and judgment. In fact, by drawing on a wide range of pedagogies, academic coursework can support not only the most clearly intellectual dimensions of moral and civic development but the full range of capacities and inclinations that make up moral and civic understanding, skills, motivation, and ultimately, action.

But to say that the curriculum *can* support moral and civic development is not to say that it usually does. In an essay on liberal education, Louis Menand (1997) commented that many curricula assume that "values, citizenship, and so on are the stuff that rubs off when students are busy learning other things" (p. 3). This assumption may be correct in some sense. Through the campus and wider cultures and the messages implicit in curricular and extracurricular experiences, some values and interpretations of human nature, morality, and social institutions may indeed rub off on students. The question is whether this inadvertent moral and civic socialization is teaching what thoughtful educators want students to learn. Too often undergraduate education also seems to assume that many of the higher-order intellectual capacities that are central to both liberal education and its moral and civic dimensions will somehow rub off. Many curricula fail to explicitly address widely acknowledged goals like judgment, integrative thinking, and facility in moving among multiple modes of inquiry. Observers of higher education have commented, for example, that in most curricula integrative learning happens only in students' heads, if at all (Anderson, 1997; Schneider & Schoenberg, 1998). Some students do make these connections, and some grow morally and civically by responding deeply to issues implicit in their courses. But more explicit attention to those goals will make moral and civic development a more reliable and widespread outcome of undergraduate education.

Unfortunately, curricular structures at most colleges and universities are not particularly well suited to the goals of moral and civic learning or of liberal education in general. The disciplinary focus and organization of the curriculum at most institutions means that courses are seldom designed to ensure the development of sophisticated cross-disciplinary capacities such as complex problem solving, integrative thinking, or judgment, all of which are central to moral and civic development. Because general education is most often organized around distribution requirements, with a wide range of courses that can fulfill these requirements, it does not usually represent a coherent or common core of undergraduate learning. As a result many students go through their entire undergraduate experience without encountering courses that speak directly to their moral and civic development. Furthermore, courses in different departments, and usually even within departments, are routinely taught in isolation from each other so that learning is not cumulative. This includes moral and civic learning, which at most institutions is sporadic at best—a service-learning course here, an ethics course there, or a teacher now and then who raises moral questions connected with her discipline. The fact that courses do not build on each other weakens their impact, because moral and civic development, like other complex learning, is best supported by multiple sources that contribute to the same goals and by clear connections among these different sources so that learning becomes cumulative.

It is not easy to structure the curriculum so that it draws all students into sustained and comprehensive moral and civic growth—but it can be done. We have seen successful efforts in all kinds of institutions, using many different curricular structures. All these institutions integrate moral and civic learning into their general education programs. In doing so they add vitality to general education at the same time that they support moral and civic growth. Most students, however, spend at least a third of their time in their majors, so schools are missing important opportunities for moral and civic learning when they restrict it to general education. Furthermore, in most disciplines, students' grasp of their major fields will be incomplete if they never grapple with the central moral issues and social implications inherent in the discipline. At many of our case study campuses and some others we learned about, moral and civic learning is threaded through the whole undergraduate curriculum, including both general education and the major. Learning of all sorts benefits when institutions treat undergraduate education as a whole rather than splitting it sharply between general and specialized or disciplinary learning. This does not mean that every course should address moral or civic themes, but it does mean that every student should have multiple experiences with these themes. The impact will be even greater when these multiple experiences are integrated and intentionally cumulative.

General Education

Almost all undergraduate curricula include some form of general education. Despite frequent laments that general education is not as highly valued as it should be, a recent survey of campuses in all Carnegie categories indicates that almost two-thirds report the general education curriculum has been a rising priority in the past ten years and only 2 percent have reported its decline. In the same survey, all institutions indicated that they were either currently engaged in a review of their general education program or had a review planned for the upcoming year (Ratliffe, Johnson, & La Nasa, 2001).

There is a significant degree of broad consensus among institutions and educators on the goals of general education, although particular programs reveal variations around these central tendencies (Stearns, 2001). In essence, general education represents a commitment to breadth in undergraduate education. It is designed to contribute to the wide range of knowledge and skills that are taken to represent the "educated person" and to provide a broad context for the specialized expertise students gain in the major. To achieve this, it seeks to endow students with some grounding in various disciplinary approaches and methodologies and an introduction to bodies of knowledge associated with different academic fields, especially in the liberal arts and sciences. It is expected to introduce students to the intellectual capacities needed for success in college, to provide experience with a range of options related to choosing a major, and at least in some configurations, to instill cross-cutting or higher-order skills and habits of mind, such as critical and independent thinking and both quantitative and verbal literacies.

The most common approach to general education is to impose *distribution requirements,* mandates that students must take one or two courses in a number of disciplinary categories (physical sciences, social sciences, literature, and so on). In another general education configuration, students are required to complete some form of shared core curriculum, which may include one or more particular courses or courses chosen from a limited set of specially designed alternatives. In yet another approach, some institutions achieve the goals of general education by requiring students to show evidence of certain competencies rather than requiring them to complete courses in prescribed categories, using models based on variants of outcomes-based or abilities-based education.

Most colleges and universities draw from several curricular models, combining them to create a configuration that is particular to that institution. Outcomes-based education, for example, is often combined with some distribution requirements or required courses. Required *core courses* are also frequently combined with distribution requirements. Some curricula with distribution requirements define some requisite categories in terms of outcomes (such as the ability to conduct an ethical analysis) and other categories in disciplinary terms.

Whatever their approach, general education programs face some common challenges, dilemmas, and tensions, all of which bear on the curriculum's capacity to support moral and civic growth: how to weigh the value of a common experience against the advantages of connecting with students' particular interests and needs; if the curriculum is to include a common experience, how to determine its content and approach; how to make general education extensive enough to accomplish its goals without encroaching on electives; how to shape the program around learning goals yet keep faculty engaged; how to make the coursework explicitly cumulative without creating so much structure that it conflicts with student choice. Answers to these dilemmas and challenges shape and constrain the means available for moral and civic education.

Distribution Requirements

The form of general education that is least conducive to systematic moral and civic education is, unfortunately, the most common curricular model—a highly decentralized system of distribution requirements. Because many courses meet these requirements, students shop around for classes, selecting according to their own personal tastes, which might mean courses that most interest them, courses that best fit their schedules, or courses they hope will require minimal effort. Much of what students learn is left to chance as they choose from a hodgepodge of diverse courses with no overall intellectual focus or integration.

If they explicitly address moral and civic learning at all, these curricula typically do so by requiring that students take a course in ethics. Sometimes this requirement is broad, and students can fill it with either an ethics or a religion course or with any philosophy or religion course. Required ethics courses can help students learn to articulate moral questions, assess competing claims, form and defend their own views, and engage in critical reflection and decision making. These are worthwhile goals, and many ethics courses do accomplish them. But unless specially designed to help students connect what they learn with their own lives and roles as citizens, these courses may provide little support for the development of usable moral and civic understanding and skills and are unlikely to influence the motivational dimensions of moral and civic development. In fact, in their most common form, they may even contribute to students' moral relativism and other confusions, as we discussed in Chapter Five.

If the requirement is defined more broadly, to include any course in religion or philosophy, it may not expose students to moral or civic issues at all. Courses in the philosophy of language or church history, for example, are unlikely to address moral and civic concerns. At one faith-based institution we visited, the required introductory theology course was generally taught as a historical review of church doctrine, with little discussion of how these doctrines reflected and shaped the church's worldview or their implications for the contemporary world and students' own lives. This was surprising because the institution views this course as a foundation for students' spiritual commitments and personal values. The problem, perhaps, is the assumption that this course automatically engages moral and spiritual issues, and therefore there is no attempt by faculty to provide a clear spiritual or moral focus for the course, nor does the department or institution provide guidelines suggesting this.

Distribution Requirements That Meet Explicit Criteria

Some institutions deal with just this kind of problem by establishing criteria courses must meet if they are to satisfy a requirement. Proposed courses are screened with reference to their intended learning goals and sometimes their pedagogies. Duke University's Curriculum 2000, for example, requires students to take two courses in Ethical Inquiry as part of its distribution requirements (see Chapter Three). In order for courses to qualify as Ethical Inquiry they must address some specific objectives (as we also described in Chapter Three): they must attempt to instill the capacity for discernment and choice about diverse systems of values and competing courses of action; a critical understanding of diverse meanings of justice, goodness, and virtue; and the capacity to articulate ethical questions, to assess competing claims and approaches to ethical thought, and to engage in careful and critical reflection about individual and social behavior, institutions, and ways of life. Ethical Inquiry courses must also do one or more of the following:

- Explore ethical arguments and beliefs in one or more cultures, religions, or philosophical, dramatic, or literary texts or traditions from a critical standpoint.

- Examine ethical and political issues and controversies in a particular historical, disciplinary, professional, or policy context.

- Combine coursework and service experiences with rigorous reflection and writing on ethical issues.

Explicit guidelines like these make the purposes of the requirement clearer to both students and faculty and establish a template for new courses built on a wide range of subject matter. Duke faculty design their own Ethical Inquiry courses, which are offered in nearly all departments, from African studies to biology to economics, and are approved by a committee. Committee reviews are rigorous, and in the year we visited, only 23 percent of the proposed courses were judged to meet the criteria. This approach encourages a strong mix of disciplinary as well as moral and civic content, helping students learn about ethical issues inherent in particular fields of knowledge.

Like many universities, Duke also requires all freshmen to take a course in writing. This kind of requirement, too, can be used as a site for moral and civic learning if careful attention is given to its structure and guidelines. To promote this, Duke developed a set of special sections that faculty can use to integrate the values and skills of discourse into their freshman writing courses. Beginning in 1997, Elizabeth Kiss, director of Duke's Kenan Institute of Ethics, and Van Hillard, director of the First-Year Writing Program, began working together to infuse deliberative ideals and values into the writing courses. They were concerned about some common weaknesses in students' writing, including "crossfire style debate" (a failure to acknowledge nuances and complexities of issues and a tendency to trivialize opposing arguments), "avoiding discernment" (a failure to examine issues in depth and a tendency to rush to unearned conclusions), and avoiding engagement with moral disagreement. Kiss and Hillard believed that teaching "the art of deliberation" would not only contribute to students' moral and civic development, it would dramatically improve their writing. They accomplished this by structuring some sections of the writing course around the idea of "disagreement, deliberation, and community." The project has grown tremendously in the past few years. During its first year, the project included only 12 of the 120 sections of the writing course, and only one theme, race, was used to anchor course writings and discussions. Three years later, 83 sections offered a moral and civic focus, and they were structured around six issues (taught in different strands): public health, race, technology and privacy, crime, environmentalism, and celebrity culture.

We mentioned in Chapter Two that even in colleges and universities with very loosely structured general education programs, students tend to choose from the same rather limited range of courses. As a result some courses predictably reach very large numbers of students, even when they are not required. Efforts to structure these courses to incorporate moral and civic learning would have a high payoff, reaching the great majority of students without restricting their freedom of choice. For example, many colleges and universities require students to take a mathematics course. For students who expect to major in fields that are not math intensive, this can often lead to disengagement, raising the question, Why do I need to know this? Mathematics with a civic focus may be especially effective for stimulating an interest in math among students like these. In one such course, Peter Alexander, a math professor at Heritage College, teaches probability theory and other modes of mathematical analysis in social contexts. His course, Math and Social Justice, prepares students to evaluate the significance of the numbers they see attached to every aspect of U.S. society, helping them gain a deep understanding of the media's use of numbers by looking at statistical accuracy, significance, and societal implications.

Core Curricula

Some colleges and universities have moved away from the distribution model by creating a framework for general education that establishes a well defined set of goals and a program of courses specially designed to educate toward those goals. The purpose is sometimes to impart a canonical body of knowledge, but more often it is to expose students to multiple modes of thought or to accomplish some cross-cutting learning goals. Such core curricula, especially when they are extensive, require a great degree of administrative and faculty cooperation and buy-in. They require more coordination across departments, faculty development, planning, and oversight than general education that relies on distribution requirements. Efforts to establish core curricula can also run up against turf battles and faculty members' desires to protect departmental budgets and personnel. Even so, some institutions find the trade-offs worthwhile because of the value of core curricula for students.

Core curricula can be extensive or consist of only one or two courses. They can mandate one or more particular courses for all students or provide students with choices from a prescribed category (for example, freshman seminar or senior capstone courses). We have seen examples of successful integration of moral and civic learning in all varieties of core curricula.

The central advantage of requiring one or more particular courses is that it gives the entire student body a genuinely shared learning experience. This experience can increase the sense of community on campus, and because all students participate, it can establish a good basis for links between the curriculum and extracurricular activities such as public speaker series or residence hall programs. This may be more feasible for small institutions, and in fact small schools are more likely to adopt this approach.

Requiring students to take and faculty to teach particular courses can result in complaints from both, so this approach requires a strong rationale justifying the need for students to learn that particular content. Historically, proponents of required courses, which were often Western civilization courses, argued that they embody both content and principles that any educated person ought to know. Now colleges are more likely to justify the courses with reference to the value of a shared experience or their relevance to particularities of the school's mission and history. For this reason, required core courses almost always clearly reflect the institution's distinctive definition of moral and civic responsibility, as we described these definitions in Chapter Three.

Like core curricula that offer choices, core curricula that include required courses vary in scope, but because they limit student and faculty choices, it is rare for them to be very extensive. A more common practice is to provide a number of choices within each category of required core courses. The alternatives are designed to be parallel, embodying the same general goals, though pursuing these goals through varied subject matter. This approach has the distinct advantage that students can choose courses in which they have a special interest. Equally important is that this approach allows faculty to create courses that engage their enthusiasm rather than requiring them to teach courses they have not designed themselves. The key to making sure these courses support moral and civic development or other particular goals is to specify the course guidelines clearly and carefully review course proposals.

Comprehensive Core Curricula

It was once common for colleges to have extensive core curricula, and those programs typically incorporated moral and civic themes. Although this approach to general education is now unusual, some contemporary institutions do have comprehensive core curricula that pay sustained attention to students' moral and civic development. This was the case in two of our case study schools—Portland State University and Tusculum College. It is noteworthy that both these curricula arose out of institutional need, even crisis in the case of Tusculum, as we described in Chapter Three. The adoption of a core curriculum as extensive as that at Tusculum may seem a rather high-risk strategy, but both faculty and students there seem happy with the decision.

Tusculum's program, the Commons Curriculum, is unusual in that it is a comprehensive core curriculum composed of particular required courses. Students are not offered multiple alternatives because the Commons Curriculum is intended to provide intellectual common ground and create a community by involving all students and most of the faculty in a shared experience. The curriculum focuses centrally on issues of citizenship, skills of reflection and deliberation, and ethical decision making as well as other academic skills and substance. This core curriculum, which is combined with outcomes-based education, includes ten required courses. All new students arriving at Tusculum take Our Lives in Community, in which they explore and experience their roles as citizens in their local communities, in part through a service project and extensive writing. The core curriculum also includes a two-part history course, The People Shall Judge, which examines the evolving meaning of self-government and citizenship in the United States from the first settlements in North America to the present. Athens to Philadelphia, another required course, asks students to explore how Greek and Roman ideas of self-governance and democracy were taken up and reworked by Enlightenment thinkers and ultimately by the authors of the U.S. Constitution.

Portland State's University Studies program also tracks students through all four years of college, requiring students to complete at least one course and sometimes several from the program each year. University Studies integrates goals such as communication and critical thinking with a strong emphasis on moral and civic learning. A central goal throughout the program is to help students develop ethical and social responsibility and community connections in the context of interdisciplinary courses that also foster the capacity for integration. The program offers students choices at each stage, and also ensures that the courses in each category share a common design and goals. All courses must meet an established set of criteria and are reviewed by a committee before they are adopted.

The program begins with Freshman Inquiry, a yearlong, interdisciplinary course that is required for all students. The alternative offerings for Freshman Inquiry are developed and taught by interdisciplinary faculty teams, and their content varies widely. An example illustrates the way that substantive material from a number of disciplines; a wide range of academic skills; and moral and civic understanding, skills, and motivations are integrated in these first-year courses. The Columbia Basin: Watershed of the Great Northwest, draws from economics, water resource management, forest ecology, native wildlife populations, environmental concerns, local art and literature, and Native American heritage. These diverse topics are explored from an informed citizen's perspective to build a holistic understanding of the Columbia River and its continued influence on the region's social and biological ecology. If this set of issues does not interest them, students can choose from a number of other courses, including Embracing Einstein's Universe: Language, Culture, and Relativity and The City: Visions and Realities.

The second phase of University Studies is Sophomore Inquiry, in which students select one lower-level course from each of three interdisciplinary *clusters*. These courses are designed to introduce students to research and perspectives that are central to each cluster and that serve as gateways to more advanced work in related disciplines. In the junior year, students choose three courses from a single upper-division cluster that is linked with their majors.

The final requirement is a senior capstone that involves interdisciplinary student teams in work on in-depth community-based projects, usually over two quarters. These projects provide students with opportunities to apply, in a team context, both the academic and moral and civic learning from their majors and other University Studies courses to a real challenge emanating from the Portland community. For example, students in a capstone course on refugees and immigrants learn about the diverse immigrant populations of the Pacific Northwest; study the historic, legal, and political aspects of U.S. immigration policy; and learn about current challenges to assimilation. In one community-based project, students created a newsletter for the Refugee and Immigrant Consortium.

Required Courses

A much more common pattern than the comprehensive core curriculum such as we saw at Portland State and Tusculum is the more modest core curriculum that requires all students to take from one to three designated courses, usually along with other courses as prescribed by distribution requirements. Most popular among these courses are freshman seminars, Western civilization or great books courses (which are often offered in the freshman year as a variant of the freshman seminar), and senior capstone courses. As with comprehensive core curricula, these more limited cores may require the same particular courses for all students or may offer choices among parallel courses structured around different content. Although freshman seminars, great books and Western civilization courses, senior capstones, and other core courses are all ideally suited to incorporate moral and civic learning, many do not take advantage of this opportunity. Nevertheless, at our case study institutions and elsewhere we saw many engaging and intellectually demanding core courses that do centrally address moral and civic issues.

Freshman seminars can be inspiring and memorable introductions to the intellectual life of college, providing a moral and civic frame that sensitizes students from the outset to connections between their classroom learning and larger moral, civic, and political questions. Some (though by no means all) colleges and universities with academic freshman seminars capitalize on this opportunity by focusing the seminars on social or ethical issues, cultural diversity, leadership, or the history and purposes of higher education or the institution (Barefoot & Fidler, 1996, pp. 13–16). These courses almost always use the format of a small discussion seminar, allowing students to engage deeply with concepts and to develop perspectives from which to think about and debate difficult issues.

Frequently, freshman seminars are designed as inquiries into influential books and ideas of Western (and, increasingly, world) civilizations or as explorations of the various modes of knowledge and methods of inquiry found in different disciplines. Like other freshman seminars, these courses are designed to provide an intellectual foundation for college life, introduce the goals and ideals of liberal arts education, and link intellectual issues to various disciplinary perspectives and methodological approaches. The subject matter of great books and Western civilization courses naturally raises age-old questions about human existence—the nature of humanity, heroism, friendship, truth, justice, the soul—that also have great relevance for contemporary life. Some great books courses use these themes to highlight the moral and civic issues inherent in the material.

Capstone courses or senior seminars are currently offered at about one in twenty U.S. colleges and universities and are growing in popularity as a means for enriching the senior year (Henscheid, 2000). Like the purposes of freshman seminars, the purposes of senior capstones and seminars differ from one institution, and even one department, to another. Capstones are comprehensive, summative courses that synthesize learning within a major or across disciplines, sometimes offering opportunities for advanced work in the major or attempting to bring coherence to the academic experience by linking the major to general liberal arts learning. Capstones often require final projects, theses, research projects, recitals, or internships, and some institutions offer a final seminar that extends the major into the real world via a field experience, practicum, internship, or community project. More often than not, however, capstones are missed opportunities for integrating learning across disciplines and incorporating moral and civic learning. Those within the major, for example, are often treated as preparation for graduate study rather than as an opportunity for integration. Even so, we learned of many that help students see how they can use what they have learned in college to contribute to something beyond themselves.

COMMON REQUIRED COURSES. Most colleges are reluctant to require more than one or two common courses. A typical pattern is to require both a freshman course and a capstone or other senior year course. At the College of St. Catherine, for example, the core consists of the interdisciplinary bookend courses we introduced in Chapter Three: The Reflective Woman, a first-year course, and The Global Search for Justice, a senior capstone. All St. Kate's students take these courses, including transfer, returning, and weekend college students, thus receiving a shared introduction to issues central to the college's mission, in essence its distinctive definition of moral and civic responsibility, which centers on feminism and the Catholic social justice tradition.

The Reflective Woman helps students draw from several moral, spiritual, and intellectual traditions to create frameworks for thinking about their lives. Its thematic sections address aesthetics, the search for truth, the individual, and the person in the constellation of communities. The course requires participation in structured controversies (as discussed in Chapter Five), a reflective journal, and several papers and other writing exercises. In connection with this course, students must also attend the college's Core Convocations, a series of public lectures and creative events that link the core's themes of social justice and diversity with the arts and life beyond the campus. Recent speakers have included Sister Helen Prejean, author of the book *Dead Man Walking,* who works with death row inmates, and Dennis Halliday, former U.S. undersecretary of state for the Middle East.

St. Kate's multidisciplinary senior seminar, The Global Search for Justice, helps prepare students for meaningful work and the pursuit of systemic social change after college. Faculty teaching the course work together in five-person interdisciplinary teams, creating a shared syllabus around three organizing topics: the Catholic social justice tradition, feminist perspectives, and non-Western, global, or multicultural perspectives. Topics for recent sections included women and work, immigration, the environment, and voices of dissent. Although the syllabus is shared by all sections of the course, some activities vary across sections. One section takes students to Mexico, where they spend two weeks learning Mexican political, social, and economic history, followed by two weeks of doing manual labor together with families in the rural hillsides. A special summer section, Overground Railroad, brings together students and faculty from six colleges to travel to Underground Railroad and civil rights sites in the American south. Students study the emancipation and civil rights movements, meet people involved in the civil rights movement, and consider how strategies from these movements, such as community-based leadership and nonviolent conflict resolution, can be applicable today.

Spelman College also relies on an interdisciplinary, designated course curriculum to provide an overall framework for students' learning and for their college experiences beyond the classroom. Like required courses at

St. Kate's, those at Spelman clearly reveal the college's distinctive mission and conception of moral and civic responsibility. Spelman's core also combines curricular and cocurricular components, but it focuses on students' first two years of college, in contrast to St. Kate's' bookend approach. Spelman's combined curricular-cocurricular core consists of a full-year, one-credit freshman orientation program (described in Chapter Eight); a yearlong, interdisciplinary, writing-intensive first-year course, The African Diaspora and the World; and a full-year sophomore assembly program. All components center around the theme of black women as world citizens, with the first year focusing primarily on historical, social, and economic issues and the second year focusing on empowerment and culture.

The African Diaspora and the World is designed to help students understand the African diaspora from historical, cultural, philosophic, artistic, and scientific perspectives. The course provides a common intellectual experience relating to the college's mission, helps students develop a sense of community, and introduces them to some intellectual, moral, and civic values central to Spelman's mission—"sisterhood, leadership, a love of learning, a sensitivity to cultural differences, the use of diverse methods of scholarly investigation, and the association between learning and social change." The first semester of the course investigates the political, economic, and social systems of the diaspora; the history of African and Native American societies, the emergence of colonialism, the slave trade, and the Enlightenment; and connections between cultural expression and political resistance in the United States, the Caribbean, and Latin America. The second semester focuses on the aftermath of slavery in political, cultural, and economic terms, including a consideration of Marxism, the industrial revolution, African independence movements, social upheavals in the Caribbean and Latin America, and the U.S. civil rights movement. Students complete at least four writing assignments each semester, including a research paper at the end of the course. They are also required to participate in group projects involving class presentations during both semesters.

Linked to these classroom assignments is a set of cocurricular *common presentations* that include a freshman convocation speaker series and an Africana film series. The common presentations range from explorations of traditional and modern African and African diaspora art and literature to films on topics such as the Harlem Renaissance to studies of historical and contemporary social, economic, and political issues. All freshmen and sophomores are required to attend at least two commons and freshman convocation programs and at least two films each semester as part of the core program, but many students, including a large share of upper-class students, choose to attend most of them.

Another college that requires both a freshman and a senior year course is Eckerd College in Tampa, Florida. At Eckerd, all first-year students take a two-course sequence called Western Heritage in a Global Context. Each year the faculty who teach the course help select the texts, which must be "classic and enduring" in some way and must include a mix of traditional Western sources and nontraditional and non-Western sources. The course addresses such themes as heroes and journeys; justice, truth, science and nature in the ancient world; power; freedom; and the sacred. Students explore the theme of power, for example, by reading works that portray different uses, perceptions, and contexts of power: *The Prince; King Lear; Chushingura: The Treasury of Loyal Retainers; A World of Art,* by Dorothy Sayre; and Elie Wiesel's *Night.* Each course segment is designed to foster cross-cultural conversation and understanding, so the unit on the sacred includes readings from the Bible; the Qu'ran; the Tao Te Ching; *The Buddhist Tradition in India, China, and Japan;* and Dante's *Inferno.* All students in the course complete action projects. They work in groups on projects that are meant to lead to personal growth and contribute to the local community. At the end of the year, students present their projects to each other in the campuswide Festival of Hope. Eckerd's senior capstone, Quest for Meaning, returns to the theme of social action, with students reading texts that examine various conceptions of value, meaning, and action, such as Václav Havel's "A Sense of the Transcendent" and Martin Luther King Jr.'s "Letter from Birmingham Jail."

Other colleges require only a common freshman seminar. All first-year students at Lewis and Clark College, for example, take a yearlong course, Inventing America, that engages students and faculty in sustained conversation about citizenship, justice, equality, freedom, authority, and related issues. The course asks students to consider how the core ideas, values, and conflicts that animated the founding and development of America can help them define their place in a rapidly changing world. The first semester focuses on the competing ideas, values, and interests behind the American founding, drawing on political, constitutional, and economic history and philosophy. The second semester explores the ideas and practices of "the American experiment," in part by focusing on the struggles of groups such as women, Native Americans, and African Americans to achieve equality, citizenship, and cultural recognition.

REQUIRED COURSES WITH ALTERNATIVE CONTENT. Many colleges that require students to take freshman seminars, capstones, or other core courses offer a wide range of choices. At some colleges virtually none of the offerings include a moral or civic focus; at others students can choose from a pool of courses in which some address moral and civic issues and others do not. Only a few institutions build moral and civic issues into all the alternatives. One of these is Gustavus Adolphus College, a Lutheran college in Minnesota.

Gustavus Adolphus requires students to take a First Term Seminar (FTS), which links disciplinary learning with larger issues of values and ethics by "encourag[ing] students to reflect on the values inherent in a particular body of knowledge, to recognize the social, moral, and ethical implications of that knowledge, and to move toward intellectual, emotional, and relational commitments" (E. Carlson, personal communication, October 12, 1998). Each fall more than sixty tenured and tenure track faculty from nearly every department teach between thirty-five and forty First Term Seminars on a wide range of topics. One recent FTS in the social sciences, AIDS: The Modern Plague, examined the AIDS epidemic and how society and individuals have responded to it. Although FTS faculty design their own seminars and choose their own topics, all must meet a common set of criteria in order to be approved by the FTS director and Curriculum Committee.

Outcomes-Based Education

Out of the conviction that what really matters in a college education is not the courses students take but what they learn, a number of colleges and universities have developed curricula that are organized around the achievement of certain outcomes or competencies. Rather than requiring students to complete a requisite number of credit hours in a particular set of disciplines, outcomes-based curricula require students to master certain skills and abilities (or *learning outcomes*) such as written and verbal communication and analytical and critical thinking. At many institutions that take this approach the required learning outcomes include moral and civic skills and capacities, such as various aspects of citizenship; social, civic, and global knowledge; self-knowledge; reflective judgment; and ethical reasoning.

In outcomes-based education the required abilities are meant to be explicit in the minds of both students and faculty, and ideally students receive regular feedback on their progress toward the outcomes and systematically work to attain mastery of them. In practice learning outcomes are frequently structured like distribution requirements: students demonstrate their achievement of required outcomes by completing courses that include those outcomes among their objectives. Faculty design courses with particular outcomes in mind and must justify to an oversight committee the relevance to the outcomes of the course syllabus and pedagogies, including assessments. In many programs, courses and course procedures for student assessment are designed so that students can do well only if they demonstrate the outcomes the course has been designed to satisfy. A handful of schools, including the leader in this approach—Alverno College—require students to demonstrate mastery of outcomes outside the context of any particular course, through portfolios of student work, presentations, and other assessed performances. Like core curricula, outcomes-based curricula often have greater coherence and more faculty participation in curriculum planning than do more decentralized curricular models.

Curricular approach did not enter into our choice of the twelve case study schools, and we were surprised to learn how many use some form of outcomes-based education. Alverno; California State University, Monterey Bay; Kapi'olani Community College; Tusculum College; and the United States Air Force Academy clearly rely on variants of the outcomes-based approach, often combined with core courses or distribution requirements. Several of the other seven define some of their distribution requirements around abilities rather than particular courses, illustrating how the lines between curricular approaches can sometimes blur. Duke's requirement that students take courses that foster ethical inquiry, rather than courses in ethics, is a case in point. Messiah College similarly defines some of its distribution requirements around abilities. In all these institutions the required competencies prominently include aspects of moral and civic responsibility, variously defined. In Chapter Three, we described some of these and noted their convergences.

Alverno College represents the archetype of an outcomes-based approach (or abilities-based approach, as Alverno faculty call it). Students are required to demonstrate mastery of eight abilities through their coursework, portfolios, and performances for internal and external reviewers. Four of the eight represent aspects of moral and civic learning—Valuing in Decision Making, Social Interaction, Global Perspective, and Effective Citizenship. Alverno's Effective Citizenship requirement, for example, calls for students to take these actions: "Be involved and responsible in the community. Act with an informed awareness of contemporary issues and their historical contexts. Develop leadership abilities" (Prospective Students: Alverno's Eight Abilities. Retrieved on September 27, 2002, from http://www.alverno.edu/prospective_stu/eight_abilities.html). Like many undergraduates, new Alverno students are drawn more to personal aspects of citizenship, such as being a good neighbor and following the laws, than to community participation or political engagement. The Effective Citizenship requirement helps students gain a broader view of citizenship— to view "active citizenship as something you 'just do,' or as a habit of the heart," as President Joel Read put it (personal communication, November 4, 1999). In order to demonstrate achievement of this ability, students must exhibit a number of skills, including the capacity to draw on their disciplinary learning to make sound judgments about community issues; to participate effectively in group decision making; and to "read" an organization's structure, resources, and strategies for the achievement of a common goal.

The two main ways Alverno students learn skills related to Effective Citizenship are internships and a required course that addresses a political or policy issue, such as human rights or water use, from the point of view of the globalization of the world's political and economic systems. But Alverno does not assume that abilities such as Effective Citizenship will necessarily be located in particular required courses or other predefined experience. Much civic learning takes place through dispersed, cumulative experiences and assignments in various courses rather than in a few that focus directly on that outcome. One student explained that many courses engage students in projects involving local issues, so students often seek out and talk to community members and leaders, both to understand the issues and to learn processes of change. Another commented that the goal of Effective Citizenship runs through most Alverno courses but is usually implied rather than explicit, so that only when students are far along in their education can they look back and see connections and begin to understand how thoroughly that goal is infused in the curriculum.

Kapi‘olani Community College uses a somewhat different approach to ensure that students meet the competencies around which the curriculum is organized. For example, in Kapi‘olani's General College Competencies program, Understanding Self and Community is identified as an outcome that students in every degree program must achieve. Kapi‘olani faculty submit courses for approval to a curriculum committee, and course proposals must show how they will meet collegewide competencies, but there is no requirement that every course must meet every competency or that any given course must include particular competencies. As a result, faculty have leeway to select emphases that best fit their course content and teaching goals. The Kapi‘olani faculty take very seriously the mandate to build these competencies into their courses: Some elements of the Understanding Self and Community requirement were evident in virtually all of the classes we visited, from Asian Philosophy to American Politics to Nursing, and faculty were very clear about how the course supported the development of the competency and how the course assessments evaluated progress toward it.

One of the courses we described in Chapter Five, David Takacs and Gerald Shenk's Social and Environmental History of California, illustrates the way outcomes can be represented in coursework. At California State University, Monterey Bay (CSUMB), the curricula for general education and for the majors employ specified learning outcomes, and Social and Environmental History of California partially fulfills two of these requirements, Democratic Participation and U.S. Histories. Takacs and Shenk plan the course with these outcomes in mind. The U.S. Histories university learning requirement specifies four outcomes—historical understanding, critical thinking, historical research methods, and historical writing, all of which are integral parts of the major project in the course, the Historically Informed Political Project (HIPP). There are five outcomes connected with the Democratic Participation requirement, four of which concern content covered by this and several other courses. The fifth outcome requires students to "understand and be able to use tools of political action in a political project . . . and reflect on the values and assumptions that inform their political participation" (University Learning Requirements: Democratic Participation. Retrieved on September 27, 2002, from http://www.csumb.edu/academic/ulr/ulr/democratic. html). Clearly the HIPPs and many of the steps leading to them address this outcome directly.

The Major

Although general education is a natural home for many of the cross-cutting and integrative capacities of liberal education, including moral and civic development, it is a mistake to think these learning goals can be fully accomplished there. It is equally important to weave moral and civic learning into the disciplines and into the majors, whether disciplinary or not. Drawing out these disciplinary links is crucial because disciplines and academic majors are the primary focus of undergraduate education. Students define themselves to a great extent through their majors, and it is through the major that they are most likely to explore directions for their vocational futures. Majors and departments also offer students communities of interest and close relationships with their peers and with faculty.

Likewise, disciplinary identity and departmental allegiances are definitive for most faculty. For this reason, departments and disciplines are important leverage points for promoting moral and civic education. Academic departments participate in institutional policy decisions and determine how university-wide policy decisions are implemented at the departmental level. As powerful as departments are for faculty, disciplinary identification may be even more important. For this reason, if an agenda for integrating moral and civic learning into the curriculum is to succeed, it needs widespread support not only from faculty within their departments but also from the disciplinary organizations that shape the direction of the field and determine the kind of work that is seen as legitimate or valuable. Achieving this support requires discussion both at the national level and within campus departments about what it means to address moral and civic learning in specific disciplinary contexts.

Although most academic fields do not presently consider moral and civic education central to their mandate (Association of American Colleges, 1990; Diamond & Adam, 1995), there are signs of change. Prominent scholars and leaders in some organizations, such as the American Political Science Association (1998), for example, have begun asserting the need for greater attention to civic and political education in colleges and universities, urging faculty to bring these topics into their teaching and research agendas. In a similar vein, an American Psychological Association report on undergraduate education recommended that majors include service learning. Similar recommendations for a greater commitment to service and social engagement are included in recent statements of several other disciplinary associations, including those for sociology, economics, history, and philosophy (Association of American Colleges, 1990). Sometimes these calls for more attention to moral and civic concerns in teaching and research are connected with debates about whether a field has lost contact with issues of real concern and influence—issues of "relevance"—not only for students but for the larger society. Alexander Nehamas (1997) is not alone in suggesting that the field of philosophy, for example, needs to question the dominance of analytical philosophy and logical positivism and become a "more engaged and consequential enterprise of the sort envisioned by the American pragmatists as well as by most of the great figures in its history" (p. 241).

Some disciplines offer bodies of knowledge, theoretical approaches, and methodological tools that seem especially appropriate for educating citizens. Indeed, learning about economic systems, political institutions, ethics, historical processes and contexts, public policy, and a number of other areas seems integral to the full preparation of citizens. And courses in some of these disciplines are very popular choices as majors, distribution requirements, and electives. Institutions concerned about undergraduates' moral and civic development can accomplish a great deal by creating courses in these fields that are designed explicitly to foster that development. Without such efforts, there is no guarantee that courses in these fields will contribute to moral and civic learning, because specialized and largely technical or internal debates dominate learning in many fields of study.

Although some fields may seem to offer an especially natural fit, moral and civic learning can be integrated into every discipline in a way that will strengthen rather than distort disciplinary learning. This is not to say that moral and civic learning is a good fit with every course. Students need to gain facility with the moral and civic issues of their chosen disciplines, but this can be accomplished through some strong, strategically placed courses and need not be a focus for all their coursework. In order for these selected courses to have integrity, moral and civic issues must connect seamlessly with important disciplinary questions and be grounded in careful conceptual analysis and rigorous methods. These integrations have to come from within the fields; moral and civic issues cannot be grafted on after the fact. The American Association for Higher Education offers some models for this kind of work in its extensive and well-regarded monograph series on service learning in the disciplines (Zlotkowski, 1998).

This book is not the place for a comprehensive review of moral and civic education in the disciplines. But we can offer a sampling of the kinds of things some faculty in the arts and sciences, undergraduate professional education, and interdisciplinary programs are doing to incorporate moral and civic issues into their courses.

Liberal Arts Disciplines and Fine Arts

We learned about courses in nearly every academic field that use moral and civic issues to help students deepen their mastery of the discipline and its debates, and could have discussed any of these. We offer examples from several liberal arts and fine arts disciplines to provide a sense of the range of strategies faculty use to link moral and civic learning with important disciplinary questions and approaches. Some of these disciplines, such as political science, offer obvious opportunities for moral and civic learning, while others, such as those in the sciences, may initially seem more remote from this learning, but actually they offer equally powerful ways to explore the ethical and civic dimensions of the field.

ECONOMICS. Many economics courses hold great promise for connecting moral and civic learning with disciplinary learning. These courses may address topics such as public sector economics and public goods, methods of collective decision making, labor economics and regulation, comparative economics, or the social, political, and cultural dimensions that shape distinctive economic systems. Courses that focus on the historical, international, and political contexts of economics can help students learn about real-world economic problems, and study of economic history gives them a chance to evaluate the relative strength of competing economic models, such as models of labor, by considering which provides the most accurate prediction of historical events and how noneconomic factors can influence behavior in the narrowly economic realm (Solow, 1997, p. 71).

In much current teaching of undergraduate economics, however, models that assume a narrow view of rationality coupled with sophisticated mathematical and statistical techniques are squeezing out a focus on the kinds of real-world economic problems that are most likely to contribute to moral and civic development. A strong disciplinary bias toward abstract analysis that avoids normative issues means that even the most value-laden topics rarely acknowledge or discuss the values embedded in economic models, the premises that inform them, or how phenomena such as unequal distribution of income reflect particular values (Association of American Colleges, 1990; Kreps, 1997). This approach is doubly problematic because of the influence of economics on many other disciplines, such as political science and law. Many criticize economics for assuming a narrow view of rationality, but perhaps a more serious problem is that these core assumptions are frequently presented as if they are self-evident truths, almost a kind of natural law. This approach tends to ignore the moral and social dimensions of the assumptions and methods used in economics and to overlook the limitations of economic thinking (Association of American Colleges, 1990; Kreps, 1997; Solow, 1997).

This is not the only approach possible, however. Alverno's Zohreh Emami, for example, teaches both lower- and upper-level economics courses "from a values perspective." Students not only learn the principles of micro- and macroeconomics but also come to recognize that those principles are infused with particular values that sometimes conflict with other personal and social values. Some of Emami's courses include an institutional analysis of values, in which students learn to separate out the competing values involved in institutional choices and commitments and learn that economic issues are more complex and ambiguous than theories seem to suggest. Emami says that, especially at the introductory level, her students readily accept the individualistic premises of economic theories and are quite willing to endorse their implied market values as the centerpiece of U.S. society. She wants students to learn that "this is the ethics of the market, but there is also the ethics of the public sphere, which includes other community values, such as making commitments on the basis of democracy, or paying taxes to provide public goods such as education." Emami also emphasizes that women need to understand economics and take part in conversations about economic issues. She believes this approach is particularly important at Alverno, a women's college where a large percentage of students are from low-income families. Emami's approach has the added benefit of increasing her students' interest and academic performance. For many students, economics can feel abstract and disconnected from their experience, so "making the course relevant, both in terms of values and in terms of touching students personally has made [students] more interested in learning the techniques and the math, and the micro and macro theories, no matter how abstract."

POLITICAL SCIENCE AND PUBLIC POLICY. Among the best courses for establishing the base of substantive knowledge required for responsible citizenship are those in U.S. politics, public policy, and political philosophy. There has been much disagreement, however, about whether civic education should be a focus of political science as a discipline, sometimes in connection with other internal debates, such as that over the increasing emphasis on quantitative analysis and mathematical modeling in the field (Lindblom, 1997; Smith, 1997). In recent years the American Political Science Association's Task Force on Civic Education in the Next Century (1998) has led efforts to make civic engagement and civic education priorities for research and teaching. The task force has sponsored panels, lectures, and workshops at the association's annual conferences and has been working to change faculty reward structures to make civic education a more valued professional pursuit. Although some political scientists have disparaged these goals as "pure futility and waste," others have embraced them as a return to the original purposes of the discipline (American Political Science Association, 1998; Bennett, 1999; Leonard, 1999; Schacter, 1998).

Some courses in politics are relatively detached from real-world social and political issues, but many political scientists have designed courses around important questions in the discipline that also involve topics that can contribute to students' civic education (Reeher & Cammarano, 1997). In Chapter Five, for example, we described a course in political theory, taught by Rick Battistoni at Providence College, which uses creative pedagogies to ensure that students are able to really use what they learn.

Another political theory course with a special focus on moral and civic learning is James Farr's Practicing Democratic Education, which he teaches at the University of Minnesota. This course addresses a number of longstanding debates about democracy, politics, and the education of citizens through both theoretical and practical investigations. In addition to discussing major texts concerned with these debates, students put their learning into practice by serving as "coaches" for Public Achievement, a program at a local middle school where younger students are researching their own questions about democracy and implementing projects that address problems in and around their school. Many of Farr's students continue to serve as Public Achievement coaches long after the course is over, and they report that the course has changed their understanding of their own responsibilities as citizens.

Public policy and other courses focused on social problems such as homelessness or welfare can teach students how to draw together diverse knowledge and perspectives to understand a complex problem and begin thinking about and evaluating possible solutions. For example, Tom Ehrlich has taught a service-learning course at San Francisco State University that studied the effects of welfare reform on several San Francisco neighborhoods (Ehrlich, 1999). At Portland State University, Sy Adler teaches Theory and Philosophy of Community Development, a course that includes a civic engagement requirement. To fulfill this requirement, students become active in such venues as neighborhood associations in their home community or associations where they work or study; watershed stewardship councils; and the offices of elected officials, labor unions, and various advocacy organizations, including electoral campaign organizations.

SCIENCES. Many critical social problems in the areas of world population, energy production, pollution, and biodiversity involve an interaction between science, public policy, and human values and belief systems. Topics that involve such connections among science, technology, and society and that consider the ethical implications of scientific work can be very effective vehicles for teaching science, and there are signs that some science disciplines are broadening their focus to embrace not only applied research but also *public science* and participatory action research, in which research is carried out in and with communities.

Science courses also present valuable opportunities to expose both majors and nonmajors to the values that are foundational for science—open-mindedness, honesty, risk taking, and the idea that convictions must be arrived at "by examination of evidence, not through coercion, personal argument, or appeal to authority" (Rapoport, 1957, p. 796). This is a goal of Emory University's Hughes Science Initiative, which includes a course for science majors that focuses on the values and ethics of scientific work. The initiative also sponsors the Summer Research (SuRE) program, which teaches science majors about the way laboratories work, the potential for conflicts of interest, the ethical issues surrounding experimentation, and the demands of collegiality and partnership in research. Students in this program are also encouraged to consider the social significance of their research projects, exploring how they may be important to society. At California State University, Monterey Bay (CSUMB), students can choose from a number of science courses that include a focus on moral and civic learning. One example is Water and Humanity, a team-taught interdisciplinary science course that analyzes the scientific, cultural, economic, political, and ethical issues related to water usage and access, pollution, and conservation at local, state, regional, national, and global levels. The course combines classroom learning with field studies on ways to prevent degradation of watersheds and oceans and to promote water resources management, and on biodiversity and equitable access to clean water.

LITERATURE. There is no question that great literature, from *King Lear* to *Anna Karenina, Pride and Prejudice,* and *The Invisible Man,* is shot through with deep and enduring moral dilemmas and insights. Although there are often sharp divisions in English and other fields of literature among different and competing theoretical frameworks and between literature and composition faculty, almost any approach can be used to engage students in reflection on questions of responsibility, honor, worldview, cultural and historical context, human connectedness, and the relation of the individual to the community and the state.

Stephen Feldman, professor of English at the University of Notre Dame, teaches several literature courses that try to reach students "at every level of their being"—integrating moral and spiritual learning into their study of literature. Students say that his course Modern Jewish Writers not only challenges them intellectually but also causes them to think more deeply about the ways their religious upbringing has shaped their perspectives on the world and the extent to which they view their moral lives and those of others through a particular religious lens. Feldman tells of an incident in that course triggered by a story in Art Spiegelman's *Maus,* in which a Jew refuses to pick up a black hitchhiker, calling him a racial epithet in German. A black student in the class raised the question of how a Jew could be so prejudiced after all the suffering Jews have experienced as the result of ethnic hatred. The ensuing discussion explored the differences in Jewish and Christian understandings of suffering, including the idea that suffering as redemptive is central in Catholicism and many Protestant denominations but not in Judaism.

THE ARTS. At CSUMB, the fine arts are connected with moral and civic learning in many courses. One such course is Ways of Seeing: Seminar on Philosophy and Ethical Thinking in Public Art, a highly participatory, hands-on course that combines study of contemporary public art with ethical theory in visual and public arts. Students in the course read case studies of controversies over public art, such as those that surrounded the

Vietnam Veterans Memorial in Washington, D.C., for example. The course addresses questions of access, empowerment, cultural criticism, censorship, and the politics of aesthetics. Students work in teams on creative productions, with guest artists, slide lectures, videos, portfolio projects, and field trips providing numerous ways to frame the controversies surrounding contemporary public art.

Undergraduate Professional Fields

Integral to the very idea of a profession is the responsibility to serve the public good and to follow the ethical norms of one's professional community. Organizations that accredit professional education programs recognize this, and therefore they typically require students to learn the ethical guidelines of the field. In this sense, moral and civic development is acknowledged as essential to undergraduate professional education in such areas as accounting, business, education, engineering, journalism, and nursing and other health care fields. But this does not mean that these majors offer deep and sustained experience with ethical judgment, responsibilities, and dilemmas. Course requirements for these majors can be especially heavy, and too often this leads professional education programs to be satisfied with a single ethics course, which may or may not be tailored to address issues in that professional field. Some institutions go further, however, attempting to shape professional identity and character as well as to teach official ethical codes and regulations.

EDUCATION. At Spelman College, for example, issues of civic engagement and responsibility are at the heart of several courses required for education majors, including courses on urban education and research in child development. Moreover, both faculty and students frequently bring local and national issues related to education into the classroom. One class focused for example on the implications of a *Dateline* report on the impact of disparate school funding on the quality of education. Every education course at Spelman has a field component—by the time they graduate, majors will have completed three hundred hours of fieldwork in local classrooms. Because students spend so much time in local schools, they regularly confront some of the most troubling issues of education. This firsthand experience makes them assertive in raising issues related to their fieldwork, stimulating passionate debates that connect their learning with broader social issues. Some of these debates generate so much interest that they spill onto the campus. After a heated discussion of biracialism, cultural identity, and social acceptance, some students decided the topic was so important and touched so many of their peers that they organized a campuswide forum on the subject.

One Spelman education professor told us he challenges his students in every course to think about leadership and vision and "how you will lead the next generation." Many faculty in the department believe that helping students reflect on "how we can try to give back to and revitalize the community" is a necessary part of teacher education at Spelman, revealing the way that the college's distinctive definition of moral and civic responsibility—community connections—is played out in this major.

ENGINEERING. Messiah College created a program that allows engineering students to practice what they are learning through an international service application. The first team of students and faculty in this program traveled to Burkina Faso, Africa, to install a photovoltaic power system. Two current service-learning projects are the West Africa Pump Project, a two-part project to supply water to a clinic and improve the irrigation system in a rehabilitation garden for the handicapped, and the Tricycle Project, which focuses on improving the design of a hand-powered tricycle used by polio victims in West Africa.

Some engineering courses at the Air Force Academy and the University of Notre Dame also involve moral and civic learning. Senior capstones in design are typical of engineering programs nationwide, but in most cases they involve considerations of service tangentially if at all. In contrast, at the Air Force Academy all engineering students complete a capstone project that will benefit an individual or a group, such as designing and building a house for a low-income family or a special wheelchair for a handicapped child. Notre Dame has strong elements of moral and civic learning concentrated in its Engineering Projects in Community Service (EPICS) program. Through this program, which partners with Notre Dame's Center for Social Concerns, undergraduates work on engineering projects in the local and sometimes international communities under faculty supervision. One of the founders of EPICS, Stephen Bass, described the program as animated by the desire to show students what it means to "practice a life of virtue" and apply the theoretical knowledge they have acquired to the concrete needs of a community.

HEALTH CARE. At the Minneapolis campus of the College of St. Catherine, a campus that specializes in preparing students for health care occupations, the curriculum emphasizes not only academic and practical expertise but also diversity, ethics, and spirituality. The introduction of these goals several years ago was partly a response to an influx of Hmong, Somali,

Ethiopian, and other immigrant groups into the Twin Cities area. St. Kate's faculty believed that in order to provide quality health care, students needed to learn to negotiate cultural differences. In nursing, physical therapy, occupational therapy, and other health care programs, St. Kate's faculty try to help students learn to deal with the ethical dilemmas that arise when patients from immigrant communities enter health care institutions that are structured around very different cultural assumptions and practices. They stress the importance of the advocacy role graduates will need to play, negotiating the complexities of cultural interfaces between patients and health care providers.

Health care faculty also emphasize the importance of meaningful and compassionate relationships with clients, families, and neighborhoods, rather than simply teaching students "how to deal with 'the gallbladder in Room 213.'" Some have been particularly creative in developing new strategies for teaching the ethics of health care, using drama, fiction, simulations, and other media to foster in their students compassion for patients or clients and a deeper comprehension of the complexity of the human situations they will face in their work. In many cases these courses are taught in connection with practicums and other clinical experiences.

Finally, in addition to instilling cultural awareness, sensitivity, and ethical responsibility, many St. Kate's faculty try to increase their students' understanding of the economic, political, and policy contexts of their work, looking, for example, at pending legislation such as Minnesota's Alternative Health Care Bill and policies such as those governing federal funding for health care.

Interdisciplinary Majors and Minors

Despite the enduring power of the disciplines, more and more faculty research and professional identities are now interdisciplinary, and interdisciplinary teaching is becoming commonplace. Reflecting the growing importance of this work, many colleges and universities offer interdisciplinary courses and programs for students, including academic majors, minors, and honors programs. These programs may reside in interdisciplinary departments or, more frequently, may draw from several discipline-based departments.

Stanford's interdisciplinary Ethics in Society Program, for example, offers a minor or an honors concentration to students in any department who want to enrich their studies through the exploration of moral issues in personal and public life. Students must complete six courses centered on moral and civic themes, and course configurations often cluster around ethics and politics, ethics and economics, or biomedical ethics. Students in the honors program must also complete an honors thesis; some recent titles are "Distribution of Costs in a National Health Insurance System: Should Some People Pay More for Their Health Insurance," "Genetic Manipulation in Humans as a Matter of Justice," and "Native Hawaiian National Self-Determination."

The Kenan Institute for Ethics is working to establish a cross-disciplinary ethics minor at Duke. The minor would require students to take specially designed introductory and capstone courses and five additional ethics courses, with distribution requirements to ensure that students are exposed to courses that focus on philosophical ethics, religion and ethics, applied ethics, and ethics in a historical context. The proposal has been approved by the chairs of philosophy, political science, religion, divinity, public policy, and history.

Emory University's Violence Studies Program also offers a minor. It requires the completion of six courses including Introduction to the Comparative Study of Violence, which considers the major literature on violence in various disciplines and features guest speakers on topics such as the Vietnam War and evolutionary perspectives on violence. The program involves seventy faculty from twenty departments, programs, and schools, including psychology, sociology, political science, anthropology, economics, women's studies, and education. Students can enroll in a wide range of courses that deal with violence, including both individual and collective violence in the United States and abroad, with a special focus on the causes, representations, effects, prevention, and control of violence. Two examples of these courses are Latin American Revolutions (political science) and Evil: Philosophical and Literary Approaches (religion). In some Violence Studies courses, including the capstone internship, students carry out applied work like creating a violence-prevention program on campus or serving community organizations concerned with violence.

Curricular Strategies Supporting Integration of Learning and Cumulative Learning

Like the learning of other complex capacities, moral and civic learning is strengthened by educational experiences that are integrative and cumulative. One of the important advantages of the holistic, intentional approach characteristic of our case study schools is that it provides experiences that reinforce and build on each other and helps students integrate what they learn across different contexts. Even institutions that are not prepared to mount that kind of full-scale, holistic effort sometimes offer programs that provide some of the same benefits, at least for some of their students. In fact this is an important reason why curricular efforts such as those we have reviewed here are so valuable—they contribute to the integration of accumulated learning.

Interdisciplinary Course Clusters and Crosscutting Themes

Many required courses, like The Reflective Woman at the College of St. Catherine or Sophomore Inquiry at Portland State University, are multi-disciplinary and intentionally designed to foster students' integrative capacities. By introducing this experience in the first year of college, fresh-man seminars show students that integrative thinking is a valued part of academic life and gives them some early practice in this possibly unfa-miliar set of skills. Clusters of courses, such as those in interdisciplinary majors, minors, and honors programs and in Portland State's core cur-riculum, carry this experience through in upper-level courses, integrating study within the major or minor and teaching students how to enrich their understanding of issues in a field by drawing on relevant work in a wide range of disciplines. And of course integration is the raison d'être of many senior capstone courses. Similarly, outcomes-based education programs are intentionally designed to highlight the learning of complex capacities by pulling together experiences across a wide array of courses, as the Alverno student observed about her learning for the Effective Citizenship requirement.

In an effort to foster more integration of learning and cumulative learn-ing across the curriculum, Kapi'olani Community College established six across the curriculum emphases that faculty in all departments incorporate into their courses, giving students sustained experience with these emphases, which include service learning and Hawaiian–Asian Pacific values. Leaders in the service-learning program were concerned that brief, sporadic involve-ment in unconnected service experiences did not support deeply meaning-ful student learning or provide responsible service to the community. For that reason they further organized the service learning across the curricu-lum emphasis around a set of ten *pathways,* organized into two clusters— school based and community based. Students generally remain on a single pathway or move among closely related pathways within a cluster during the whole of their time at Kapi'olani. Most students choose pathways related to their primary academic interests. The school-based cluster, which works closely with the Education and English Departments, engages stu-dents in teaching and mentoring local K–12 students through such means as tutoring programs at two middle schools, literacy programs at twenty local elementary schools, and a program in which Kapi'olani students work with local teens in literacy circles. The community-based cluster offers pathways such as Promoting Health/Preventing HIV; Education for Citizenship, in which students work with immigrants; and Caring Long-Term, in which students work with home-bound elderly and HIV-positive individuals, learning about long-term care issues from both personal and public health perspectives and studying the impact of these issues on the community. The pathway Adopting an *Ahupua'a* (the Hawaiian term for a unit of land from the mountains to the sea) is linked to the Hawaiian Studies Program and involves students in environmental stewardship projects in east Honolulu, such as watershed and taro restoration.

Learning Communities

Another approach to increasing the integration of learning and cumulative learning in undergraduate education, one that has gained significant currency in recent years, is the *learning community*. These programs provide opportunities for integration not only across the curriculum but also with the cocurriculum. A variant of learning communities that capitalizes on these connections is the *living-learning community*, in which students both live and take courses together. We say more about living-learning communities in Chapter Eight.

There are many types of learning communities, with different names on different campuses, ranging from learning clusters to linked writing courses to freshman interest groups to honors and "experimental" colleges such as those created at the University of Wisconsin, Madison and University of California, Berkeley. Learning communities typically address issues of curricular coherence, civic leadership, student retention, active learning, and faculty development and often incorporate team teaching, interdisciplinary themes, and active, collaborative pedagogies (Gabelnick et al., 1990). Learning communities treat courses and disciplines as connected rather than as separate, discrete experiences. Through curricula organized around a common purpose, they also create close, ongoing fellowship among students and faculty and ensure that day-to-day interactions reinforce classroom learning. Among the most intensive and best-known examples of learning communities linked to moral and civic learning are those at Evergreen State College. In 1970, the college's founding faculty designed the new college around yearlong, team-taught learning communities called *coordinated studies*, with interdisciplinary themes (Jones & Newman, 1997). This program was to be a "moral curriculum," grounded in the humanities and social sciences, that would prepare students to participate actively in a democratic society (Cadwallader, 1994). The Evergreen experience inspired the creation of dozens of learning communities on other campuses in the 1970s and 1980s.

At most institutions learning communities draw on regular course offerings rather than specially designed courses as at Evergreen. This makes learning communities an attractive option for campuses of every size and type, from large state universities to community colleges, because they do not require massive infusions of money or large-scale reorganization. At the State University of New York, Stony Brook, for example, students can select *federated learning communities* that pull together courses from many fields around a common theme. In addition to taking these courses together, students participate in a three-credit seminar that draws connections between the courses. The learning community World Hunger, for example, includes courses such as The Ecology of Feast and Famine, The Economics of Development, and The History of Latin America. Social and Ethical Issues in the Life Sciences, a learning community designed for upper-division students majoring in biology or psychology, includes courses such as General Genetics, The Healer and the Witch in History, and Philosophy and Medicine (Gabelnick et al., 1990, pp. 26–27).

Learning communities can be especially useful for students at community colleges and other institutions with many part-time students who are often also working and caring for families. The intellectual communities these programs provide can give part-time students a common sense of purpose as well as stronger connections with the faculty, their fellow students, and the institution. In Daytona Beach Community College's Quanta Program, for example, students work in teams with faculty from several departments, with coursework integrated around a theme. In the fall semester the theme is Quest: The Search for Intimacy and Identity, and in spring semester it is Values and Visions: Creating a Better World. The program satisfies general education requirements as it also helps students explore connections among seemingly unrelated subjects and develop closer relationships with faculty and other students.

Faculty Roles and Expertise

Clearly, the curricular approaches we recommend demand a lot from faculty. When core courses are offered, someone has to teach them—year after year. Multidisciplinary courses require faculty with many disparate areas of knowledge. The specialized faculty in U.S. higher education may find this requirement daunting and uncomfortable, which means that the requisite expertise must typically be brought to bear through collaborative planning, faculty development, or team-teaching. Such approaches require difficult decisions about deployment of departmental resources and involve a level of cooperation and compromise in the design and teaching of courses that is outside the experience of most faculty. When we call for faculty to integrate moral and civic issues into their courses in the disciplines, we are well aware that this requires a high level of expertise with those issues, expertise that few faculty have before beginning this kind of integration. In the next chapter we look at why some faculty take on challenges like this and what institutions can do to support them.

7

FACULTY: THE CORNERSTONE

DURING ALEXANDER Astin and Helen Astin's study of values, authenticity, and stress in the lives of college faculty, one professor at a state university told them: "Until this January I worked almost every night and every weekend. Last year I took three weekends that I did not work on academic stuff the entire academic year. That's how it's been, and I just can't do it any more" (Astin & Astin, 1999, pp. 18–19). This exhausted professor was typical of many in the study. Most respondents reported a lot of stress in their professional lives, and virtually all said they did not have time to meet all their professional and personal responsibilities. Large surveys have revealed the same results as the Astins' qualitative study (Sax, Astin, Korn, & Gilmartin, 1999).

The many demands on their time require faculty members to set stringent priorities, and at most institutions faculty are not encouraged to place students' moral and civic development high on this list. Incentives to make the moral and civic agenda, or even teaching more generally, a high priority are not built into the reward systems at many campuses, although this varies a great deal across different kinds of institutions. Institutional pressures make many faculty feel as if they are swimming upstream when they focus their attention on innovative undergraduate teaching. As Stanford professor Rob Reich told us: "It takes an active resistance to channel a lot of your energy into teaching, which doesn't get rewarded institutionally. I don't bemoan the fact, but I recognize that given my own interests in teaching, I'm swimming against a current that's strong on occasion."

The kind of teaching we have described in this book requires a lot of time and energy. Given the barriers to participation, it is remarkable how many faculty do make serious commitments to undergraduate moral and civic education. Faculty at many different types of institutions go to great lengths to teach in ways that will engage students actively in working through difficult moral concepts, learning to operate in the complicated and ambiguous contexts of the community, and finding ways of thinking and feeling that will change their sense of who they are and what they can contribute to the world. Over the past decade or so growth in the popularity of service learning, for example, has been dramatic. Service learning just began to have some currency in the mid-1980s, and yet the 1998–99 survey of undergraduate faculty by the Higher Education Research Institute reports that almost a fifth of faculty at two-year colleges (19.8 percent) and almost a quarter at four-year colleges (24.1 percent) said they had taught at least one service-learning course in the past two years (Sax et al., 1999).

What is it that motivates faculty to invest the creative energy and sustained effort it takes to teach for moral and civic learning, often in the absence of institutional recognition and reward? Faculty who are considering a foray into this kind of work might want to know why others do it, the ways in which these others find it rewarding, and the kind of institutional support they need. A better sense of why faculty are willing to make these investments and what helps support their commitment to the work might also be useful to administrators and program planners who care about moral and civic education. Of course, administrative leaders who want to make this a real priority on campus would do well to work toward changes in well-known institutional impediments. We did see some of this work going on at the case study schools. But in many institutions these structures are deeply entrenched, and dramatic changes are not on the horizon. Fortunately, moral and civic education does not need to wait for those changes.

To understand the motivation of faculty, it is important to recognize the centrality of *their* moral and civic understanding, goals, and identities. In our earlier discussion of vocationalism in higher education (Chapter Two), we remarked on how important it is to understand the moral and civic significance work has for many people (Colby, Sippola, & Phelps, 2001). This is especially true for faculty who are teaching for moral and civic responsibility. Of course institutional rewards are important to faculty. Few can afford to ignore considerations of tenure, promotion, compensation, and collegial respect. But this kind of external incentive is not the only thing driving their choices and directions. Perhaps even more important is how they think about their work, what they believe in, care about, and find meaningful and personally rewarding on a more human level. This sense of meaning is what sustains them when the work is hard. If an understanding of the various forms of faculty motivation does not inform the work of administrators hoping to engage faculty or designing faculty development programs, there may be a disconnect between them and the faculty they are trying to reach.

The work of most academics is central to their sense of who they are and their desire to contribute something important to the world. In interviews that the Astins conducted with faculty from public and private colleges and universities, many respondents described their work as having a kind of transcendent meaning for them. For example, when asked about the meaning of his work and its possible connections with a sense of spirituality, a scientist said: "I don't know what greater respect I could pay to a creator than to be so interested in the world that lives. I'm still in awe of [the natural world] so if there's any spirituality, then I guess I'm exercising it to some degree when I see the biological world as being amazing and beautiful, and I'm very fortunate to be studying its parts and pieces and learning about it" (Astin & Astin, 1999, p. 7).

This sense of transcendent meaning is also an important part of what students learn from their connections with these faculty. By conveying the personal significance their academic work has for them, faculty can help students understand the broader, more inspiring meaning of scholarship and learning in almost any field.

Faculty Motives

Faculty who make the kinds of efforts we have been describing here derive motivation primarily from their beliefs in the value of undergraduate education, their sense of community, their satisfying relationships with students, and their connections with research.

Conceptions of Undergraduate Education

If they are to invest themselves in their work as moral and civic educators, faculty must believe that this kind of teaching is legitimate and important. In fact faculty in large numbers do believe in the value and importance of undergraduate moral and civic education. In a recent national survey, 36 percent of faculty said they believe it is important to "instill in students a commitment to community service," and 60 percent believe it is important to "prepare students for responsible citizenship" (Sax et al., 1999). Another national survey found that 45 percent of faculty rated promoting "firm moral values" in students as a "very important" learning outcome, and these numbers were even higher when only faculty at baccalaureate institutions were considered. In addition, 20 percent of faculty at all institutions "strongly agree" and 41 percent "agree" that their own institution "should be actively engaged in solving social problems," and a strong majority of faculty "agree" or "strongly agree" that undergraduate education would be improved by making it more relevant to contemporary life and that "faculty in my discipline have a professional obligation to apply their knowledge to problems in society" (Huber, 1998).

Many faculty we talked to spoke of their conviction that undergraduate education should address the "whole person" and said that they take very seriously the broader goals of liberal education, including education for effective citizenship. Anything less would be too narrow, shortchanging both the students and the worlds they will enter. This conception of higher education clearly shaped the courses we described in Chapter Five. In talking about why he teaches the way he does, for example, Stanford's Rob Reich referred to his understanding of the meaning of a liberal arts education:

> The ideal of a liberal arts education is one that exposes you to and engages you with the history of important movements, thinkers, thoughts, and ideas. It's not only instrumental in making you a more free person but also probably making you a better person. . . . I think the tendency among most faculty is to resist the claim that you have some agenda for improving humanity, but I think in the final analysis you have to have some hope for that. And it's not as if you're trying to transmit to students the way to live, but you're hoping to transmit to them an engagement with the variety of ways to live in the hope that they may be better able to realize, on their own terms, a better life. If push came to shove, I think I'd give you the naked admission that the university should be engaged in making students better human beings.

David Takacs and Gerald Shenk talk about their teaching at California State University, Monterey Bay (CSUMB), as educating for the transformation of their students and ultimately of contemporary society. Takacs comments:

> For me, the purpose of my life is to envision an ideal world, think about what the real world looks like, and think about ways to bridge the gap between real and ideal. At the same time I'm thinking about an ideal me, I'm thinking about the flawed human being I am, I'm thinking about how to bridge the gap between the real me and the ideal me and to find joy in doing that personal development while making the world look more like the ideal world. . . . That's what motivates me, because teaching this way does that. At the same time, all my classes make students try to do that same thing: to envision who

they want to be, who they really are, and what they want the world to look like . . . and to empower them to bridge that gap between the real and ideal them while finding joy in making the world more like the ideal place it could be. . . . That's what motivates me.

Almost without exception the overriding concern of the faculty we talked to was *education*—how to foster students' learning, in the most encompassing sense of that term. They really care about this; they think hard about their goals for students and how to achieve them. Pedagogies that support moral and civic development are understood as means to the ends of both broad and specialized academic learning as well as ways to educate responsible citizens. On many campuses, faculty say their original interest in service learning, for example, arose from a belief that it could help their students learn academic material more effectively.

In institutions that use outcomes-based learning, faculty help establish institution-wide learning goals, including those relating to moral and civic development. At Alverno College, for example, faculty have been instrumental in creating and shaping the abilities-based learning program, and there is widespread faculty interest in thinking about how to help students achieve the abilities selected. These faculty are outspoken in their conviction that educating for citizenship and academic preparation more generally are mutually enhancing.

Just as the faculty we talked to believe in undergraduate education that engages more of the student, they also appreciate the fact that they can bring more of themselves to their teaching. Many say they have cared about some transcendent value for a long time—it may be social justice, community participation, or spirituality—and are grateful for a way to bring their work and personal values together. Many faculty may have entered education because they thought it would support this kind of integration and were disappointed to find that in many settings it did not. They are later delighted when they find themselves in an institution that supports and encourages it. At CSUMB, for example, many faculty said they were drawn to teach there because of CSUMB's distinctive mission. A member of the Social Sciences Division echoed others' statements that they had been attracted by CSUMB's vision statement, saying that CSUMB had allowed her to "come out of the closet as a humanist"—a social scientist who cares about values of multiculturalism, social justice, and community commitment. In her previous job she had longed to be at a campus where she would be listened to instead of marginalized for her views. At CSUMB she appreciated that she could be valued and respected for her commitments and really be herself.

Sense of Community

Faculty who incorporate moral and civic issues into their teaching also derive tremendous satisfaction from the collaboration and sense of community this work engenders. Many new faculty look forward to joining a community of scholars but are disappointed to find their work lives isolating and private, with few opportunities to share their experience and learn from others (Shulman, 1993). In almost every case, participation in moral and civic education results in a change in that traditional pattern. As they start to bring moral or civic issues into their courses, faculty begin talking to each other about their teaching, something they had not done before, and they see this as an unexpected institutional as well as personal benefit of the work. On campus after campus we saw these faculty in regular communication, working to create something together. As a result, they said, their teaching had improved and become more satisfying, not only in the courses that specifically addressed moral and civic learning but in their other courses as well.

At several of the campuses we visited, including the College of St. Catherine, Kapi'olani Community College, and Alverno College, campuswide interest in moral and civic education has been stimulated through study groups for faculty. The widely attended faculty study groups at St. Kate's led to new patterns of interacting and teaching that persisted long after the formal groups had ended. One outcome of this process was the establishment of the Teaching-Learning Network, which fosters collaboration among faculty and even encourages them to sit in on each other's classes.

On other campuses, required courses with a moral or civic dimension provide similar opportunities for faculty fellowship because they have multiple sections taught by faculty from many departments. In order to take a unified approach to these classes that involve material outside their primary areas of expertise, faculty work together closely to develop the syllabi and bring each other up to speed on unfamiliar subject matter. At Spelman College there are about fifteen sections of the core course, The African Diaspora and the World (ADW), taught mainly by tenured or tenure track faculty from several disciplines. Many initially find teaching the interdisciplinary course daunting. As one faculty member noted, a sociology professor may feel completely unprepared to teach the section on *The Tempest,* just as an English professor might feel uncertain about teaching Marx and Engel's *Communist Manifesto.* In the end, however, faculty involved with ADW value the opportunity to stretch themselves beyond traditional disciplinary boundaries, and wind up enjoying the challenges. Instructors typically teach ADW for several years before "cycling out," so from year to year some ADW faculty remain the same and others are new to the program. This has proved a useful system for ensuring continuity and expertise in the program and for preventing faculty burnout. Each spring the faculty who will teach ADW the following year begin weekly workshops in which they plan the content and organization of the course and discuss teaching strategies. Because the course covers topics as disparate as Shakespeare, the blues music culture, medical anthropologists' research on early African American burial grounds, and Caribbean history, sharing expertise across disciplines is essential, and each person teaches the others about the areas in which she is knowledgeable, sometimes sharing lecture notes or teaching techniques. Many faculty find that involvement with ADW promotes "intellectual talk across disciplines" and has informed and improved their research as well as their teaching. And by teaching the course together these faculty are led to talk to each other about teaching in much greater depth than they ever have before, and they say that the process has been energizing. Faculty who are working collaboratively on other campuses are similarly enthusiastic.

Depending on the nature of the institution, the sense of community created through participation in moral and civic education can encompass just a few people, who may feel somewhat out of step with the central priorities of their university, or most of the faculty on the campus. On campuses like Alverno, Tusculum, and Messiah, students' moral and civic learning is so central to the college's mission that it draws the majority of faculty together in a common purpose. On these campuses where moral and civic education is aligned with the central mission of the institution, it is easier to achieve recognition for this work, to be publicly recognized for contributing something valuable to the institution. Likewise, faculty at community colleges, urban universities, and some land grant universities (that is, the great majority of faculty) find that the goal of connecting with the local communities is well aligned with the institution's mission.

In more research-focused institutions, however, faculty who pursue the goals of moral and civic education often echo Rob Reich's comment that they feel as though they are swimming upstream. We heard this at Emory University, for example, which places a strong emphasis on scholarly productivity. But even there and at other research institutions, such as Duke University, faculty who seriously pursue moral and civic education experience a valuable sense of community—they tend to know and support each other, forming an important network of like-minded colleagues.

Satisfying Relationships with Students

Another powerful source of satisfaction for faculty who engage in moral and civic education is their relationships with and impacts on their students. In a large survey of college and university faculty, Sax et al. (1999) found that this was the source of professional satisfaction that faculty mention most often. Many of the faculty with whom we talked echoed this sentiment. Student responses to his course were very satisfying to Rob Reich, for example, and it is no wonder, with reactions like these:

> He creates an environment of energy and interaction that motivates you to learn. He is challenging but at the same time radiates warmth and commitment. Prof. Reich, in his honest criticism and sincere support, has made me a better writer, thinker, citizen, and person.

> Prof. Reich is the only professor at Stanford to make me seriously think about this issue. I had thought about service before but had failed to realize the implications of all types of service, particularly in international arenas. The class forced me to ask myself some questions that I did not necessarily like the answer to.

When he taught the course for the first time, Reich was awarded the Distinguished Teaching Award of the Associated Students of Stanford University. Similarly, at Tusculum College we heard that "faculty here really care about their students. It is not a place for people who want to teach a few hours and leave. It is more like doing social service than teaching in a research school." Despite these heavy demands, many faculty say they stay at Tusculum *because of*, not in spite of, these aspects of its mission.

In our campus visits we heard many faculty talk about their efforts to form guiding relationships with their students, and we heard students speak of the power those relationships have for them. Richard, a student at Kapi'olani Community College, talked about his transformation from an uninvolved and underachieving high school student to a leader on his college campus through the influence of Kapi'olani faculty. He said that one of his teachers "saw things in me that I didn't know I had and led me to get more involved." When we saw him in his second year at Kapi'olani, he was doing well academically and was student body chairman and an active member of the campus honor society and several other clubs. Civic engagement has become central to his life. Similarly, a CSUMB student said that her classes are all quite small so she has had a chance to get to know her teachers, and she respects them a great deal. She knew that she was missed when she did not attend class and was not surprised that the professor let her know, via e-mail, that the professor and the other students missed her. Another student at CSUMB said that he knew the faculty were there "out of passionate commitment," that they really cared about their students, and that he and other students frequently had dinner with some of their teachers.

The power of these relationships is also clear in student letters supporting teaching award candidates. In a program sponsored by The Carnegie Foundation for the Advancement of Teaching and the Council for the Advancement and Support of Education, colleges and universities nominate "exceptional faculty members" as U.S. Professors of the Year. Most of the nominees have not only inspired students with a passion for their field and for learning in general but have also served as powerful role models of caring, compassion, and a deep commitment to students' learning and achievement. In a typical letter of support to the review committee, one former student described her political science professor as having changed her choices for her education, work, and life:

> As a student at . . . I was very heavily influenced by Steve's brilliant work in the classroom. Late at night, when I was talking with my classmates about their lives, they routinely spoke about how Steve was the one teacher who seemed to care for them. Many who were the first in their families to attend college spoke of his respect for their lives and the hope he seemed to have for them as individuals. I worked on numerous faculty and student committees on which he also served. In those venues, he was also a teacher, always calling us to be a more caring, responsive, and honest community, showing us what that community would be. I also participated in his seminar focusing on work, justice, and economic democracy in the United States. In that class, I came to reevaluate my life's goals, the kinds of relationships I wanted for my life, the kind of work I wanted to do, the kind of community and society I wanted to build. So profound was that experience that it has continued to shape my choices and my education a decade later.

Connections with Research

Many faculty who engage in this kind of teaching were drawn to it in the course of doing research or scholarship that addresses moral or civic issues. Questions of social justice, and more recently of social capital and civic participation and renewal, are of both professional and personal interest to many faculty. Many are redefining their work in public terms (or have always defined it that way) and want to use their teaching and research to contribute to the long-term revitalization of U.S. democracy. Because much contemporary research and scholarship addresses issues of public concern such as globalization, the environment, health care, education, aging, and social and public policy, many faculty find that their scholarly interests feed directly into teaching that addresses moral and civic issues.

Academic life often reflects and contributes to social movements, directly through the incorporation of new perspectives into the work of faculty who are personally engaged in movements and reciprocally through the academy's power to shape public consciousness and debate. Many faculty who have taken a special interest in various forms of moral and civic learning have done so because of their interest or participation in larger social movements, both personally and in their scholarly work. This of course does not mean it is legitimate for faculty to use their classrooms to indoctrinate students in the pursuit of their own ideological agendas. When faculty bring their passion for social change into their teaching, they should take extra care to invite dissent and diversity of opinion.

Such faculty interests can be clearly seen in the tremendous increase in feminist scholarship and teaching over the past couple of decades. From the beginning, feminist analyses across the full range of disciplines have been accompanied by large-scale programs of curriculum reform. This reform has included concerted (and fairly successful) efforts to "mainstream" gender studies into many disciplines as well as the creation of interdisciplinary women's studies courses and programs. Feminist scholarship and teaching has consciously sought to contribute to social change, often focusing not only on gender equality but also on issues of race and class as they intersect with gender. Although not typically billed as moral or civic education, this work attempts to expand students' social and moral perspectives and foster their concern for gender, racial, and social equality.

Sometimes faculty involved in this kind of work become leaders in persuading colleagues in other fields to raise issues of social justice in their teaching. At Spelman College, for example, Beverly Guy-Sheftall, professor of women's studies and founding director of the Women's Research and Resource Center, repeatedly called her colleague's attention to the need to take a critical perspective on their fields and the educational experience, identifying patterns that reinforce inequality. This led many faculty outside women's studies to take a greater interest in moral and civic education.

In part spurred by the moral concerns and continuing influence of the civil rights movement and in part by a pragmatic recognition of this country's dramatic demographic shifts, many faculty have become interested in issues of racial, ethnic, religious, and other forms of diversity. Because multiculturalism is of institutional concern on many campuses, there is considerable support for this kind of work. Furthermore, many faculty have incorporated a multicultural perspective into their scholarship and so find it is natural to extend this focus to their teaching.

The environmental movement has also inspired many faculty to focus on moral and civic issues in their teaching. It has spawned new cross-disciplinary departments and curricular programs, and environmental issues are well represented among service-learning courses and other curricular and extracurricular approaches to moral and civic education. Because issues of individual and organizational responsibility and public policy arise naturally in these courses, faculty working in this domain can incorporate moral and civic issues quite seamlessly into their teaching.

For all these faculty, moral and civic issues are an especially good fit with their disciplines and at least some of their courses. For them, this kind of teaching often can be cast in a way that serves multiple purposes as the lines between their scholarship, teaching, and personal commitments are blurred by the strong substantive connections among them.

Supports for Moral and Civic Education

When the president or others in an institution's administration want to make moral and civic education a priority, they can provide institutional support in a number of ways. We have already talked about reward structures and will not elaborate on those issues here, except to say that rewards need not always be formal. Sincere expressions of appreciation or visible, public references to good teaching that addresses moral and civic issues can contribute significantly to faculty morale. Other strategies include faculty development, logistical support, and support for faculty engagement with relevant national communities and organizations. Attention should be paid to non-tenure track as well as tenure track faculty, because instructors and adjuncts play important roles in undergraduate moral and civic education at many colleges and universities.

Faculty Development

Faculty development is essential to high-quality moral and civic education. Many faculty lack the expertise to incorporate these issues into their teaching in a sophisticated way. Faculty in fields like ethics may feel they lack the substantive knowledge they would need to address the complexities of contemporary social or policy questions. Conversely, faculty with the content knowledge often lack experience with ethical or policy analysis. Faculty may also lack the pedagogical expertise needed to organize a course around complex, open-ended problems, coach students in simulations, or connect student learning to experiences in the community. Good faculty development programs can address these challenges.

Informal opportunities for faculty development are present at all the schools we visited and form a regular structure at many. For example, at Alverno College there are no classes on Friday afternoons so that faculty can get together in small working groups to take up issues relating to the curriculum, pedagogical practices, assessment, and other topics of broad concern. Because moral and civic development is so central to Alverno's mission, these conversations often focus on ways to support students in that development.

At Portland State University, the Center for Academic Excellence offers several ongoing discussion groups so that faculty can support each other and learn from each other's experiences. A monthly breakfast series, Celebrating Practices of Civic Responsibility in Higher Education, brings in outside speakers, such as William Grace, executive director of the Center for Ethical Leadership, who talked to the group about ethics, leadership, and service and the creation of a just society. The breakfast series sometimes draws on shared readings, such as books by John Dewey (1916), Amy Gutmann (1987), and Harry Boyte (1989) that focus on moral and civic education. In addition to fostering discussions of literature in the field, the meetings provide a chance for faculty to talk about such practical pedagogical issues as how to manage heated debates in community-based learning courses and make sure that all perspectives are heard. Despite the demands of heavy teaching loads, committee work, and their own research, more than 150 faculty, administrators, staff, and community partners have participated in the breakfast series.

Campus centers and campuswide programs can play critical roles in facilitating these kinds of conversations and can also offer seminars and other tools to help faculty gain new expertise and design new courses. When Tufts University received a $10 million gift to incorporate civic concerns into undergraduate education, one of the first steps the new University College of Citizenship and Public Service took was to establish seminars for faculty interested in redesigning one or more of their courses. Participants were drawn from physics, chemistry, biology, engineering, literature, international relations, political science, and history. Initially faculty thought teaching related to citizenship would be an "add-on," layered on top of the material already in their courses. The seminar asked them to think instead about how integrating a concern for active citizenship throughout their courses could help them achieve their academic goals as well as help the students develop as engaged and informed citizens. Seminar participants worked together in small groups to develop a new model for each course being redesigned. The teams worked on pedagogy as well as content and also began to rethink their own roles, asking, Who am I as a teacher?

Just as a large gift was pivotal in the development of the ambitious new program at Tufts, even modest amounts of grant money or internal funding can enable faculty development seminars and small grants to faculty who are designing new courses. Follow-up support is equally important, because faculty who are inspired and enriched by a seminar with their peers may lose steam quickly if they try to implement their new ideas in settings that provide little validation or practical support.

Faculty development programs must be of high quality if they are to be useful, and this may be particularly true of programs designed to help faculty bring moral and civic issues into their teaching because these issues are complex and require careful attention to course content, pedagogical approaches, and the classroom atmosphere. Good faculty development programs provide participants with the understanding and tools that allow them to be both experimental and reflective in identifying the issues and pedagogical approaches best suited to their goals. In designing a course on ethical issues, for example, instructors need opportunities to think about and discuss such questions as, What is the right balance between discussions of difficult dilemmas and cases where the right course of action is fairly easy to discern but perhaps more difficult to carry out? What implicit messages do different answers to this question convey?

Faculty who are engaged in moral and civic education also need structured opportunities to confront the place of their own values in their teaching, sorting out those values on which they believe it is legitimate to take a firm stand and those that represent their own take on issues that are more debatable. Often it is easier for faculty to see the values they are directly and explicitly affirming (you must be respectful of others, everyone can find some way to contribute to improving society, and so forth) than those that are present but unstated (such as personal attitudes toward religion or politics).

Faculty development programs can also be useful for devising strategies to manage interactions among students. Faculty need to understand that the teacher is not the only social force at play in the classroom. In order to deepen the discourse among students while keeping the conversation open to dissent, they will sometimes need to play devil's advocate or support students' articulation of positions with which they strongly disagree, helping students make a case as well as it can be made (as we described in Chapter Five).

Sometimes faculty development programs that focus on moral and civic learning are too watered down to be very helpful. These programs need to be intellectually engaging as well as useful on a very practical level. For this reason it may be helpful to offer several different programs from which faculty can choose, so that, for example, a "layperson" teaching an ethics course for the first time has opportunities to learn about basic theories and techniques; a teacher with expertise in teaching these theories can select a more sophisticated program.

Supportive Infrastructure

In addition to opportunities for continuing education about moral and civic issues and unfamiliar pedagogies, faculty need a supportive institutional infrastructure. Without institutional support, they may be too busy to design new courses, especially courses that are quite different from those they have taught in the past. Logistical support, ethics centers, service-learning offices, and teaching and learning centers make it possible for busy faculty to focus on their students' learning rather than being consumed by the practical complexities of teaching that connects with the community. Some campuses have centers specifically charged with supporting moral or civic education; on others, teaching and learning centers with broader missions play this role. In Chapter Three we talked about the important leadership role these centers can play. Moral and civic education at Duke University, the University of Notre Dame, and the United States Air Force Academy, for example, would not be the same without these institutions' very powerful centers that catalyze and support faculty work in this domain.

Logistical support is especially important for service learning, because establishing relationships with community organizations is time consuming and benefits greatly from continuity over time. This kind of infrastructure helps faculty with many things they may not have thought about at all, including student safety and liability issues, transportation, and guidelines for protecting community partners from well-intentioned but inexperienced students. Often the more advanced students play key roles in providing logistical support while developing further their capacities as leaders, gaining a sense of competence, and serving as guides for other students.

National Ties

The sense of community and participation in a shared endeavor that we saw on so many campuses can extend well beyond the campus when faculty members engage with national educational movements and the associations that support them. Conferences, cross-institutional networks, organizations such as Campus Compact, and publications such as the *Michigan Journal of Community Service Learning* and the American Association for Higher Education's monograph series on service learning in the disciplines (Zlotkowski, 1998), along with visible national leadership on the importance of the issues, help to sustain a national community of people working to develop effective approaches to undergraduate moral and civic education. Achieving recognition beyond one's campus for this kind of work can also consolidate support for it at home. Robert Franco and others at Kapi'olani Community College have led the development of service learning in the wider University of Hawaii system and among community colleges nationally. This not only ties Franco and his colleagues into the national network but makes their work a source of pride for Kapi'olani, thus stimulating greater interest in service learning there.

Sometimes these collegial networks are facilitated by regional and national meetings of higher education organizations such as the American Association for Higher Education (AAHE) and the Association of American Colleges and Universities as well as by meetings of organizations whose missions are specifically targeted toward moral and civic education like Campus Compact, the Association for Practical and Professional Ethics, and the Society for Ethics Across the Curriculum. AAHE, for example, sponsors three major conferences every year, each drawing many faculty and administrators from across the country. One is the full annual meeting, the second focuses on faculty roles and rewards, and the third addresses assessment. For each conference, groups of faculty interested in particular issues propose sessions on topics of interest. The meetings typically include sessions focused on service learning, problem-based learning, and faculty participation in learning communities.

Enlistment of Non-Tenure Track Faculty

At many institutions, adjunct and other non-tenure track faculty play a central part in undergraduate moral and civic education. In fact, adjunct faculty are doing about 40 percent of the teaching throughout higher education. It is not surprising then that many service-learning courses are taught by adjunct, usually part-time, faculty. At CSUMB, where this number has increased significantly over time so that now almost half of the service-learning courses are taught by adjuncts, Seth Pollock, director of service learning, is worried about what appears to be a trend: "It's frustrating because a lot of our strongest supporters, who are really grappling with how to do service learning and be a good service-learning practitioner, are our part-timers. I have a graph that tracks it from the beginning—first semester almost everyone teaching it was full-time faculty, and now we're at about 50 percent, which is the university average for courses being taught by adjuncts. That's where the trend is headed, but I don't know if we'll stay at the average or keep sliding. It's a real concern."

Portland State University has also seen a decreasing proportion of community-based learning and core curriculum (University Studies) courses taught by tenure track faculty. This is especially true of the labor-intensive senior capstone courses. Portland State's former provost, Michael Reardon, believes it is critical to engage more senior faculty in University Studies in order to avoid segregating University Studies from the rest of the curriculum. A primary danger of such segregation is that it can create a division of labor in which tenured and tenure track faculty consider their work "the real work" of the campus and fail to understand fully or value the work of adjunct faculty. We heard at other institutions, such as St. Kate's and Kapiʻolani Community College, that a major concern among faculty has been the struggle to ensure fair compensation and benefits policies for adjunct faculty and to ensure that these teachers are fully incorporated into the life of the campus and respected for their contributions, which often go far beyond classroom teaching.

Although it is undesirable for moral and civic concerns to be represented only in courses taught by lecturers and adjuncts, these faculty can be an extremely valuable resource for and play important roles in moral and civic education because they offer a wider range of backgrounds and expertise than that of tenure track faculty. Many of them, especially those who teach part-time, have strong ties to the local community, many bring pedagogical skills and interests that are not well represented among the tenure track faculty, and most are free of the pressures imposed by departmental politics.

At Emory University as at other campuses, many of the faculty who have played leadership roles in introducing ethical and civic issues into their courses are on a lecture track, though most are on long-term, full-time contracts. There is considerable solidarity among the lecture track faculty and a sense that they can have real impact on teaching at Emory by bringing in foundation and government grants to support new programs that bring ethical concerns into undergraduate science education and into other fields that have not previously given these issues much attention. It may be that having the stability of long-term contracts and the flexibility afforded by operating outside the research-dominated tenure and promotion system puts these faculty in a strong position to do this kind of work.

Faculty Recruitment

Some campuses that take a holistic and intentional approach to moral and civic education explicitly or implicitly include faculty interest and experience in this area among their hiring criteria. At the two-year Minneapolis campus of the College of St. Catherine, search committees look explicitly for people with a desire to educate for moral and social responsibility. As one administrator said: "We're very deliberate about it. We have developed a 'profile of a mission-oriented teacher' here at St. Kate's Minneapolis to use for recruiting candidates." Both the hiring and the promotion programs at Alverno College emphasize the institution's commitment to moral and civic learning. All faculty who apply for teaching positions are asked to provide a *philosophy of education statement.* Alverno is conscious that it takes a particular kind of person to be happy there and that it is important to find the right fit. The college pays a great deal of attention to cover letters, looking to see whether applicants emphasize their interest in teaching or focus primarily on their research. At the Air Force Academy, "the development of officership" is brought up during hiring interviews and the impression among current faculty is that the academy's *whole person* model of education is an attraction for many civilians as well as military faculty. At community colleges, involvement with the local community is generally a criterion for evaluating faculty performance, so it is not surprising that evidence of commitment and expertise in this area plays an important part in hiring decisions at Kapi'olani and Turtle Mountain Community Colleges. Nevertheless, many institutions, especially research-intensive universities, do not consider it appropriate to use an interest in moral or civic education as a criterion for evaluating prospective faculty (except for those who will teach in special programs with this kind of focus).

When hiring criteria seek "mission-oriented teachers" of various sorts but do not specify the need to adhere to any particular values or ideology, policies that give preference to candidates with an interest in moral or civic education should not pose any threat to academic freedom. To ensure that this so, campuses must be careful that this kind of recruitment does not impose an unspoken filter, that criteria have been made explicit to candidates and reviewers (and the larger community), and that a rationale is offered for using these criteria. For example, some institutions may recruit faculty with a particular religious affiliation, as Roman Catholic institutions may do, and this is generally recognized as legitimate because these preferences are a matter of public record and are justified as a means of preserving the religious identity and mission of the schools.

The Rewards of This Work

There is no question that the kind of teaching we described in Chapters Five and Six is demanding. And there is no question that many faculty in higher education feel stressed, too busy, even burned out in many cases. But paradoxically, many faculty who feel too busy to take on one more thing actually feel energized when they do decide to incorporate moral and civic concerns and more engaged pedagogies into their teaching. This kind of teaching is deeply rewarding for many who do it, fully justifying its considerable costs. Faculty who teach service-learning courses, for example, say they are constantly renewed when their students are learning outside the classroom—that is, outside what the faculty members themselves know. Students bring these new insights into discussions with their teachers, thus enriching the faculty and enlarging their understanding. This feeling that they are learning from their own teaching is another of the many rewards that faculty report when they do this work.

In talking about the inspiration he has drawn from Socrates, Rob Reich expresses the personal meaning this kind of engaged teaching has for him and for many who practice it: "In an immediate sense, I think Socrates is a guiding light, a beacon both pedagogically and substantively in the sense that everything should be submitted to critical thought and reflection and nothing should be taken for granted. And the result of that makes education itself into a spiritual enterprise in a way, because ultimately it's about reflecting upon who you are and how you fit into the universe." For many faculty we met, the spiritual or moral enterprise, the sense of pursuing something they believe in, is not only the students' enterprise but their own.

8

MORAL AND CIVIC LEARNING
BEYOND THE CLASSROOM

WHEN COLLEGE GRADUATES think back on their undergraduate years, especially when they reflect on the experiences that changed them personally, they may remember a few special courses or professors as having been especially powerful, but they are more likely to recall important relationships with friends, the general feel of being at college, and perhaps some especially engaging activity, like involvement with the theater, a musical group, or the student newspaper. This is especially true for people who attend residential colleges, but memories of powerful experiences outside the classroom are also salient for many at commuter campuses. This makes sense, because undergraduates spend the majority of their time in pursuits other than their classes and related work. Not all of this time of course is discretionary. The majority of students work in paid jobs (Boyer, 1987; National Center for Education Statistics, 1996), and many also have family responsibilities. Yet even for the busiest undergraduate, who commutes to campus and has both a job and a family, learning in college can be significantly enriched by experiences beyond the classroom.

Summarizing a number of studies, Alexander Astin (1985b) concluded that extracurricular involvement is directly linked to the amount of time students spend on campus, the quality of that experience, and students' persistence in college. More recent research also reveals that involvement in extracurricular activities has a strong positive influence on students' satisfaction with their college experience. An extensive survey of Harvard students found that a commitment to one or two activities other than coursework—for as much as twenty hours per week—does not affect students' grades, but such commitments are related strongly to satisfaction with college life. The more involved students are, the more satisfied they are with their college experience (Light, 2001, p. 26). This finding is consistent with earlier studies of undergraduates at a range of institutions (Kapp, 1979; Kegan, 1978; Pascarella, 1980). Even more striking, there is a strong indication that the only factor that predicts adult success—whatever outcome measure is used, including income—is involvement in extracurricular activities during college (Krumboltz, 1957; Power-Ross, 1980).

Many students spend their out-of-class time in activities that contribute to their well-being and intellectual and personal development. But some extracurricular pursuits are less benign. The corrosiveness of big league, intercollegiate sports is well known. A study of intercollegiate athletes by Sharon Stoll (1995), for example, concludes that "the present competitive model is doing more harm than good" (p. 12) in the realm of moral development (see also Shulman & Bowen, 2001). As early as 1929, a Carnegie Foundation study reported that "more than any other force, [intercollegiate athletics have] tended to distort the values of college life" (Savage, 1929, p. 307). Boyer (1987) concluded that the situation had not improved in the six decades between his and Savage's studies: "The tragedy is that the cynicism that stems from the abuses in athletics infects the rest of student life, from promoting academic dishonesty to the loss of individual ideals" (p. 184).

The commercialism on many campuses is fed by but extends beyond intercollegiate competition in sports and is reinforced by aspects of the U.S. culture beyond the campus. The many hours some students spend watching television help promote this commercialism (Boyer, 1987). The hazing and racism that characterize some fraternities is well known, and the long-standing problem of binge drinking among college students is growing (Wechsler et al., 2002). It is clear that not all activities outside the classroom are productive and educationally valuable. The challenge for higher education is to find ways to capitalize on the potential of positive out-of-class experiences. Efforts to involve a majority of students in a systematic way that has real educational impact, however, are impeded by some of the trends we outlined in Chapter Two. These include the increased number of older students and students who work, commute, or have family responsibilities, as well as the huge increase in the sheer number of students in higher education. The new student profile makes it much more difficult to engage students in a coherent set of extracurricular experiences. Complicating matters further, student autonomy has increased dramatically, largely as a result of activism in the 1960s and 1970s, leading colleges to set aside close regulation of residence halls, compulsory chapel services, convocations, and other required extracurricular activities.

In Chapter Two we also pointed to the unity of early American higher education—its holistic approach to educating the mind, body, and spirit—and the sharp separation between academic affairs and student life that emerged in the twentieth century. Although the value of integrating curricular and extracurricular learning is widely recognized, these two domains are distinctly bifurcated in contemporary higher education. The dichotomy found at most colleges and universities is rooted in the administrative separation of the two domains. Provosts and presidents rarely have firsthand experience in student affairs until their appointments, and few are able to develop a coherent vision of student development that integrates academic with nonacademic learning. Faculty do not see student affairs as their responsibility, and student affairs staff are generally disconnected from the faculty and curricular matters. Graduate training for faculty and for student affairs professionals establishes areas of expertise for these two groups that intersect very little, and perpetuates a conception of the two domains as almost entirely distinct.

As a result, student life and academic life are rarely integrated productively, and students are given relatively little guidance in their extracurricular involvements (Kuh, Douglas, Lund, & Ramin-Gyurnek, 1994). On most campuses the many cultural events available to students receive little attention or support from faculty. Faculty seldom urge students to attend important lectures or other events and seldom connect these out-of-class educational events to ongoing classroom teaching (Boyer, 1987). On virtually every campus there are many worthwhile extracurricular activities, but whether students will get involved in programs that support their development is generally left to chance. In addition, some activities that have great potential to support moral and civic development, as well as other kinds of learning, fail to realize that potential. Students generally need support and guidance in order to make the most of activities they choose. For example, help from a journalism professor or other adviser can stimulate the integration of journalistic ethics into the work of a student newspaper, but this kind of guidance is rare. Unfortunately, many faculty and staff members are hesitant to provide moral guidance, as David Brooks (2001) recently suggested in *The Atlantic Monthly*. In extensive discussions at Princeton and other elite university campuses, Brooks found that "when it comes to character and virtue, these young people have been left on their own. . . . We assume that if adults try to offer moral instruction, it will just backfire, because our children will reject our sermonizing. . . . We assume that such questions have no correct answer that can be taught. Or maybe the simple truth is that adult institutions no longer try to talk about character and virtue because they simply wouldn't know what to say" (pp. 40, 53).

Given all these complexities, the steps colleges and universities might take to make most of campus life beyond the classroom supportive of students' moral and civic development are not at all obvious. Developing strategies to provide a positive developmental experience for more students requires careful thought. A heavy-handed approach will not work. Students will not give up their autonomy and adult status, especially when so many have been out of high school for years. Furthermore, there is clear evidence that students engage longer in and learn more from activities they choose themselves (see, for example, Cordova & Lepper, 1996). Many of the important out-of-class experiences for college students are generated by the students themselves, especially informal activities involving interactions with their fellow students, and are therefore largely outside the control of the institution. Despite these challenges, there are things that colleges and universities can do if they want to take best advantage of the time and energy students spend on pursuits other than attending and preparing for their classes.

At our case study campuses and some others we learned about, we saw many creative attempts to ensure a positive extracurricular experience for students while still respecting their freedom to follow their own interests and inclinations. These efforts begin early—even before freshman year—through setting a tone in literature about the school, asking students to prepare the summer before entering college, and establishing clear expectations when students arrive on campus, including the articulation of an honor code on some campuses. In Chapter Three we described the cultural climates the case study schools have developed. In their daily lives at these schools, students encounter not only the kinds of cultural symbols and routines we described earlier but also administrators and faculty who are prepared and able to take advantage of the "teachable moments" for moral and civic learning that arise naturally in any complex community. On campuses where student bodies are racially or religiously diverse, students need help connecting across the lines of ethnic division. Structured programs to encourage these connections begin early at most of the campuses we visited. And perhaps the heart of developmental out-of-class experiences is found in the huge variety of clubs and other organizations available to students, including many that involve students in service to others. Finally, recognizing that college is only one segment of an ongoing developmental process—some colleges and universities have put programs in place to help students maintain their commitment to social responsibility beyond their college years.

Hallmarks of Quality

How can all these approaches best be accomplished? George Kuh and his colleagues (1991, 1994) have studied campuses that have especially positive effects on students, and their research reveals a number of hallmarks of high-quality extracurricular programs. They are *intentionally designed* with specific learning outcomes in mind, they are *aligned with the mission* of the campus as a whole so that the various academic and extracurricular programs reinforce each other, their organizers *collaborate* with each other, they are overseen and *guided by student affairs staff or faculty,* and they are regularly *assessed* to document and guide program improvement. We found evidence of these hallmarks on the campuses we visited and on some we learned about in other ways, and the presence of these hallmarks is part of what we mean when we call moral and civic education on these campuses holistic and intentional. Although Kuh and his colleagues' hallmarks represent an ideal that few campuses, even our case study schools, can fully achieve, they provide a sense of direction for institutions that are trying to move toward more effective programming.

On most campuses extracurricular activities are not intentionally designed with specific developmental goals in mind nor are they coordinated with each other or with the curriculum. We were struck by the special efforts taken at many of the campuses we chose for site visits to think about the goals of their student life activities and to integrate the work of faculty and professional staff, linking academic learning with extracurricular life. Alverno College, for example, is characterized by a high degree of collaboration between faculty and student services. Members of the student affairs staff are often invited by faculty to talk about their work at regular Friday afternoon faculty discussions, and student affairs staff are also involved in faculty-led revisions of the curriculum. It is common for Alverno faculty and staff to work together on both curricular and extracurricular matters. For instance, members of Alverno's counseling office often collaborate with academic programs, working for example with nursing students to create a poster session on breast cancer for their spring health fair. The counseling office also partners with some faculty members in courses and special programs. When counseling staff learned that a faculty member had invited leaders from Legal Action of Wisconsin to speak to her class about domestic violence and services for victims of domestic violence, the counseling office worked with the professor to open the program to all Alverno students, staff, and faculty.

Messiah College has also worked hard to build cooperation and linkages among a wide array of programs. The Office of External Programs oversees a number of curricular and extracurricular programs and centers that reach beyond the borders of the campus, including the Agapé Center for Service and Learning, the Career Center, International Programs, the Internship Center, and the Latino Partnership Program. Each has articulated student development objectives that complement and build on students' academic learning. The staff of the Office of External Programs work closely with faculty and other administrators to ensure that strengthening moral and civic learning along the lines of the college's mission statement is a common goal and that all programs and centers develop strategies for connecting those goals with their work (Messiah College, 2001, pp. 8–9). Messiah is able to link all these programs and centers around a common set of moral and civic themes partly because its evangelical Christian mission attracts students, faculty, and staff who are prepared to help build a community dedicated to a common vision built on faith as well as reason. Nevertheless, this kind of integration does not come naturally at any institution, and most faith-based campuses have not achieved Messiah's level of intentional collaborations. Size is a key factor as well. Its small, residential campus gives Messiah obvious advantages over larger campuses, especially commuter campuses, in promoting a coordinated approach to student life.

Another hallmark of good practice for powerful extracurricular activities is careful involvement, guidance, and oversight by faculty, student affairs staff, and administrators. Some students come to college knowing that they want to be engaged in the theater or the student newspaper or some other area. But most are unsure. Campuses where students receive guidance not only about curricular choices but also about extracurricular choices and the ways these choices can complement each other are much more likely to find that their students choose a positive path that matches their interests and the institution's educational goals. At Messiah College, for example, all first-year students enroll in a fall semester seminar, and as part of this seminar the director of the EpiCenter (Experiential Programs Information Center) makes presentations about the college's off-campus program opportunities.

Although every campus can benefit from programs that help students plan their extracurricular involvement, these programs are particularly important at commuter campuses, which have more obstacles to student involvement than other schools and which lack the residences that are natural settings for small-group activities. Alverno College's efforts are

notable in this regard, because Alverno has a high proportion of returning and commuting students.

Developmental Impact

The power of extracurricular and other out-of-class experiences for moral
and civic development derives from their multiplicity, their emotional
immediacy, and their encompassing quality. They are both figure and
ground in campus life. They can be experienced as the sea in which students swim as well as the dives and explorations those students make.
Experiences outside the classroom can change students' frameworks for
interpreting reality, their sense of what is important, their confidence in
their own ability to affect the world around them, and their sense of who
they are and who they want to be. Because extracurricular and other student life activities so often involve action as well as reflection, students
engaged in them can learn skills that they may not be likely to derive from
classroom learning. These activities also allow students to consolidate and
extend skills such as critical thinking and writing that are important to
their academic coursework.

Campus culture, student life broadly construed, and structured extracurricular programs all provide opportunities for the institution to
embody its distinctive understanding of moral and civic development,
focusing on connections with various communities, establishing expectations of integrity and personal responsibility in all pursuits, and supporting efforts to contribute to positive social change. But the multiplicity of
student life also makes it an arena in which an institution can reasonably
broaden its conception of what is morally and civically important, going
beyond its dominant themes to incorporate other themes and goals that
are valuable for full development even though less obviously central to
the institution's identity.

From a developmental point of view, it is important for student life to
contribute to students' moral and civic learning for some of the same reasons that it is important for faculty to take advantage of the wide array
of pedagogies we described in Chapter Five. Learning how the world
works, learning to resolve problems and make judgments in the world beyond the academy, and learning in a deep and flexible enough way to remember and use what they have learned requires students to engage in
complex practices in settings that include uncertainties, uncontrolled vari-
ance, and unpredictable forces, things academic study too often filters out
(Menand, 1997; Shulman, 1997). Depth and persistence of learning are
enhanced by opportunities to consolidate and apply new ideas in more

complicated situations, in multiple contexts, and in actual practice. In fact extracurricular activities and other experiences outside the classroom can be vitally important for the development of the full range of understanding, motivation, and skills that is entailed in moral and civic maturity. Research confirms this impact. George Kuh and his colleagues (1991, 1994) have examined carefully the ways in which learning outside the classroom can contribute directly to students' development. As their work and extensive national studies by Alexander Astin (1984, 1985a) show, the more engaged students are in multiple, mutually reinforcing activities, the more likely they are to learn in a variety of areas. Extracurricular activities can also have a significant influence on students' personal development and acquisition of important values and skills, including development related to moral and civic learning (Harnett, 1965; Kuh et al., 1991; Whitla, 1981). Not surprisingly, the nature of the activity in which students engage is directly related to its developmental impact. Activities that offer leadership experiences, for example, are more likely than more individually focused activities to enhance abilities to work with and motivate others (Kuh et al., 1991; Schuh & Laverty, 1983).

Many students engage in some form of community service as an extracurricular activity, and this participation has been shown to have a positive effect on their moral and civic development. A survey of more than 3,000 students from forty-two institutions found that (compared to nonparticipating students and adjusting for preexisting differences) student involvement in community service is associated with gains in academic engagement (such as aspirations for advanced degrees), civic responsibility (such as sense of efficacy to change society, commitment to influence social values, and future plans to volunteer), and life skills (including leadership, interpersonal, and conflict resolution skills) (Astin & Sax, 1998). A study of more than 12,000 alumni of college programs, funded by the Corporation for National and Community Service, also shows that undergraduate volunteer experiences have a positive influence on many behavioral and value outcomes, including frequency of socializing with diverse people, helping others in difficulty, developing a meaningful life philosophy, and volunteering and participating in community action programs; these experiences also promote racial understanding and a sense of efficacy (Astin, Sax, & Avalos, 1999). Other studies show that democratic political attitudes are enhanced among students who participate in extracurricular activities such as community service and that involvement is positively related to the development of high levels of political efficacy, increased valuing of democratic processes, and greater community and political activism (see, for example, Hepburn, Niemi, & Chapman, 2000).

Further, a landmark study on civic voluntarism found that student participation in extracurricular activities was a powerful predictor of subsequent involvement in political activities (Verba, Schlozman, & Brady, 1995).

Extracurricular activities that encourage interactions with diverse peers show particular promise for promoting moral and civic development. Students who reported interactions with diverse peers in terms of race, interests, and values showed greater openness to diverse perspectives and a willingness to question their own beliefs (Pascarella, Edison, Nora, Hagedorn, & Terenzini, 1996). Longitudinal studies of undergraduates also indicate that interaction with racially diverse peers is associated with many moral and civic values and skills, including increases in cultural knowledge and understanding, commitment to promoting racial understanding, acceptance of people from different races and cultures, tolerance of people with different beliefs, and leadership abilities (Antonio, 1998b; Hurtado, 1997; Milem, 1994). Evidence suggests that the most effective forms of interaction with diverse peers reflect engagement on a range of topics, participation in activities that focus on social diversity and intergroup dialogue, and participation in race awareness workshops that promote communication (Antonio, 1998b; Springer, Palmer, Terenzini, Pascarella, & Nora, 1996).

There is a lot that institutions can do to create an environment conducive to this kind of moral and civic development. They can set the stage for incoming students from the very beginning, calling attention to moral and civic goals as integral to students' understanding of the undergraduate experience. They can create a community based in positive values and establish a cultural fabric rich in moral and civic learning opportunities. They can connect with and build on the values and interests students bring to college, broadening, deepening, and sometimes transforming those values and interests. And in various ways they can support the persistence of moral and civic learning beyond the college years.

Setting the Stage: Introduction to Campus Life

Most colleges and universities send prospective students materials about course selection and other aspects of the academic work and also about the nuts and bolts of beginning college. But many of these colleges fail to use those introductory materials to articulate specifically what the faculty and administration expect students to gain in terms of either their academic or moral and civic development. A few institutions, with a strong commitment to the moral and civic dimensions of undergraduate education, use their early contacts with students to establish a frame of expectations that encompasses themes of community, integrity, diversity, respect, and moral and civic growth. Even at this early stage they begin calling attention to the values the institution stands for, the standards and expectations for students, what is most important in the college experience, and what is likely to be exciting and inspiring about it. These messages encourage students to view their experience through a moral and civic lens from the start, alerting them to pay attention to the moral and civic aspects of their education and conveying the idea that "we are a community; we are in this together; we have high expectations for you; and here are some of the big ideas that college life will address." When conveyed memorably and powerfully, these messages can shape the interpretive frame through which students will make sense of their educational experience.

Miami University, a public residential campus of about 16,000 students in Oxford, Ohio, carefully articulates expectations for students' academic and moral and civic learning through a series of summer newsletters sent to incoming students and titled "First Things First." Soon after admission, students receive the first of several newsletters. It stresses key dimensions of the Miami undergraduate experience and is written in a vivid style that encourages new students to read them carefully and consider their suggestions. As part of the recurring theme of academic excellence, this newsletter includes engaging stories of students with outstanding academic records, and lively faculty profiles are added as a way to invite students to form relationships with their teachers. Students are urged to explore the entire range of the liberal arts, and not to choose a major, let alone a career, too quickly. The importance of being responsible, active members of the Miami campus community is a second key theme, emphasized in stories that show how extracurricular activities relate to students' academic and personal interests and their overall college experience. A third theme is the history and traditions of Miami University, stressed to strengthen the sense of campus community. The fourth theme is the responsibility of every student to discover and appreciate racial, ethnic, and cultural differences.

These themes are emphasized throughout Miami University's orientation programs. In order to engage students in thinking about diversity, the members of each incoming class are asked to read a provocative book in the summer before they begin college. In 1998, for example, students read *The Lone Ranger and Tonto Fistfight in Heaven,* a series of twenty-two interlinked stories about life on the Spokane Indian Reservation, by Sherman Alexie (1993). Then Alexie spoke at the freshman convocation that year, and students discussed the book and its insights in small groups led by faculty and staff. In part because Miami University is named for an indigenous tribe, Native American culture is a frequent focus for helping students appreciate the value of diverse cultures. In other years other cultures and perspectives have been highlighted by summer reading books such as Cornel West's *Race Matters* (1993), Julia Alvarez's *How the García Girls Lost Their Accents* (1991), and Abraham Verghese's *My Own Country* (1994). As these titles suggest, Miami University's summer reading program stresses issues of racial, ethnic, and socioeconomic diversity. This is a crucial part of introduction to college life, because most students at Miami University, like those at many colleges and universities, come with little experience outside of the towns where they grew up, and many have had no interactions with people from different racial or ethnic groups.

Many campuses have similarly found that summer reading programs and student discussions draw students together around complex issues that relate to larger questions of student life and learning. Harvard University, for example, sends incoming freshmen a series of essays. A typical packet included pieces by then-president Neil Rudenstine on civility, faculty member Henry Louis Gates Jr. on the conflicting pressures faced by those entering college, Henry David Thoreau on self-reliance, and Anne Fadiman on keeping an open mind, particularly when reading literature. The packet also included several essays written by undergraduates with different backgrounds about their experiences at Harvard. Incoming students read these essays during the summer, and soon after they arrive on campus they meet in small groups with a faculty member to discuss the readings and issues such as how they will grapple with the diversity of their fellow students and society as a whole (Light, 2001).

Colleges can also set the stage for students' moral and civic learning through orientation programs, which may last from a day or two to a week and are designed to help acclimate students to college life. Many campuses use orientation programs to inform students about expectations for student behavior such as campus regulations and policies, and some use them to introduce newcomers to the college's values by emphasizing themes such as community involvement, personal growth, and respect for diversity. A growing number of campuses are incorporating opportunities for student volunteerism and community service into their orientation activities. Duke University's orientation week, for example, includes an open house at the community service center and a scheduled opportunity to participate in Project Child, a program to support Durham Public Schools. Building community service activities into orientation programs can be an excellent way to introduce students to the idea of service and community involvement as a valuable and natural part of the undergraduate experience.

In addition to short orientation programs, an increasing number of campuses offer yearlong freshman seminars that serve as extended orientation, or "college survival," seminars. Although the primary focus of these seminars is enhancing students' overall academic success, many also cover topics such as diversity and gender issues, academic integrity, student rights and responsibilities, drug and alcohol use, the values of academic life, and other campus policies and expectations (Barefoot & Fidler, 1996). The quality of these extended orientation seminars varies widely, and many seem to have little careful planning or overarching structure. They usually do not offer the same kinds of opportunities for linking deep academic work with moral and civic learning as do standard courses. If they are taught well, however, extended orientation seminars can be effective methods for introducing new students to the campus mission and values and helping them think about what is important to them during and after college. For example, Emory University freshmen take part in a six-week advising and mentoring program that involves self-exploration as well as orientation to the university and local community. Among other things, students are helped to think about what they are good at, what they like doing, and what it is important to do for the well-being of the world. They are asked to think about the points where two or three of these categories might intersect and the ways their experiences in college might expand the first two categories and their understanding of the third as well as increasing the all-important intersection among all three. Spelman College recently transformed its one-week orientation into a year-long, one-credit course linked to the core academic program. Freshman Orientation begins with an intense week of activities for incoming students prior to the start of classes, followed by a yearlong series of freshman convocation speakers and biweekly classes with a professor who serves as a mentor to the group. During recent years the theme of the program has been Women as Citizens of the World: Demonstrating Vision, Integrity, Values and Involvement, focusing on urgent issues confronting world citizens in the twenty-first century.

Creating a Community Based in Positive Values

Not all important elements in student life are located in formal programs such as orientation seminars or clubs and organizations. Some are part of the ethos of campus life and the campus's sense of community. Institutions of higher education, like all communities, have expectations for and make demands on their members as well as providing them with benefits. Various constituencies, subcultures, and incidents convey both consistent and conflicting messages to students. Prominent among these messages are the reactions of administrative leaders and faculty to problems that arise when cherished values conflict, as they inevitably will. Intentional efforts to create ongoing conversations about actual and potential conflicts constitute another important element in the moral and civic environment, as do intentional communities formed to enhance the experience of those undergraduates who live as well as study together. It is the richness and flux of this array that leads us to call student life the encompassing ocean and the ground as well as the figure of the college experience.

Honor Codes and Other Codes of Conduct

In searching for values around which higher education in a pluralistic society can find common ground, there is perhaps none clearer than academic integrity. It therefore provides a credible entry point for almost any institution that wants to strengthen its moral and civic climate. It is undeniable that honesty, including intellectual honesty, is indispensable to the academic enterprise, and educational institutions universally tell students that they must be honest in their academic work. Although campuses make this value highly explicit, it is nevertheless violated with growing frequency. National studies show that cheating in college has increased considerably since the 1960s (Pavela, 1997). Research suggests that many students do not understand or share the values of academic integrity. They excuse their cheating on the grounds that their studies are not relevant to their goals or that they need good grades in order to get jobs or acceptance to graduate school. They say that cheating is easy and the risks are low (Gehring, Nuss, & Pavela, 1986).

Unfortunately, many faculty are not fully committed to campus policies on academic integrity and do not follow established procedures and policies regarding cheating (Jendrek, 1989). The reasons for this are numerous: the time and effort required to monitor cheating, the high burden of proof needed, a lack of clarity in the judicial system or guidelines, dissatisfaction with judicial board proceedings, and a focus of attention on research rather than teaching (McCabe, 1993; McCabe & Trevino, 1993). Faculty at colleges with honor codes are much more likely to adhere to established procedures, but only 68 percent of faculty even in those schools say they consistently report students who cheat to the designated authority (versus 33 percent at non-honor code schools) (McCabe, 1993). This widespread failure to enforce campus codes and policies is unfortunate, because it sends a message to students that these matters are not important. It can even encourage cheating, because students' behavior is greatly influenced by their perceptions of faculty attitudes and behavior toward cheating (McCabe & Pavela, 1997).

In response to this alarming situation more institutions are adopting honor codes and paying serious attention to how these codes can be implemented effectively. Many campuses are recognizing the need for serious conversations about the important connections among fundamental values, campus rules, and student behavior. This is a positive development for moral and civic education more broadly, because strong honor codes and the kinds of conversations they stimulate not only help deter academic dishonesty[1] but also seem to raise an interest in a wider range of moral issues and foster a climate of trust, civility, self-restraint, and mutual respect (Bok, 1990; Cole & Conklin, 1996). Honor codes work partly by promoting a campus culture of integrity. One study asked students at thirty-one campuses, half of which had honor codes, what they thought about academic integrity. Students at honor code campuses frequently referred to the honor code as an integral part of a broader culture of integrity that permeates their institutions, a culture based on community values, communication, the influence of positive peer pressure, mutual responsibility, and respect. Students at institutions without honor codes rarely engaged in this type of discussion (McCabe, Trevino, & Butterfield, 1999).

One of the oldest traditions at Rhodes College, in Tennessee, is its Honor System, which goes beyond academic honesty to address "the spiritual, moral, and intellectual development of the individual student" and of the college as a whole. Rhodes emphasizes that the Honor System, which applies to students, faculty, and staff, contains "a moral ideal by which to guide [our] actions. This ideal is absolute honesty to oneself and to others in all aspects of life. It is not only a guide for college life, it is also a principle which Rhodes students believe to be fundamental in ethical life, both during and after college" (Rhodes College, 2001). Surveys show that the Honor System enjoys wide support and that most students take it seriously.[2] Responses to a series of controversies on campus indicate that many students have thought deeply about the significance of the code for the campus community. In one campus newspaper article criticizing a prank involving the rigging of student government elections, a student journalist noted: "This is not a moral plea, but rather an explanation of attitude. If you choose to break the Honor Code . . . you will be held accountable. This sounds like a lecture, but is a simple application of the responsibility and repercussions at work in a functioning society like ours (i.e. the 'real world'). The 'deeper meaning' of the code might not be freedom and trust alone, but a sense of campus unity and potential for personal growth" (Bogner, 1996). The Honor System fosters a sense of concern and respect among community members, said another Rhodes student: "It is this sense of respect which leads to a feeling of belonging and unity. This idealism provides an opportunity to tie the group together as one" (May, 1996). Exchanges like these indicate the extent to which honor codes, conduct codes, and other campus guidelines can shape students' understandings of the campus community and their responsibilities to it. They also reveal that making these policies salient to students—emphasizing their values and purposes and creating a strong sense of student ownership in them—can result in valuable opportunities for moral learning when problems arise, as they do at all campuses.

Duke's Center for Academic Integrity has been a leader in efforts to study and improve honor codes. To foster an ethic of responsibility, the center advocates policies that require students to recognize their own responsibilities to the campus community and take responsibility for the actions of others. It recommends making as few conduct rules as possible, stating them broadly, and ensuring—through persuasive public justifications and rationales for rules, procedures, and decisions—that they make sense to students. The recommended model explicitly links clear expectations of honorable student behavior with the idea of responsible citizenship, helping students understand that the values and behaviors required of them as members of their campus community parallel the requirements of good citizenship in any community.

A crucial factor in building effective codes is involving all members of the campus community in honest discussions about academic values (Pavela & McCabe, 1993). Research suggests that guidelines for student conduct should not be created and imposed by an administration acting in isolation but should represent collaborations among students, faculty, and administrators. Because some students graduate and others enter every year and some faculty and staff leave and new faculty and staff are hired, these processes should operate continually rather than as one-time events.

Strong faculty involvement in honor and conduct codes is important not only in helping to determine rules but also in maintaining and applying them. Instructors can emphasize the importance of the policies by discussing them in their classes and making explicit the relationship between academic integrity in scholarly work and student honesty in their courses (Cole & Conklin, 1996). Clearly, having an honor code significantly increases the likelihood that faculty will maintain and apply the rules, but the fact that almost a third of faculty even at honor code institutions do not consistently follow established procedures for reporting breaches of the code indicates that many campuses could benefit from more effective communication with faculty about how they can best foster academic integrity and why it matters.

The participation of students in the process is at least as critical. Recognizing this, Connecticut College has engaged students actively in every aspect of the college's code. At the beginning of each year all new and returning Connecticut College students sign the C-Book, which contains the Honor Code Pledge. This pledge states that students are honor-bound to report their own violations to the judiciary board and that students who are aware of violations by others must remind them to report themselves. Students also have the primary responsibility for deciding what is covered by the Honor Code Pledge—a student committee meets once or twice each semester to review what goes into the C-Book, and faculty review all decisions. The Student Judiciary Board deals with all infractions (for the C-Book text and further information about the Connecticut College Honor System, see Connecticut College, Student Government Association, 2002). Former Connecticut College president Claire Gaudiani (1995) emphasizes that the student-run honor code provides students "an opportunity to live under a set of rules and to judge themselves within its framework." The honor code "makes clear to students the moral choices they have—to cheat or not to cheat, for instance—to meet or not to meet the expectations of the community. They see the repercussions of their personal choices on the quality of everyone's common life. It shapes opportunities for students to live the values that connect the college community members: self-discipline, self-reliance, fairness, trust, patience, compassion, and loyalty." The expectations of personal integrity expressed in the Honor Code Pledge yield ongoing campus discussions about justice, consideration for the dignity of others, individual rights, and personal and community responsibilities. Students feel a strong sense of ownership of the code and its values and realize the benefits of meeting these expectations, including the freedoms and leadership opportunities they gain as a result of having the trust of the faculty and administration.

Students' perception that their institution's honor system has value and legitimacy is essential because peer attitudes are among the most important factors affecting student behavior in a range of areas, including cheating (McCabe & Trevino, 1997). Integrated, comprehensive, and student-centered approaches to academic integrity are vital because students learn what is acceptable through talking to other students as well as by interacting with faculty and administrators and participating in many different subcultures on the campus and beyond. Students will understand and accept responsibility for their own and others' conduct only when all campus "signals" are sending this message, from the president welcoming freshmen, to faculty talking with students and advisers with advisees, to students talking to each other at midnight in a residence hall corridor (Cole & Conklin, 1996).

For these reasons, it is beneficial for the returning students to serve as the primary educators of new students about honor and conduct codes. Duke University's student-run Honor Council, for example, sponsors a freshman orientation to the honor code and judicial system, dormitory discussions on academic integrity, campuswide symposia featuring leading thinkers in ethics, surveys gauging the status of academic integrity at Duke, and town hall meetings to establish dialogues on honor code issues. At the United States Air Force Academy, student honor representatives help mediate conflicts related to the honor system, working with individuals on both sides of a case in the discovery and negotiation phases of a hearing, and serve on the honor board that decides honor code cases. At many other schools, student groups such as judicial boards or honor councils have primary responsibility for hearing and handling some or all complaints.

High standards for student conduct have little influence unless they are consistently and fairly enforced. At the Air Force Academy, sanctions for violating the honor code are severe although they have been tempered somewhat over time. In the past, any cadet found in violation of the academy's honor code was immediately and summarily *disenrolled*. This policy was revised in the 1980s, and a more *developmental* system was instituted, allowing cadets to be put on probation in some circumstances, depending on the severity of the offence, whether the cadet turns himself or herself in voluntarily, and the cadet's year in school. (Usually, probation is an option only for freshmen and sophomores.) A cadet on probation is confined to the campus for six months, which is considered a very stern penalty, and participates in a number of developmentally oriented activities, including working with a mentor, writing a regular journal, undertaking special projects, and working to make other students aware of the importance of the honor code. In the view of the program staff and some cadets we talked to, this set of disciplinary and developmental experiences is positive and powerful for most who go through it.

Penalties for violating honor codes and other campus policies should provide students with structured opportunities to learn from their mistakes, as the academy program does. The University of Maryland program Citizenship and Ethical Development includes the Academic Integrity Seminar, a six-week, noncredit educational seminar sponsored by the Student Honor Council and taught by staff members or graduate assistants. Students who violate the school's honor code are often required to complete this course, which uses provocative short readings to engage students in ethical dialogue around academic integrity issues. Student violations of honor codes are opportunities—teachable moments—for moral learning not only for the offending student but also for those who know about the violation, those who struggle with their own responsibility in the situation, and those who are involved in administering the disciplinary systems. Honor codes and similar codes of conduct, when they are broadly construed and thoughtfully implemented, can help a student develop habitual behaviors of scrupulous honesty, a sense of identity as a person of integrity, and a deeper understanding of the responsibilities and constraints entailed in being a member of a community. For students involved in establishing and administering the codes, this experience constitutes an apprenticeship in democracy.[3]

Teachable Moments and Campus Conversations

Disciplinary incidents represent just one of many kinds of moral and civic teachable moments that arise in academic life. Often these moments arise out of clashes of values within or across groups, real dilemmas with no obvious right answers. These conflicts can be public and contentious and therefore are not generally welcomed by college and university administrations. But if handled well, the very fact that they are so public enhances their scope and impact. Handling them well is far from easy, however, and highlights the importance of the moral qualities of the president and others in leadership roles, that is, the need for administrative leaders to have wisdom and judgment themselves.

An incident that faced Tom Ehrlich when he was president of Indiana University illustrates the kind of clash that can become a teachable moment. An alumnus had bequeathed a farm in Mississippi to the Indiana University Foundation, a nonprofit organization that raises funds for the university. But the farm was losing money, and the president and board were eager to sell it. After some years a buyer was found—a waste disposal company that promised its new plant would not only add jobs in one of the state's poorest counties but also be environmentally sound. The local city council and the National Association for the Advancement of Colored People (NAACP) supported the plant, and the sale promised needed funds for the university. But an environmental group charged that this was a case of environmental racism and that the farm was seen as an appropriate location for the plant only because the local population was largely African American. A small but vocal student group took up these arguments and urged President Ehrlich to reject the sale, threatening a sit-in. When the student newspaper also took up the cause, the issue threatened to explode. In response Ehrlich asked a member of the foundation board, who was also a popular teacher at the Law School and a leading lawyer, to conduct an open inquiry into all the facts and issue a report. The lawyer held extensive meetings with student groups and many others over the course of several weeks, during which time they explored the facts of the situation from the perspectives of those living near the farm, those involved with the waste disposal company, and others who had a stake in the outcome. This was a learning experience for all involved, and when the lawyer issued his report supporting the sale, complete with extensive analysis and clear articulation of his reasons, there was campuswide support for his conclusion, even among many of those who had previously opposed the sale.

Student activism frequently provides a catalyst for teachable moments. Over the past four decades student groups on many campuses have held protests against the Vietnam War and for civil rights; demonstrations to urge colleges and universities to divest their investment portfolios of holdings in businesses connected with South Africa in the days of apartheid; rallies in support of organizing agricultural workers, many of whom are immigrants; and protests demanding better working conditions and wages for college service workers. Most recently, campuses have experienced clashes between students supporting the Israelis and those supporting the Palestinians in the Middle East conflict.

When the issues are directly related to the campus, as they are in many student protests (Levine & Cureton, 1998), the protests often entail conflicts between groups of students. These conflicts can produce especially powerful teachable moments, because they require students to learn how to deal constructively with competing interests in a community. A recent incident is a case in point. In the spring of 2001, a full-page advertisement was offered to many student newspapers. It was titled "Ten Reasons Why Reparations for Slavery Is a Bad Idea for Blacks—and Racist Too." The ten points included the claims that blacks as well as whites benefited from slavery and that reparations have already been paid to African Americans in the form of welfare benefits and racial preferences. Most student newspapers rejected the ad, generally on the grounds that it was racist. But some papers printed it, often with explosive results. At Brown University "student activists . . . trashed 4,000 copies of the paper . . . nearly the entire press run. . . . Papers bearing the ad were (also) shredded at the University of California at Berkeley and burned at the University of Wisconsin at Madison" (Brownstein, 2001, p. A55).

The antireparation ad raised complicated issues and competing values— the right to freedom of speech and of the press on the one hand and the use of words that deeply offended some members of campus communities on the other. When issues of race are involved, as in this case, it is enormously difficult to avoid polarizing a campus. But students at some campuses recognized that this ad could also be the occasion for promoting serious dialogue about complicated social and economic issues related to the legacy of slavery and about the nature of a campus community: What is owed the descendants of slaves and why? What should be the limits on viewpoints expressed on college campuses and in student newspapers? What should happen when those limits are exceeded? And so forth. At Stanford University, for example, the student paper ran the ad as a guest column on one page and printed a response by the Stanford Black Student Union on the facing page ("Ten Reasons . . .," 2001; Stanford Black Student Union, 2001). This approach opened the issue to discussion in an atmosphere of reasoned debate, and although there were strong negative responses to the arguments offered in the ad, these responses occurred as part of an ongoing exchange and did not involve the angry thefts and attacks that occurred on other college campuses.

Some campuses have created ongoing forums, or campus conversations, that encourage sustained attention to the kinds of issues raised by episodic teachable moments. Several of our case study campuses offer regular, structured opportunities for campuswide dialogue about controversial issues throughout the year. Every month or two the College of St. Catherine sponsors community meetings open to all students, faculty, and staff. There are clear guidelines for discussion that center on three rules: speak for yourself, not others; be civil; and don't take more than two minutes. Each meeting is evaluated at its conclusion. Many of the community meetings are proposed, organized, and run by students, sometimes in connection with issues that arise in classes and particularly in St. Kate's core courses, The Reflective Woman and The Global Search for Justice. Others are triggered by controversial events on campus. One well-attended meeting was organized after feminist activist and author Gloria Steinem gave a talk on campus to promote voting. During the question period a student asked Steinem about her views on abortion, and Steinem responded that she had had an abortion herself and believed every woman should have the freedom to make that choice. The local St. Paul newspaper ran a story the next morning with the headline "Steinem Promotes Abortion at St. Kate's," even though this topic represented only a few minutes of the talk. The newspaper story prompted the local archbishop to chastise the college, resulting in a call for a community meeting focused on the meaning of the college's Catholic identity, an issue complicated by the fact that less than half of St. Kate's students are Catholic.

The meetings at St. Kate's have two goals that are sometimes difficult to balance. One is to create a sense of community. The other is to educate students for a public culture in which they will encounter people who are different from themselves. Neither goal is easy to achieve. Discomfort with open disagreement and controversy is evident on nearly every college campus. This was apparent in a St. Kate's community meeting on gay and lesbian issues, in which some new students said they did not feel "safe" at the session. Upper-class students, however, viewed the discussion differently and pressed younger students to clarify the meaning of the word *safe* and the idea of a *safe place* for discussion. This prompted a follow-up meeting at which students talked more about what *safe* means and how people can feel comfortable while expressing divergent views.

Making this kind of forum productive is extremely difficult, and the community meetings at St. Kate's are still evolving. Problems include participants' hesitation to challenge each other sharply enough, imbalances in attendance such that one side of a controversy is sometimes much better represented than the other, and lack of continuity in the discussion when speakers make independent statements rather than building on or engaging with the prior comments. As one student said, "Sometimes we just run out of time and we think, 'What did we really accomplish here?' We all got in what we wanted to say, but we didn't really answer anything." Despite the flaws in the community meetings, the very task of working together to improve them is a valuable learning experience, requiring participants to pay conscious attention to the dynamics that lead to deep and productive debate and to work on implementing strategies to move the group toward more effective interactions.

At Emory University, sustained conversations about campus issues or cultural events like visiting speakers are carried out electronically, through the campus's LearnLink e-mail network. LearnLink enables students, faculty, and staff to hold public conversations about issues on campus, to reflect together about recent campus speakers and other events, and to interact about coursework. The system is widely used, drawing into shared discourse even some people who would be reluctant to engage in face-to-face interchange and debate. Often the exchanges begun electronically are followed by in-person discussions that pursue the issues further.

Residential Learning

Part of the value of mechanisms like community meetings and LearnLink is the community-building function they serve. Especially in large institutions, creating a strong sense of community across the entire campus is difficult, so many schools work to foster community in smaller units. Portland State University's Freshman Inquiry courses (see Chapter Six) intentionally create close-knit groups of first-year students, which is important on this nonresidential campus because it is particularly difficult for students on such campuses to connect with each other and the institution. Residential colleges and universities have community-building opportunities not available to campuses where students commute. Unfortunately, most residential institutions do not take full advantage of these opportunities. We have seen several that do, however, and the benefits are clear. In Chapter Three, we mentioned for example that one of Nannerl Keohane's first decisions as president of Duke University was to bring all the freshmen together into one group of dormitories in order to create a stronger sense of community among them at the outset of their college experience.

The University of Notre Dame brings its strong Roman Catholic identity to the task of making residential life central to students' moral and spiritual development. All freshmen are assigned to one of the twenty-seven single-sex residences, each of which has a distinct character. Students usually remain in the same residence for all four years, forming small, close communities that serve as the backbone of the larger campus community. Even the few students who move off campus later in their college careers maintain their residence hall affiliations. Each residence has scores of teams, clubs, and other organizations, and the student government is residence hall based. Each residence also has a *service commissioner,* and service is a dominant focus of activity, particularly in the women's residences. Notre Dame's residences are also important arenas for developing students' moral and spiritual life. The university consciously decided not to use the student life model of staffing, staffing the residences instead with full-time *rectors,* most of whom are priests or nuns. The rectors live in the halls, often staying for a decade or more, serving as spiritual advisers and attending to the spiritual life of the community. They see themselves not only as religious advisers but also as counselors, helping students work through moral and spiritual challenges. "We are in the business of character development," one rector explained, "and most of it takes place when someone steps in a chuckhole." By this he meant that rectors find teachable moments in students' missteps.

A number of campuses are finding effective ways to link the intellectual life of students in their academic work and the residences through living-learning programs. In Vanderbilt University's Mayfield Living/Learning Lodges, for example, groups of ten students live together and pursue a self-directed, yearlong program of educational cocurricular activities that include community service projects. These educational programs often feature moral and civic issues. Some of the titles of the 1999–2000 lodge programs were A Living History—Nashville's Multicultural Past, Building Relationships with the Homeless, Commitment to Companionship, Friendship Foundation, Project Share, and Urban Poverty. Each lodge sponsors lectures by professors and other staff, regular meetings and dinners with advisers, and participation in an educational program for the entire campus community (for more information, see Vanderbilt University Office of Housing and Residential Education, 2002).

Many residential campuses include one or more theme dormitories, some of which focus on moral and civic issues such as peace, community service, or environmental stewardship or on a culture or ethnicity, such as Asian-Pacific culture or, more generally, multiculturalism. Hobart and William Smith Colleges in Geneva, New York, for example, has designated one residence as the Community Service House; residents are selected for their service activities and interests. Each member of the house completes at least five hours of service each week and also participates in planning and implementing a house project. At Stanford University, students who live in theme houses, such as the Multicultural Theme House, are responsible for teaching both their own house members and the larger campus community about their theme by sponsoring speakers, seminars, and other theme-related activities. Each of these living-learning programs provides important ways for students to connect their intellectual and academic learning with their lives beyond the classroom.

Building on Students' Values and Interests

Students come to college with a great variety of values and interests and a huge range of experience with and commitment to civic and political engagement—from none at all to a very great deal. A few students are extremely activist and politically concerned. Many are less politically oriented but idealistic nevertheless and accustomed to participating in community service. A growing number, even on secular campuses, are deeply religious and looking for ways to maintain and express their spirituality. There are many opportunities on campus for students like these. Their interests lead them into activities that deepen these commitments, offer them a more mature and sophisticated understanding of the issues they are confronting, sharpen and broaden their skills, and engage them with people who are different from them in many ways. Interests also create solidarity among the like-minded. Joining friends in intense experiences around civic and political issues can help students develop a "love of the game" and can solidify their moral and civic identities as people who cannot stand on society's sidelines.

Sometimes students engage with these activities not because they have done so before and are committed to service, social change, or spirituality, but because the friends they have fallen in with are doing it or they "want to meet girls" (or boys), as many activists in the 1960s later admitted. Many students pursue community service at least in part because it makes their résumés more competitive for jobs or graduate school. No doubt most have mixed motives. But if they become engaged in activities that broaden their horizons and connect them with people they respect and can learn from, some will undergo what we have called a "transformation of goals." They may form relationships with people they admire who push them toward new ways of thinking about what they are doing or new commitments. By engaging in community service or other broadening pursuits, even if initially for largely pragmatic or self-interested reasons, they may be surprised to find that they begin to care about issues and people that had not previously concerned them.

Other students come to college with interests that have no obvious relevance to moral and civic issues; they want to become involved in clubs and activities that will support their passions, advance their careers, or provide social connections or entertainment. Many of these clubs and organizations, however, can also awaken a concern for moral and civic issues or a desire to contribute to the campus or the wider community. Sometimes the impetus for this broadening of organizational aims comes from vocal and influential students who convince the others to add community service or a political slant to a club's repertoire. Sometimes creative faculty or staff mentors see how a group can incorporate more inspiring goals without distorting or diminishing its original focus. When that happens, these organizations can awaken moral and civic concern in the many students who are not invested in these issues when they come to college. This is not to say that clubs and organizations always achieve this potential. Many do not. In order for organizations to have a lasting effect on students' moral and civic development, they have to connect with students' existing passions and convictions and then expand those passions and convictions through powerful relationships and experiences and new ways of understanding what one is doing.

Whether or not students choose extracurricular activities that are directly relevant to moral and civic issues, their participation in any extracurricular activity can have important developmental benefits if it teaches them to work with people different from themselves, connects them with both peers and adults who inspire them and offer new models of the type of person they would like to be, helps them learn or extend a wide variety of skills, and gives them a sense of their own effectiveness. Participation in clubs and other activities can also give students a sense of solidarity or community within the broader campus, an outcome that is important at any institution but especially in large universities and nonresidential institutions. Many extracurricular activities also have the potential to help students integrate their academic and personal interests, enhancing their learning in both domains.

The very multiplicity of student clubs and organizations gives them enormous potential to connect with a wide range of students. Some students are attracted to programs that balance their academic interests and offer relief from academic pressure. Others seek out programs that enhance their disciplinary work or career aspirations or affirm the value they place on academic excellence. These programs may not have any connection with moral or civic issues, but many do make this connection and can be influential in supporting moral and civic growth. The Stanford Film Society, for example, cosponsors the United Nations Annual Film Festival (UNAFF), which brings to the campus documentaries dealing with human rights and other United Nations issues, made by filmmakers from many countries. This kind of program benefits both the students who organize the series and those who attend.

Student organizations based in academic disciplines, majors, or professions, such as history and premed clubs, can be a powerful bridge between students' classroom experiences and their personal lives. They can also help students explore dimensions of their majors beyond the curriculum, including the moral and civic dimensions. Sassafras, the sociology and anthropology club at Spelman College, began with a strictly disciplinary focus but quickly became extremely active both on the campus and in the local community, evolving a mission that "bridges scholarship and activism." The group, which has strong faculty involvement, has raised awareness and concern about the gentrification of the local community near the campus, sponsored programming for local youths, and demonstrated outside Spelman's annual fashion show to protest the overemphasis on appearance and materialism at Spelman and in the culture more broadly.

Disciplinary and other academically oriented clubs can be especially helpful on nonresidential campuses, where students often feel their strongest affiliation is to their major. Turtle Mountain Community College, for example, offers the Health Careers Opportunity Program, which is designed to increase the number of Native Americans in health professions, with the further goals of providing better health care on the Turtle Mountain reservation and training medical staff who are sensitive to traditional cultural beliefs about holistic medicine and community health.

Students in the Kapiʻolani Community College chapter of Phi Theta Kappa, the main honor society for two-year colleges, are concerned not only about their own academic excellence but also academic achievement by others. Among other things, they mentor underprepared students in a program called Holomua, which pairs underprepared high school students with chapter members who become friends and guides to college life, offering advice, counseling, study tips, and campus information to help smooth the transition to college. This is just one of many service activities that Kapiʻolani's Phi Theta Kappa chapter sponsors, and members describe the club as promoting an attitude of lifelong service.

In addition to the almost endless array of topical clubs and organizations, there are also many organizations that focus directly on issues of citizenship or moral concern. The most prominent among them are community service programs, political clubs and organizations, religious clubs and activities, and leadership programs.

Community Service Programs

Young people's increasing interest in performing community service is one of the most characteristic features of the current generation of college students. Linda Sax (1999), for example, reports that the percentage of incoming freshmen who had done volunteer work during their senior year in high school reached a record high of 74.2 percent in 1998, and one of the most important predictors of service involvement during college is having been similarly involved in high school. It is not clear how many high school students have performed community service in order to help their case for college admissions, how many have been required to participate, and how many gain real personal satisfaction from their service. But those who do participate, no doubt for a variety of reasons, are known to be likely to continue and to experience developmental benefits as a result.

Community service in some sense is part of many, maybe even most, student clubs and organizations, especially if one considers activities like the public performances of music and plays and the publication of campus newspapers and literary magazines to be a service to the campus community. There are also many clubs and organizations that are more centrally defined by their service mission. These cover a huge variety of causes, may be local or connected with national organizations, and can lead to short- or long-term student involvement.

Generally, service programs are organized around particular issues and activities, which can connect with varied interests or tastes and lead to particular kinds of learning as well as learning that is common across different kinds of service. Many address some aspect of poverty. These include both national programs such as Habitat for Humanity and Christmas in April and local efforts to staff homeless shelters, tutor low-income children, and the like. Other service programs focus on the environment or social issues such as the death penalty or discrimination against particular racial or ethnic groups. Moreover, many student service organizations are linked together through a national student organization focused on civic engagement, the Campus Outreach Opportunity League (COOL, 2002).

Many campuses have centers that coordinate student community service programs and offer support for faculty using service learning. Stanford University's Haas Center for Public Service, for example, houses over forty service organizations and a variety of staff-run programs. They vary considerably in size, focus, ideology, and the level of time commitment required. Through the center, students can get involved in hands-on action, government service, policy research, service-related work-study, fellowships, and leadership programs. The Haas Center was established by former Stanford president Donald Kennedy, who was especially supportive of educating undergraduates for active citizenship. Student groups have also been active in the creation of these service program centers, particularly during the 1960s and 1970s. Student-initiated centers include the Center for Social Concerns at Notre Dame, the Community Involvement Center at San Francisco State University, and the Community Action Volunteers in Education at California State University, Chico.

Housed near the center of the Notre Dame campus, the Center for Social Concerns brought together a number of disparate programs and is now linked with about forty student groups. The center offers many extracurricular service experiences, including short programs such as Urban Plunge during break periods and more extensive service projects in the summer. Most students in summer service projects live with alumni families. We talked with a group of students involved with the center, and they told us that the Center for Social Concerns represents values such as social conscience and commitment to one's community that often seemed to get lost in the highly ambitious, career-driven atmosphere of the campus. Many also said that the center is one of the best places on campus for developing mature and enduring friendships, including friendships that cross racial, gender, and cultural lines. Several said that their involvement with the center had made them change their minds about their majors or career goals, making them decide they wanted "a career that includes service."

On just about any campus, students can participate in community service during a single weekend, regularly over the course of the year, or very intensively during spring break or over the summer. Spring break and summer programs can be especially transformative for students because they are so completely absorbing. When these programs involve travel to an unfamiliar part of the world, either in this country or abroad, they often open students' eyes to vivid new realities. The College of St. Catherine offers the spring break program Reaching Out for Justice, in which students travel with members of the Sisters of St. Joseph of Carondelet, the college's founding order, to Denver to work in homeless shelters. The program represents a partnership among the Sisters, Campus Ministry, and Multicultural and International Programs and Services. Students are asked to write journals about the experience, and their reflections reveal the extent to which the experience touched their lives, often producing discomfort and challenging earlier views, in some cases even leading them to question whether they are capable of helping in any meaningful way. One student wrote: "I feel frustrated about the world we live in and its emphasis on consumerism, profits, and wealth, frustrated that I'm very much a part of that world, frustrated that there is so much I can't do." This student and others struggle to think about what they can do that will make a difference in problems of such enormous proportions. As another student said: "One thing I can do about [this problem] is to educate people about issues, talk about it with people, and be aware and question all that is going on around me and in the world. I may not be able to change all the unfairness and injustices that are going on in this world, but if I can change one person's perception about an issue, it's worth the effort."

Reactions like this call attention to the challenge of helping students make sense of their experiences in a way that will foster their development of a mature understanding of the relationship of individual responsibility to major social issues, supporting their engagement even when their potential impact in the short run is in question. Structured reflections on their experiences, including discussions guided by faculty or staff, can be crucial in helping students make sense of their newfound appreciation of the depth and complexity of the social problems they are trying to address. The program at the College of St. Catherine includes this kind of reflection, as do others that have been shown to have a strong positive impact. The kind of extended consideration of the meaning, potential, and limits of service that was exemplified in Alma Blount's course Integrating Community and Classroom, at Duke, and Rob Reich's The Ethics and Politics of Public Service, at Stanford (discussed in Chapter Five), can be especially helpful. Many institutions recognize this and connect some of their intensive service experiences or internships with courses. Some summer programs are not only connected with courses the student participants will take, they also prepare the students to take real responsibility on campus by assisting faculty who are incorporating community service into their teaching. One such program is the Summer of Service Leadership Academy (SOSLA) at California State University, Monterey Bay, an intensive four-week internship program that trains a group of about fifteen students in effective community involvement and leadership. Students apply for the program after taking the introductory service-learning course required of all students, and they receive a small stipend for their living expenses. They can also enroll concurrently in advanced service-learning courses, which allows them to earn academic credit for the internship.

Participants in SOSLA train to be University Service Advocates, or USAs, who assist with service-learning courses and are responsible for raising student awareness of service opportunities and issues. They develop communication abilities and other leadership skills and learn from a variety of community leaders in the Monterey area. The program includes activities such as a *community scan,* in which students visit local community agencies and organizations to learn about them and their roles, and volunteering in various local organizations. Working in small teams, students engage in a number of service projects over the course of the summer, such as helping to restore a park and chaperoning youths on a visit to an amusement park. The whole group also works together to plan and implement a larger project in collaboration with a community organization or group of organizations. Each of these projects involves preparation, reflection, and evaluation. After the summer program ends, students design action projects they will complete in the fall term. One student, for instance, worked to raise awareness of hunger issues in the local community. New USAs serve as assistants for introductory service-learning courses and help facilitate other students' involvement with community organizations as well as continuing to work in those organizations themselves. Many students we spoke to love the SOSLA program and feel that it has changed them dramatically. They emphasized that the experience had influenced their studies and thinking about their future careers and life goals. Many affirmed the sentiments of the student who said: "Service isn't something that's done from two to four on Monday and Wednesday; it's a way of living and being, an attitude."

Service organizations vary greatly in the extent to which they incorporate policy or political concerns as well as provide direct service to those who need help. In fact the relative legitimacy and value of these two approaches is a subject of debate among students on many campuses. In our view it is beneficial to students' learning when direct service programs do find ways to connect their work with policy or other systemic analysis, though this effort need not be the central focus. Students themselves are the ones who most often press for these political connections. Many environmental groups, for example, are adamant in their commitment to policy agendas that they see as essential for long-term success in protecting the environment. And many see themselves as political activists working for social as well as environmental justice. Members of Students for Environmental Action at Stanford University (SEAS), for example, describe themselves as "a group of activists dedicated to fighting for environmental and social justice on campus, in the surrounding communities and beyond." One of their recent campaigns has been "to stop the Stanford Medical Center from incinerating its medical waste at a dioxin spewing incinerator in East Oakland (a low-income community of color, classic environmental racism)" (Students for Environmental Action at Stanford, 2002).

Political Clubs and Organizations

It is sometimes difficult to distinguish between organizations that focus on service and those that take an overtly political approach, because the degree of focus on systemic issues and policy solutions is a continuum and may even fluctuate over time within the same organization. For some clubs, however, the focus is clearly political. Many campuses have political clubs tied to specific political organizations in the surrounding community or state or linked to national political parties. Although these clubs reach primarily the relatively few students who already care about politics, they provide enormously valuable learning experiences for those students.

George Washington University, for example, has an active chapter of College Democrats of America, which was recently chosen as the university's Student Organization of the Year. In addition to the campaign volunteering, voter drives, and speaker series that most political clubs host, these College Democrats engage in both political action and community service. Similarly, at Texas A&M University an active College Republicans club hosts speakers, sponsors get-out-the-vote drives, and organizes debates on controversial issues such as abortion and gun control. During the 2000 campaign, this club registered over 2,000 students to vote and campaigned actively for Republican candidates. Many of these groups, particularly those connected with political parties, contribute to the political interest and understanding of their peers by publicizing local political issues, such as Proposition 209, an anti-affirmative action measure in

California, or by helping organize voter registration drives on campus or in local communities.

Student governments would seem to be among the most obvious training grounds for future political and civic leaders, but involvement in student government is generally in decline, even among residential campuses. Too often these organizations are (perhaps correctly) seen as lacking any real power on campus and so are not taken seriously. The failure of higher education institutions to take full advantage of student governments is unfortunate because these groups can provide important apprenticeships in the democratic process not only for the elected leaders but also for the students that form their constituencies. There are exceptions to the general pattern, however, and they can provide models of what this kind of organization can achieve. The Associated Students of Missouri, for example, links the student governments of the four campuses of the University of Missouri not only to each other but also to the state legislature. This network is coordinated by a board of directors from each campus. These boards, supported by a staff of student interns, meet once each month to discuss issues and decide what action to take on legislation and other matters. The student interns lobby at the state capitol and make a trip to Washington, D.C., each year to represent University of Missouri undergraduates' interests. The student internships are coordinated through each campus's political science department so academic credit may be earned. Student "ambassadors" also help with student government events and activities, with the express aim of building interest in politics and informing students of active campus issues and what they can do to be heard on those issues. A Web site, the Internet Headquarters for Student Government, provides a steady source of information about issues to all students on the four Missouri campuses.

Religious Organizations and Activities

As much as fifteen years ago, Boyer (1987) noted the marked increase in student religious organizations and activities. He and his colleagues were surprised by the frequency of religious revivals, study groups, and songfests even at public colleges and universities. These events drew many students from evangelical Christian denominations but were not limited to that group. Jewish, Roman Catholic, and some mainstream Protestant students were also quite active. Since that time, voluntary religious activity among college students has surged even more. Membership in the major evangelical student groups has almost doubled in the past five years

(Mahoney, Schmalzbauer, & Youniss, 2001). But evangelical Christians do not account for all of the growth in attention to religion and spirituality. Student religious life is characterized by striking and growing religious pluralism, and many schools have multifaith chapels serving their remarkably diverse student bodies, which may include Muslim, Buddhist, and Hindu students as well as Christians and Jews.

A recent study found that despite the visibility of conservative Christian groups, the majority of undergraduates prefer to use the word *spirituality* instead of *religion* when describing their attitudes and practices and were drawn more to personal experience of God or ultimate values than to organized religion. The study concluded that most undergraduates are better characterized as "spiritual seekers rather than religious dwellers," constructing their spirituality without much regard to denominational or organizational boundaries (Cherry, DeBerg, & Porterfield, 2001, p. 10). Many students have moved away from organized religion because they are offended by the idea that only one religious tradition can have a monopoly on the truth. But this skepticism of orthodoxy has not stood in the way of the strong revival of interest in spiritual matters. At all kinds of institutions, including the most secular, students take religious studies courses, organize prayer groups and discussion groups focused on the Bible and other religious texts, and participate in interfaith gatherings (Kiely, 2001). As religion professor Robert Kiely (2001) says about his campus: "at Harvard [these activities] would have been quite rare twenty-five years ago. Today they are commonplace. Whereas in the not-too-distant past, religion was regarded as a private matter not to be displayed in public (and, in many cases, not even to be acknowledged), it is now very much out in the open" (p. 24). Because of students' strong interest in understanding the theological and historical traditions as well as the practices of religion and spirituality, this is an ideal set of issues around which to connect curricular and extracurricular life. As in other areas of student life, the engagement of faculty and staff can be extremely valuable in helping students make these connections.

In these endeavors, religious pluralism on campus and in U.S. society is often seen as a valuable cultural resource. But religious convictions can also come into conflict with each other and with secular perspectives. We have already mentioned the tension around Gloria Steinem's reference to abortion at the College of St. Catherine. Reproductive rights and other issues of sexuality are sites of potential conflict on many campuses. Students often need help in working through these and other religious conflicts in ways that make the disputes learning experiences rather than sources of alienation and bitterness.

Leadership Programs

Like community service programs and religious and spiritual activities, leadership development programs have multiplied in recent years at every type of institution across the country. Why have they become so popular? On the face of it, leadership programs need not concern themselves with moral and civic issues, and it is reasonable to assume that much of their appeal lies in the promise of personal advancement or at best in the idea of "doing good by doing well." This is no doubt part of the reason for their popularity. And some "leadership training" programs or workshops respond to this demand by offering skills development with an instrumental approach that pays little attention to the moral and civic underpinnings and aims of responsible and authoritative leadership. We believe that these programs not only neglect participants' moral and civic learning but also fail even to support leadership development in any meaningful sense. Fortunately, recognition of the moral and civic character of effective leadership does seem to inform the goals of most undergraduate leadership programs. A recent study (Zimmerman-Oster & Burkhardt, 1999) of leadership programs at thirty-one campuses showed that the outcomes expected of participants nearly always include goals involving civic responsibility and engagement: civic, social, and political awareness was at the top of the list (92.6 percent), with civic and political efficacy (78.6 percent) and civic and political activity (70.4 percent) not far behind.

Naturally, leadership development efforts vary in quality and in the extent to which they incorporate experiences and state goals that foster morally and civically responsible leadership. Some of the strongest have multiple components that entail deep and extended involvement. Many, whether curricular or extracurricular, include an intellectual or theoretical component, so that students are stimulated to think carefully about what leadership means. This component may include discussion of influential theories and models from different cultures and historical eras as well as those of the present culture and era and their relationship to leadership in the contemporary world. It is also important to offer opportunities to practice leadership and to connect this practice with theoretical understanding. The more ambitious programs draw together and integrate students' academic coursework, their structured extracurricular activities, and often their more spontaneous campus engagements. At their best the programs can have significant developmental impact, leading to intellectual learning, more mature judgment in complex situations, practical skills, passionate commitments, a strong sense of efficacy, and a sense of self organized around moral and civic engagement.

Miami's Leadership Commitment is the title for a cluster of programs at Miami University, in Ohio, including programs for prospective and new students, many curricular programs (including service-learning courses and courses taught in the residence halls), a wide array of extracurricular programs, and several programs designed to "launch students into the work of active community citizenship." Students undertaking Miami's Leadership Commitment are also encouraged to engage in multiple reinforcing experiences. No student could take part in all these programs, but many undergraduates participate in several, and the cumulative impact is impressive. The staff and faculty who lead the various components work together around a set of common goals to ensure that programs complement and reinforce each other. The student life staff monitor the impact of Miami's Leadership Commitment through surveys of freshmen and seniors. These surveys indicate high levels of participation in and satisfaction with the program (Roberts, 2001).

The story of one student we talked to illustrates the way extended involvement in this kind of multifaceted program can lead to the transformation of students' goals, especially when the program enables them to establish important relationships with people they admire. This student's initial motivations and interests were superceded as he moved from instrumental to moral and social concerns, and other students we interviewed showed a similar pattern. Steven Wittman Jr. (class of 2001) came to Miami University from a sheltered, homogeneous community and had not had much occasion to question his values and beliefs. Financial and career success and recognition were his primary goals when he entered college. In order to move this personal agenda forward, Steven decided in his freshman year that he would like to organize a public lecture on campus, bringing in a corporate CEO to talk about leadership. Steven approached Denny Roberts, the director of Miami's Leadership Commitment, to propose the idea. As Steven said, "I was just this little kid with a crazy idea, but Dr. Roberts believed in me. He taught me a lot about dealing with people, and we had long philosophical discussions about character and leadership development." Roberts supported the idea of a lecture, and as a result of these discussions, Steven invited the CEO of Procter & Gamble to come to campus to talk about leadership and character. At Roberts's urging, Steven attended an institute on leadership the following summer, where he was asked to develop a vision of something he would like to accomplish and make it happen the following year. Steven's vision was to increase awareness of character on the Miami campus, and he accomplished this by organizing the lecture series Character Counts. After the success of that series, several campus groups, such as the Diversity Affairs

Council, wanted to collaborate with Steven in creating some events for the following year. This resulted in Miami Celebrates Character—a week-long series with a broader range of speakers and a "multicultural fest."

Due to his own evolving thinking and his collaborations with Denny Roberts and various student groups, the focus of the programs that Steven organized evolved from corporate leadership to the moral dimensions of leadership to a multicultural theme: "Character is not just about you but also about affirming other people's dignity." The audience for the events also changed, expanding beyond the business students who were attracted to the first lecture to become a very large and diverse group. Steven derived tremendous satisfaction not only from his own sense of personal growth but also from the feeling that he had been able to contribute something important to so many other students. In his senior year, Steven moved into a living-learning community organized around leadership, where he lived and worked with a more diverse group of students than he had ever encountered before. His relationships with these students, many of whom saw moral, social, and political issues very differently than he did, challenged his thinking anew. Thus each step Steven took, each project he took on, led to another, quite different set of developmental opportunities and learning experiences. In some ways he left college a different person from the person he was when he had entered, and these changes will help determine the experiences he chooses after college and what he will make of them.

Like the program at Miami, Duke University's Hart Leadership Program mixes many elements and leads to long-term participation for many students. The most intensive of Duke's programs is the twelve-month sequence of academic coursework and internships called Service Opportunities in Leadership (SOL). According to its director, Alma Blount (2001), SOL is designed to help students become "engaged citizens in a democratic society," to help them develop a rich understanding of public life and ultimately to deepen their commitments to service, philanthropy, and civic participation no matter what careers they choose (p. 3). Blount and her colleagues have identified five outcome goals for the SOL program, all of which revolve around moral and civic learning. These goals include learning to negotiate with community partners, developing an appreciation for the complexities of working with people from different backgrounds, and understanding the links between leadership and systemic change.

Service Opportunities in Leadership begins with a service-learning course in the spring that explores a series of questions about "reinventing democracy at the grassroots." Studying theoretical frameworks and case studies in which value differences hinder or help public problem-solving efforts, students analyze the ethical dimensions of decision making in a democratic society. Students then participate in summer internships in community service organizations across the country. The internships are customized for each student to ensure a good fit between student interests and community needs and to offer students sustained opportunities to develop a wide range of understanding, skills, and personal qualities. These include the abilities to negotiate and to collaborate toward common goals; an appreciation of the complexities of working with people from different cultural, economic, and racial backgrounds; and development of an identity that includes agency for social change. The substantive focus of students' work varies depending on their interests and the organizations with which they work. Past internships have included creating a microlending program for immigrant families in Charlotte and assisting a refugee resettlement program in Boston. In addition to their service work some of the students also conduct research designed to benefit the organizations for which they are working. When the SOL interns return to Duke in the fall, they participate in the research seminar we described in Chapter Five (Integrating Community and Classroom: Internship Reflection), in which they reflect on their work experiences and integrate what they have learned with concepts about service, social change, citizenship, and leadership. The course involves extensive reading, discussions, essay writing, and research on a policy issue connected with the summer internship.

The story of a recent participant illustrates the transformative impact of this kind of extended program and its complex relationships with other sources of moral and civic learning during college. Like most other college students, Tico Almeida, a first-generation American from a Cuban immigrant family, had no serious interest in politics or social justice prior to his SOL internship in the summer after his sophomore year (see Baerman, 1998; Blount, 2001; Kiss, n.d.). He spent that summer working with the Union of Needletrade, Industrial and Textile Employees (UNITE) in New York City, teaching English and citizenship classes to Latino garment workers. He also helped workers prepare complaints to the U.S. Department of Labor about back wages owed, forced overtime, and subminimum pay, and even did undercover work for the department by pretending to be an immigrant and working in a substandard garment factory. Tico's interest in the conditions of low-wage workers led him to collaborate that summer with students from other colleges to plan the Sweatshop-Free Campus Campaign. The group members studied international labor standards and monitoring mechanisms as they drafted a code of conduct to be adopted by college campuses that license apparel manufacturers. When Tico returned to Duke in the fall, he helped organize Duke Students Against Sweatshops (SAS), which sought meetings with the university administration to discuss the group's concerns. Although the administration initially did not agree with the group's recommendation, over time administrators came to recognize the moral legitimacy as well as the educational value of the issue and invited students to participate in drafting a new code of conduct for Duke licensees. As a result, in 1998, Duke became the first campus to adopt a code of conduct requiring a process for monitoring manufacturers of college-licensed products.

Almeida and Duke Students Against Sweatshops then redirected their efforts, putting pressure on the Collegiate Licensing Company, the licensing agent for 170 institutions, to adopt the Duke code. When the company released a draft code that did not require public disclosure of factory locations, Almeida and other students waged a strong campaign, urging President Keohane to reject it. They publicly confronted her on the campus one cold winter day, arguing that the code would be ineffective without a provision requiring public disclosure of factory locations. Almeida then held a megaphone for Keohane to respond. She said she recognized the code's weaknesses, but argued that it was an important first step and that a stronger code was simply not feasible at that point: "For Duke to back out now would make the best the enemy of the good" (Kiss, n.d., p. 2). Disappointed with that decision, Almeida and other SAS students spent a month educating, organizing, and planning and then marched into the administration building and confronted Keohane again. They were allowed to stay in the building, and after thirty-one hours of negotiation, SAS and the administration were able to work out a compromise: Duke would sign the code but would also press the Collegiate Licensing Company to strengthen it. University administrators wrote to each of Duke's licensees notifying them that they would have one year to publicly disclose factory locations, and if they chose not to do so they would no longer be eligible to sell products with the Duke trademark. One student involved with the protests said she felt that "we've just written a new page in history" (Kiss, n.d., p. 2).

Supporting Persistence of Moral and Civic Learning

Clearly, Tico Almeida went through a dramatic transformation on a par with that of the students Douglas McAdam (1988) chronicled in *Freedom Summer* (see Chapter Four). It is not surprising that after college he continued to pursue his passion for workers' rights, doing student outreach around sweatshop issues for the AFL-CIO and then using a Fulbright Fellowship to study international trade and labor rights. He is now attending Yale Law School with the expectation of continuing that work. This level of personal transformation during college is unusual, however. Even Virginia Durr, who went on to become a powerful leader in the civil rights movement, experienced much more subtle, incremental shifts that changed her partly by increasing her susceptibility to later influences; she did not complete her transformation during college (see Chapter One). For most students, the stability of learning and personal growth is at greater risk. When they leave the college setting and face intense pressure to achieve career success and provide for themselves and their families, they may pull back from the commitments they developed in college.

Many factors combine to determine the extent to which positive changes in college will be enduring and generative of further development in later life. Moral and civic learning outside the classroom can contribute to this persistence in a number of ways. The kinds of activities and experiences we have described in this chapter have the potential to establish deeply engrained patterns of behavior, irreversibly profound changes in ways of understanding the world, expert skills, and a sense of oneself as a morally and civically concerned and engaged person—an identity tested and consolidated in multiple and intersecting contexts.

Some institutions try to bolster the stability of these shifts by providing some scaffolding for the transition to postcollege life. Many incorporate moral and civic values explicitly in graduation ceremonies. In order to reach beyond that one-day event, a group of graduating seniors at Humboldt State University in 1988 started a movement that has since spread to scores of campuses and many thousands of students throughout the country, from Whitman College to the University of Kansas to the University of Notre Dame and to Harvard University. Students at Humboldt State took the Pledge of Social and Environmental Responsibility, in which each one promised he or she would "explore and take into account the social and environmental consequences of any job I consider and will try to improve these aspects of any organizations for which I work." The pledge has been modified in minor ways from campus to campus, but always underscores a public commitment that moral and civic concerns will be part of decisions about employment and about how work is conducted. Graduates who signed the pledge have turned down jobs about which they had moral qualms and have worked to make changes in their workplaces. For example, they have promoted recycling, removed racist language from a training manual, and helped convince an employer to refuse a contract to work on chemical weapons (Manchester College Peace Studies Institute, 2002).

Some institutions also educate students about postcollege opportunities that connect moral and civic values with academic, career, or personal interests. Career centers can play an important role by ensuring that there are internship and job recruitment opportunities for students interested in careers that involve public service, nonprofit work, or other forms of community leadership and service, such as teaching. Too often college career centers are strongly focused on attracting corporate recruiters and helping students find jobs in business rather than also working to ensure that students carefully consider which jobs best match their own interests and values. The Messiah College Career Center is particularly focused on helping students integrate their personal faith and values with their career decisions, and some other institutions bring their own distinctive approaches to bear in helping their students bridge the transition from college to full-time work.

Duke, Stanford, and some other universities and colleges offer fellowships for graduating students who want to pursue research or action projects related to social or ethical concerns. Stanford's Ethics into Action prize provides $3,000 to support a graduating senior in any department in developing an idea from his or her honors thesis that seeks to improve some aspect of society; one such idea was to create a Web site that tracks environmental hazards. In addition, Stanford's Haas Center for Public Service works with the university's Career Center to provide workshops for students who want to pursue careers in public service or nonprofit organizations. As we mentioned in Chapter Three, Notre Dame's Center for Social Concerns sponsors the Alliance for Catholic Education, which supports students who become teachers in low-income schools in the South.

Even after students have graduated, colleges and universities can still provide important opportunities for their former students to pursue moral and civic learning and community improvement. At Indiana University and Notre Dame, for example, alumni clubs in cities throughout the country are focused on service, and this sends a clear signal to graduates about the expectations their alma maters have for them. Other colleges work with local alumni association chapters to sponsor guest lectures or special alumni trips that involve learning as well as sight-seeing, both of which can place special emphasis on social issues and problems.

Some institutions also provide regular opportunities for alumni engaged in public life to connect with the students currently attending their college or university. For example, Stanford's Haas Center and the Stanford Alumni

Association cosponsor the Visiting Mentor Program, which brings back to the campus Stanford alumni with distinguished accomplishments in public and community service. These "mentors," who are an ethnically and professionally diverse group, share their public service experiences with students, providing a perspective on public service from the "real world" and helping them think about directions for their service work beyond college. Visiting mentors have included a lawyer working for Amnesty International, the director of San Francisco Peer Resource Programs, a civil rights attorney and policy consultant, a former Republican Congressman from California, and a member of the Arizona State Legislature.

In these and other ways, colleges and universities can increase the chances that the development they have fostered will be only one phase, albeit a pivotal phase, in a much longer story of deepening commitment and effective action.

Notes

1. Surveys in 1990, 1995, and 1999, involving over 12,000 students on forty-eight campuses, all show that honor codes, especially those with high student involvement, reduce academic dishonesty. Cheating on tests, for example, is typically 30 to 50 percent lower at honor code campuses: 53 percent of undergraduates at non-honor code campuses self-reported one or more instances of cheating on tests compared to 29 percent of students at honor code schools (see, for example, McCabe & Trevino, 1993, 1997).

2. For example, a survey performed by the student newspaper, *Sou'wester,* showed that the honor code enjoys widespread support among students. Over 80 percent of respondents agreed both that the code is effective and that the student Honor Council is effective; 63 percent stated that they take the code "very seriously," and 34 percent said they take it "somewhat seriously" (*The Sou'wester Online,* 1996).

3. It is notable in this regard that in the late 1970s, after becoming disenchanted with moral dilemma discussions as a sufficient means of moral education, Lawrence Kohlberg moved to what he called "just community schools," in which students make and administer their own systems of rules. Kohlberg believed that changes in moral conduct as well as thinking required this more experiential approach, and subsequent research supports this conviction (Kohlberg & Higgins, 1987; Power, 2002).

9

ASSESSMENT IN MORAL AND CIVIC EDUCATION

AS IN EDUCATION generally, in moral and civic education quality varies and quality matters. But what is quality, and how do you measure it? Taking this question seriously requires us to take a look at assessment—assessment of courses, programs, and student learning.[1] Higher education is struggling with these issues, and there are no easy answers even for disciplinary learning, let alone for moral and civic learning. We cannot offer answers or prescriptions. And we are heedful of the wisdom in the reminder that Albert Einstein is said to have had hanging above his desk at Princeton: "Not everything that counts can be counted, and not everything that can be counted counts." So here we suggest some general directions, offer some caveats, and describe some efforts to assess teaching and learning that we saw in our campus visits. Overall, we learned that programs to foster students' moral and civic development are seldom assessed, like most programs in higher education. This is too bad, because more attention to assessment would strengthen programs and enlighten the field. But we do not call for more assessment lightly. Quality matters in assessment too, and we are well aware how hard it is to achieve.

Student Assessment

In student assessment, problems are legion, and some issues, such as grade inflation, are particularly explosive at the moment. In the moral and civic domain these problems are complicated further by the question of what should count toward grades, course credit, and program completion. In this area we have more caveats than answers.

Students are assessed for three quite different purposes, and it is important to keep the purposes distinct even though they intersect in practice. First, assessment of student learning provides a basis for specific feedback, which can help students improve their performance. Second, assessment provides the grounds for assigning course credit and grades. And third, assessment of student learning lets faculty know whether they need to adjust their teaching. We introduce the first two purposes here and discuss the third later in this chapter.

Feedback to Students

The American Association for Higher Education's "Principles of Good Practice for Assessing Student Learning" (Astin et al., 1992) suggest that student assessment should address knowledge, abilities, values, attitudes, and habits of mind that affect academic success and performance beyond the classroom. In order to do that, these principles recommend assessments "that use a diverse array of methods, including those that call for actual performance, using them over time to reveal change, growth, and increasing degrees of integration" (p. 2). This kind of assessment recognizes the complexity of learning and provides feedback on many developmental dimensions.

Informative feedback is essential for learning, and many students say they would like feedback more regularly. Teaching and learning are often represented as an apprenticeship, and regular feedback leading to adjustments of performance, followed by additional feedback, is a critical element of a successful apprenticeship. It is important to recognize, however, that expressions of approval or disapproval (that answer was right or wrong, that performance was good or bad) do not constitute *informative* feedback. Students need more detail and precision than that for feedback to support learning. It is noteworthy that when undergraduates at Harvard University were asked to describe their best course, their answers pointed to courses that gave regular, immediate feedback (Light, 2001).

When courses incorporate moral and civic learning, the scope of understanding and skills on which students may benefit from feedback broadens, and it can be especially important for them to receive feedback not only from teachers but also from peers, supervisors in field placements, and others with whom they work. When managed well, service learning, experiential learning, collaborative work, and other kinds of active learning include systematic feedback. This feedback, especially when it is disconnected from the assignment of grades, helps students progress on the many dimensions that make up moral and civic maturity. Feedback on unexamined assumptions and social, civic, and political skills can be especially helpful. When students are learning skills for reasoned discourse about controversial issues, for example, they will often know whether they have succeeded in convincing their classmates through other students' reactions, so informative feedback is built into the task. This is akin to Wiggins and McTighe's (1998) suggestion that in golf a key piece of feedback is whether the ball goes into the hole, and in writing, whether readers fall asleep while reading the paper.

Assignment of Grades and Course Credit

It is not easy to assess substantive knowledge, communication skills such as persuasive writing and speaking, or aspects of analytical or critical thinking such as the capacity to formulate and defend positions on difficult issues or the ability to take multiple perspectives into account. But faculty ought to assess progress toward these educational goals in any case, whether the content is relevant for moral and civic development or not. And that content should not change the assessment criteria. Including moral and civic goals in coursework should not affect the way grades are assigned.

Many dimensions of moral and civic development should not contribute to a student's grade, even if they are goals of the course. A faculty member might expect and hope that her service-learning course will lead to a greater sense of political efficacy, for example, but she should not give lower grades to students who still believe at the end of the course that their political actions cannot have a significant impact. This is especially true for dimensions of moral and civic motivation—values, convictions, moral identity, and the like—but it holds for some aspects of moral and civic understanding as well, including maturity of moral judgment or beliefs about political issues. It is often useful for students to take part in activities, such as journal writing, that help them become more aware of their values, moral identity, sense of political efficacy, and the like, but it should be made clear to them that the content of their responses does not contribute to their grades.

Sometimes students think that their teachers unfairly assign grades based on the moral or ideological content of students' views, favoring papers or other products that conform to the faculty member's beliefs. A student at one of the case study campuses, for example, suspected that he had received a lower grade on a course paper because he had argued that homosexuality is morally wrong. His teacher denied that this entered into the grade. In such cases it is incumbent upon the faculty member to define clearly the grading criteria and to show the student the particular features of his or her product (features that are presumably independent of ideological content) that did not fully meet those criteria.

Assessment of Abilities-Based or Outcomes-Based Education

Alverno College and other institutions that have adopted an outcomes-based approach place systematic, carefully designed feedback to students at the center of undergraduate education. In these institutions both external and self-assessment are understood to be essential to learning (Alverno College Faculty, 1994). This approach requires explicit articulation of required learning outcomes and innovative strategies for assessing those outcomes.

Alverno, which does not use grades, has been a leader in arguing that traditional testing is not adequate for plumbing the depths of an individual's developing abilities (Alverno College Faculty, 1994). Instead, it uses a multidimensional process in which active student performances are observed and judged on the basis of public, developmental criteria. These assessments may involve the creation and analysis of portfolios of student work and performance observations in real and simulated situations as well as more traditional approaches such as feedback on student papers. In one of these performance assessments, students are asked to demonstrate capacities relating to their responsibilities as citizens by participating in a simulated board meeting. Students act as members of a Citizens Advisory Council convened to address a controversy about the kinds of books that should be used in teaching high school students, the ways decisions about books for courses should be made, and the individuals who should have a voice in those decisions. Students are evaluated by a trained outside panel and also assess themselves on their abilities to do the following things: take a position, consider alternative ideas (show awareness of multiple perspectives), contribute to group problem solving, communicate with an awareness of their audience, think through and organize ideas, define problems and plan for solutions, and formulate appropriate action. Specific criteria further define each of these abilities. Students who perform well at "defining problems and planning for solutions" are said to show these characteristics: identifies and sets priorities among key tasks, demonstrates accurate awareness of major goals of the advisory council, shows informed awareness of constraints, identifies pertinent relationships between issues in different parts of the simulation, identifies meaningful implications, effectively organizes ideas, and suggests feasible alternative strategies.

Proponents of outcomes-based education argue that assessment is fairer in this kind of system. Because the criteria for passing at each level are publicly articulated and students are given many opportunities to demonstrate what they have learned, outcomes-based approaches are said to reduce subjectivity and arbitrariness in assessment. The outcomes and criteria are sometimes described as a kind of contract between students and faculty. Faculty assure students that they will have the learning opportunities necessary to achieve the outcomes and as many assessment opportunities as they need to demonstrate that learning (A. Driscoll, personal communication with T. Ehrlich, March 8, 2002). Another advantage of outcomes-based assessment is that it makes the learning goals and requirements explicit so both faculty and students can look at them critically. This allows them to determine whether the outcomes require of students more mature intellectual capacities than they can reasonably be expected to possess or the adoption of particular moral beliefs, ideologies, or interpretations of social problems, which would not be legitimate. This kind of review is essential when the assessments have high stakes attached, such as assignment of grades, granting of course credit, or college graduation.

Assessment of Courses and Teaching

Faculty teaching courses that are meant to foster moral and civic development often want to know whether the courses are achieving their goals. Teachers can go a long way toward assessing the quality of their courses by thinking carefully about what they are trying to accomplish and how they are going about it. If they pay explicit and scrupulously honest attention to a few key criteria of quality and go to some effort to find out whether the course seems to meet the criteria, their teaching is very likely to benefit, even if the assessment effort is quite informal or impressionistic. We saw faculty looking carefully at their courses in this way at some of the campuses we visited, but most could benefit from more explicit reflection. (See Chapter Five for some examples of faculty efforts to evaluate and improve their courses. Also, the Assessment Forum of the American Association for Higher Education has published numerous materials that may be helpful for these purposes; see, for example, Gardiner, Anderson, & Cambridge, 1997.)

Faculty interested in pursuing this informal assessment should ask whether the course goals, including moral and civic goals, are clearly articulated and whether their students understand and accept them. It is not possible to learn whether the course needs adjustment or what kind of adjustment it might need without clarity and specificity about its goals.[2] It is especially important to review specific course goals and strategies when an institution is relying on distribution requirements to ensure students' exposure to moral and civic education. Otherwise, courses that fulfill the requirements may not address students' moral or civic development at all (see Chapter Six).

In thinking about the effectiveness of their courses, faculty must also ask themselves whether their students seem to be learning what the course is intended to teach. Even teachers who are not evaluating their courses systematically routinely use indicators from class discussions, student questions, papers, and tests to gauge student learning and adjust their teaching. Evaluating the success of a course entails assessing student learning, so the more explicit faculty can be about identifying evidence of student learning (or its absence) on all dimensions represented in the course goals, the more useful the course evaluation will be.

Faculty should also think carefully about whether the pedagogical approaches they are using to pursue particular goals are consistent with what is known about student learning and development (see the initial sections of Chapter Five and the works cited there). Among other things, faculty should ask themselves whether they are asking students to practice what they hope the students will learn, including practice in understanding moral and civic concepts and in intellectual and practical skills. As we said in Chapter Five, if teachers want students to develop genuine understanding of a difficult concept, they must ask students to explain it, represent it in new ways, apply it in new situations, and connect it to their lives, rather than asking students simply to recall the concept in the form in which it was presented. Moral and civic issues should be integrated thoroughly with disciplinary material so that growing understanding in each domain enhances learning in the other. Sharing syllabi and talking with colleagues who are teaching related courses at the same or another institution can be very helpful to this kind of exploration.

Teachers can also ask students whether they think the course had a positive effect on the targeted dimensions of their moral and civic development. For example, do students believe at the end that they have developed an increased understanding of and interest in ethical or social issues? Do they expect to pursue these issues further, either intellectually or in some practical activity? Has the course changed the way they think about their own beliefs or goals?

The extensive research on service learning has provided useful criteria for evaluating service-learning courses: Are the service placements challenging (providing growth in important moral and civic skills)? Are students well prepared for the placements? Do the field experiences contribute directly to the academic goals of the course? Does the course have a structured reflection component that examines the issues addressed by the service in terms of systemic causes and policy responses as well as in interpersonal terms? Do students use the reflection opportunities to think through their assumptions, values, and identities when appropriate as well as to focus on the substantive issues raised in the service experience? Was the student participation effective from the point of view of the community partners?

Assessment of service-learning courses and programs has been more fully developed than assessment of other approaches to moral and civic education, just as service learning has been more fully examined in research. Two monographs, both published with support from Campus Compact, provide a great deal of information about how to approach this kind of evaluation. The first, a workbook, was issued as a "companion volume" to the Michigan Journal of Community Service Learning (2001). It is intended to help faculty members design service-learning courses that will promote civic learning as well as enhance academic learning goals. The second, published by Campus Compact, is *Assessing Service-Learning and Civic Engagement,* by Sherril B. Gelmon, Barbara A. Holland, Amy Driscoll, Amy Spring, and Seanna Kerrigan (2001). It outlines a rich array of methods for assessing student learning and the impact of service-learning programs on faculty, the campus, and participating community organizations as well as on students. These methods include surveys, interviews, focus groups, various modes of observation and documentation, and student journals. To assess an institution's commitment to service, for example, the book suggests examining the centrality of the service commitment to the institution by looking at such key indicators as the school's mission statement; promotion, tenure, and hiring standards; and organizational structure.

The Scholarship of Teaching and Learning

If individual faculty members are conscious of exactly what they hope their students will learn, including their goals for moral and civic development, and attempt to specify how they will know whether that learning is taking place, this preparation should go a long way toward ensuring quality in moral and civic education, as it does for teaching and learning more generally. Even so, we believe that if some institutions and faculty are in a position to move beyond individual and impressionistic reflections on their own teaching to more systematic and potentially public methods, this shift will improve not only their own teaching but the field of moral and civic education as well.

In writing on the scholarship of teaching and learning, Patricia Hutchings and Lee Shulman (1999) have discussed the private nature of teaching and the fact that creative teaching is too seldom documented and shared in ways that allow others to build on it. As we said in Chapter Two, the scholarship of teaching and learning involves purposive reflection, documentation, assessment, and analysis in a public and accessible manner. Its purpose is to make teaching public: to subject it to peer review and critique—as other scholarship is—and to share it with others in order to move toward the improvement and understanding of learning and teaching in a given discipline or field. Objects of investigation include particular courses, student learning across courses, and aspects of teaching that transcend any particular course context.

The kinds of questions faculty are addressing through the scholarship of teaching and learning are also pertinent to the pursuit of quality in moral and civic education. Answering these questions requires investigations of the relative effectiveness for student learning of different pedagogical approaches; descriptive studies that explicate the constituent features of a course (for example, the dynamics of class discussions of contested issues); documentation of what Lee Shulman calls "visions of the possible" (for example, close examination of a course with an unusual and ambitious goal, Hutchings, 2000); and studies that attempt to formulate a new conceptual framework for illuminating teaching and learning in a particular area. Faculty conducting these investigations into their own teaching use a wide array of methods, with both questions and methods shaped to a large extent by their own disciplines (Huber & Morreale, 2002). The scholarship of teaching and learning draws on course portfolios, the collection and systematic analysis of student work (often by secondary readers), focus groups, ethnographic interviews and observations, questionnaires, and standardized instruments. Communities of faculty interested in the scholarship of teaching and learning are emerging on many campuses and in some professional associations, and the American Association for Higher Education offers rich programming in this area as well.

This new field has just begun to address the moral and civic goals of undergraduate education. Barbara Mae Gayle, for example, professor of communication at the University of Portland, uses her public speaking courses to teach students to conduct reasoned interactions on divisive topics such as school vouchers, animal rights, or Megan's law. Students choose an issue, conduct extensive research on the topic, and make several presentations to the class, arguing for different points of view in each presentation. Through structured attitude change instruments and thematic coding of presentations and journal entries, Gayle learned that students actively engaged in investigating the issue and speaking about it from multiple perspectives were more likely to change their opinions than students who listened to the presentations. Some listeners did change their opinions, however, and both the speakers and the listeners whose attitudes changed said they were most influenced by the evidence presented and by an increased understanding of the consequences of adopting a particular position. Those who did not change their minds referred to their personal experience or personal opinion as the primary reason for the maintenance of their original views. Although attitude change is not always a desirable outcome, if one takes attitude change in this case as a rough proxy for open-mindedness on the issue, it appears that active involvement in making the case for multiple perspectives on highly charged issues may support students' capacity for open-minded civil discourse. The study also highlights the probability that an emphasis on personal experiences as grounds for opinion formation on complex social policy issues may get in the way of open-minded consideration of evidence. This has important educational implications, because students can no doubt learn to recognize the limitations of their personal experiences with complex issues and develop the capacity to integrate these experiences better with a broad range of evidence. Importantly, Gayle also found that the public speaking skills of the students in courses that focused on discourse about divisive issues improved as much as the skills of students in comparison courses that focused more explicitly on teaching those public speaking skills.

If more faculty begin to address moral and civic learning goals in their investigations into teaching and learning, their assessments will build a rich base of insights about what works to support development along the various dimensions of moral and civic maturity, what methods are most useful for documenting and evaluating that development, and how best to integrate moral and civic learning with academic learning so that both benefit. The field of moral and civic education could be advanced significantly if faculty had the resources and motivation to build on each other's work.

Program Assessment

We described in Chapter Eight a rich array of extracurricular programs that are as important to students' moral and civic development as curricular programs. Very few of these programs are being evaluated systematically, which means that we have only an impressionistic sense of which ones are engaging and effective. Likewise, it is rare for schools to assess formally curricular programs consisting of collections of courses, such as general education programs with moral and civic goals or programs that enable the teaching of ethics across the curriculum. This kind of assessment is extremely labor intensive and difficult to do well. We are not recommending that administrative leaders require assessment of these programs. Even so, we believe that high-quality program assessments can be very fruitful.

Program assessment can take very different forms, depending on its purpose and audience. Most often the purpose is clarifying program goals, reviewing progress toward those goals, and identifying areas in which the program can be improved. This kind of assessment may have multiple audiences: program leaders and staff, administrative leaders with oversight for the program, funders, and people interested in replicating or adapting the program for use at other institutions. Sometimes assessments are conducted for the purpose of demonstrating a program's value to a specific audience (for example, policymakers, funders, or skeptics). Growing demands for "accountability" in education often motivate this kind of assessment.

Assessment for Program Improvement

One form of program assessment that can be very useful is the visiting committee, which involves bringing in *critical friends* to take a close look at the program's goals, strategies, and products (including evidence of student learning and development). Critical friends are people who are deeply knowledgeable about the kind of work the program and others like it are doing, who are sympathetic with the program goals, and who have enough distance from the program to see things about it that may be invisible to someone who is thoroughly immersed in it. When well done, visits like this can be very productive—clarifying goals, gathering information about whether these goals are being met, delineating strengths and weaknesses, and producing a broad perspective on the program through comparison with other, related efforts. As in the case of institutional accreditation visits, the external group can be a catalyst for self-examination, and preparation for the visit, though time consuming, can force staff to clarify their thinking in ways that would not otherwise happen. The Center for Social Concerns at the University of Notre Dame and the Center for Character Development at the United States Air Force Academy have both used this approach.

For program evaluators who want to go beyond the advice of a visiting committee to look more systematically at the program's processes and outcomes, the long tradition of educational program assessment provides a rich literature on how to evaluate the quality of programs and investigate their dynamics in ways that can strengthen them. Systematic assessment of programs intended to foster moral and civic development can lead to significant program improvement as well as deepening educators' understanding of what works and why, what it means when something is said to "work," and even how educators conceive of moral and civic development. But in order for assessment to accomplish these things, it is essential that educators use descriptive, often qualitative methods to look at the processes through which the program operates, the nature of students' experiences, and the changes students undergo, and that they do not rely entirely on outcome measures, especially measures remote from the phenomena for which these measures are indicators. This kind of approach represents what we might call *high-yield* assessment.

In contrast, assessments that examine a few outcome measures and do not look closely at the processes underlying the program's operation cannot say much about the nature of the program, the specific experiences of participating students, the processes that may be operative, and the nature of changes the students may undergo. This is especially true when assessments rely on outcomes measures that are highly condensed indicators of an underlying dimension, often standardized measures that are chosen for convenience or economy of use despite the fact that they are not authentic representations of the learning and development the course or program seeks to foster (Shulman, 2000). These *low-yield* assessments provide little information that can be used to improve the programs being evaluated. When the expected increases on outcome measures are not obtained, it is very difficult to interpret the significance of the finding. It may have resulted from an ineffective program, an inappropriate choice of measures, or an important but correctable weakness in an otherwise strong program. Unfortunately, evaluations that rely entirely on assessment of a few outcomes do not provide any information about which of these factors might be the operative one.

Low-yield assessments include not only this kind of program evaluation but also such assessments of individuals as screening and selection tests like the SAT and GRE, the standardized tests required for high school graduation, and many institutional assessments meant to hold education accountable to standards generated at the state or national level. Low-yield assessments are frequently applied in both K–12 and higher education to individuals and institutions, and in many cases these assessments have very high stakes attached, determining admission to selective programs, certification, accreditation, allocation of resources within an institution or across institutions, and elimination of programs.

There are a number of risks associated with these high-stakes, low-yield assessments. One risk is that they may drive programs in the wrong direction. When there are high stakes attached for the institution, it is natural that faculty will begin to "teach to the test." Teaching to the test can be a good thing when the test captures faithfully the skills and other learning outcomes it is most important for the course or program to impart. But it is very difficult for low-yield assessments to do this, and most do not. Because low-yield assessment is so ubiquitous, many people assume it is the only option, which makes them reluctant to assess the impact of their programs. With some justification they fear that they will learn little that is useful or, worse, that the evaluation might seriously underestimate a worthwhile program's impact and thus result in loss of support. This may be especially true for moral and civic education programs because the outcomes of interest are so difficult to measure, especially with instruments that can be used economically on a large scale.

Portland State University is unusual in the degree to which it conducts ongoing assessments of the courses in its general education program, University Studies. Participating faculty see these assessments as not only acceptable but worthwhile, in part because they are high yield and have relatively low stakes attached. The course assessments are designed to provide immediate, usable feedback to faculty and to provide the university administration and the Center for Academic Excellence (the teaching and learning center) with a sense of how well this relatively new program is doing. The overall assessment initiative is built around asking faculty to articulate student learning expectations and connect them to assignments that demonstrate learning. Somewhat different assessments are used for each of the components of University Studies (Freshman Inquiry, Sophomore Inquiry, and capstone courses), but all use multiple methods, including student self-report, standardized scales, and analyses of student work.

Freshman Inquiry courses, the first component of University Studies, are interdisciplinary explorations of issues such as community, the environment, faith and reason, and personal and social change. In any academic year, students choose from among six or seven Freshman Inquiry courses, each with a different content focus but all sharing the more general goals of University Studies to teach inquiry and critical thinking, communication, the variety of human experience, and ethics and social responsibility (see the description in Chapter Six). Evaluation of each section of Freshman Inquiry involves a guided "free write" by students in about the fifth week of the term, a student focus group, administration of the Classroom Environment Scale around the middle of the term, a course evaluation and survey of students' perceptions of their progress toward the stated learning objectives at the end of the year, and a portfolio review in which a random sample of student portfolios is scored using rubrics for writing, critical thinking, appreciation of diversity, and understanding of ethics and social responsibility. During the summer after the course, faculty teams teaching comparable sections of Freshman Inquiry meet to review the results of the previous year's assessment and give the Freshman Inquiry Coordinator a report of the team's course improvement goals. The Freshman Inquiry Coordinator uses these reports, along with information from the assessments, to plan faculty development efforts for the following year (Portland State University, Office of University Studies, 1994).

Although all Freshman Inquiry courses share some overarching goals and common assessment strategies, more specific learning objectives are spelled out in each particular course. The course called Metamorphosis, for example, investigates the process of change in human existence: How do people envision and experience transformation in their bodies, their minds, and their social lives? How do they shape and interact with the environments they inhabit? What are the processes of social, political, and paradigmatic change? What types of change are likely to affect individuals, systems, and society? Among other assessment efforts, the faculty who teach the two sections of Metamorphosis developed a scoring rubric for analyzing students' final research papers in order to assess the extent to which students had achieved this central course goal: "Students will be able to describe and evaluate the probable success of various means of promoting personal, social/cultural/political, and paradigmatic change." Participating faculty found the process of developing the scoring rubric very useful because it gave them a common language for codifying the dimensions of good research writing and grasp of the concepts in the course. The application of the rubric revealed that students varied greatly in the extent to which they had achieved the specified learning outcomes but that the majority had not fully achieved the course goals by the end of the year. For example, most students still had difficulty seeing multiple sides of an issue, and most tended to avoid dealing with structures and mechanisms of social change, focusing instead on personality changes and on the outcomes of change. This was important information for faculty thinking about how they might teach the course somewhat differently in the future.

Because many elements of the program assessments are common across sections and across academic years, it is possible to look at variation across sections and across time. This has helped faculty see which aspects of which courses need strengthening. For example, in end-of-year course evaluations, students consistently report that their Freshman Inquiry courses helped them to improve their critical thinking and writing skills, to explore ethical issues, and to examine their understanding of social responsibility, but many fewer believe the courses helped them use numbers, charts, tables, or graphs to communicate, another stated objective of Freshman Inquiry.

Methods and Tools

In conducting assessments that are useful in understanding the dynamics of a program and the ways to strengthen it, careful identification of outcomes and thoughtful, creative approaches to measuring those outcomes are critical. Informal assessments of courses and programs can involve questioning student focus groups, conducting quick checks of student learning, like the "minute papers" that students are sometimes asked to complete at the end of class (Cross, 1995), or reading student papers with a rubric that highlights features of interest to the faculty member. For both formal or systematic program assessments and research on moral and civic development and education, instrumentation is a major challenge. There are twin dangers here to be avoided. The first danger is the temptation to use a standardized measure that is not quite appropriate in order to avoid costly investment in instrument development. Even an outcome like critical thinking, which has been studied fairly extensively, takes different forms in different fields; so the adoption of a rubric that was developed for another purpose may generate misleading results. Paradoxically, the second danger is the misguided assumption that each campus or assessment effort must invent its own instruments de novo. Instrument development and validation are extremely difficult, and few projects are in a position to do them well. Furthermore, when different studies use different instruments, it is very difficult to integrate the findings across the field. These twin dangers create a dilemma for research and program assessment, pointing to the need for a *shareable toolkit* that includes a wide array of valid measures of important dimensions of moral and civic development.

In the past few years there have been a number of efforts to develop catalogues of the relevant instruments and new instruments that are best able to assess important aspects of moral and civic development. For example, Robert Bringle and his colleagues (Bringle, Phillips, & Hudson, in press) at Indiana University-Purdue University Indianapolis are compiling a book of instruments that measure constructs associated with student learning in service-learning classes. Although of particular interest to service-learning practitioners, this volume will be useful to a wide range of faculty as many of the scales are not specific to service-learning experiences and may be used to assess student outcomes in other courses or programs. A particularly useful instrument was developed by Scott Keeter at George Mason University (sponsored by Pew Charitable Trusts) to elaborate a set of "youth civic engagement indicators." Research and evaluation are only as good as the instruments they use, so all of this instrument development work should make very useful contributions to the field.

Making the Case for a Program

One purpose of assessment for most educational innovations, including moral and civic education programs, is to persuade others, including skeptics, of new programs' value. At many institutions there are faculty who demand evidence that new curricula or teaching methods are effective. As Judith Ramaley (2000) has pointed out, these skeptics often assume the effectiveness of the old approaches without offering any support for that assumption, thus applying a double standard to the question of what does and does not require justification. Moreover, in attempting to show the effectiveness of educational innovations, program proponents often allow their critics to define the terms of what will count as evidence, designing assessments that will yield simple quantitative results, even when this gives a distorted picture of a program's effectiveness, because some of the intended outcomes cannot be readily quantified. The problem with too strong an emphasis on quantitative evidence of effectiveness is that this approach is likely to reduce complex phenomena to oversimplified indicators rather than rich representations of process or outcomes that capture something important about the work itself.

An alternative to the reductionist approach to persuading skeptics is to create exhibitions of student work and performance that show the learning that has occurred and to ask the evaluative questions in the context of rich documentation of a program or course. For example, student journals or papers written over the course of a semester may be analyzed to highlight important changes in students' understanding that have emerged during the program or course. This kind of analysis can be especially convincing when it uses independent coders. Similarly, documentation of student performances early and late in the course can reveal dramatic changes in skills. It is sometimes appropriate to supplement these exhibitions with numbers, but it is difficult for numbers alone to demonstrate the value of a complex educational undertaking. In order for this kind of demonstration to be convincing to skeptical audiences, it may be necessary to educate audiences so they are better able to interpret what they are seeing. Increasing an audience's understanding of a program's goals and methods opens productive communication in a way that a more narrowly defined presentation of statistical results does not. It is also important to bear in mind, however, that it may not be possible, or even necessary, to persuade all of a program's critics (Ramaley, 2000). Complete consensus on the value of new educational approaches is no doubt an unrealistic goal on most campuses.

Research on Moral and Civic Education

In general, program assessments are intentionally local, contextually bounded (closely tied to the particular intervention being assessed), and not centrally concerned with results that can be generalized beyond that local context. Unlike program assessment, educational research *is* centrally concerned with generalization to the broader universe of which the particular programs being studied are representative instances. For this reason, additional methodological issues become important, often involving designs that control for confounding variables, ensure comparability across different sites of data collection, and address a range of competing interpretations of the results. High-quality educational research is not limited to experimental design and hypothesis testing approaches, but even when methods such as ethnographies and case studies are used, a concern for generalization beyond the particular instance is central. It must be clear in case studies, for example, what the instance under study is "a case of" (Shulman, 1981) and why it is valid or useful to treat this case as representative of that larger class.

Systematic empirical research is usually resource intensive, and not all institutions are in a position to undertake such research on moral and civic learning. But this research is very important in giving educators a better understanding of the development of moral and civic maturity, the kinds of educational experiences that foster it, and the reasons these experiences are important. We urge both foundations and higher education institutions to invest in this research, which we believe has already had tremendous payoff, most notably through the extensive research on service learning. Even educators' conceptions of what constitutes quality in service learning have been shaped by research comparing service-learning experiences that lead to the desired student outcomes with those that do not. As a result of this work it is known that participating students' academic performance improves, their concern for and involvement with social issues and political efficacy grows, and other aspects of their moral and civic maturity increase only when the courses include such key features as challenging service placements and structured reflections on the course content (Eyler & Giles, 1999). More recent research suggests that students benefit even more when they have leadership responsibility in their service placements, adding another factor to educators' understanding of high-quality service learning (Morgan & Streb, 2001).

Longitudinal research is especially valuable in helping educators understand the way moral and civic development unfolds over time and the long-term impact of various experiences. Longitudinal studies of moral and civic education (and of naturally occurring experiences thought to affect moral or civic development) demonstrate that assessments conducted immediately following an experience or program can overstate the apparent impact. It is not unusual for effects to disappear over time as graduates leave college and enter new contexts (Astin, Sax, & Avalos, 1999). Conversely, short-term assessments can understate the impact of the experience or program. Sometimes developmental effects are exhibited gradually over time or emerge only later in life. Jennings and Stoker (2001) report that their longitudinal analyses show that adolescent experiences in civic organizations have a positive effect on adult involvement in voluntary organizations but the effect is delayed, emerging gradually and increasingly strongly as individuals approach middle age. In psychology, this is known as a "sleeper effect." Longitudinal studies that have looked at college students' development over time have contributed greatly to the understanding of moral and civic development (we reviewed some of these findings in Chapter Four).

Longitudinal research is extremely resource intensive and requires well-developed social science expertise, so it should not be undertaken lightly. But if researchers or program evaluators expect that they may want to conduct longitudinal follow-ups later, there are some simple things they can do initially to make these follow-ups more feasible. First, it is important to prepare and ask students to sign a form by which they consent to be recontacted. Second, to make it easier to find the participants later, the form should ask them for the names and addresses of one or two people (usually close relatives) who are likely to remain at the address given and who will always know where to find the participant. Finally, it is important that the data collected in the initial study be documented and stored in an orderly way so they will be available for comparison if a follow-up is conducted. This applies to both computer-coded data and the original materials when they are qualitative (for example, interview transcripts) and therefore not entirely redundant with the coded data.

Investing in Assessment

Assessment is an area of relative weakness as well as heated debate in education generally, and assessment of moral and civic learning is even more difficult, even less well developed. Nevertheless, some institutions have worked hard to create innovative methods for assessing student performance along moral and civic dimensions or for evaluating the effectiveness of their programs that enhance moral and civic development. As we discussed in Chapter Five, some faculty routinely evaluate their own teaching and improve it based on what they learn. At most of the institutions we reviewed, however, programs addressing moral and civic development were not assessed at all. Although we recognize how difficult such assessment is, we believe that more systematic efforts to assess program effectiveness would be worth the considerable investment they require. The development of instruments and methods and the careful documentation of courses and programs, along with empirical research on different modes of moral and civic education, would yield more effective program design, better understanding of what works for which students, increased communication among educators so they could build on each other's work, and more useful feedback to students and thus more reliable learning.

NOTES

1. Some writers in higher education use the term *evaluation* rather than *assessment* to refer to some aspects of each of these categories or to course and program evaluation, reserving the term *assessment* for the assessment of students. The terms are not consistently distinguished in the field, however, and because assessments (or evaluations) of courses, programs, and students intersect, we use same term (*assessment*) to refer to all three.

2. In their book *Understanding by Design*, Grant Wiggins and Jay McTighe (1998) suggest a process faculty may employ to think through what they want students to learn, how they can best ensure that learning, and how to assess it. Wiggins and McTighe's framework centers on a conception of genuine understanding much like the one we discussed in Chapter Five.

10

BRINGING MORAL AND
CIVIC LEARNING
TO CENTER STAGE

IN CHAPTER ONE we compared undergraduate education to preparing for an expedition, with the explorers mastering bodies of knowledge and scientific techniques they will need, collecting tools and learning to use them, establishing collaborative relationships with team members, studying maps, and working out routes. Most educators hope and expect that like the explorers Meriwether Lewis and William Clark, college graduates will not just be traveling forward and trying to survive the journey but also learning and accomplishing valuable things along the way. They may also hope that the college experience will shift graduates' life trajectories just a bit and give them new ways of responding to later experiences, as Lewis's preparation did, so that the shift in direction will be magnified over time and the long-term impact significant.

Both personally and professionally, today's college graduates will be doing many things in their lives, and even they cannot predict the many roles they will take on. But whatever else students do, we hope they will also be active citizens and positive forces in the world. The central premise of this book is that this expectation and hope of engaged and responsible citizenship should enter into the preexpedition preparation students undertake. Whatever specific life patterns and occupations they choose, these will be enriched and strengthened if they conduct their personal and professional lives with integrity and a sense of purpose. Their preparation will benefit from taking the moral and civic dimensions of their tasks and destination into account as well. In the view of many educators, especially those who draw on the traditions of liberal education, the preparation for citizenship, honorable work, and personal integrity lies at the heart of preparation for life.

This goal was central to American undergraduate education in its early years but has been pushed aside in many colleges and universities today, in practice if not in principle. If the undergraduate years are to contribute fully to the well-being of students and the world, this agenda must be brought back from the margins into the front and center of higher education. Overall, however, students' moral and civic development is not a high priority in U.S. higher education today. We have been struck again and again by the many lost opportunities for moral and civic growth in curricular and extracurricular programs on most campuses. But despite the number of challenges and impediments this developmental work faces, some colleges and universities have made education for moral responsibility and engaged citizenship an integral part of their undergraduate programs. They are institutions of every type—large urban universities, religiously affiliated and secular colleges, highly selective research universities, community colleges, historically black and tribal colleges, residential and commuter campuses, and institutions with mostly older students as well as those whose students come straight from high school. Like any complicated enterprise, these efforts require strong leadership. Often, though not always, this includes leadership from the highest administrative levels. But leadership can also come from interested faculty and campus centers, in collaboration with administrative leadership or in its absence (see Chapter Three). Many faculty believe in educating for moral and civic growth and go to great lengths to take it on, but they are almost invariably stretched too thin and need support in this work (see Chapter Seven).

We have described twelve institutions that make moral and civic education a central priority (see Chapter Three). All twelve are characterized by approaches that are intentional, holistic, and designed to reach all of their students. Although there has been no research comparing them to colleges and universities with less far-reaching programs, our site visits gave us the strong impression that this more comprehensive, intentional approach has a greater impact on more students. But this comprehensive approach is not the only way to provide effective moral and civic education to undergraduates. Complete institutional buy-in is not necessary for a college or university to take this agenda seriously. There is a lot that interested administrative and faculty leaders, and even individual faculty and staff members, can do even when they are at schools where the climate is receptive to moral and civic learning but where that focus is not a central institutional commitment.

Although we have made many suggestions for designing and improving undergraduate moral and civic education, we do not mean to imply that institutions must act on the full array of these suggestions in order to have a significant impact on students. Clearly, some of these ideas will be more feasible and appropriate than others on any given campus, and even targeted programs can be very important to the students they reach.

Both in our case study institutions and in the many others we reviewed, we saw a great deal of exceptionally creative and engaging programming, including classroom teaching, extracurricular programs, and rich cultural practices, that supported students' moral and civic growth. We have described in some detail what we consider to be some of the best of these efforts. In this concluding chapter we lay out in condensed form some basic principles we derived from our observations and analyses of these programs. These principles are offered as a framework for strengthening efforts currently in place and for planning future directions. The parameters and guidelines that interested faculty and administrators should keep in mind can be seen as answers to three questions:

1. How can educators be sure that programs address the full range of developmental dimensions we have called moral and civic understanding, motivation, and skills?

2. How can educators take advantage of the most useful sites for moral and civic education in institutions of higher education?

3. How can educators be sure to touch on the three basic themes spelled out in Chapter Three, all of which are important to a full conception of moral and civic maturity: moral and civic virtue, systemic social responsibility, and community connections?

Developmental Goals and Dimensions (Question 1: Are All Important Dimensions Addressed?)

Moral and civic maturity is not a unitary phenomenon. It is made up of multiple dimensions, and undergraduate education can address the full range of these dimensions (see Chapter Four). It may be helpful for campuses to create an inventory of their existing programs as they begin thinking about which developmental areas are well represented, which need strengthening, and which are not being addressed at all. The dimensions fall into three broad categories:

• *Moral and civic understanding.* Moral and civic understanding includes moral interpretation and judgment; the understanding of key ethical concepts such as equity and moral relativism and civic concepts such as civil liberties and procedural impartiality; knowledge of democratic principles and institutions; and substantive expertise in the fields with which one becomes engaged.

- *Moral and civic motivation.* Moral and civic motivation arises out of emotions such as hope and compassion; the adoption of such values as an interest in politics and a desire to be an engaged citizen; a sense of political efficacy; and a sense of one's own identity that places moral and civic responsibility at the core of one's self-definition.

- *Moral and civic skills.* Moral and civic skills include well-developed capacities for communication of various kinds; the ability to collaborate, compromise with, and mobilize others; and various skills of democratic participation.

Sites of Moral and Civic Education (Question 2: Are All Useful Sites Exploited?)

There are three main sites of moral and civic education, and all are important: the curriculum, including both general education and the major; extracurricular activities and programs; and the campus culture, including honor codes, residence hall life, and spontaneous teachable moments, as well as various cultural routines and practices—symbols, rituals, socialization practices, shared stories, and the like. Although we discuss them separately, some of the most effective programs integrate learning from at least two of the sites—usually curricular and extracurricular—and sometimes all three. In fact part of what we mean when we say the case study institutions use a holistic approach is that moral and civic education takes place in all major sites and is well aligned and dynamically interconnected across sites.

The Curriculum

If curriculum planners want to be sure that courses intended to serve the purpose of moral and civic education actually accomplish that purpose, it is helpful to establish clear goals and criteria and review the courses to determine whether they meet these ends. In addition, if institutions wish to connect with students who arrive on campus with no particular interest in moral and civic issues, they need to make sure that those issues are not dealt with only in electives that will be chosen only by students who already show a strong interest in ethical concerns or social responsibility.

- *Mutual enhancement.* Moral and civic learning, touching not only on understanding but also on motivation and skills, should be thoroughly integrated with the rest of academic learning. When this is done successfully, moral and civic learning and academic learning are mutually enhancing (see Chapters Five and Six).

- *Pedagogies.* Both moral and civic learning and academic learning benefit from a wider array of pedagogies than lecture and discussion. Faculty teaching for moral and civic development should consider using a wide range of pedagogies, including service learning and other field placements, simulations, collaborative work, and projects that grapple with complex, open-ended problems (see Chapter Five).

- *General education.* There are several effective ways to incorporate moral and civic issues into the general education curriculum (see Chapter Six).

> *Distribution requirements.* Highly decentralized distribution requirements are often the least effective way to ensure that moral and civic learning is represented in general education. This can be corrected when courses that satisfy requirements intended to represent moral and civic education are carefully screened with reference to clearly articulated criteria. In addition, even in very loosely structured general education programs, some courses predictably reach very large numbers of students. Whenever possible, it is especially useful to incorporate moral and civic learning into those courses.

> *Core courses.* A second option is to require particular courses designed to foster moral and civic development. These are often interdisciplinary but need not be. Institutions may require one or more core courses that are *common to all students,* thereby providing a shared learning experience for the whole student body. Alternatively, students may be offered *choices within a given category* of required course, such as the freshman seminar or senior capstone. This approach allows students and faculty to choose subject matter of particular interest to them while ensuring that parallel sections, even though they have different content, embody the same goals and general approach.

- *Abilities- or outcomes-based education.* A third way to ensure that moral and civic learning in the curriculum reaches all students is to establish certain moral and civic competencies (along with other competencies) as requirements for graduation. These competencies can be assessed directly both within and outside the classroom context or faculty can build them into the criteria for success in their courses. A centralized or departmental curriculum committee should review the courses to make sure they address the educational outcomes in question. Required outcomes should not be defined to include particular moral and civic values, beliefs, or interpretations of social or political issues.

• *Academic majors.* It is also important to incorporate moral and civic issues into the major. Almost all fields naturally raise these issues, and education in the major is incomplete if they are not addressed. Faculty can be encouraged to weave these issues into the many courses in the major for which they are relevant, or department faculty can design common required courses, particularly entry-level courses and senior capstones, that address the ethical issues and social implications of the disciplinary content. It can be especially beneficial to employ both entry-level and capstone courses.

• *Faculty development.* Many faculty are interested in incorporating moral and civic learning into their courses but lack the substantive knowledge and pedagogical expertise to do so. They can benefit from structured faculty development seminars, ongoing discussion groups, and connections with national programs that support moral and civic education, such as Campus Compact. They should also have regular opportunities to collaborate with and learn from colleagues on their own or other campuses who are doing this kind of work (see Chapter Seven).

• *Logistical support.* Faculty also need logistical support, especially when they are using service learning or other field placements. This support may include help with service placements, liability issues, transportation to field sites, and guidelines for protecting community partners. Even modest amounts of funding for course development and assessment can also be very helpful.

• *Campus centers.* Campus centers are often very effective in providing both faculty development and logistical support. Several kinds of centers can provide these services: teaching and learning centers, which are present on most campuses; centers for service learning, which are growing in popularity; and centers charged with stimulating and overseeing moral and civic education on the campus, a relatively unusual but very powerful model. (In Chapter Three we discuss the important leadership in moral and civic education that campus centers provide.)

• *Non-tenure track faculty.* It is also important to recognize the contributions of non-tenure track faculty to undergraduate moral and civic education and offer these teachers development opportunities and logistical support. They can be a valuable resource for moral and civic education because they bring a wide range of backgrounds and expertise to their efforts.

Moral and Civic Learning Beyond the Classroom

Moral and civic learning beyond the classroom occurs both through structured extracurricular programs and activities and many aspects of the environment or culture. All are important potential sites for moral and civic education (see Chapters Three and Eight).

• *Extracurricular programs.* Leadership programs; service activities; disciplinary, religious, and political clubs; and programs designed to foster communication and respect among diverse individuals and groups are most directly relevant to students' moral and civic growth, but moral and civic learning can be incorporated into virtually any kind of student activity with sensitive guidance and support from faculty and staff advisers.

• *Precollege efforts.* Programs that foster moral and civic development should begin even before students arrive on campus with precollege readings that introduce a moral and civic lens. Then new student orientations can include discussions of institutional values and expectations, including respect for ethnic, religious, political, gender, and other kinds of diversity.

• *Postcollege efforts.* Programming can also continue after college if campuses reach out to alumni, helping sustain their interest in serving the public good in the midst of the pressures of postcollege life and connecting them with current students around public service issues and activities.

• *Campus culture.* Campus cultures convey many, often conflicting, messages. It may be useful to review some of the campus's most prominent physical symbols, iconic stories, socialization practices, and widely shared ideas, and to talk with students about what aspects of the culture are salient to them and how they understand their meaning. Although efforts to manipulate these features of the culture intentionally may be perceived as artificial and thus be ineffective, an increased awareness can lead naturally to changes that will benefit students' moral and civic development. When institutions have a vibrant tradition of social contribution, a rich set of public events that explore social and political issues, or a faculty that is especially engaged with the local or national community, they should highlight and build on these strengths.

• *Spontaneous opportunities.* Campus life also presents many teachable moments for moral and civic learning, opportunities for wise administrators and faculty to use even conflicts or serious infractions of civility to developmental advantage. Conflicts directly related to the campus can produce especially powerful teachable moments, because they help students learn to deal constructively with competing interests in a community.

• *Honor codes.* Honor codes are an important way to highlight some of the central values of higher education—honesty, trust, self-restraint, civility, and mutual respect. In order for an honor code to contribute to a climate that supports these values, it should involve faculty support, student participation in its development and implementation, thoughtful discussions of its meaning and rationale, discussion that makes explicit the links between honorable student behavior and responsible citizenship in the campus and broader communities, and fair and consistent enforcement.

• *Residence halls.* Residence halls can be effective sites for moral and civic learning through community building within the residential unit, residence-based service programs, links with the curriculum, and theme-oriented residences that focus on diversity, community service, leadership, active citizenship, or particular social issues.

Assessment

• *Student assessment.* Validly assessing student learning is complex and difficult in any domain, and this is especially true in the domain of moral and civic development (see Chapter Nine). Informative feedback is essential to student learning and is as appropriate in the moral and civic domain as in other areas. That feedback can come from peers, field placement supervisors, and community partners as well as from faculty. Many areas of moral and civic learning, including substantive knowledge in fields such as ethics, political theory, or government and skills such as well-argued and persuasive writing, are already evaluated in coursework, and the incorporation of moral and civic issues does not affect criteria for assessing these areas.

• *Course assessment.* Faculty members and program directors should not be routinely expected to assess formally the impact of their courses and programs. That will not be feasible in many cases. All should, however, make sure that their intended learning goals are clear to and accepted by students and make at least informal efforts to determine whether the program as designed and implemented seems to be accomplishing those goals, making changes when some aspects of the course or program seem problematic (see Chapter Five for examples).

• *Program assessment.* For more systematic course or program evaluations, we recommend employing descriptive, often qualitative methods (high-yield assessments) that document students' experiences and the processes through which the program operates as well as learning outcomes, rather than relying entirely on quantitative outcome measures (see Chapter Nine).

Thematic Perspectives
(Question 3: Are the Three Basic Themes Represented?)

In our analyses of observations at the twelve case study institutions, we identified three themes, or emphases, that represent different conceptions of what is important to moral and civic responsibility: *community connections, moral and civic virtue,* and *social justice* (which we also call *systemic social responsibility*). These three emphases represent different aspects of fully developed moral and civic education. For reasons we articulated in Chapter Three, we believe that moral and civic education is incomplete if it does not somehow take account of all of these themes.

• *Community connections.* It is important for students to develop a sense of being members of various communities, to understand the responsibilities entailed in community membership, and to have both the inclination and capacity to contribute in important ways to those communities. Relevant communities include the campus itself or some part of the campus, local neighborhoods, particular groups to which students feel allegiance and responsibility, groups to which the institution feels such allegiance and duty, and the broader national or international communities.

• *Moral and civic virtue.* A full program of moral and civic education must include support for the central values and virtues of the educational enterprise and a democratic society. As in the case of community connections, different institutions will bring distinctive approaches to their interpretation of key values, but some are important for all. These include intellectual integrity and concern for truth, mutual respect and tolerance, open-mindedness, concern for both the rights and the welfare of individuals and the community, and commitment to rational discourse and procedural fairness. Adoption of core values connected with more specific cultural or religious traditions can also be appropriate, as long as these are consistent with fundamental democratic values and made clear to prospective students and faculty.

• *Systemic social responsibility.* When drawing on the theme of systemic social responsibility, it is important to have curricular and extracurricular programs that help students learn how democratic processes work and how citizens can have influence, encourage them to take responsibility for participating actively in the democratic process, and make connections between moral and civic values and social policy analyses. Few students bring an initial interest in policy, electoral, or more broadly political issues, and without explicit efforts to foster that interest, institutions will reach only those few students who are already active. It is also important to reach the large numbers of students who begin from a position of distaste for or lack of interest in politics.

Extending coverage. Although a systemic, social policy, or political focus will not be relevant for all courses and programs, many can be enriched and strengthened through the incorporation of that focus. This area is currently relatively neglected on many campuses and should be given greater attention.

Freedom of opinion. Faculty should not pressure students to adopt a particular partisan or ideological point of view but should rather encourage political participation from a broad range of perspectives, beliefs, interpretations, and explanations of or solutions to social problems.

• *Creating a distinctive yet comprehensive approach.* In order to create approaches to moral and civic education that are well suited to their institutional mission, history, philosophy, strengths, and student body characteristics and needs, it is appropriate for colleges and universities to specialize to some extent in the relative emphasis they place on these three different ways of framing moral and civic education and on the way each of the three is defined. Although it is important for programming to touch on all three, every institution should create its own individual approach.

Renewing the Importance of Moral and Civic Education

This book was completed less than a year after the terrorist attacks in New York and Washington, D.C., and the war in Afghanistan and other events that followed. Those happenings were a jolting example of the way that historical events can present teachable moments for moral and civic development. In response to the tragic events of September 11, 2001, most college and university campuses held memorial services and discussion sessions. Many sponsored informational programs about Islam in efforts to promote religious respect and tolerance. Some sponsored extensive and searching inquiries on the causes and nature of terrorism, U.S. foreign policy, global interdependence, and civil liberties. Students throughout the country contributed to the national outpouring of support for and solidarity with the victims of the attacks. The power of this educational opportunity was heightened by the extraordinary degree to which the issues engaged people's passionate feelings. Whether in the long run the new interests that were kindled will lead to sustained learning and increased social concern and civic engagement remains to be seen. But in the short run the responses of campuses and their students have been heartening.

Surveys in the immediate aftermath of September 11, 2001, suggest that the attacks led to shifts in the civic attitudes of college students (Lake Snell Perry & Associates, Inc., 2002). For some those events elicited feelings of national pride and patriotism, which were previously largely absent in the overwhelming majority of undergraduates. Numerous earlier polls had shown that most students had little pride or trust in their country and less in its government. They were cynical about public affairs, particularly on the national level. In the wake of the attacks many campuses have sought to capitalize on emerging civic feelings of students and also to address the complexities of nationalism, international affairs, military and legal responses, and the historical background to the events.

These recent events are also a reminder that students, like all other individuals, are developing in a particular historical context and that historical events can affect their moral and civic development in important ways for better or for worse. National crises often trigger significant changes in the ways students, along with the public more generally, view public issues and react to those issues. The rise of student involvement in the civil rights movement during the first half of the 1960s and the protests against U.S. involvement in the Vietnam War are two prime illustrations.

When historical events dramatically affect the lives of a generation of young people, as in the case of the two World Wars, for example, they can create a generational identity that becomes key to the way members of that generation understand themselves and their stance toward the world as well as toward their country and its government. As Kathleen Newman (1996) has written, "An intense generational identity shapes and defines the individuals who fall within its boundaries and separates them from others who have no claim on its immediacy" (p. 374). Generally, the creation of this kind of intense generational identity requires political, economic, or cultural upheavals that force dramatic and sustained departures from the normal course of daily life for a large group of people in a given generation. For example, in *The Generation of 1914,* Robert Wohl (1979) traces the impact of World War I on the young men who fought in it. According to Wohl, the pointlessness and unprecedented brutality of the Great War in the minds of its survivors led them to adopt a worldview characterized by cynicism and disengagement from society's institutions.

In contrast, Putnam (2000) and others (for example, Brokaw, 1998) have described the very different response of the generation that fought in World War II. The civic engagement of that generation marked a high point from which U.S. citizens have been declining with every succeeding generation.

As we write, it is too early to know whether terrorism or any other set of social or economic events will create a clear-cut generational identity for the young people of today. Likewise, the moral and civic architecture of their generational identity is unpredictable. We do know, however, that historical contexts and events affect people's lives in part through the meaning they have for those who experience them. Colleges and universities do not create the cataclysmic events that create generational identity, but they can have enormously important roles in shaping the meaning their students make of those and other experiences, including the implications of these experiences for students' moral and civic sense of themselves.

Finally, terrorist attacks and the military and political responses to them underscore the importance of the moral and civic life of this nation at every level. They make it very clear that if we are fighting to protect our basic moral values, our freedoms, and our democracy, we had best do all we can to ensure that succeeding generations gain the understanding, skills, and motivations needed to preserve and promote those values and freedoms. This book has been written with that purpose at center stage.

REFERENCES

Adelson, J., & O'Neil, R. P. (1966). Growth of political ideas in adolescence: The sense of community. *Journal of Personality and Social Psychology, 4,* 295–306.

Alexie, S. (1993). *The Lone Ranger and Tonto fistfight in heaven.* New York: Atlantic Monthly Press.

Alvarez, J. (1991). *How the García girls lost their accents.* Chapel Hill, NC: Algonquin Books of Chapel Hill.

Alverno College Faculty. (1994). *Student assessment-as-learning at Alverno College.* Milwaukee, WI: Alverno College Institute.

Ambrose, S. (1996). *Undaunted courage: Meriwether Lewis, Thomas Jefferson, and the opening of the American West.* New York: Simon & Schuster.

American Commitments Program. (1995). *American pluralism and the college curriculum: Higher education in a diverse democracy* (Third in the American Commitments Series). Washington, DC: American Association of Colleges and Universities.

American Political Science Association, Task Force on Civic Education in the Next Century. (1998). Expanded articulation statement: A call for reactions and contributions. *PS: Political Science and Politics, 31,* 636–637.

Anderson, C. W. (1997). Pragmatism, idealism, and the aims of liberal education. In R. Orrill (Ed.), *Education and democracy: Re-imagining liberal learning in America* (pp. 111–130). New York: College Entrance Examination Board.

Antonio, A. (1998a). *The impact of friendship groups in a multicultural university.* Unpublished doctoral dissertation, University of California, Los Angeles.

Antonio, A. (1998b, April). *Student interaction across race and outcomes in college.* Paper presented at the American Educational Research Association, San Diego, CA.

Association of American Colleges. (1990). *Reports from the field:* Vol. 2. *Liberal learning and the arts and sciences major.* Washington, DC: Author.

Astin, A. W. (1977). *Four critical years: Effects of college on beliefs, attitudes, and knowledge.* San Francisco: Jossey-Bass.

Astin, A. W. (1984). Student involvement: A developmental theory for higher education. *Journal of College Student Personnel, 25,* 297–308.

Astin, A. W. (1985a). *Achieving educational excellence: A critical assessment of priorities and practices in higher education.* San Francisco: Jossey-Bass.

Astin, A. W. (1985b). Involvement: The cornerstone of excellence. *Change, 17*(4), 35–39.

Astin, A. W. (1993). *What matters in college: Four critical years revisited.* San Francisco: Jossey-Bass.

Astin, A. W. (1997). Liberal education and democracy: The case for pragmatism. In R. Orrill (Ed.), *Education and democracy: Re-imagining liberal learning in America* (pp. 207–223). New York: College Entrance Examination Board.

Astin, A. W. (2000). The civic challenge of educating the underprepared student. In T. Ehrlich (Ed.), *Civic responsibility and higher education* (pp. 124–146). Phoenix, AZ: Oryx Press.

Astin, A. W., & Astin, H. S. (1999). *Meaning and spirituality in the lives of college faculty: A study of values, authenticity, and stress.* Los Angeles: University of California, Los Angeles, Graduate School of Education and Information Studies, Higher Education Research Institute.

Astin, A. W., Banta, T., Cross, P., El-Khawas, E., Ewell, P., Hutchings, P., Mentkowski, M., Miller, M., Moran, T., & Wright, B. (1992). *Principles of good practice for assessing student learning.* Washington, DC: American Association for Higher Education.

Astin, A. W., Parrott, S. A., Korn, W. S., & Sax, L. J. (1997). *The American freshman: Thirty year trends.* Los Angeles: University of California, Los Angeles, Graduate School of Education and Information Studies, Higher Education Research Institute.

Astin, A. W., & Sax, L. J. (1998). How undergraduates are affected by service participation. *Journal of College Student Development, 39,* 259–263.

Astin, A. W., Sax, L. J., & Avalos, J. (1999). Long-term effects of volunteerism during the undergraduate years. *Review of Higher Education, 22,* 187–202.

Astin, A. W., Sax, L. J., Ikeda, E. K., & Yee, J. A. (2000). *Executive summary: How service learning affects students.* Los Angeles: University of California, Los Angeles, Graduate School of Education and Information Studies, Higher Education Research Institute.

Baerman, P. (1998). Giving voice to the campus conscience: Students Against Sweatshops. *Duke Magazine.* Retrieved September 25, 2002, from http://www.dukemagazine.duke.edu/alumni/dm18/dm18.html

Bandura, A. (1977). *Social learning theory.* Upper Saddle River, NJ: Prentice Hall.

Bandura, A. (1986). *Social foundations of thought and action.* Upper Saddle River, NJ: Prentice Hall.

Bandura, A. (1997). *Self-efficacy: The exercise of control.* New York: Freeman.

Bardacke, F. (1994). *Good liberals and great blue herons: Land, labor and politics in the Pajaro Valley.* Santa Cruz, CA: Center for Political Ecology.

Barefoot, B. O., & Fidler, P. P. (Eds.). (1996). *The 1994 National Survey of Freshman Seminar Programs: Continuing innovations in the collegiate curriculum* (Monograph No. 20). Columbia: University of South Carolina, National Resource Center for the Freshman Year Experience.

Barrows, H. S. (1980). *Problem-based learning: An approach to medical education.* New York: Springer.

Battistoni, R. M. (2000). *Democracy, learning, and power: Reflections from the margins of academic political science.* Paper presented at the annual meeting of the American Political Science Association, Washington, DC.

Beerbohm, E. (1999). *Why are we teaching ethics?* Paper presented at the Teach-In on Moral Relativism, Stanford University, Stanford, CA.

Bellah, R., Madsen, R., Sullivan, W., Swidler, A., & Tipton, S. (1991). *The good society.* New York: Vintage Books.

Bender, T. (1997, Winter). Politics, intellect, and the American university. *Daedalus,* pp. 1–38.

Bennett, D. C. (1997). Innovation in the liberal arts and sciences. In R. Orrill (Ed.), *Education and democracy: Re-imagining liberal learning in America* (pp. 131–149). New York: College Entrance Examination Board.

Bennett, S. E. (1999). The past need not be prologue: Why pessimism about civic education is premature. *PS: Political Science & Politics, 32,* 755–757.

Bennett, S. E., & Rademacher, E. W. (1997). The "age of indifference" revisited: Patterns of political interest, media exposure, and knowledge among Generation X. In S. C. Craig & S. E. Bennett (Eds.), *After the boom: The politics of Generation X* (pp. 21–43). Lanham, MD: Rowman & Littlefield.

Bennett, W. J. (1992). *The de-valuing of America: The fight for our culture and our children.* New York: Summit Books.

Berberet, J. (1999). The professoriate and institutional citizenship. *Liberal Education, 85*(4), 33–39.

Bergman, R. (2002). Why be moral? A conceptual model from developmental psychology. *Human Development, 45*(2), 104–124.

Blasi, A. (1995). Moral understanding and the moral personality: The process of moral integration. In W. Kurtines & J. Gewirtz (Eds.), *Moral development: An introduction* (pp. 229–253). Boston: Allyn & Bacon.

Blatt, M., & Kohlberg, L. (1975). The effects of classroom moral discussion upon children's level of moral judgment. *Journal of Moral Education, 4,* 129–161.

Bligh, D. A. (1972). *What's the use of lectures?* Harmondsworth, England: Penguin Books.

Bloom, A. (1987). *The closing of the American mind: How higher education has failed democracy and impoverished the souls of today's students.* New York: Simon & Schuster.

Blount, A. (2001). *Service and leadership: Our pedagogy for moral and civic education.* Unpublished manuscript.

Bogner, J. (1996). The illusion of community. *The Sou'wester Online.* Retrieved November 19, 2001, from http://www.students.rhodes.edu/sw/2~21~96/opinion/illusion.html

Bok, D. C. (1986). *Higher learning.* Cambridge, MA: Harvard University Press.

Bok, D. C. (1990). *Universities and the future of America.* Durham, NC: Duke University Press.

Bowen, W. G., & Bok, D. (1998). *The shape of the river: Long-term consequences of considering race in college and university admissions.* Princeton, NJ: Princeton University Press.

Boyer, E. L. (1987). *College: The undergraduate experience in America.* New York: HarperCollins.

Boyer, E. L. (1990). *Scholarship reconsidered: Priorities for the professoriate.* Menlo Park, CA: The Carnegie Foundation for the Advancement of Teaching.

Boyte, H. C. (1989). *Commonwealth: A return to citizen politics.* New York: Free Press.

Boyte, H. C. (2001, September). *A tale of two playgrounds: Teaching a different kind of politics and the obstacles.* Paper presented at the annual meeting of the American Political Science Association, San Francisco.

Bransford, J. D., Franks, J. J., Vye, N. J., & Sherwood, R. D. (1989). New approaches to instruction: Because wisdom can't be told. In S. Vosniadou & A. Ortony (Eds.), *Similarity and analogical reasoning* (pp. 470–497). New York: Cambridge University Press.

Bransford, J. D., & Stein, B. (1993). *The ideal problem solver: A guide for improving thinking, learning, and creativity.* New York: Freeman.

Bringle, R. G., & Hatcher, J. A. (1995). A service-learning curriculum for faculty. *Michigan Journal of Community Service Learning, 2,* 112–122.

Bringle, R., Phillips, M., & Hudson, M. (in press). *Measurement instruments for service learning: Students.* American Psychological Association.

Brokaw, T. (1998). *The greatest generation.* New York: Random House.

Brooks, D. (2001, April). The organization kid. *Atlantic Monthly,* pp. 40–53.

Brown, A. L. (1989). Analogical learning and transfer: What develops? In S. Vosniadou & A. Ortony (Eds.), *Similarity and analogical reasoning* (pp. 369–412). New York: Cambridge University Press.

Brown, J. S., Collins, A., & Duguid, P. (1989). Situated cognition and the culture of learning. *Educational Record, 18,* 32–42.

Brownstein, A. (2001, March 30). Race, reparations, and free expression: A dispute at Brown and other universities reflects divisions among liberal students. *Chronicle of Higher Education,* pp. A48–A55.

Cadwallader, M. (1984). The uses of philosophy in an academic counter-revolution: Alexander Meiklejohn and John Dewey in the 1980s. *Liberal Education, 70*(1), 275–292.

Calabrese, R. L., & Schumer, H. (1986). The effects of service activities on adolescent alienation. *Adolescence, 21*(83), 675–687.

Callan, E. (1997). *Creating citizens: Political education and liberal democracy.* New York: Oxford University Press, Clarendon Press.

Candee, D. (1975). The psychology of Watergate. *Journal of Social Issues, 31*(2), 183–192.

The Carnegie Foundation for the Advancement of Teaching. (2000). *The Carnegie classification of institutions of higher education.* Menlo Park, CA: Author.

Chase, W. G., & Simon, H. A. (1973). Perception in chess. *Cognitive Psychology, 4*(1), 55–81.

Cherry, C., DeBerg, B. A., & Porterfield, A. (2001). Religion on campus. *Liberal Education, 87*(4), 6–13.

Clement, J. (1982). Students' preconceptions in introductory mechanics. *American Journal of Physics, 50,* 66–71.

Colby, A., & Damon, W. (1992). *Some do care: Contemporary lives of moral commitment.* New York: Free Press.

Colby, A., & Kohlberg, L. (1987). *The measurement of moral judgment.* New York: Cambridge University Press.

Colby, A., Kohlberg, L., Gibbs, J., & Lieberman, M. (1983). A longitudinal study of moral judgment. *Monographs of the Society for Research in Child Development, 48*(1–2), 1–96.

Colby, A., Sippola, L., & Phelps, E. (2001). Social responsibility and paid work in contemporary American life. In A. Rossi (Ed.), *Caring and doing for others: Social responsibility in the domains of family, work, and community* (pp. 463–501). Chicago: University of Chicago Press.

Cole, S., & Conklin, D. (1996). Academic integrity policies and procedures: Opportunities to teach students about moral leadership and personal ethics. *College Student Affairs Journal, 15*(2), 30–39.

Connecticut College, Student Government Association. (2002). *The C-Book.*

Retrieved August 22, 2002, from http://oak.conncoll.edu/~sga/ CBook/index.html

COOL (Campus Outreach Opportunity League). (2002). [Homepage.] Retrieved August 20, 2002, from http://www.cool2serve.org

Cordova, D. I., & Lepper, M. R. (1996). Intrinsic motivation and the process of learning: Beneficial effects of contextualization, personalization, and choice. *Journal of Educational Psychology, 88*(4), 715–730.

Corsaro, W. A. (1997). *The sociology of childhood.* Thousand Oaks, CA: Pine Forge Press.

Council on Civil Society. (1998). *A call to civil society: Why democracy needs moral truths.* A Report to the Nation from the Council on Civil Society. New York: Institute for American Values.

Cross, P. (1995, July 23–26). *Educating for the 21st century.* Paper presented at the annual international conference of the League for Innovation in the Community College and the Community College Leadership Program, San Francisco.

Csikszentmihalyi, M. (1990). *Flow: The psychology of optimal experience.* New York: HarperCollins.

Damon, W. (1975). Early conceptions of positive justice as related to the development of logical operations. *Child Development, 46*(2), 301–312.

Damon, W., & Hart, D. (1988). *Self-understanding in childhood and adolescence.* New York: Cambridge University Press.

Davidson, P., & Youniss, J. (1991). Which comes first, morality or identity? In W. Kurtines & J. L. Gewirtz (Eds.), *Handbook of moral development and behavior* (Vol. 1, pp. 105–121). Hillsdale, NJ: Erlbaum.

Dewey, J. (1916). *Democracy and education: An introduction to the philosophy of education.* New York: Macmillan.

Dewey, J. (1998). The moral self. From his *Ethics* (1932). In L. A. Hickman & T. M. Alexander (Eds.), *The essential Dewey* (Vol. 2, pp. 321–354). Bloomington: Indiana University Press.

Diamond, R. M., & Adam, B. E. (1995). *The disciplines speak: Rewarding the scholarly, professional, and creative work of faculty.* Washington, DC: American Association for Higher Education.

Diamond, R. M., & Adam, B. E. (1998). *Changing priorities at research universities, 1991–1996.* Syracuse, NY: Syracuse University.

Diamond, R. M., & Adam, B. E. (2000). *The disciplines speak: II. More statements on rewarding the scholarly, professional, and creative work of faculty.* Washington, DC: American Association for Higher Education.

Dionne, E. J. (1991). *Why Americans hate politics.* New York: Simon & Schuster.

Durr, V. F., & Barnard, H. F. (1985). *Outside the magic circle: The autobiography of Virginia Foster Durr.* Tuscaloosa: University of Alabama Press.

Ehman, L. (1980). The American school in the political socialization process. *Review of Educational Research, 50,* 99–119.

Ehrlich, T. (1997). Dewey versus Hutchins: The next round. In R. Orrill (Ed.), *Education and democracy: Re-imagining liberal learning in America* (pp. 225–262). New York: College Entrance Examination Board.

Ehrlich, T. (1999). Civic education: Lessons learned. *PS: Political Science and Politics, 32,* 245–250.

Erikson, E. H. (1968). *Identity: Youth and crisis.* New York: Norton.

Eyler, J., & Giles, D. E. (1999). *Where's the learning in service-learning?* San Francisco: Jossey-Bass.

Fadiman, A. (1997). *The spirit catches you and you fall down: A Hmong child, her American doctors, and the collision of two cultures.* New York: Farrar, Straus & Giroux.

Fenstermacher, G. D. (1990). Some moral considerations on teaching as a profession. In J. Goodlad, R. Soder, & K. Sirotnik (Eds.), *The moral dimensions of teaching* (pp. 130–154). San Francisco: Jossey-Bass.

Finkel, D. (2000). *Teaching with your mouth shut.* Portsmouth, NH: Boynton/ Cook; Heinemann.

Flanagan, C. A., & Sherrod, L. R. (1998). Youth political development: An introduction. *Journal of Social Issues, 54*(3), 447–456.

Fowler, J. (1991a). Stages in faith consciousness. In F. K. Oser & W. G. Scarlett (Eds.), *Religious development in childhood and adolescence* (New Directions for Child Development, No. 52, pp. 27–45). San Francisco: Jossey-Bass.

Fowler, J. (1991b). *Weaving the new creation: Stages of faith and the public church.* San Francisco: Harper San Francisco.

Fowler, J. (1994). Moral stages and the development of faith. In B. Puka (Ed.), *Fundamental research in moral development* (pp. 344–374). New York: Garland.

Franco, R. (1999). *The community college conscience: Service-learning and training tomorrow's teachers.* Unpublished manuscript.

Gabelnick, F., MacGregor, J., Mathews, R. S., & Smith, B. L. (1990). *Learning communities: Creating connections among students, faculty, and disciplines* (New Directions for Teaching and Learning, No. 41). San Francisco: Jossey-Bass.

Galston, W. (1991). *Liberal purposes: Goods, virtues, and diversity in the liberal state.* Cambridge, England: Cambridge University Press.

Gardiner, L. F. (1994). *Redesigning higher education: Producing dramatic gains in student learning* (ASHE-ERIC Higher Education Report No. 7). Washington, DC: George Washington University, Graduate School of Education and Human Development.

Gardiner, L. F., Anderson, C., & Cambridge, B. L. (Eds.). (1997). *Learning through assessment: A resource guide for higher education.* Washington, DC: American Association for Higher Education.

Gardner, H. (1983). *Frames of mind: The theory of multiple intelligences.* New York: Basic Books.

Gardner, H. (1991). *The unschooled mind: How children think and how schools should teach.* New York: Basic Books.

Gaudiani, C. L. (1995). *An honor code in 1995.* Retrieved March 22, 2002, from http://clairegaudiani.com/writings/honorcode.html

Geertz, C. (1973). *The interpretation of cultures: Selected essays.* New York: Basic Books.

Gehring, D., Nuss, E., & Pavela, G. (1986). *Issues and perspectives on academic integrity* (NASPA Monograph Series). Columbus, OH: National Association of Student Personnel Administrators.

Gelmon, S., Holland, B., Driscoll, A., Spring, A., & Kerrigan, S. (2001). *Assessing service-learning and civic engagement: Principles and techniques.* Providence, RI: Campus Compact.

Gilligan, C. (1982). *In a different voice: Psychological theory and women's development.* Cambridge, MA: Harvard University Press.

Glassick, C. E., Huber, M. T., & Maeroff, G. I. (1997). *Scholarship assessed: Evaluation of the professoriate.* San Francisco: Jossey-Bass.

Graff, G. (1987). *Professing literature: An institutional history.* Chicago: University of Chicago Press.

Gray, M. J., Ondaatje, E. H., Geschwind, S., Fricker, R., Goldman, C., Kaganoff, T., Robyn, A., Sundt, M., Vogelsang, L., & Klein, S. (1999). *Combining service and learning in higher education: Evaluation of the Learn and Serve America Higher Education Program.* Santa Monica, CA: Rand Education.

Greeno, J. G., Collins, A. M., & Resnick, L. B. (1996). Cognition and learning. In R. C. Calfee (Ed.), *Handbook of educational psychology* (pp. 15–46). New York: Simon & Schuster; Macmillan.

Gutmann, A. (1987). *Democratic education.* Princeton, NJ: Princeton University Press.

Gutmann, A. (1996). Democratic citizenship. In J. Cohen (Ed.), *For love of country* (pp. 66–71). Boston: Beacon Press.

Habermas, J. (1993). *Justification and application: Remarks on discourse ethics* (C. Cronin, Trans.). Cambridge, England: Polity Press.

Haidt, J. (2001). The emotional dog and its rational tail: A social intuitionist approach to moral judgment. *Psychological Review, 108*(4), 814–834.

Harnett, R. T. (1965). Involvement in extracurricular activities as a factor in academic performance. *Journal of College Student Personnel, 6,* 272–274.

Hart, D., & Fegley, S. (1995). Prosocial behavior and caring in adolescence: Relations to self-understanding and social judgment. *Child Development, 66*(5), 1346–1359.

Harvard University, Committee on the Objectives of a General Education in a Free Society. (1945). *General education in a free society.* Cambridge, MA: Harvard University.

Haskell, T. L. (1996). Justifying the rights of academic freedom in the era of "power/knowledge." In L. Menand (Ed.), *The future of academic freedom* (pp. 43–90). Chicago: University of Chicago Press.

Helwig, C. C. (1995). Adolescents' and young adults' conceptions of civil liberties: Freedom of speech and religion. *Child Development, 66*(1), 152–166.

Henscheid, J. M. (2000). *Professing the disciplines: An analysis of senior seminars and capstone courses.* Columbia: University of South Carolina, National Resource Center for The First-Year Experience and Students in Transition.

Hepburn, M. A., Niemi, R. G., & Chapman, C. (2000). Service learning in college political science: Queries and commentary. *PS: Political Science & Politics, 33,* 617–622.

Hersh, R. H. (1997). Intentions and perceptions: A national survey of public attitudes toward liberal arts education. *Change, 29*(2), 16–23.

Hoffman, M. (1981). Is altruism part of human nature? *Journal of Personality and Social Psychology, 40,* 121–137.

Huber, M. T. (1998). *Community college faculty attitudes and trends, 1997.* Menlo Park, CA: The Carnegie Foundation for the Advancement of Teaching.

Huber, M. T. (2002). *Faculty evaluation and the development of academic careers.* In C. Colbeck (Ed.), *Evaluating faculty performance* (New Directions for Institutional Research No. 114). San Francisco: Jossey-Bass.

Huber, M. T., & Morreale, S. P. (2002). *Disciplinary styles in the scholarship of teaching and learning: Exploring common ground.* Washington, DC: American Association for Higher Education.

Humphreys, D. (2000). Diversity, democracy, and civic engagement: Higher education and its unique opportunity. *Higher Education Exchange,* pp. 82–90.

Hurtado, S. (1997). *Linking diversity with educational purpose: College outcomes associated with diversity in the faculty and student body.* Paper commissioned by the Harvard Civil Rights Project, Harvard University.

Hurtado, S. (2001). Linking diversity and educational purpose: How diversity affects the classroom environment and student development. In G. Orfield (Ed.), *Diversity challenged: Evidence on the impact of affirmative action* (pp. 187–203). Cambridge, MA: Harvard Education Publishing Group.

Hutchings, P. (Ed.). (1998). *The course portfolio: How faculty can examine their teaching to advance practice and improve student learning*. Washington, DC: American Association for Higher Education.

Hutchings, P. (Ed.). (2000). *Opening lines*. Menlo Park, CA: The Carnegie Foundation for the Advancement of Teaching.

Hutchings, P., & Shulman, L. (1999). The scholarship of teaching: New elaborations, new developments. *Change, 31*(5), 10–15.

Illich, I. (1968). *To hell with good intentions*. New York: A CVSA Publication.

Jackson, P. W. (1968). *Life in the classroom*. New York: Holt, Rinehart, and Winston.

Jankowski, T. B. (1992). Ethnic identity and political consciousness in different social orders. In H. Haste & J. Torney-Purta (Eds.), *The development of political understanding: A new perspective* (New Directions for Child Development No. 56, pp. 79–93). San Francisco: Jossey-Bass.

Jendrek, M. P. (1989). Faculty reactions to academic dishonesty. *Journal of College Student Development, 30,* 401–406.

Jennings, M. K., & Stoker, L. (2001). *Dynamics of social capital: A longitudinal multiple-generation analysis*. Paper presented at the annual meeting of the American Political Science Association, San Francisco.

Jones, L., & Newman, L. (1997). *Our America: Life and death on the south side of Chicago*. New York: Scribner.

Kadel, S., & Keehner, J. A. (Eds.). (1994). *Collaborative learning: A sourcebook for higher education* (Vol. 2). University Park, PA: National Center on Postsecondary Teaching, Learning, & Assessment.

Kagan, J. (1984). *The nature of the child*. New York: Basic Books.

Kapp, G. J. (1979). *College extracurricular activities: Who participates and what are the benefits?* Unpublished doctoral dissertation, University of California, Los Angeles.

Kegan, D. L. (1978). The quality of student life and financial costs: The cost of social isolation. *Journal of College Student Personnel, 19,* 55–58.

Kiely, R. (2001). Out of the closet and into the classroom, the yard, and the dining hall: Notes on religion at Harvard. *Liberal Education, 87*(4), 24–29.

Kimball, B. A. (1986). *Orators and philosophers: A history of the idea of liberal education*. New York: Teachers College Press.

Kimball, B. A. (1997). Naming pragmatic liberal education. In R. Orrill (Ed.), *Education and democracy: Re-imagining liberal learning in America* (pp. 45–67). New York: College Entrance Examination Board.

Kirlin, M. K. (2000). *The role of experiential programs in the political socialization of American adolescents*. Paper presented at the meeting of the American Political Science Association, Washington, DC.

Kiss, E. (n.d.). *A tale of two disagreements: Examining campus issues through a deliberative lens.* Unpublished manuscript.

Knefelkamp, L. (1974). *Developmental instruction: Fostering intellectual and personal growth in college students.* Unpublished doctoral dissertation, University of Minnesota, Minneapolis and St. Paul.

Knox, W., Lindsay, P., & Kolb, M. (1988). *Higher education institutions and young adult development.* Unpublished manuscript, University of North Carolina at Greensboro.

Kohlberg, L. (1969). Stage and sequence: The cognitive-developmental approach to socialization. In D. A. Goslin (Ed.), *Handbook of socialization theory and research* (pp. 347–480). Skokie, IL: Rand McNally.

Kohlberg, L. (1971). Indoctrination and relativity in value education. *Xygon, 6,* 285–309.

Kohlberg, L., & Higgins, A. (1987). School democracy and social interaction. In W. M. Kurtines & J. L. Gewirtz (Eds.), *Moral development through social interaction* (pp. 102–128). New York: Wiley.

Kreps, D. M. (1997). Economics: The current position. In T. Bender & C. Schorske (Eds.), *American academic culture in transformation* (pp. 77–103). Princeton, NJ: Princeton University Press.

Krumboltz, J. (1957). The relation of extracurricular participation to leadership criteria. *Personnel and Guidance Journal, 35,* 307–313.

Kuh, G. D. (1993). In their own words: What students learn outside the classroom. *American Educational Research Journal, 30*(2), 277–304.

Kuh, G. D., Douglas, K. B., Lund, J. P., & Ramin-Gyurnek, J. (1994). *Student learning outside the classroom: Transcending artificial boundaries* (ASHE-ERIC Higher Education Report No. 8). Washington, DC: ASHE-ERIC.

Kuh, G. D., Schuh, J. H., Whitt, E. J., Andreas, R. E., Lyons, J. W., Strange, C. C., Krehbiel, L. E., & MacKay, K. A. (1991). *Involving colleges: Successful approaches to fostering student learning and development outside the classroom.* San Francisco: Jossey-Bass.

Lagemann, E. C. (1997). From discipline-based to problem-centered learning. In R. Orrill (Ed.), *Education and democracy: Re-imagining liberal learning in America* (pp. 21–43). New York: College Entrance Examination Board.

Lake Snell Perry & Associates, Inc. (2002). *Short term impacts, long term opportunities: The political and civic engagement of young adults in America* (Analysis and Report for The Center for Information and Research in Civic Learning & Engagement (CIRCLE) and The Center for Democracy & Citizenship and The Partnership for Trust in Government at the Council for Excellence in Government). Washington, DC: Author.

Lampert, M. (1985). How do teachers manage to teach? Perspectives on problems in practice. *Harvard Educational Review, 55*(2), 178–194.

Lave, J. (1988). *Cognition in practice: Mind, mathematics and culture in every-day life.* New York: Cambridge University Press.

Leonard, S. T. (1999). "Pure futility and waste": Academic political science and civic education. *PS: Political Science & Politics, 32,* 749–753.

Lepper, M. R., & Green, D. (1978). Overjustification research and beyond: Toward a means-ends analysis of intrinsic and extrinsic motivation. In M. R. Lepper & D. Green (Eds.), *The hidden costs of reward: New perspectives on the psychology of human motivation* (pp. 109–148). Hillsdale, NJ: Erlbaum.

Levine, A., & Cureton, J. S. (1998). *When hope and fear collide: A portrait of today's college student.* San Francisco: Jossey-Bass.

Light, R. J. (2001). *Making the most of college.* Cambridge, MA: Harvard University Press.

Lindblom, C. (1997). Political science in the 1940s and 1950s. In T. Bender & C. Schorske (Ed.), *American academic culture in transformation* (pp. 243–270). Princeton, NJ: Princeton University Press.

Loeb, P. R. (1999). *Soul of a citizen: Living with conviction in a cynical time.* New York: St. Martin's Press; Griffin.

Lucas, C. (1994). *American higher education: A history.* New York: St. Martin's Press.

Lutkus, A. D., Weiss, A. R., Campbell, J. R., Mazzeo, J., & Lazer, S. (1999). *The NAEP 1998 civics report card for the nation.* Washington, DC: National Center for Education Statistics.

Lynton, E. A. (1995). *Making the case for professional service.* Washington, DC: American Association for Higher Education.

Macedo, S. (2000). *Diversity and distrust: Civic education in a multicultural democracy.* Cambridge, MA: Harvard University Press.

Mahoney, K., Schmalzbauer, J., & Youniss, J. (2001). Religion: A comeback on campus. *Liberal Education, 87*(4), 36–41.

Manchester College Peace Studies Institute. (2002). *Graduation Pledge Alliance.* Retrieved August 20, 2002, from http://www.manchester.edu/academic/programs/departments/peace_studies/files/gpa.html

Markus, H., & Nurius, P. (1986). Possible selves. *American Psychologist, 41*(9), 954–969.

Mason, J. L., & Nelson, M. (2000, September 22). Selling students on the elections of 2000. *Chronicle of Higher Education,* p. B16.

May, E. (1996). A community defined: Rhodes faces challenges to campus unity. *The Sou'wester Online.* Retrieved November 19, 2001, from http://www.students.rhodes.edu/sw/1~31~96/scene/defined.html

McAdam, D. (1988). *Freedom summer.* New York: Oxford University Press.

McCabe, D. L. (1993). Faculty responses to academic dishonesty: The influence of student honor codes. *Research in Higher Education, 34,* 647–658.

McCabe, D. L., & Pavela, G. (1997). Ten principles of academic integrity. *Synthesis: Law and Policy in Higher Education, 9*(1), 645.

McCabe, D. L., & Trevino, L. K. (1993). Academic dishonesty: Honor codes and other contextual influences. *Journal of Higher Education, 64*(5), 522–538.

McCabe, D. L., & Trevino, L. K. (1997). Individual and contextual influences on academic dishonesty: A multicampus investigation. *Research in Higher Education, 38,* 379–396.

McCabe, D. L., Trevino, L. K., & Butterfield, K. D. (1999). Academic integrity in honor code and non-honor code environments: A qualitative investigation. *Journal of Higher Education, 70*(2), 211–234.

McCullough, D. (2001). *John Adams.* New York: Simon & Schuster.

McKeachie, W. J., Pintrich, P. R., Yi-Guang, L., & Smith, D.A.F. (1986). *Teaching and learning in the college classroom: A review of the research literature.* Ann Arbor: Regents of the University of Michigan.

Meadows, D. M. (1991). The question of leadership. *In Context, 30,* 48.

Menand, L. (1997). Re-imagining liberal education. In R. Orrill (Ed.), *Education and democracy: Re-imagining liberal learning in America* (pp. 1–19). New York: College Entrance Examination Board.

Menand, L. (2001, October 18). College: The end of the golden age. *New York Review of Books,* pp. 44–47.

Mentkowski, M., & Associates. (2000). *Learning that lasts: Integrating learning, development, and performance in college and beyond.* San Francisco: Jossey-Bass.

Messiah College. (2001). *Integrative developmental model for contextual learning.* Grantham, PA: Messiah College, Office of External Programs.

Michigan Journal of Community Service Learning. (2001). *Service Learning Course Design Workbook.* Ann Arbor: University of Michigan, OCSL Press.

Milem, J. F. (1994). College, students, and racial understanding. *Thought & Action, 9*(2), 51–92.

Moore, D. T. (2000, Fall). The relationship between experiential learning research and service-learning research. *Michigan Journal of Community Service Learning* (Special issue), 124–128.

Morgan, W., & Streb, M. (2001, August–September). *The impact of service learning on political participation.* Paper presented at the annual meeting of the American Political Science Association, San Francisco.

Most admissions letters go to minority students. (2002, March 29). *San Jose Mercury News,* p. 3B.

National Center for Education Statistics. (1996). *Digest of education statistics* (Report No. NCES 96-133). Washington, DC: U.S. Government Printing Office.

National Commission on Civic Renewal. (1998). *A nation of spectators: How disengagement weakens America and what we can do about it.* College Park, MD: University of Maryland.

Nehamas, A. (1997). Trends in recent American philosophy. In T. Bender & C. Schorske (Ed.), *American academic culture in transformation* (pp. 227–241). Princeton, NJ: Princeton University Press.

Newcomb, T. M., Koenig, K., Flacks, R., & Warwick, D. (1967). *Persistence and change: Bennington College and its students after 25 years.* New York: Wiley.

Newman, D., Griffin, P., & Cole, M. (1989). *The construction zone: Working for cognitive change in school.* New York: Cambridge University Press.

Newman, K. (1996). Ethnography, biography, and cultural history: Generational paradigms in human development. In R. Jessor, A. Colby, & R. A. Shweder (Eds.), *Ethnography and human development: Context and meaning in social inquiry* (pp. 371–393). Chicago: University of Chicago Press.

Noddings, N. (1984). *Caring: A feminine approach to ethics and moral education.* Berkeley: University of California Press.

O'Meara, K. (2000). *Scholarship unbound: Assessing service as scholarship in promotion and tenure.* Unpublished dissertation, University of Maryland, College Park.

Orrill, R. (Ed.). (1997). *Education and democracy: Re-imagining liberal learning in America.* New York: College Entrance Examination Board.

Palmer, P. J. (1992). Divided no more: A movement approach to educational reform. *Change, 24*(2), 10–17.

Panetta Institute. (2000). *Institute poll shows college students turned off by politics, turned on by other public service* (Mellman Group). Retrieved February 15, 2001, from http://www.panettainstitute.org/news1.html

Pascarella, E. T. (1980). Student-faculty informal contact and college outcomes. *Review of Educational Research, 50,* 545–595.

Pascarella, E. T., Edison, M., Nora, A., Hagedorn, L. S., & Terenzini, P. T. (1996). Influences on students' openness to diversity and challenge in the first year of college. *Journal of Higher Education, 67*(2), 174–195.

Pascarella, E. T., Ethington, C. A., & Smart, J. C. (1988). The influence of college on humanitarian/civic involvement values. *Journal of Higher Education, 59,* 412–437.

Pascarella, E. T., Smart, J., & Braxton, J. (1986). Postsecondary educational attainment and humanitarian and civic values. *Journal of College Student Personnel, 27,* 418–425.

Pascarella, E. T., & Terenzini, P. T. (1991). *How college affects students: Findings and insights from twenty years of research.* San Francisco: Jossey-Bass.

Patel, V. L., Arocha, J. F., & Kaufman, D. R. (1994). Diagnostic reasoning and medical expertise. In D. L. Medin (Ed.), *The psychology of learning and motivation: Advances in research and theory* (Vol. 31, pp. 187–252). San Diego, CA: Academic Press.

Pavela, G. (1997). Applying the power of association on campus: A model code of academic integrity. *Synthesis: Law and Policy in Higher Education, 9*(1), 637–651.

Pavela, G., & McCabe, D. L. (1993). The surprising return of honor codes. *Planning for Higher Education, 21*(4), 27–32.

Pederson-Randall, P. J. (1999). *The effects of active versus passive teaching methods on university students' achievement and satisfaction* (Doctoral dissertation, University of Minnesota, 1999). *Dissertation Abstracts International, 60,* 1014A.

Perkins, D. N. (1992). *Smart schools: From training memories to educating minds.* New York: Free Press.

Perkins, D. N., & Martin, F. (1986). Fragile knowledge and neglected strategies in novice programmers. In E. Soloway & S. Iyengar (Eds.), *Empirical studies of programmers* (pp. 213–229). Norwood, NJ: Ablex.

Perkins, D. N., & Simmons, R. (1988). Patterns of misunderstanding: An integrative model of misconceptions in science, mathematics, and programming. *Review of Educational Research, 58*(3), 303–326.

Perry, W. G., Jr. (1968). *Forms of intellectual and ethical development in the college years: A scheme.* New York: Holt, Rinehart and Winston.

Piaget, J. (1932). *The moral judgment of the child* (M. Gabain, Trans.). New York: Free Press.

Piliavin, J. A., & Callero, P. L. (1991). *Giving blood: The development of an altruistic identity.* Baltimore: Johns Hopkins University Press.

Portland State University, Office of University Studies. (1994). *Portland State University, University Studies Program. Faculty summary: A new program for undergraduate education.* Portland, OR: Portland State University.

Power, F. C. (2002). Building democratic community: A radical approach to moral education. In W. Damon (Ed.), *Bringing in a new era in character education* (pp. 129–148). Stanford, CA: Hoover Institution Press.

Power-Ross, S. K. (1980). Co-curricular activities validated through research. *Student Activities Programming, 13,* 46–48.

Putnam, R. D. (1995, January). Bowling alone: American's declining social capital. *Journal of Democracy,* pp. 65–78.

Putnam, R. D. (2000). *Bowling alone: The collapse and revival of American community.* New York: Simon & Schuster.

Raaijmakers, Q.A.W., Verbogt, T.F.M.A., & Vollebergh, W.A.M. (1998). Moral reasoning and political beliefs of Dutch adolescents and young adults. *Journal of Social Issues, 54*(3), 531–546.

Rahn, W. M. (1992). *The decline of national identity among young Americans: Diffuse emotion, commitment, and social trust.* Unpublished manuscript, University of Minnesota.

Rahn, W. M. (2000). Panel discussion at the advisory board meeting of the Civic Identity Project, Grand Cayman, Bahamas.

Rahn, W. M., & Hirshorn, R. M. (1999). Political advertising and public mood: A study of children's political orientations. *Political Communication, 16,* 387–407.

Ramaley, J. (2000). Embracing civic responsibility. *AAHE Bulletin, 52*(7), 9–13, 20.

Rapoport, A. (1957). Scientific approach to ethics. *Science, 125,* 796–799.

Ratliffe, J. L., Johnson, D. K., & La Nasa, S. M. (2001). *The status of general education in the year 2000: Summary of a national survey.* Washington, DC: Association of American Colleges and Universities.

Read, S. J., & Sharkey, S. (1985). Alverno College: Toward a community of learning. In J. Green, A. Levine, & Associates, *Opportunity in adversity: How colleges can succeed in hard times* (pp. 195–214). San Francisco: Jossey-Bass.

Reeher, G., & Cammarano, J. (Eds.). (1997). *Education for citizenship: Ideas and innovations in political learning.* Lanham, MD: Rowman & Littlefield.

Resnick, L. B. (1987). *Education and learning to think.* Washington, DC: National Academy Press.

Rest, J. R. (1979). *Development in judging moral issues.* Minneapolis: University of Minnesota Press.

Rest, J. R. (1986). *Moral development: Advances in research and theory.* New York: Praeger.

Reuben, J. A. (1996). *The making of the modern university: Intellectual transformation and the marginalization of morality.* Chicago: University of Chicago Press.

Rhodes College. (2001). *The meaning of the honor system.* Retrieved November 26, 2001, from http://www.stuaffairs.rhodes.edu/handbook/honor.html

Ricks, V. (1999). *Introduction: How not to teach moral relativism.* Paper presented at the Teach-In on Moral Relativism, Stanford University, Stanford, CA.

Roberts, D. C. (2001). Miami's leadership commitment. In C. L. Outcalt, S. K. Faris, & K. N. McMahon (Eds.), *Developing non-hierarchical leadership on campus: Case studies and best practices in higher education* (pp. 77–89). Westport, CT: Greenwood Press.

Rowe, S. (2001, February). *Not in a vacuum: Teaching ethics at Kapi'olani Community College*. Paper presented at the Promoting Moral and Civic Responsibility in American Colleges and Universities Conference, Tallahassee, FL.

Rudolph, F. (1990). *The American college and university: A history*. Athens: University of Georgia Press.

Salomon, G., & Perkins, D. N. (1989). Rocky roads to transfer: Rethinking mechanisms of a neglected phenomenon. *Educational Psychologist, 24*(2), 113–142.

Satz, D. (2001, February). *What are the most effective ways to weave together rigorous learning within the disciplines and moral and civic learning?* Paper presented at the Promoting Moral and Civic Responsibility in American Colleges and Universities Conference, Tallahassee, FL.

Savage, H. J. (1929). *American college athletics*. Menlo Park, CA: The Carnegie Foundation for the Advancement of Teaching.

Sax, L. J. (1999). Citizenship development and the American college student. In T. Ehrlich (Ed.), *Civic responsibility and higher education* (pp. 3–18). Phoenix, AZ: Oryx Press.

Sax, L. J., Astin, A. W., Korn, W. S., & Gilmartin, S. K. (1999). *The American college teacher: National norms for the 1998–1999 HERI faculty survey*. Los Angeles: University of California, Los Angeles, Graduate School of Education and Information Studies, Higher Education Research Institute.

Sax, L. J., Astin, A. W., Korn, W. S., & Mahoney, K. M. (1999). *The American freshman: National norms for fall 1999*. Los Angeles: University of California, Los Angeles, Graduate School of Education and Information Studies, Higher Education Research Institute.

Schacter, H. L. (1998). Civic education: Three early American political science association committees and their relevance for our times. *PS: Political Science & Politics, 31*, 631–635.

Schneider, C. G., & Shoenberg, R. (1998). *Contemporary understandings of liberal education*. Washington, DC: Association of American Colleges and Universities.

Schuh, J. H., & Laverty, M. (1983). The perceived long term effect of holding a significant student leadership position. *Journal of College Student Personnel, 24*, 28–32.

Selman, R. L. (1980). *The growth of interpersonal understanding: Developmental and clinical analyses*. New York: Academic Press.

Selnes, F., & Troye, S. V. (1989). Buying expertise, information search, and problem solving. *Journal of Economic Psychology, 10*(3), 422–428.

Shedd, J. (2002). *Results of the survey of the relation between SCH and class time* (Working Papers for the SCH Project). Washington, DC: Institute for Higher Education Policy.

Shulman, J. L., & Bowen, W. G. (2001). *The game of life*. Princeton, NJ: Princeton University Press.

Shulman, L. S. (1981). Disciplines of inquiry in education: An overview. *Educational Researcher, 10*(6), 5–12.

Shulman, L. S. (1993). Teaching as community property: Putting an end to pedagogical solitude. *Change, 25*(6), 6–7.

Shulman, L. S. (1997). Professing the liberal arts. In R. Orrill (Ed.), *Education and democracy: Re-imagining liberal learning in America* (pp. 151–173). New York: College Entrance Examination Board.

Shulman, L. S. (2000). From Minsk to Pinsk: Why a scholarship of teaching and learning? *Journal of Scholarship of Teaching and Learning, 1*(1), 48–52.

Shweder, R. A. (1996). True ethnography: The lore, the law, and the lure. In R. Jessor, A. Colby, & R. Shweder (Eds.), *Ethnography and human development* (pp. 15–52). Chicago: University of Chicago Press.

Shweder, R. A., Mahapatra, M., & Miller, J. G. (1987). Culture and moral development. In J. Kagan & S. Lamb (Eds.), *The emergence of morality in young children* (pp. 1–83). Chicago: University of Chicago Press.

Sills, D. L. (Ed.). (1972). *International encyclopedia of the social sciences*. New York: Macmillan.

Singer, P. (1998). *Ethics into action: Henry Spira and the animal rights movement*. Lanham, MD: Rowman & Littlefield.

Smith, R. M. (1997). Still blowing in the wind: The American quest for a democratic, scientific political science. In T. Bender & C. Schorske (Eds.), *American academic culture in transformation* (pp. 271–305). Princeton, NJ: Princeton University Press.

Solow, R. (1997). How did economics get that way and what way did it get? In T. Bender & C. Schorske (Eds.), *American academic culture in transformation* (pp. 57–76). Princeton, NJ: Princeton University Press, 1997.

The Sou'wester Online. (1996). Rhodes College Honor Code Survey results. Retrieved April 16, 1999, from http://elvis.rhodes.edu/SW/3~28~96/news/results.html

Springer, L., Palmer, B., Terenzini, P. T., Pascarella, E. T., & Nora, A. (1996). Attitudes towards campus diversity: Participation in a racial or cultural awareness workshop. *Review of Higher Education, 20,* 53–68.

Stanford Black Student Union. (2001, May 3). Ten reasons why you shouldn't be fooled by David Horowitz's ad—and why it's racist too. *Stanford Daily,* p. 7.

Start of art? (1996, November).*Tusculumnus,* pp. 3–7.

Stoker, L. (2000). Panel discussion at the advisory board meeting of the Civic Identity Project, Grand Cayman, Bahamas.

Stoll, S. K. (1995). *Moral reasoning of Division III and Division I athletes: Is there a difference?* Paper presented at the annual meeting of the American Alliance of Health, Physical Education, Recreation, and Dance, Portland, OR.

Students for Environmental Action at Stanford. (2002). *About SEAS.* Retrieved August 20, 2002, from http://seas.stanford.edu/frames.html

Sullivan, W. (1999). *The university as citizen: Institutional identity and social responsibility.* Washington, DC: Kettering Foundation.

Sullivan, W. (2001). *Sizing up the predicament of liberal education.* Unpublished manuscript.

Takacs, D., & Shenk, G. (2001). *Teaching to inspire political participation in communities: Praxis pedagogy and changing ideas about politics* (Final report for the Carnegie Academy for the Scholarship of Teaching and Learning [CASTL]). Menlo Park, CA: The Carnegie Foundation for the Advancement of Teaching.

"Ten Reasons Why Reparations for Slavery Is a Bad Idea for Blacks—and Racist Too." (2001, May 3), *Stanford Daily,* pp. 6.

Trosset, C. (1998). Obstacles to open discussion and critical thinking: The Grinnell College Study. *Change, 30*(5), 44–49.

Turiel, E. (1997). The development of morality. In N. Eisenberg (Ed.), *Social, emotional, and personality development* (5th ed., Vol. 3, pp. 863–932). New York: Wiley.

Turiel, E. (2002). *The culture of morality: Social development, context, and conflict.* Cambridge, UK: Cambridge University Press.

U.S. Census Bureau. (1975). *Historical statistics of the United States: Colonial times to 1970* (Vol. 1, Bicentennial ed.). Washington, DC: U.S. Government Printing Office.

U.S. Census Bureau. (2000). *Statistical abstracts of the United States* (120th ed.). Washington, DC: U.S. Government Printing Office.

Vanderbilt University Office of Housing and Residential Education. (2002). *Mayfield Living/Learning Lodges.* Retrieved August 20, 2002, from http://www.vanderbilt.edu/ResEd/4may_pro.html

Verba, S., Schlozman, K. L., & Brady, H. E. (1995). *Voice and equality: Civic voluntarism in American politics.* Cambridge, MA: Harvard University Press.

Verghese, A. (1994). *My own country: A doctor's story of a town and its people in the age of AIDS.* New York: Simon & Schuster.

Walker, J. S. (2000). Choosing biases, using power and practicing resistance: Moral development in a world without certainty. *Human Development, 43*(3), 135–156.

Webster, N. (1965). On education of youth in America. In F. Rudolph (Ed.), *Essays on education in the early republic* (pp. 41–77). Cambridge, MA: Harvard University Press, Belknap Press. (Original work published 1788.)

Wechsler, H., Lee, J. E., Kuo, M., Seibring, M., Nelson, T. F., & Lee, H. (2002). Trends in college binge drinking during a period of increased prevention efforts: Findings from 4 Harvard School of Public Health college alcohol study surveys: 1993–2001. *Journal of American College Health, 50*(5), 203–217.

Weigel, V. (2000). E-learning and the tradeoff between richness and reach in higher education. *Change, 33*(5), 10–15.

West, C. (1993). *Race matters.* Boston: Beacon Press.

Whitehead, A. N. (1929). *The aims of education and other essays.* New York: Macmillan.

Whitla, D. K. (1981). *Value added and other related matters.* Washington, DC: National Commission on Excellence in Education.

Wiggins, G., & McTighe, J. (1998). *Understanding by design.* Alexandria, VA: Association for Supervision and Curriculum Development.

Wohl, R. (1979). *The generation of 1914.* Cambridge, MA: Harvard University Press.

Youniss, J., & Yates, M. (1997). *Community service and social responsibility in youth.* Chicago: University of Chicago Press.

Zimmerman-Oster, K., & Burkhardt, J. C. (1999). *Leadership in the making: Impact and insights from leadership development programs in U.S. colleges and universities.* Battle Creek, MI: W. K. Kellogg Foundation.

Zlotkowski, E. (Ed.). (1998). *Service-learning in the disciplines.* Washington, DC: American Association for Higher Education.

Zlotkowski, E. (1999). Pedagogy and engagement. In R. Bringle, R. Games, & E. A. Malloy (Eds.), *Colleges and universities as citizens* (pp. 66–120). Boston: Allyn & Bacon.

NAME INDEX

A

Adam, B. E., 47, 186
Adelson, J., 105
Adler, S., 190
Alexander, P., 174
Alexie, S., 227
Almeida, T., 253–255
Ambrose, S., 5
Anderson, C., 262
Anderson, C. W., 168
Antonia, Sister, 87
Antonio, A., 44, 226
Arocha, J. F., 112
Astin, A. W., 8, 20, 42, 44, 99, 113, 134, 200, 201, 202, 218, 225, 259, 274
Astin, H. S., 200, 202
Avalos, J., 225, 274

B

Bandura, A., 120, 121
Bardacke, F., 162–163, 164
Barefoot, B. O., 178, 229
Barnard, H. F., 1–4, 5, 6, 83
Barrows, H. S., 135
Bass, S., 193
Battistoni, R. M., 157–160, 189
Beerbohm, E., 144
Bellah, R., 7
Bender, T., 32
Benhabib, S., 89–90
Bennett, D. C., 26, 29, 31, 33
Bennett, S. E., 7, 189

Bennett, W. J., 110
Bergman, R., 117, 121
Bernstine, D., 75
Bethune, M. M., 3
Blasi, A., 121
Blatt, M., 108
Bligh, D. A., 133
Bloom, A., 110
Blount, A., 155–156, 245, 252, 253
Bogner, J., 231
Bok, D. C., 27, 44, 231
Bowen, W. G., 44, 219
Boyer, E. L., 5–6, 25, 46, 57, 218, 219, 220, 248
Boyte, H. C., 70–71, 82, 211
Brady, H. E., 118, 122, 226
Bransford, J. D., 20, 133
Braxton, J., 114
Bringle, R. G., 135, 271–272
Brody, R., 115, 116
Brokaw, T., 287
Brooks, D., 220–221
Brown, J. S., 137
Brownstein, A., 236
Burkhardt, J. C., 250
Butterfield, K. D., 231

C

Cadwallader, M., 198
Calabrese, R. L., 123
Callan, E., 13, 15
Callero, P. L., 119
Cambridge, B. L., 262

SUBJECT INDEX

A

Academic disciplines. *See* Majors and disciplines, academic

Academic freedom, 28–29, 216–217, 285

Academic integrity, 76, 78, 232, 234

Academic life, service learning integration with, 20–21, 149–154, 154–156, 187, 214

Academic prestige and competition, 41–42

Access and Success (program), 69

Activism, social, 70–71, 287; and environmental issues, 160–165, 176, 185, 210, 235, 247; levels of student, 114, 118–119; student protests, 118–119, 145, 235–238, 253–254. *See also* Students

Adjunct faculty. *See* Faculty

Admissions, higher education, 38, 44

Advertising, 12, 125

Africa, service learning in, 193

African American colleges, 146; Emory University, 190, 195, 206, 215–216, 229, 238; Spelman, 58–60, 179–180, 192–193

African American students, 236–237

African Diaspora and the World (course), 97, 180, 205–206

Age: and education levels, 129n.5; and moral judgment, 107–108; of students, 39, 100

AIDS: The Modern Plague (course), 182

Air Force Academy. *See* United States Air Force Academy

Alliance for Catholic Education, Notre Dame's, 68, 256

Altruism, 118, 131

Alumni-student connections, post-college, 256–257, 282

Alverno College, 52, 95n.1, 222; about, 53–54; courses and faculty, 183–184, 188–189, 204, 211, 216, 261–262; presidential leadership at, 74

Ambiguity: of moral situations, 108; in public service, 123–124, 151–152, 153

America, Inventing (course), 181

American Association for Higher Education (AAHE), 45–46, 187, 214, 259, 262, 265

American Commitments Program, 44

American Political Science Association, 160, 186, 189

Ancients and Moderns: Democratic Theory and Practice (course), 156–160

Antipoverty work, 123, 124

Apathy, political, 6–7, 99, 125, 165, 285, 286

Argumentation, moral, 145

Assessing Service-Learning and Civic Engagement (Gelmon et al.), 264

Assessment: course, 160, 267–271, 275n.2, 283; institutional investment in, 275; methods and tools, 271–272

F

Faculty: academic disciplines and departments, 185–191; adjunct and non-tenured, 41, 214–216, 281–282; advancement and rewards, 45, 47–48, 200, 201; assessment of teaching by, 28, 57, 60, 262–271, 283; autonomy of, 34–35; centers (on campus), 46–47, 211; community involvement of, 213, 216–217, 282; credits for courses taught, 35–36; development of, 46–47, 210–213, 281; fellowship and community, 205–206; honor codes involvement of, 232; idealism of, 201–202, 203–204, 209–210; leadership by, 80–83, 277; in the modern university, 28–29; and multidisciplinary courses, 160–165, 179–180, 185, 196–197, 198–199, 205–206, 208–210; national ties supporting, 186–187, 214; orientation, 90–91, 91–92; pedagogical strategy case studies, 148–165; preparing future, 47; pressures on, 48, 200–201; recruitment, 216–217; religious affiliations, 217; rewards systems for, 35–36, 208, 217; as role models, 11; roles in pedagogies of engagement, 122, 141–142; satisfaction in student relationships, 207–208, 262; scholarship of teaching and learning, 36, 46–47, 148–165, 208–210, 264–271; specialization by, 33–34, 198–199; student feedback to, 207–208, 263; study groups and meetings, 82, 88, 205; U.S. Professors of the Year, 208; work motivations of, 201–202, 207–208, 262

Faculty teaching moral and civic education, 200–202; community among, 205–206; and conceptions of undergraduate education, 202–204; connected to research, 208–210; and faculty development, 210–213; logistical support for, 213, 274–275, 281; motivations of, 202–210; patterns impeding, 33–36; pedagogical strategy case studies, 148–165; student guidance relationships, 207–208; and work rewards, 35–36, 217

Fellowships, graduating student, 256

Feminist scholarship and teaching, 209

Fine arts majors and disciplines, 191–192

"Flow" in civic activities, 124

Freedom: of speech and opinion, 236–237, 285; to teach and study, 29

Freedom Riders, 1964, 118–119

Freshman courses and seminars, 57–58, 78, 145, 173, 176, 177–178, 182, 228–229, 238–239, 269–271; convocations, 180

Freshman students, 97–98; developmental issues confronting, 99–127; orientation materials, 226–229

Funding: competition for, 42; of moral and civic education, 211–212, 281

G

Gay and lesbian issues, 238

Gender equality values, 3, 209

General education, 34, 169–182; assessment, 269–271; core curricula, 30–31, 170, 174–177, 280; distribution requirements, 36, 66–67, 170, 171–174, 183, 263, 280; goals of, 170; moral and civic courses restricted to, 169. *See also* Freshman courses and seminars